BANKING AND CAPITAL MARKETS

BANKING AND CAPITAL MARKETS

David Adams LLB, Solicitor

Published by

College of Law Publishing,
Braboeuf Manor, Portsmouth Road, St Catherines, Guildford GU3 1HA

British Library Cataloguing-in-Publication Data
A catalogue record for this book is available from the British Library.

ISBN 978 1 905391 61 5

Typeset by Style Photosetting Ltd, Mayfield, East Sussex
Printed in Great Britain by Ashford Colour Press, Gosport, Hampshire

Preface

The hardest part in writing this book was deciding what should be left out; a work entitled 'Banking and Capital Markets' could justifiably run to a dozen volumes. However, from a solicitor's perspective, banking practice is essentially 'document driven', and so Part I of this book is devoted to the fundamentals behind drafting loan facility documentation. Probably the most legally complex area of a banking solicitor's practice is that of security: Part II therefore explains the fundamental issues of secured lending. Finally, Part III of the book introduces capital markets financing and, in particular, the process of issuing a eurobond. The reader should be aware that this book is primarily designed as an integral part of the Legal Practice Course elective, 'Banking and Debt Finance'.

In true preface tradition, I must record my thanks to the people who saved me from making countless mistakes. In particular, I must thank ex-client Ian Brown, colleagues Patrick O'Connor, David Dunnigan and Julia Machin, and ex-colleague Frances George. Following preface tradition still further, I take all responsibility for the mistakes that remain. This book is dedicated to Jayne, who supported me through the pregnancy pains of its creation whilst suffering her own, and to little Tabitha and Francesca for giving me the best incentive to finish writing.

In the interest of brevity, the masculine pronoun is used throughout to include the feminine.

The law is stated as at 1 October 2008 (unless indicated otherwise). The Companies Act 2006 is not fully in force at the date of publication; therefore, where section numbers from the Companies Act 1985 are used in the text, the Table of Statutes shows CA 2006 equivalents in square brackets. This edition aims to detail where the law has actually changed and where it is likely to change.

Finally, the *Financial Times* articles reproduced throughout the book are from various years and are intended to provide contextual illustrations of topics rather than current market positions.

DAVID ADAMS
London

Contents

Table of Cases

Table of Statutes

International legislation

Table of Secondary Legislation, Accounting Standards and Rules

Table of Abbreviations

ACT	Association of Corporate Treasurers
AIBD	Association of International Bond Dealers
CA 1985	Companies Act 1985
CA 1989	Companies Act 1989
CA 2006	Companies Act 2006
CAD	Capital Adequacy Directive
CAO	Company Announcements Office
CD	certificate of deposit
CDDA	Company Directors Disqualification Act 1986
COMI	Centre of Main Interest
CP	conditions precedent
EA 2002	Enterprise Act 2002
EEA	European Economic Area
EPA 1990	Environmental Protection Act 1990
FRN	floating rate note
FRSs	Financial Reporting Standards
FSA	Financial Services Authority
FSA 1986	Financial Services Act 1986
FSAP	Financial Services Action Plan
FSMA 2000	Financial Services and Markets Act 2000
GAAP	Generaly Accepted Accounting Practice
IA 1986	Insolvency Act 1986
IAS	International Accounting Standard
ICMA	International Capital Markets Association
ICTA 1988	Income and Corporation Taxes Act 1988
IFRS	International Financial Reporting Standards
IPMA	International Primary Markets Association (now part of ICMA)
IRB	internal ratings-based
ISIN	International Securities Identification Number
ISMA	International Security Markets Association (now part of ICMA)
LCA 1972	Land Charges Act 1972
LECB	large exposure capital base
LIBID	London Interbank Bid Rate
LIBOR	London Interbank Offered Rate
LIMEAN	London Interbank Mean Rate
LMA	Loan Market Association
LPA 1925	Law of Property Act 1925
LRA 2002	Land Registration Act 2002
LSE	London Stock Exchange
MAC	material adverse change
MBI	management buy-in
MELs	modified eligible liabilities
MTN	medium term note
NIF	note insurance facility
OECD	Organisation for Economic Co-operation and Development
P & L account	profit and loss account
PSM	Professional Securities Market
RCF	revolving credit facility
RIS	Regulatory Information Service (Listing Rules, Rule 12.5)
RUF	revolving underwriting facility
SA 1891	Stamp Act 1891
SDRT	stamp duty reserve tax
SEC	Securities and Exchange Commission
SPV	special purpose vehicle
SSAPs	Statements of Standard Accounting Practice
TLC	transferable loan certificate
TLI	transferable loan instrument
UKLA	UK Listing Authority

Chapter 1

Raising Finance: An Overview of Players and Products

> 'We're in the risk business. We take positions. We lend money. We get most of it back.'
>
> Martin Taylor, Chief Executive, Barclays Bank, reporting losses of £325m
> (Source: *Financial Times*, September 1998)

1.1 Introduction

Most people will never be party to litigation. Many of us, including a good few lawyers, will die without making a will. Some people will never own property, and so avoid the nuances of conveyancing, and very few people will run their own business. Almost all of us, however, will borrow money.

Whether it is to buy a car, a house, to fund education, or to bridge from one payday to the next, borrowing is almost a 'requirement' of our society. Banking services available to individuals have grown in number and sophistication over recent years, with innovations such as telephone and internet banking making borrowing increasingly more accessible.

However, borrowing is not the sole preserve of the individual. Businesses must also borrow money, and they usually require more versatile, more complex, and far larger loans than individuals. Banks and business borrowers will therefore frequently rely on the skills of specialised solicitors to help establish their required financing.

This book is not about banking for individuals. It is about financing a business; and in particular it is about the solicitor's role in the two dominant forms of corporate financing: commercial loan facilities and capital markets finance. Beyond this chapter the book is divided into three parts: the first part concentrates on raising money by way of a commercial loan facility, the second deals with taking security for a commercial loan, and the third part considers raising money on international capital markets.

1.2 Borrowers

1.2.1 Types of borrower

The most common borrowers of capital on a commercial basis can conveniently be placed into the following three broad categories.

1.2.1.1 Governments

All governments borrow. The borrowing may be short term, to bridge a shortfall between their income (primarily from taxation) and the money they require to fulfil their policies and meet their general obligations, or it may be long term (eg, to fund specific projects). When a government borrows, it is usually referred to as 'sovereign debt'. Examples of recent sovereign debt issues include a $200 million note issue by the Republic of Austria, and a US$6 billion loan arranged for Canada.

1.2.1.2 Local authorities and municipalities

Part of a government's borrowing may be used to fund local authorities; however, those authorities will also usually have the capacity, and the need, to raise their own money. For example, in September 2007, the London Borough of Barnet was looking to issue a bond for up to £360 million (see the article below). Meanwhile the City of Moscow made its debut on the syndicated loan market in 1997, borrowing $50 million over three years.

1.2.1.3 Companies

By far the most prevalent borrowers are companies. These range from public companies with diverse interests and a vast network of subsidiaries to small local businesses. Furthermore, banks and other financial institutions are voracious corporate borrowers. Companies, particularly public companies, enjoy a broader range of techniques for raising money (and providing security for borrowing) than any other type of borrower. Since they are so numerous, corporates usually account for the majority of a solicitor's borrower clients. The following chapters will therefore concentrate on borrowing by a limited company, and references to 'borrower' should be read accordingly.

1.2.1.4 Others

Whilst the three categories above cover most of the entities raising substantial finance, it should not be thought that they account for every type of borrower: partnerships, sole traders, the few nationalised industries that remain in the UK, and supranational organisations (eg, the World Bank or the European Investment Bank) will all borrow capital.

1.2.2 The need for finance

It is not difficult to think of reasons why a *new* business might require considerable 'start up' capital. Assets such as premises, office equipment, and plant and machinery must be purchased or leased. Manufacturing businesses will need to buy raw materials, and almost all businesses must pay employees' wages. They will need to pay electricity bills, advertise to attract customers, and initially they may even have to run at a loss to win business from competitors.

Most existing businesses will also need to borrow capital in order to trade successfully. Consider BP plc (BP), holding company of one of the world's largest petroleum and petrochemicals groups. According to its latest (2007) accounts, the BP group had a net worth of around US$94.6 billion, with profit before tax in 2007 of over US$31 billion. It might be thought that a well-established company generating such immense profit would have little need for borrowing. However, the group had outstanding borrowing of more than US$30 billion. BP almost certainly has continuing working capital requirements not dissimilar to those listed above for a newly-formed business (albeit on a larger scale!). But the BP group will also have required capital to expand its businesses through acquisitions, to replace obsolete assets, to finance exploration, and to fund research and development. The group also required financial programmes enabling it to convert its revenue, which was primarily in US dollars, into other currencies to meet its worldwide financial commitments.

1.2.3 Financing a company

There are, broadly, four methods by which a large company might raise the money it requires to run its business:

(a)   share capital;

(b)   retained profits;

(c)   loan facilities; and

(d)   capital markets instruments.

1.2.3.1 Share capital

All companies have 'ordinary' shareholders who invest money in the company in return for a 'share' in the business. This money is effectively 'non-returnable' so far as the company is concerned (other than on a winding-up), and so it can be used to invest in the company's assets on a long-term basis. Furthermore, while most shareholders expect to share in some of the profits their company makes (by way of a dividend), there is no absolute obligation on the company to provide a return on its shares.

Most companies will issue shares both on incorporation (to provide initial capital) and at a future date (to raise additional capital). However, each time a company issues more shares it will generally entail any profit which is distributed to the shareholders being spread more thinly. The existing shareholders may therefore prefer their company to borrow capital on which it pays a 'fixed' return, rather than a return linked to profits. In other words, the company can borrow money at a (relatively) fixed cost, and use it to make greater profits for its shareholders. This is known as 'gearing', or 'leverage'. (A fuller explanation of share finance is given in *Business Law and Practice*.)

1.2.3.2 Retained profit

Once a company starts trading successfully, it will make a profit. The directors will decide how to use any profit, and a substantial amount will usually be distributed to the shareholders as a return on their investment in shares. However, part (and occasionally all) of a company's profits will be retained in the company to provide working capital and to finance other funding requirements. These retained profits are shown in a company's balance sheet as 'retained profits', or 'profit and loss reserve' (see **6.3.5**).

1.2.3.3 Loan facilities

Whilst share capital and retained profits can provide substantial levels of funding, they are unlikely to be entirely sufficient for all a company's needs. For example, share capital cannot generally be raised in small amounts on a regular basis, and only public limited companies may offer their shares to the general public. Meanwhile, the timing and amount of a company's profits are often unpredictable.

Borrowing by way of a loan (usually known as a 'loan facility') can provide a company with a flexible and 'reliable' source of funds, and allow very diverse methods of borrowing capital. An overdraft facility, for example, provides an instant source of variable borrowing, helping a company with its cash flow. Alternatively (or additionally), a company might borrow a lump sum for a period of time (known as a 'term loan') to fund a specific project. Loan facilities can cater for borrowing in a choice of currencies. Interest may be payable at a fixed or variable rate, whilst the capital may be repayable in stages through the life of the loan, or in one repayment when the loan 'matures'. The most common forms of loan facility are dealt with more fully in **Chapter 3**.

1.2.3.4 Capital markets instruments

Large companies may obtain financing from another source of funds known as the 'capital markets'. In simplistic terms, this will involve a company issuing a series of instruments (ie, a form of certificate) to investors in acknowledgement of an amount of capital it has borrowed from them (these instruments are known generically as 'debt securities'). The most common forms of capital markets debt security involve the issuer agreeing to repay the borrowed capital on a specified date (on 'maturity') and to pay interest on the borrowed capital in the meantime. The debt security may be sold by the original investor to subsequent investors at any time, allowing it to recover some or all of its capital investment before the maturity date. The subsequent investor will then be entitled to claim any remaining interest payments, and to receive the borrowed capital on maturity. The debt security can be re-sold any number of times; the issuer simply pays interest to the current owner, and repays capital to the owner at maturity.

Debt securities issued on the capital markets include bonds, notes, commercial paper, certificates of deposit, and loan stock. Raising finance through issuing debt securities is dealt with in **Part III**.

1.3 Lenders

For most people the word 'lender' is probably synonymous with 'bank'. There are, however, two main types of lender: banks and so-called 'institutional' lenders (also known as 'non-bank lenders' or, rather loosely, 'funds'). Both are intermediaries, that is they generally lend money raised from others rather than their own capital. Banks raise money primarily from depositors (eg, you and I opening savings accounts), from issuing debt securities and by borrowing from each other (see **4.9.1.2**). Individuals also 'lend' through their contributions to pension funds and insurance policies, because the institutions which receive the contributions invest them in order to raise the money they need to meet their obligations under the funds and policies. Institutional lenders usually raise money from investors by creating a series of 'funds' which then reinvest the money in various ways. These 'funds' have become prominent participants in term loans in recent years, commonly making up at least half the syndicate (by value) once a loan is in secondary syndication (see **3.3.2**).

In basic terms, therefore, individuals and companies fund all the forms of borrowing outlined above by putting 'spare' cash with banks or into investment funds, and by buying debt securities. However, it is usually a bank, of one type or another, with which a borrower must initially deal in order to arrange most types of borrowing. For the sake of brevity, the generic term 'bank' is used throughout this book to refer to the financial institution which acts as lender. The main types of bank are examined below.

1.4   A bank is a bank is a bank

It is inconceivable that any of us will go through life without some form of interaction with a bank. To some extent, the high street banks with which we deal are also the bankers to businesses. However, substantial commercial borrowing will usually involve other kinds of bank and financial institution with specialist knowledge and specialised products.

In common with many other industries over the last few years, bankers have subscribed to the theory that 'biggest is best'. Takeovers and mergers, as well as organic growth fuelled by deregulation, have led to large organisations with a multiplicity of interests. The leading banks now deal with almost every facet of commercial lending, and even the smaller banks will rarely offer just one type of service. For this reason, the labels that were traditionally given to different banks are becoming increasingly meaningless. Designations such as 'accepting houses', 'clearing banks', 'commercial banks', 'discount houses', 'finance houses', 'longterm credit banks' and 'retail banks' have become blurred as institutions vie for each other's business. It is, however, useful to distinguish the traditional labels for a few different kinds of bank according to the main type of activity in which they are involved.

1.4.1   Commercial banks

The major UK commercial banks such as Barclays, Lloyds, HSBC and National Westminster are familiar institutions, because they have branches on most high streets (they are often known as the 'high street banks'). The traditional role of these banks is taking deposits and making loans to individuals ('retail' or 'private' banking) and businesses ('corporate banking'), and providing related services. They attract depositors by paying interest on their deposit accounts, and by offering 'products' such as ISAs and other high-yield investments. On the premise that only a fraction of depositors will want their money back at any one time, the majority of the deposits made with the bank are lent on to borrowers. The bank charges sufficient interest on those loans to pay its depositors and make a profit for itself (or, more precisely, its shareholders). That is why, in general terms, the cost of borrowing a given amount from an institution is higher than the return on a corresponding investment.

The 'high street' commercial banks are characterised by providing general banking services through a national network of branches, which serve a wide customer base (including businesses and the general public), which in turn provides the banks with a vast pool of assets. The larger commercial banks also organise the system for clearing (ie, processing) cheques, and are therefore sometimes referred to as the 'clearing banks'. Many foreign commercial banks have a presence in the UK in order to service larger-scale deposit taking and lending, although they do not provide a 'high street' service. Examples include Citibank (USA), Mizuho Corporate Bank (Japan), and Calyon (France).

1.4.2   Merchant banks

The term 'merchant bank' is now rarely used, institutions preferring the label 'investment bank'. The 'concept' is important though. Merchant banks (also known as 'accepting houses' from their traditional role of accepting bills of exchange, see **17.6.4**) originated from 18th-century trading houses. These banks provide specialist advice in arranging financing, primarily for corporate clients, rather than lending money themselves. The main services offered by merchant banks include advice for companies on raising capital (eg, through issuing securities), underwriting and assisting in selling a securities issue, managing investments (eg, for pension funds), advising on launching and defending takeovers and mergers, and sometimes organising venture capital. Some merchant banks have also become involved in the stock market by acquiring stockbroking firms.

Most of the original merchant banks are now subsidiaries of commercial or investment banks, for example, Barings (part of ING) and Hambros (part of Société Générale). Those that remain as independent entities include Close Brothers, Lazard Brothers and NM Rothschild & Sons, but only Close Brothers still use the label 'merchant bank'.

1.4.3   Investment banks

The term 'investment bank' originally referred to American institutions which were the equivalent to UK merchant banks, for example Goldman, Sachs & Co and Merrill Lynch. However, the term is increasingly used by any bank offering a wide range of financial services and advice to corporates (see **1.4.2**). Investment banks buy and sell corporate and government securities, underwrite securities issues and also advise companies on raising capital, but do not accept deposits or make loans in the traditional sense.

1.4.4   Private banks

This term usually refers to banks which act for high net worth individuals rather than businesses. Private banks are usually owned by commercial or investment banks, one of the world's largest being JP Morgan Private Bank with around £209 billion in client assets in 2007.

1.4.5   Central banks

All countries with developed economies have a central bank, although the functions performed by that institution will vary between jurisdictions. The central bank of the United Kingdom is the Bank of England, which was founded in 1694 as a private bank and nationalised under the Bank of England Act 1946. The main functions of the Bank of England are to act as the Government's banker (holding its main account and borrowing on its behalf) and adviser on monetary policy, to issue bank notes, to regulate the money markets by lending or borrowing and to set interest rates (the Bank's historic function as regulator of other banks has now been almost entirely transferred to the Financial Services Authority (FSA)). The Bank of England will also help other banks with short-term liquidity problems as a lender of last resort (eg, in September 2007 the Bank provided a short-term 'emergency' facility to the Northern Rock bank which feared it could not borrow sufficient short-term funds in the markets because of a general liquidity crisis). Longer-term problems are more likely to be met with advice than money (when Northern Rock's depositors decided an 'emergency facility' signalled time to withdraw their savings, the Government had to nationalise the bank).

1.5   The finance solicitor's role

This chapter has provided a very brief overview as to why a business might need to borrow money, how that money might be raised, and the role of various banks in the financing process. What part does a finance solicitor play? Newly-formed companies will usually require relatively straightforward financing: typically a simple term loan to supplement their initial shareholders' capital, together with an overdraft facility to aid cash flow and provide flexibility. Many banks provide their own specialist small business advisers, and will usually insist that basic loans are transacted on their standard form documents, with minimal negotiation. There is little requirement at this stage for a specialist finance solicitor.

Larger companies, however, will tend to have more complex financial requirements, and so both the company and the bank will frequently instruct their own specialist finance solicitors. The depth of a solicitor's involvement depends upon the stage at which he is instructed by his client. In very complicated facilities, or for specialised transactions such as an acquisition finance, project finance or securitisation, the finance solicitors will be involved at a very early stage assisting with the structure of the deal. For more straightforward facilities, the structure and basic terms of the facility will usually be agreed between the director with executive responsibility for supervising the company's finances (the 'finance director') and the company's bankers. The finance solicitors will then be instructed to draft and negotiate the loan documentation. Together with good drafting and negotiation skills, a finance solicitor must also be aware of current market practice, since this will dictate the terms that most banks are likely to accept.

Most City firms will split a large finance department into a number of areas with specific responsibilities. The common divisions are:

(a)   general banking (ie, loan facilities – acting for bank or borrower);

(b)   capital markets and securitisation (see **10.10** for a brief explanation);

(c)   project finance (ie, the financing of specific projects in which the return on investment is linked to the project itself) and asset finance (ie, the financing of the purchase or lease of specific assets such as aircraft or ships).

1.6 Perspectives

Banking practice is usually a particularly constructive form of legal work; both parties will be anxious for the loan transaction to go ahead, and this invariably results in a fair degree of co-operation between them. It is important to remember, however, that each party will see certain matters from a slightly different perspective, with various matters up for negotiation. As a finance solicitor, your perspective on certain matters will therefore depend on your client. Where appropriate, this book will try to give a brief summary of both the borrower's and the bank's perspectives.

'Barnet bond' proposed to fund services

**By John Willman,
Business Editor**

A bond to raise up to £360m for transport, schools and other local services will be proposed by a north london borough as it looks for new ways to raise money.

The "Barnet bond" would provide as much as half the £733m the London suburb says it needs to improve its infrastructure to cope with expected housing growth over the next 10 years.

The bond would be financed by earmarking extra income created by expanding housing stock, including higher council tax and business rate receipts. The borough also says it could raise money from the expansion of Brent Cross shopping centre, with a £1 a day levy on each parking space among the options.

An article illustrating a local authority proposing bond finance. Source: *Financial Times*.

Part I
FACILITY AGREEMENTS

Chapter 2

Due Diligence, Commitment Letters and the Term Sheet

'Every journey begins with a single step.'

Mao Tse-Tung

2.1 Introduction: understanding the context

Before considering loan documentation, it is important to understand that the context in which a loan facility is to be used will influence its final terms and the process of its creation. The three main contexts are:

(a) *investment grade loans (or 'corporate credit')* – where the borrower is typically a large established company requiring cash to run and expand its business, and possibly make small acquisitions;

(b) *leveraged loans* – where the borrower's debt is a multiple of its share capital (equity). Because this involves greater risk for a bank, the controls in the facility agreement are usually tighter. Leveraged loans are usually used for 'acquisition finance' in which companies, or private equity funds, buy other companies or groups.

(c) *cross-over credit* – where a borrower is borderline investment grade and so subject to controls in the facility agreement stricter than usual investment grade loans but not usually as strict as leveraged loans.

Almost as important as the context is the liquidity of the market: the more money available to borrow, the more borrowers can dictate the terms of the loan facility, whatever the context. For example, investment grade borrowers traditionally demand more relaxed terms than a leveraged loan. The last few years have seen leveraged markets flooded with cash from institutional lenders ('funds') resulting in certain terms being more relaxed than investment grade loans. Then, since August 2007, the so-called 'credit crunch' has made negotiating borrowing difficult for almost all borrowers.

This book generally explains the process and terms relevant to an investment grade loan, but with an indication of certain leveraged terms, and relaxations that a strong borrower might request.

If a borrower is refinancing an existing loan it will probably approach its current syndicate. Not only will there be an existing relationship, but the current facility agreement will usually form the basis of the new loan document. If it has no existing facilities, is dissatisfied with its current bank, or even requires a loan facility of a type that the current bank cannot or will not provide, then the borrower will have to approach a new institution. It should not be assumed, however, that the borrower is always the 'suitor'. When the lending market is flush with money, banks are generally more pro-active and may approach businesses with the offer of a loan (usually the approach is to existing borrowers, but cold-calling is not unknown).

Once initial contact has been made, a bank cannot proceed further without obtaining approval for the transaction in accordance with its internal credit procedures. Approval must always be obtained before a loan is offered. If the loan is approved, the next stage involves the drafting of an initial summary of terms (the 'term sheet') from which the loan facility will grow. This chapter explains the first steps in the lending process with a review of a typical credit procedure and term sheet.

2.2   Due diligence

Before lending several hundred million pounds, it is necessary to know a little bit about the borrower! When a bank considers lending to a would-be borrower, its initial job is to assess the credit risk: put simply, what is the risk that the borrower will be unable to pay interest ('service' the loan), or be unable to repay the capital? If the credit risk is small, many banks will be prepared to lend to that borrower, and so the fees and margin (ie, profit) that can be charged will be driven down. Conversely, the higher the chance of default, the larger the fees and margin a bank will demand to compensate for the greater risk, and at some point the risk will become too great for the bank to offer a loan. The more information about a borrower that a bank can get, the better it can assess the risk. A bank will therefore conduct a fact-finding exercise known as 'due diligence'.

The breadth and depth of any due diligence process will depend on a number of factors (see **2.2.1**), but in broad terms it will initially be in two parts.

2.2.1   Initial investigation

The format and scope of the investigation will vary with the identity of the bank and the borrower as well as a number of factors, including:

(a)   the size of the loan;

(b)   the type of loan and its purpose;

(c)   whether the loan is to be secured;

(d)   whether the borrower is already known to the bank;

(e)   market liquidity (ie, whether there are numerous or few lenders willing to lend); and

(f)   whether the loan is an integral part of a larger transaction, such as a flotation or an acquisition (where the due diligence process will have to take account of the larger transaction).

There is no 'standard' due diligence procedure applied by all banks. However, a typical initial investigation for an existing borrower requiring a loan for general corporate purposes might be as follows.

2.2.1.1   Account officer

Each borrower is assigned a particular individual (usually known as an 'account officer') within the bank who provides a consistent point of contact and someone with whom the borrower's officers (in particular its Finance Director) can build a relationship. The account officer will put together a very basic package of terms for the proposed loan. This will usually cover matters such as the amount and term of the loan, repayment dates and principal financial covenants, and will be based largely on the account officer's knowledge of the borrower.

2.2.1.2 Credit analysis

The account officer's proposal will then undergo a credit analysis. Some banks will have a separate department which analyses the proposal. Many banks will rely on the account officer to create his own assessment, often with the help of a credit assessment manual which provides checklists of the points to be covered. This will also include any policy guidelines peculiar to the bank, for example, the mandatory inclusion of a material adverse change, or cross-default clause (see **Chapter 8**). The source of information for the credit analysis depends on the borrower and the proposed deal. The borrower's most recently published accounts will always be reviewed. Since a public company has six months after its year end in which to publish accounts (a (London) listed company has four months, and a private company has nine months), the information they contain could legitimately be 18 months old. Smaller borrowers will, therefore, probably be asked to produce interim accounts or management accounts. Larger borrowers (eg, those in the FTSE 250) would treat such a request with derision if the loan was for general purposes. Generally, the better credit rating the borrower has, the less information it is likely to provide. If a borrower provides sensitive unpublished information, it will ask the bank to give an undertaking not to disclose it to third parties (a 'confidentiality letter').

As mentioned above, the scope of the analysis will also depend on the size of the loan. It is also important for any analysis to take into account the 'global' exposure the bank will have with respect to the borrower, its affiliated entities and that business sector, since these factors may affect the risk assessment.

2.2.1.3 Credit clearance

Once the credit analysis has been completed it will be sent to a credit department for sanctioning by a more senior officer of the bank. The credit department (or a 'credit committee') will see all credit requests and therefore have an overview of overall lending. They will also check that internal limits and policies, as well as any external restraints (eg, for exposure), will not be breached. Occasionally, they may defer the analysis to an industry department (which has expertise in a particular industry) or Area Credit Officer (with geographical expertise) to obtain a more specialised view of the borrower in the context of contemporary businesses.

The credit department might reject the proposal. Alternatively, they may either approve a loan on the basis of the analysis, or make approval subject to revised terms being agreed (eg, a smaller loan, stricter undertakings, or a shorter term). Once clearance has been given, the account officer can finalise a draft term sheet. If the deal is particularly complex, the account officer might involve a solicitor at this stage, to help construct the term sheet.

2.2.2 Subsequent investigation

The borrower may immediately accept the bank's draft of the term sheet, or there may be a small amount of negotiation (any major changes would require reapproval by the credit department). Once the bank and borrower have agreed the term sheet, a second phase of the due diligence process will begin. It is at this point that the bank is most likely to involve advisers (although smaller loans and 'repeats' may be dealt with largely 'in house'). The bank will instruct solicitors to put together an initial draft facility agreement on the basis of the term sheet. The bank may also instruct accountants to compile a report on the borrower.

During this stage, a solicitor might obtain copies of the memorandum and articles, the charges register and company records relating to the borrower. Obtaining a copy of a corporate borrower's registered documents (typically from the Companies Registry online service) is a quick and cost-effective way of getting information. However, the register does have its limitations. For example, the borrower may not have filed its returns properly. Whilst this may result in a fine for a company and its officers, there is no provision for compensating a third party who suffers any loss. Primarily, therefore, the bank and its advisers will turn to the borrower to supply information.

2.2.3 Ongoing information

It is important to realise that a bank's information gathering does not end with the signing of the loan document. Once it has paid the money out, a bank must monitor the borrower to ensure it has a reasonable chance of getting the money back. This is the practical reason behind the repeated representations and undertakings in a facility agreement (see **Chapters 5** to **7**).

2.2.4 Acquisition finance

The position is different here. Traditionally, acquisition financings involve greater due diligence since they are leveraged financings with increased risk. However, in very liquid markets, with multiple bidders for each target company, due diligence is usually very limited. In particular, if the target is already owned by a private equity house, due diligence may consist of just a few documents and reports about the target company made available to view for a limited time in a 'data room' (either a 'virtual' data room – ie, online – or a designated room at the vendor's solicitor). In a hostile acquisition of a public company, information will also be limited.

2.3 The term sheet and commitment letter

2.3.1 What are they?

A term sheet is a document which records, in writing, the principal terms of a transaction. It is signed by the parties to the transaction, but it is not usually intended to be contractually binding (see **2.5**). Term sheets are often attached as an Appendix to a short letter (the 'commitment letter' or 'mandate letter'), which contains any legally binding terms required at the outset of the lending process (see **2.4**).

After initial meetings with the borrower to discuss the fundamentals of the proposed loan, the bank will produce a commitment letter and term sheet reflecting the terms on which it is prepared to lend. The borrower will then be given a date by which it must accept those terms by signing and returning the commitment letter (known as granting the bank a 'mandate'). Occasionally, the bank will instruct solicitors to assist in drafting the commitment letter and term sheet, but more frequently it will be produced by the bank's in-house legal department. It is important to realise that the term sheet aims to provide an overview and will not include substantial detail.

2.3.2 Why have a term sheet?

2.3.2.1 Clarity

Undoubtedly the most compelling reason for producing a term sheet is to focus the minds of bank and borrower on the fundamental issues of the deal. If the pricing and structure of the loan cannot be agreed in outline then there is little point instructing solicitors or performing substantial due diligence.

If the proposed facility is to be syndicated, it will be helpful for the bank which is arranging the loan to have an accurate summary of the main terms when trying to sell the deal to early syndicate members before an information memorandum has been produced (see **Chapter 3** for further explanation).

Finally, when markets are flush with cash (as is currently the case for acquisition finance, for example) borrowers tend to have the whip hand in negotiating terms. This may result in borrowers drafting their own term sheets in an attempt to dictate terms to prospective lenders.

2.3.2.2 Summary

If a loan facility is likely to be particularly complicated, a term sheet serves as a helpful summary of the main provisions, both for the parties and their advisers. This can be useful for a number of reasons. First, whilst solicitors charge at an hourly rate, they will often be required to give an estimate of their fees for a large transaction. This may extend to putting a ceiling on the total amount they can bill (a 'fee cap'). The term sheet provides a useful guide for a solicitor to judge the complexity of a transaction, and so estimate his fee.

Secondly, the term sheet acts as an outline from which the bank's solicitor can extract the key information necessary to prepare the first draft of the facility agreement. Whilst not usually intended to be legally binding, neither party will expect any derogation from the broad outline of the term sheet, and so the solicitor has some certainty on which to begin his drafting.

2.4 What should the commitment letter cover?

The commitment letter (also known as a 'mandate letter') is a letter sent from the bank which is arranging the facility to the borrower. It contains any terms which need to be legally binding before the loan itself is executed, and usually has the term sheet attached as an appendix. The key points covered in the letter are:

(a) whether the bank's obligation to arrange the facility are 'best efforts' or 'underwritten';

(b) any general conditionality to the offer to arrange, eg time limit for executing the facility document, obtaining credit committee approvals, completion of satisfactory due diligence, etc;

(c) a material adverse change provision allowing the bank to withdraw from the offer if there is a material adverse change to the market generally (known as the 'market mac') or to the borrower's situation specifically (known as the 'business mac');

(d) a 'clear market' clause in which the borrower agrees not to raise other finance whilst this facility is being arranged;

(e) a 'market flex' clause which allows the bank to change aspects of the negotiated facility agreement if it is necessary to attract other banks to participate; and

(f)   provisions for the bank to recover fees, costs and expenses if the deal does not go ahead, as well as an indemnity for any losses the bank might suffer.

The intention is that the commitment letter is signed and returned by the borrower within a few days, although it must be said this is often overlooked in practice.

2.5   What should a basic term sheet cover?

A 'sample' of a straightforward bilateral, investment grade type term sheet appears at **2.10**, although many are more complex (see **2.7**). As explained at **2.3.2.2**, a signed term sheet is usually the first thing a solicitor will know about the transaction. If called upon to help draft the term sheet, however, there are a number of general points a solicitor should keep in mind.

2.5.1   What the term sheet should not cover

A term sheet is not a facility agreement, neither is it a first attempt at drafting. Too much detail will neutralise its purpose. For example, the term sheet may specify the *type* of undertakings (see **Chapter 7**) that are to appear in the final agreement, but it will not include a draft clause.

The aim is towards brevity; the details will need careful negotiation at a later stage. For example, the term sheet might state:

> Guarantees will be given by all material subsidiaries of the borrower.

It is not usually necessary to define what is meant by 'material subsidiary' at this stage: the term sheet simply makes it clear that guarantees will be required between companies within the borrower's group; which companies actually give the guarantees will be a focus of subsequent negotiation.

2.5.2   'Inclusive' lists

There is a danger, when listing specific points to be included in the agreement, that one party might claim during later negotiation that they believed the list to be exhaustive. Where appropriate, therefore, language such as '... including, but not limited to ...' should be used to preface a list of requirements.

2.5.3   Only specify 'unusual' provisions

It is quite common to see the following in a term sheet:

> Conditions Precedent:
> The facility agreement will contain the usual conditions precedent applicable to this type of facility.

This wide language can also be used with other generic, terms such as undertakings, events of default or representations and warranties. Any provisions peculiar to the deal, for example a condition precedent that a borrower must win a particular contract before the loan facility can be utilised, should be referred to specifically in the term sheet.

2.6   Legal effect of the term sheet

The term sheet is not usually intended to be legally binding. This is because it is drafted in broad terms, and based on limited information. More detailed investigation by the bank and its advisers will follow the signing of the term sheet (see **5.2**). These investigations will guide the bank as to the terms required in the facility agreement, and occasionally may cause it to withdraw from the deal altogether although this would be unusual: term sheets have considerable 'moral' authority.

Term sheets are usually not binding as a matter of English common law. An 'agreement to agree' will not be legally enforceable if there is a material term of the future contract which has not been expressly or impliedly agreed (this is not the same as an ambiguous or meaningless term, which might be disregarded whilst the remaining terms stand). A binding contract would also require proper consideration, in other words one party's promises must be paid for by the party benefiting from them. This could be achieved, however, if the document is made under seal, or if the benefiting party makes a promise or other gesture in return.

The only safe course, therefore, is to state clearly that the parties do not intend the term sheet to bind them legally. This may be achieved by heading the document 'subject to contract', a formula borrowed from conveyancing practice but widely recognised in its intention (a longer version is 'subject to documentation mutually acceptable to all parties'). More explicitly, a clause stating 'This arrangement is not entered into as a formal or legal agreement and shall not be subject to legal jurisdiction in the law courts' was held to mean precisely that (*Rose & Frank Co v JR Compton & Bros Ltd* [1925] AC 445).

On the other hand, if any parts of the term sheet are intended to be binding, they should be specifically identified as such, and the common law requirements mentioned above must be complied with. Alternatively they might appear in a separate 'commitment letter' (see **2.4**).

2.7 Private equity term sheets

In acquisition finance deals, the private equity house borrowing to finance the acquisition commonly produces its own term sheet from which to negotiate the loan. In contrast to the traditional term sheet described above, these private equity (or 'sponsor') term sheets are long (90–100 pages), detailed (containing complete definitions and clauses) and favour the borrower. This strong borrower position was the result of high market liquidity in recent years, which brought stiff competition to lend but also easy syndication, allowing banks to sell almost any loans. As at September 2008, the 'credit crunch' is still curtailing most acquisition financing, and borrower positions are relatively weaker.

2.8 From commitment documents to loan: duty to negotiate in good faith?

The commitment letter and term sheet are usually intended to set parameters for negotiating the facility agreement. There is no implied duty to negotiate in good faith under English law (although many other European jurisdictions do imply some sort of duty): in other words, either party may withdraw at any time without reason. Until recently, it was thought that even if the documents specifically agreed the parties should negotiate in good faith, this would be unenforceable for uncertainty. However, in *Petromec Inc v Petroleo Brasileiro SA Petrobras and Others* [2006] 1 Lloyd's Rep 121 the Court of Appeal stated that an express obligation to negotiate in good faith may be enforceable in some cases. The point was *not* a point of appeal before the Court and so its statements are not binding precedent, but they do indicate that a court may give weight to the clause in the future.

2.9 Sample term sheet

The format of a term sheet will depend on the type of loan facility being proposed. Set out below is an imaginary term sheet for a simple bilateral term loan to illustrate typical content and structure.

DATE 1 March 2009   SUBJECT TO CONTRACT

Borrower:	Bashum Car Rental Co Ltd (the 'Company').
Lender:	Loadido Bank plc.
Facility:	£10,000,000 term facility to be drawn in advances of sterling.
Fees:	Commitment fee at 50 basis points on daily unused and uncancelled amount (payable monthly in arrear).
Purpose:	To finance part of cost of acquisition by the Company of entire issued share capital of Wrecker Rent Ltd ('Target'), together with costs and expenses in connection therewith.
Availability:	The facility will be available for utilisation for 2 months after execution of documentation.
Interest:	Floating rate interest at Loadido Bank plc's (prime bank) LIBOR + 85 basis points + Mandatory Cost (payable quarterly in arrear).
Maturity:	5 years from execution of loan documentation.
Repayment:	The facility will amortise as follows:

Repayment date:	Amount:
years 1–3	zero
42 months	2,000,000
48 months	2,000,000
54 months	2,000,000
60 months	4,000,000

Prepayment:	Prepayment permitted with 5 business days' notice to coincide with any interest payment. Prepayment amounts to be no less than £50,000 or a multiple thereof, and may not be redrawn.
Security:	The facility will be secured by:

a. First ranking security over all shares in Target being acquired by the Company.

b. First ranking fixed and floating security over all current and future assets (including revenues) of the Company.

c. Guarantee from Target supported by first ranking fixed and floating security.

Conditions Precedent: All conditions precedent which are customary for such financings including, without limitation:

a. Payment of Arrangement fee.

b. Satisfaction with the terms of the acquisition documentation in connection with Target.

c. Satisfaction with the terms of financing for the balance of Target's acquisition cost, in particular as regards the equity contribution.

d. All documentation required to comply with the Financial Assistance Relaxation Procedures.

Representations: The usual reps and warranties in connection with this type of facility shall be included in the loan documentation, including but not limited to:

a. No withholding taxes on payments.

b. Pari passu ranking.

c.   No material adverse change.

Undertakings: The loan documentation will include standard undertakings for this type of facility, including, without limitation, restrictions on:

a. Liens and encumbrances.

	b. Guarantees.
	c. Sale of assets.
	d. Loans and advances.
Financial Covenants:	The loan documentation will contain financial covenants to be negotiated, including, without limitation:
	a. Minimum net worth to be £10 million at all times.
	b. Borrowings not more than 1.5 times net worth.
Events of Default:	Customary events of default for a facility of this type, including, but not limited to:
	a. Default in payment or other obligation.
	b. Cross-default.
	c. Material adverse change.
Taxes:	All payments to be free of withholding and other taxes.
Costs:	Notwithstanding that this term sheet is 'subject to contract', the following provision shall be binding on the Company from the date hereof. All expenses in the preparation, negotiation, execution and delivery of the facility, including, but not limited to, legal fees, to be paid by the Company whether or not the facility is put in place. All expenses associated with administering the facility to be paid by the Company.
Assignment:	Loadido may transfer or assign all or part of the facility at any time.
Other:	All other standard terms for documents of this nature shall be included.
Available:	These terms will be available until 11 March 2009. In the event that documentation is not executed within 30 days of acceptance of this offer, Loadido reserves the right to renegotiate the term sheet, or withdraw the offer.
Law:	English law and jurisdiction shall apply.

Accepted by:

....

on behalf of Bashum Car Rental Co Ltd   Date ....

2.10   Confidentiality letter

A bank may, at some stage in the loan negotiation, be given information about the borrower which is highly confidential. This may be information about the purpose for which the borrower requires the loan, such as a project finance, management buy out, or funding for a flotation. Alternatively, it may be information specifically concerning the borrower which the bank requires to enable it to make a decision on whether it can lend, or to enable it to form a syndicate to provide the loan (see **3.3**).

Whilst a bank is subject to common law confidentiality obligations (based on agency principles) due to the banker/customer relationship (see **8.3.4**), most borrowers will require the bank to sign a confidentiality letter. The short letter contains an undertaking by the bank not to disclose confidential information other than in limited circumstances to aid syndication. Any bank which is considering participating in the facility will have to sign the confidentiality letter before receiving any information.

Chapter 3

Plain Vanilla or Bells and Whistles?

'The Golden Rule is that there are no golden rules.'

George Bernard Shaw

3.1 Introduction

A facility agreement is a contract. In order to be valid under English law, it will require offer and acceptance, consideration, an intention to create legal relations and agreement on all material terms. In common with most commercial contracts, the detailed provisions of a facility agreement will be tailored to the specific requirements of the parties. From a wider perspective, however, there is a handful of categories within which most loan facilities can be placed. This chapter explains the most common types of facility, before providing a broad anatomy of a facility agreement as a preliminary to more detailed review in the ensuing chapters.

3.2 Common types of facility

The three most common types of general purpose loan facility are:

(a) overdraft;

(b) term loan;

(c) revolving credit facility.

The feature which distinguishes one type of loan from another is the way in which it allows the borrower to utilise credit. Facilities with relatively straightforward mechanics were traditionally referred to as 'plain vanilla' loans, whilst any additional features were known as 'bells and whistles'. Which particular loan is appropriate for a borrower will depend largely on the purpose for which the money is required.

Before looking more closely at the features of different loan facilities, it is important to understand a further categorisation: a loan facility may be either 'committed' or 'uncommitted'. A facility is committed if the facility agreement, once executed, obliges the bank to advance monies at the borrower's request (subject to the borrower complying with certain pre-agreed conditions – see **4.7**). If the facility agreement allows the bank some discretion before advancing any loan monies, the facility will be an 'uncommitted' facility.

3.2.1   Overdraft facility

This is the one type of facility of which most people have first-hand experience! The corporate overdraft is little different to the personal one, apart from its size.

3.2.1.1   Purpose

In the long term, a business will survive only if its income is greater than its expenditure. From day to day, however, it is very difficult for a business to ensure that it has sufficient receipts to cover all outgoings: the week in which the employees are paid will not necessarily coincide with the business selling products, or customers paying their bills. An overdraft is, essentially, a tool to aid cash flow by providing a reserve of easily accessible money to meet any shortfall in working capital (it is sometimes known as a 'working capital facility').

3.2.1.2   Basic features

An overdraft is an 'uncommitted' facility (see **3.2**). Furthermore, it will be 'on demand', which means that it must be repaid (reduced to zero) whenever the bank demands, even if the borrower has not defaulted (ie, failed to comply with a term of the loan). This position is not quite as precarious for the borrower as it first seems; there is generally an understanding that the bank will not 'pull the plug' and demand repayment without good reason. Even so, since it is technically on demand, an overdraft must appear as a current liability on a borrower's balance sheet (see **6.3.2**).

As a result of being on demand and uncommitted, an overdraft facility does not usually require substantial documentation. It is often provided on the bank's 'standard terms', with little room for negotiation by the borrower.

An overdraft will always be subject to a maximum aggregate amount which may be borrowed at any one time and may be subject to a 'clean-down' provision (see **3.2.3.3**). If a business is being run efficiently, each utilisation of its overdraft should be temporary, and once cash flow recovers, it should be used to reduce borrowing under the overdraft.

An overdraft is a relatively expensive way of borrowing capital. Interest is calculated on the amount outstanding each day, and usually charged at a fixed percentage above the bank's base rate (see **4.9** for interest rate calculations). The bank will also charge a relatively high fee for providing an overdraft, since it requires more administration than other loan facilities.

3.2.2   Term loan

A term loan (or 'term facility': both labels are used for this type of credit) essentially provides a specified capital sum over a set period (the 'term'), with an agreed schedule for repayment (see **Table 3.1** below).

TABLE 3.1   £10m one-year term loan: repayment examples

| Date | Total Drawn | Amortised | Type of repayment | |
			Balloon	Bullet
1/1	10m	[Repayment	—	—
28/2		Holiday]	—	—
31/3		1m	—	—
30/4		1m	—	—
31/5		1m	—	—
30/6		1m	—	—
31/7		1m	—	—
31/8		1m	½m	—
30/9		1m	1m	—
31/10		1m	1½m	—
30/11		1m	3m	—
31/12	Nil	1m	4m	10m

3.2.2.1   Purpose

Term loans provide a borrower with a lump sum of capital usually for a specified purpose, for example setting up a business, renewing assets ('capital expenditure'), or acquiring another business.

3.2.2.2   Basic features

Term loans are usually committed facilities (see **3.2**). Typically, a borrower is allowed a short period (the 'availability period' or 'commitment period') after executing the facility agreement during which (provided it has complied with certain pre-conditions – see **4.7**) it can draw down or 'utilise' a lump sum up to a specified amount. Sometimes, a term loan will provide for an extended availability period during which the money can be drawn in a number of portions (known as 'tranches', 'advances' or 'loans') as and when required by the borrower. This allows a borrower to borrow only what it needs, minimising interest payments, and also to spread the incidence of interest payments into manageable amounts at different times.

Term loans will be repayable in accordance with an agreed timetable. The schedule of repayment may be structured in a number of different ways (see also **9.2**), most commonly:

(a)   'amortisation' – repayment in equal amounts at regular intervals over the term of the loan. There will usually be a repayment 'holiday' at the beginning of the loan;

(b)   'balloon repayment' – repayment over several instalments where the instalment amount increases in size towards maturity;

(c)   'bullet repayment' – repayment in a single instalment at the end of the term of the loan (at 'maturity').

Once the capital has been repaid it cannot then be re-borrowed (compare revolving facilities at **3.2.3**). If the loan has a bullet repayment, the borrower might negotiate a renewal of the loan at maturity, or arrange a 'refinancing' to repay the loan by taking out other borrowings. It is unusual to see a general purpose term loan with a life of more than five years, although acquisition finance term loans are usually seven to 10 years (but invariably refinanced long before maturity) and project finance loans may be for 20 years or more.

Term loans are not usually 'on demand': the bank cannot withdraw the facility unless the borrower defaults (see **Chapter 8**). This allows the borrower to plan with certainty when it needs to fund capital repayments, and to commit borrowed money in a way that would not be possible with a loan which was on demand, such as an overdraft.

A multicurrency term loan allows the borrower to draw different tranches in different (pre-agreed) currencies. In addition, drawn amounts may be 'redenominated' (ie, converted into a different currency) at the end of an interest period. For example, a sterling tranche could be redenominated into dollars: the borrower does not receive more capital, but its interest payments and repayment would now be due in dollars.

Interest on a term loan may be at a fixed rate, but more usually floats at a fixed percentage (the bank's 'margin') above the bank's base rate or LIBOR (see **4.9**).

3.2.3 Revolving credit facility

Like a term loan, a revolving credit facility (RCF) provides a maximum aggregate amount of capital, available over a specified period. Unlike a term loan, the RCF allows a borrower to draw down and repay tranches of the available capital, almost as and when it chooses throughout the term of the loan (see **Table 3.2** below).

TABLE 3.2   £10m one-year RCF: utilisation and repayment example

Date	Total Drawn	Repayment	Available
1/1	4m	—	6m
7/2	7m	—	3m
1/4	3m	4m	7m
21/6	8½m	—	1½m
7/8	5½m	3m	4½m
31/12	Nil	5½m	Nil

3.2.3.1 Purpose

The RCF combines some of the flexibility of an overdraft, allowing the borrower to draw money when it is required, with the certainty of a term loan (the RCF is usually a committed facility: see **3.2**). Not only can the borrower save money by not drawing the whole loan at once, it can also elect to repay outstanding tranches that it no longer requires. Interest payments can therefore be kept to a minimum. Like an overdraft, the RCF is a 'working capital' facility intended to meet the short-term, fluctuating capital needs of the borrower.

3.2.3.2 Basic features

Each tranche is usually borrowed for a relatively short period (eg, one, three, or six months) after which it is technically repayable. However, if the borrower has not defaulted under the loan, the tranche to be repaid can be immediately re-drawn. This is known as a 'rollover'. The RCF might appear very similar to an overdraft facility, but there are fundamental differences. The first of these is size: an overdraft will rarely exceed a few hundred thousand pounds, whereas in late 2007, Tata Steel organised a £0.49 billion, five-year revolving credit facility for the former Corus business (British Steel). A second difference is flexibility: utilisation and repayment will usually be subject to more restrictions than an overdraft. For example:

(a)   minimum notice periods before each utilisation;

(b)   maximum and minimum amounts which may be drawn down in one tranche;

(c)   a minimum period for which an amount must be borrowed before it is repaid;

(d)   a maximum number of tranches which may be drawn at any time;

(e)   control over frequency and timing of repayment (final repayment is usually required in a bullet repayment, although an RCF can also be structured with a reducing availability through its life, mimicking term loan amortisation).

Whilst a borrower can avoid unnecessary interest costs by borrowing only as much as it requires, the bank will charge a 'commitment fee' calculated as a percentage of the undrawn facility from time to time. The commitment fee is levied to cover capital adequacy costs suffered by a bank in making a committed facility available. (Capital adequacy requirements are dealt with in more detail at **9.3.3**.)

3.2.3.3   Clean down

A clean down provision may be included to ensure the RCF (and usually any overdraft) are used for working capital rather than for 'long term' capital expenditure. The clean down provision typically requires the borrower to reduce the amount drawn under the RCF (overdraft) to a specified sum, during a specified period and for a specified number of (consecutive) days. For example, the borrower might have to reduce these facilities to zero, for at least five consecutive business days, once a year. At first sight this provision appears rather odd. It is, however, intended to ensure that the borrower is utilising its RCF and overdraft properly: they are structured for use in cash flow management, and not intended to be permanently drawn at maximum amount (contrast term loans at **3.2.2**).

3.2.4   '364 day facilities' and 'term-out options'

As the name suggests, '364 day facilities' are loans with an original maturity of up to one year. They are usually revolving credit facilities. The advantage of these loans is that, to the extent they are unutilised, they do not require regulatory capital to support them (see **9.3.3**). This makes them a cost-effective way to provide a 'standby' facility in circumstances where a borrower is unsure whether it will need funds or not.

Furthermore, the borrower can be given the right to convert any outstanding amount on the last day of maturity into a term loan without losing the benefits explained above (during the first 364 days). This is known as a 'term-out option'.

From January 2008, this favourable regulatory capital treatment was largely lost as 'Basel II' came fully into force. As a result, 364 day facilities are less common though not yet extinct.

3.2.5   Ancillary facilities

Some RCFs allow the borrower to utilise part of the commitment as a bilateral loan with one of the syndicate banks, for example an overdraft or derivatives facility. These are known as 'ancillary facilities'.

3.3 Syndicated facilities

3.3.1 Bilateral or syndicated facility

Most small loans and overdraft facilities are provided by a single bank. Because they are between two parties, they are known as 'bilateral' facilities. However, banks try to avoid the risk of making large commitments to single borrowers. In addition, the Consolidated Banking Directive generally prohibits banks lending 25% or more of their 'large exposure capital base' (LECB) to a single (or connected) source(s) and requires notification to the bank's regulator for exposures of 10% of the LECB or more. If a borrower requires a large or sophisticated facility (eg, for a project or acquisition funding), the loan monies are commonly provided by a group of banks known as a 'syndicate'. It is not unusual to find syndicates of more than 30 banks, and sometimes even larger syndicates (large facilities with multiple institutional investors, for example, may have several hundred lending entities).

3.3.2 Structuring a syndicate

The majority of syndications involve one bank, the 'arranger', organising a group of banks to participate directly in the facility agreement. This is known as 'primary syndication'. The syndicate members will participate in the syndicate on common terms, and so agree common documentation, although they may contribute different amounts. Most importantly, each syndicate member will assume liability only for its own lending obligations: it will not undertake any responsibility for other syndicate members' commitments.

An alternative form of 'syndication' occurs when a single bank is party to the loan documentation and initially provides the facility, with the intention of immediately transferring part, or all, of its commitment to other banks. These 'post-closing syndications' are dealt with in **Chapter 10**.

As with most banking terminology, the nomenclature is not set in stone, but the main roles of various syndicate members are explained below.

3.3.2.1 Arranger

The arranger is the bank originally responsible for advising the borrower as to the type of facility it requires and then negotiating the broad terms of the loan. It will either be a bank with which the borrower already has a relationship or one which has won the mandate to arrange the loan after pitching for the role (sometimes known as the 'mandated lead arranger' or 'MLA'). At the same time, the arranger will be putting together a syndicate to provide the loan.

In a large facility, syndication may be done in stages. The first stage will involve finding a further group of banks to provide a share of the facility with the arranger. These are usually known as 'lead managers' or 'co-arrangers'. The lead managers will then each attempt to find more banks to participate in the syndicate (known as 'participants') by taking a share of the lead managers' commitment (variations on these titles will appear to show banks' relative importance in the syndicate – see pp 32–33). Co-arrangers/managers commonly underwrite the loan, that is, they will have to provide the whole of the loan between them if further syndicate members cannot be found.

Once the facility is made available, the particpating banks might sell part or all of their commitment to other banks (or institutional lenders), known as 'secondary syndication'. However, a borrower will usually require the arranger to retain a substantial part of the facility (known as a 'minimum hold'), since negotiation with the arranger can become more difficult if it does not have any direct interest. The facility agreement should specifically state that the arranger does not owe the other syndicate members any common law fiduciary duties, in order to prevent any argument to the contrary.

3.3.2.2 Administrative agent

It is not difficult to imagine how the mechanics of a syndicated facility could become very unwieldy, especially if the syndicate members approached the numbers involved in the Eurotunnel facility. To avoid a logistical headache, it is common for one bank to act as agent for the others in the day-to-day running of the loan. This bank is known as the 'administrative agent' (or simply the 'agent') and, broadly, it must act as interpreter (maintaining regular contact with the borrower and representing the views of the syndicate), counsellor (dealing with any practical problems concerning the provisions of the agreement), policeman (monitoring the borrower's compliance with its obligations), postman and record keeper (it is the administrative agent to which the borrower must usually give notices (eg, of utilisation), pay interest and make repayments, and through which it will receive loan monies).

The administrative agent is simply empowered to administer the mechanics of the facility. Any material decisions, such as a waiver of facility agreement provisions, must usually be taken by the whole syndicate, or at least by a majority (see **3.3.2.4**). The administrative agent will carry the duties and responsibilities imposed on any agent under English law, but the facility agreement will contain provisions to limit the relationship (known as 'exculpatory provisions'), in particular:

(a) the agent will not want any obligation to act unless instructed by the syndicate;

(b) the agent will want the ability to delegate its functions and to take professional advice if necessary;

(c) the agent will want syndicate members to take responsibility for their own credit assessment of the borrower. It will not want responsibility for any information it passes to the syndicate members with respect to the borrower, for the efficacy of the facility agreement, or for any security or other ancillary documents (see **3.3.4** below);

(d) syndicate members will also be required to complete their own 'Know Your Customer' (or 'KYC') checks to comply with money laundering regulations;

(e) an agent must be able to take agency fees and other payments from the borrower without them being classed as secret profit (and therefore prohibited);

(f) the agent will want a right to resign, and the other syndicate members will want the right to replace it. A borrower will usually ask for a right of veto (or at least consultation) before any change is made, since its relationship with the agent is very important; and

(g) the agent will want an indemnity from syndicate members with respect to all costs incurred in its role as agent (unless they are recovered from the borrower).

3.3.2.3 Security trustee

If a syndicated loan is secured, one entity (usually one of the syndicate banks) will usually hold the security on trust for the whole syndicate. This entity is known as the 'security trustee'. In civil law jurisdictions, which may not recognise the trust, a 'security agent' and 'parallel debt' structure may be used instead (although the concepts are fundamentally different under English law, and the security document should reflect this). The fiduciary duties imposed upon a security agent/trustee will be more extensive than those of a simple agent.

3.3.2.4 Advantages of taking a role

There are several advantages for a bank in taking lead roles within a syndicated facility. The first is prestige: the most prestigious role is lead arranger. The other banks in the syndicate will then be allotted titles to reflect their standing within the syndicate (based on their contributions to the facility, financial and otherwise). A large deal might create numerous different titles which do not denote different responsibilities but simply cater for the need of a hierarchy. The second advantage to taking a leading role in the syndicate is the ability to charge fees (see **9.5**). Lastly, the 'relationship' banks within the syndicate will hope that the borrower comes to them for other financial products.

3.3.3 Tombstones

Historically, once a large deal closed, it would be announced by way of an 'advert' in the financial press with details of the borrower, deal size and main parties. This was known as a 'tombstone' (or sometimes the 'football team'), and some examples are shown at pp **32** and **33**. The tombstone would often be cast in a perspex block and given to parties and advisers as a 'memento' of the deal. Nowadays, both the adverts and mementos are uncommon, due probably to cost, alternative 'online' advertising and change in fashion.

3.3.4 Liability of arrangers

In order to persuade banks to join the syndicate, an arranger will have to provide a considerable amount of information about both the borrower and the facility. This usually takes the form of a document known as an 'information memorandum', compiled by the arranger and borrower. Since the syndicate members might reasonably be expected to rely on the facts in the information memorandum, it is an area of potential liability for the arranger.

It is market practice for the arranger to disclaim responsibility for information given to the syndicate, by including a clause in the information memorandum such as:

> The information in this document has been obtained from the borrower and other sources, and no representation or warranty, either express or implied, is given by the arranger with respect to such information.

The arranger will also want to include a warranty in the facility agreement, given by the syndicate members, to the effect that they have performed their own due diligence and are not relying on the information memorandum.

The effectiveness of the disclaimer and warranty has been questioned. First, as a general proposition, courts are reluctant to uphold exclusion clauses. More specifically, the Unfair Contract Terms Act 1977 will allow a disclaimer of liability for negligence or misrepresentation only if it satisfies a reasonableness test under the Act.

Secondly, the disclaimer and warranty clauses are often drafted too narrowly. They should cover:

(a)   excluded, as well as included, information;

(b)   oral, as well as written, information.

Thirdly, the arranger is almost certainly under a duty not to withhold relevant information, and also under a duty to answer fully any specific questions.

Furthermore, the courts have confirmed that the relationship between an arranger and the syndicate banks is a 'classic example' of a situation where a duty of care arises (see *Sumitomo Bank Ltd v Banque Bruxelles Lambert SA*, QBD (Commercial Court), 1 October 1996). However, in *IFE Fund SA v Goldman Sachs International* [2006] EWHC 2887, the Court of Appeal ruled that the disclaimer language commonly used in information memoranda is effective to deny an arranger's liability for the accuracy of information and to deny responsibility for updating it.

If the disclaimer and warranty are ineffective, the arranger may be liable to the syndicate members for misrepresentation or breach of warranty (see **5.5**).

3.4 Other forms of short-term lending

3.4.1 Standby facility

A standby facility is a generic name for a facility which a borrower does not intend using under normal circumstances but may need to utilise if other uncommitted funding is unexpectedly unavailable (see also swing-line facility at **3.4.3**). It may include a 'utilisation fee', payable (in addition to interest) if the facility is actually drawn.

3.4.2 Bankers' acceptance

A bankers' acceptance is a bill of exchange (essentially a written acknowledgement by one party that it owes a second party money at a future date) which a bank has agreed to be responsible for paying when it falls due. The borrower which asked the bank to accept its bill must eventually reimburse the bank, but in the meantime it is effectively borrowing short term from the bank.

3.4.3 Swing-line facility

A swing-line facility is a facility which is usually made available to a company which has a commercial paper programme ('commercial paper' is a short-term – between one day and one year – uncommitted debt security ('IOU') issued by a company to investors). The swing-line facility can be utilised on very short notice (eg, by a telephone request) to allow the borrower to pay back any maturing commercial paper which it is unable to re-lend ('rollover').

Chapter 17 provides a short explanation of MTNs, bills of exchange and commercial paper.

3.5 Which facility is appropriate?

This chapter has outlined the common forms of loan facility. It should be appreciated that, rather like primary colours, these can be mixed and matched to suit an individual client's requirements. Furthermore, within a particular type of facility, the mechanics of utilisation, interest payment and the repayment schedule can fundamentally alter its complexion. A banking solicitor must therefore understand his client's needs and business in order to establish the most appropriate facility and properly negotiate its terms.

3.6 Anatomy of a facility agreement

Banks must lend to make money; businesses must borrow to thrive. The ultimate aim of borrower and bank is therefore the same: both want the loan in place as soon as possible. The loan contract could of course be made orally. It is generally accepted, however, that the certainty of a written facility agreement is preferable, especially from an evidential point of view. But how can a facility agreement which might be summarised in a 10-page term sheet grow to a 150-page document? To answer that question, it is important to realise that the provisions in a loan document are almost all designed to protect the bank's position, since it is the bank which is most likely to suffer in the event of any uncertainty or ambiguity.

3.6.1   A bank's concerns

In broad terms, a bank will want to ensure three things:

(a)   its fees are paid;

(b)   it receives interest on the loan;

(c)   it eventually gets its loan capital back.

These aims may be best served by ensuring that:

(a)   the loan monies are used only for a specific purpose(s);

(b)   the borrower does not do anything which might put its ability to service and/or repay the loan at risk;

(c)   the borrower is monitored to give early warning of any possibility that it might be unable to service or repay the loan; and

(d)   all monies due to the bank are secured over the borrower's assets.

These areas of concern provide the pattern for most facility agreements (the first draft of which is usually produced by the bank's solicitor). First, the agreement will need clauses to cover the use and flow of the borrowed money, for example:

(a)   amount and purpose;

(b)   fees;

(c)   interest payment;

(d)   repayment;

(e)   maturity;

(f)   early termination by the bank.

Secondly, there will be a number of clauses designed to protect the bank's profit margin in the event that certain costs or other circumstances change, for example:

(a)   withholding tax is imposed (the 'gross-up clause');

(b)   regulatory capital costs change (the 'increased costs clause');

(c)   the interbank market costs change (the 'market disruption clause');

(d)   it becomes illegal for the bank to lend to the borrower (the 'illegality clause');

(e)   other unexpected costs are incurred (indemnities).

Thirdly, the facility agreement will usually contain provisions allowing the bank to keep a check on the borrower's 'financial health', and to deal with the possibility of things going wrong, for example:

(a)   conditions to be met before utilisation ('conditions precedent');

(b)   information from the borrower about its status and business ('representations and warranties');

(c)   promises by the borrower about things it will do, or will not do ('undertakings');

(d)   events allowing the bank to cancel the loan ('events of default');

(e) security over the borrower's assets.

Lastly, there will be a number of provisions which the bank's solicitor insists are necessary for smooth operation of the agreement, for example:

(a) a governing law clause;

(b) provisions for assignment of the loan; and

(c) provisions for serving notices.

The clauses in a facility agreement can therefore be classified into four main groups.

(a) 'Mechanics' clauses (ie, clauses dealing with the mechanics of making the money flow).

(b) Margin protection clauses (ie, clauses protecting the bank's profit).

(c) General protection clauses (ie, clauses connected with the bank's willingness initially to make the loan, and then to allow it to continue).

(d) Boiler plate clauses (ie, provisions governing the relationship between the parties, and enforcement of the agreement).

3.6.2 A borrower's concerns

The borrower's primary concern is flexibility. It wants the money to achieve its aims, and the fewer strings that are attached the better. In particular, the borrower wants the bank (and so the facility agreement) to recognise that there are bound to be highs and lows on the road to corporate success, and so if the bank sticks with it, everything will be fine in the end ... probably.

The main areas to be negotiated, therefore, will relate to the monitoring of, and restrictions on, the borrower. The solicitors must try to negotiate a document which both bank and borrower feel is an acceptable and workable compromise. The mechanics will, to a large extent, be a function of the terms agreed initially between bank and borrower, and recorded in the term sheet (see **Chapter 2**). The boiler plate will contain provisions affording protection for the bank, or (occasionally) the borrower, and provisions 'oiling' the mechanics. These will usually be included as a matter of accepted market practice. **Chapters 4** to **9** will focus on the detail of loan documentation.

3.7 Further reading

Stephen Valdez, *An Introduction to Global Financial Markets* (5th edn, Macmillan, 2006).

Geoffrey Fuller, *Corporate Borrowing: Law and Practice* (2nd edn, Jordans, 1999).

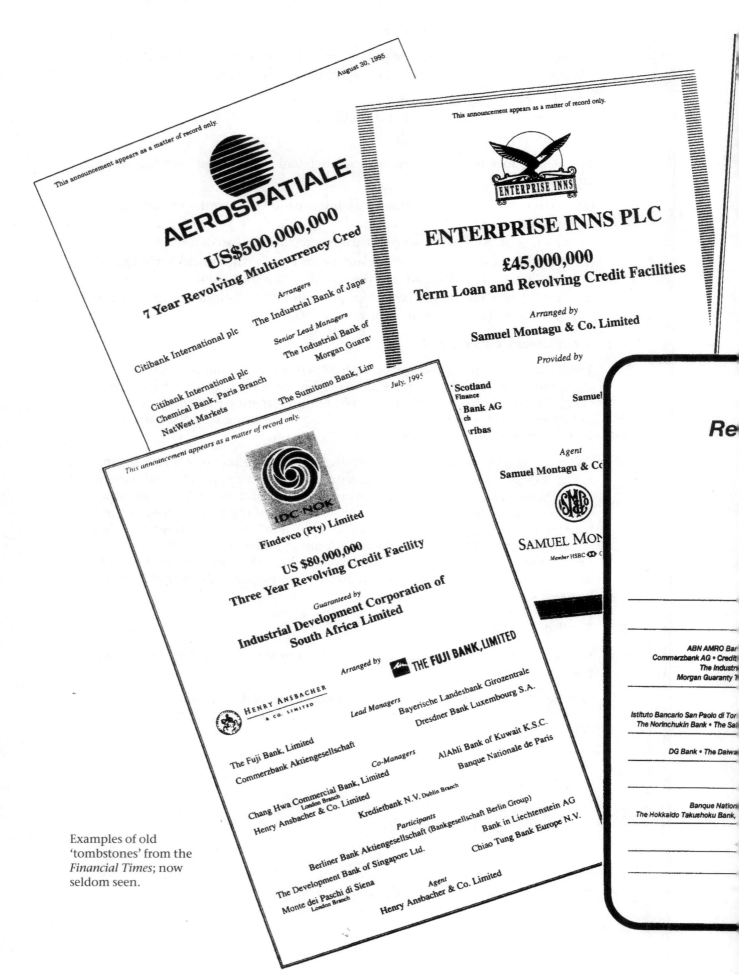

Examples of old 'tombstones' from the *Financial Times*; now seldom seen.

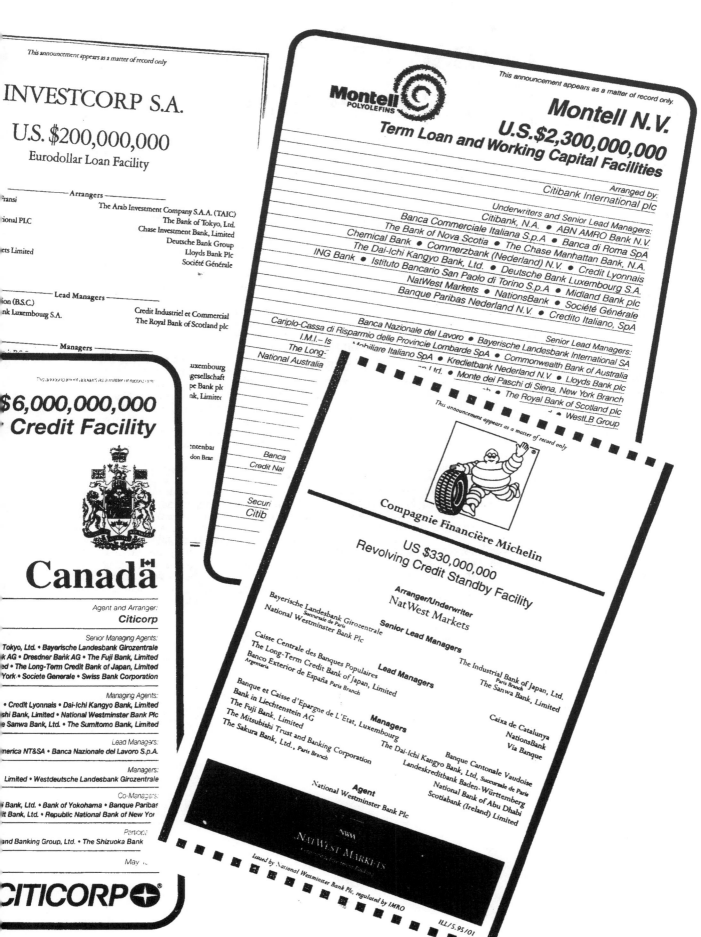

This announcement appears as a matter of record only

INVESTCORP S.A.
U.S. $200,000,000
Eurodollar Loan Facility

——— Arrangers ———

...ransi
...ional PLC
...ts Limited

The Arab Investment Company S.A.A. (TAIC)
The Bank of Tokyo, Ltd.
Chase Investment Bank, Limited
Deutsche Bank Group
Lloyds Bank Plc
Société Générale

——— Lead Managers ———

...ion (B.S.C.)
...nk Luxembourg S.A.

Credit Industriel et Commercial
The Royal Bank of Scotland plc

——— Managers ———

This announcement appears as a matter of record only

Montell
POLYOLEFINS

Montell N.V.
U.S.$2,300,000,000
Term Loan and Working Capital Facilities

Arranged by:
Citibank International plc

Underwriters and Senior Lead Managers:
Citibank, N.A. • ABN AMRO Bank N.V.
Banca Commerciale Italiana S.p.A • Banca di Roma SpA
The Bank of Nova Scotia • The Chase Manhattan Bank, N.A.
Chemical Bank • Commerzbank (Nederland) N.V. • Credit Lyonnais
The Dai-Ichi Kangyo Bank, Ltd. • Deutsche Bank Luxembourg S.A.
ING Bank • Istituto Bancario San Paolo di Torino S.p.A • Midland Bank plc
NatWest Markets • NationsBank • Société Générale
Banque Paribas Nederland N.V. • Credito Italiano, SpA

Senior Lead Managers:
Banca Nazionale del Lavoro • Bayerische Landesbank International SA
Cariplo-Cassa di Risparmio delle Provincie Lombarde SpA • Commonwealth Bank of Australia
I.M.I. – Is... ...Mobiliare Italiano SpA • Kredietbank Nederland N.V. • Lloyds Bank plc
The Long-... ...td. • Monte dei Paschi di Siena, New York Branch
National Australia ...h • The Royal Bank of Scotland plc
... WestLB Group

This announcement appears as a matter of record only

$6,000,000,000
Credit Facility

Canada

Agent and Arranger:
Citicorp

Senior Managing Agents:
...Tokyo, Ltd. • Bayerische Landesbank Girozentrale
...k AG • Dresdner Bank AG • The Fuji Bank, Limited
...ed • The Long-Term Credit Bank of Japan, Limited
...York • Societe Generale • Swiss Bank Corporation

Managing Agents:
• Credit Lyonnais • Dai-Ichi Kangyo Bank, Limited
...shi Bank, Limited • National Westminster Bank Plc
...e Sanwa Bank, Ltd. • The Sumitomo Bank, Limited

Lead Managers:
...merica NT&SA • Banca Nazionale del Lavoro S.p.A.

Managers:
...Limited • Westdeutsche Landesbank Girozentrale

Co-Managers:
...i Bank, Ltd. • Bank of Yokohama • Banque Paribas
...t Bank, Ltd. • Republic National Bank of New Yor...

Partic...
...and Banking Group, Ltd. • The Shizuoka Bank

May ...

CITICORP

This announcement appears as a matter of record only

Compagnie Financière Michelin
US $330,000,000
Revolving Credit Standby Facility

Arranger/Underwriter
NatWest Markets

Senior Lead Managers

Bayerische Landesbank Girozentrale
Succursale de Paris
National Westminster Bank Plc

Lead Managers

Caisse Centrale des Banques Populaires
The Long-Term Credit Bank of Japan, Limited
Banco Exterior de España Paris Branch
Argentaria

The Industrial Bank of Japan, Ltd.
Paris Branch
The Sanwa Bank, Limited

Managers

Banque et Caisse d'Epargne de L'Etat, Luxembourg
Bank in Liechtenstein AG
The Fuji Bank, Limited
The Mitsubishi Trust and Banking Corporation
The Sakura Bank, Ltd., Paris Branch

Caixa de Catalunya
NationsBank
Via Banque
Banque Cantonale Vaudoise
Landeskreditbank Baden-Württemberg
National Bank of Abu Dhabi
The Dai-Ichi Kangyo Bank, Ltd, Succursale de Paris
Scotiabank (Ireland) Limited

Agent
National Westminster Bank Plc

NWM
NATWEST MARKETS

Issued by National Westminster Bank Plc, regulated by IMRO

ILL/5.95/01

Hanson's £4.5bn deal closes oversubscribed

By Conner Middelmann

With bankers in much of Europe off on holiday, activity in the syndicated loans sector has slowed markedly.

"Unless there's some big acquisition, it'll stay quiet in the next few weeks," said one banker. "It's very difficult to get anything agreed. In many countries, like France and Italy, credit committees aren't even sitting – except on the beach."

Few new deals have been launched lately, but several are in general syndication.

The syndication of £4.5bn in new bank facilities for **Hanson** closed yesterday, heavily oversubscribed to the tune of £5.9bn.

"The full support of our banks for the demergers is confirmed by their oversubscription to these facilities," said Mr Derek Bonham, chief executive of the diversified industries conglomerate which is splitting into four companies. Chase Investment Bank acted as global co-ordinator.

A £500m working capital facility for the recently privatised **British Energy** has been launched into general syndication by arrangers BZW, DKB, IBJ, Midland and Royal Bank of Scotland.

The deal comprises a £225m term loan paying a margin of 35 basis points over Libor and a £275m revolving credit facility at 27.5 basis points over Libor, with a utilisation fee of 7.5 basis points if more than 50 per cent is drawn.

A presentation to banks was held last Wednesday, followed by a visit to the Dungeness power station on Friday. The deal may take

SYNDICATED LOANS

some time to evaluate and place, given that not every banker is comfortable with nuclear power.

"Nuclear power is an acquired taste," said one banker involved in the deal. "Some banks just wouldn't entertain it, but others – like French and Japanese – accept it more readily because they are familiar with it from their own countries," he said.

One new facility was the **Body Shop**'s debut loan, a $60m five-year revolving credit. The transaction is priced at 32.5 basis points over Libor and has a commitment fee of 17.5 basis points, as well as a utilisation fee of 5 basis points on drawings over 50 per cent. BZW is acting as arranger.

Elsewhere, the **Leeds & Holbeck Building Society** has asked Lloyds Bank and WestLB to renegotiate the terms of a £230m seven-year facility which it signed in April 1995. Dealers were puzzled that the borrower did not seek to lengthen the maturity of the loan, but chose simply to shave 5 basis points off the margins and reduce the commitment fees by between 1 and 1.75 basis points. The move reflects the decline in margins in the building society sector since early 1995, the borrower said.

● NatWest Markets is examining ways of structuring one of the largest foreign finance deals made to an independent Russian company. **Almazy Rossi Sakha**, Russia's leading diamond producer, last week awarded NatWest the mandate to raise $500m of funding over the next two years. The funding is expected to be made in several tranches.

An article illustrating different types of facility.
Source: *Financial Times.*

Chapter 4

When, Who, Where, What and Why?

4.1 Introduction

Broadly speaking, a facility agreement follows the same pattern as the majority of commercial agreements, namely:

(a) date, title and parties;

(b) interpretation/definitions;

(c) operative provisions;

(d) schedules;

(e) execution.

Even if they both provide the same type of facility, no two facility agreements will have identical provisions. Agreements must be tailored to suit borrowers, banks, purpose, market practice and the prevailing economic circumstances. However, **Chapters 4** to **9** endeavour to explain the main provisions that might be found in a typical bilateral or syndicated facility agreement made to an investment grade company for general corporate purposes. Contrast is made between strong and weak borrowers where appropriate. The terms are reviewed in the order in which they are likely to occur within a document, with this chapter covering the following clauses:

(a) date;

(b) parties;

(c) interpretation;

(d) the facility;

(e) purpose;

(f) conditions precedent;

(g) availability;

(h) interest.

4.2 Date

Usually the date clause will appear on the first page of the document, and should be completed, in manuscript, simultaneously with signing. If there are several parties signing on different days, the date should be that on which the last party signs. If there are conditions precedent outstanding, the document will usually become effective when signed and dated, but utilisation will not be possible (see **4.7**) until the conditions are either met or waived.

4.3 Parties

It may seem puerile even to mention this clause. There are, however, three things in a 200-page facility agreement that a bank will always check: the fee clause; the schedule of commitments; and whether the names of the bank and its representatives have been spelt correctly.

It is also important to consider who should be a party to the agreement. Privity of contract means that a party cannot usually assume obligations under a document (and so be sued for breach) unless it is a signatory to it. More complicated facilities may include companies in the borrower's group which are not borrowing directly, but which must guarantee the borrower's obligations under the loan (see **13.2**). Any such companies (eg, parent, subsidiary or sister companies of the borrower) must either be party to the facility agreement in order to bind them into its terms, or execute separate guarantee documents. Note, the Contracts (Rights of Third Parties) Act 1999 gives a third party rights to enforce a contractual term if the contract expressly so provides, or if the term confers a benefit on the third party (most facility agreements purport to exclude the effect of the Act other than allowing a bank's employees to benefit from indemnities and other 'protective' provisions).

It is usual for the names of the borrower and any guarantor to appear on the front page before the bank. If the loan is syndicated, the convention is to list the names of banks with particular roles (eg, 'Arranger' or 'Administrative Agent') at the front of the document, but to record the other banks by reference to a schedule at the back. If one party has two or more roles under an agreement, it is usual for it to execute the document separately in each capacity. One signature will be legally binding, however, as long as each capacity is specified.

If several companies are executing the facility (for example, as borrowers or guarantors) they must each have a separate execution clause, even if they share the same directors and/or secretary (see the Regulatory Reform (Execution of Deeds and Documents) Order 2005 (SI 2005/1906)).

4.4 Interpretation/definitions

This clause marks the beginning of the operative part of the document. The use of a definitions clause is particularly prevalent in facility agreements because there is a great deal of repetition of terms. However, if they are used excessively, definitions can make the document front-heavy and difficult to follow. If a term appears several times in one clause but not in any others, it should be defined in the clause where it appears rather than in the definitions section (this is often the case for financial covenants). Defined terms should always appear in the document with their initial letters in upper case. Beware, however – most documents have an 'interpretation' section (defining common words, eg, month, year, etc) immediately after the 'definitions' section, and this may include 'lower-case' definitions. Complex definitions are almost mini-clauses and they should be drafted with great care, particularly since any mistake is likely to occur more than once. Finally, you should not negotiate a definition before checking where it is used and thus the full effect of any changes.

4.5 The facility

The facility clause outlines the type of facility (or facilities) the bank will provide under the agreement, as well as the amount to be made available. From a borrower's perspective it is important to include this clause to create an obligation on the bank to lend (albeit conditional – see **4.7**). It may require just one sentence, for example:

> THE FACILITY
>
> Subject to the terms of this Agreement, the Bank agrees to make available to the Borrower a term loan up to an amount of £5,000,000.

For more complicated facilities, perhaps providing several loans in different currencies and from a syndicate of banks, the clause may be considerably longer. Each bank in a syndicated loan will agree to provide a proportion of the total facility, and this is known as the bank's 'commitment'. The agreement will specify that their obligations are 'several' (and not 'joint and several') to ensure that each bank is liable to provide only its own commitment.

4.5.1 Why 'facility'?

In common usage, the terms 'loan facility' and 'facility agreement' tend to be interchangeable. There are, however, two technical reasons why the use of 'loan facility' might be more appropriate in the document:

(a) The term 'agreement' suggests that the borrower has agreed to borrow money, and is obliged to draw down. The term 'facility' reflects the fact that the loan is available if the borrower wants to use it, but without an obligation to borrow.

(b) Any written acknowledgement of a company's indebtedness is classified as a 'debenture' under the Companies Act 1985 (CA 1985) (because the definition at s 744 includes the common law meaning). If a facility agreement was held to be a 'debenture', the consequences might include authorisation under the Financial Services and Markets Act 2000 (FSMA 2000). This is probably not an issue unless money has already been lent at the time the document is signed. Use of the word 'facility' is generally considered more helpful than 'loan' in this context.

How, then, can a bank prove that a borrower owes it any money? The account records kept by a bank showing the total amount outstanding (the bank's 'book') and certified by an appropriate officer of the bank are, under English law at least, prima facie evidence of the borrower's obligations (the facility agreement will usually require the borrower to accept the account records as conclusive evidence). In some jurisdictions (eg, the United States) the bank's account records would be insufficient evidence of debt. In that case, a certificate is issued acknowledging each utilisation (known as a 'promissory note').

4.5.2 Facility office

The facility office (or 'lending office') is the particular branch of a bank through which a loan is made ('booked'). The facility office will be specified in the facility agreement, and is the place where the borrower must make interest payments and capital repayments. The location of the facility office is of particular concern to a borrower for tax reasons (see **9.3.4**).

4.6 Purpose clause

4.6.1 Control

The bank will want the facility agreement to state explicitly how the loan monies can be used. It is the first point of control which a bank can use to protect its money and maximise the probability of being repaid. The wording may be relatively wide, for example:

> The Facility is to be used for general corporate purposes.

or

> The proceeds of the Facility will be used to support the general corporate requirements of the Borrower.

This would at least make it clear that the borrower must not place the first utilisation on the '2.30' race at Epsom.

Sometimes, however, a purpose clause will be more specific. For example, restricting the use to 'working capital' purposes will probably exclude making a substantial acquisition. If the bank has assessed its credit risk (see **2.2**) on a particular project which the borrower is to finance with the loan monies (known as 'project finance'), or it has taken security over particular assets on which it will want the loan monies spent, the purpose clause should be drafted accordingly.

Some purpose clauses state that money should not be used for certain purposes (eg, an investment in particular companies). The purpose clause might also contain restrictions which are driven by the bank's constitution or policy.

Two matters closely connected with the purpose clause are those of capacity and authority. The questions of whether a borrower has the capacity to enter into a transaction, and who is authorised to bind the borrower, are invariably determined in accordance with the law of the borrower's domicile (for companies, this is the country of incorporation). The position for companies incorporated under English law is considered briefly below.

4.6.2 Capacity

The CA 1989 attempted to clarify the position with respect to a company's capacity to enter into a transaction, by introducing a new s 35 to the CA 1985. The law on ultra vires acts prior to the new s 35 was complicated, and is now largely obsolete (although it still applies to transactions completed before 4 February 1991, and to certain acts of charitable companies (see CA 1989, ss 111, 112)). However, a brief summary of the pre-s 35 law with respect to borrowing is given at **4.6.2.1**, since it formed the basis of the new law.

4.6.2.1 The position pre-CA 1989

Prima facie, a company could pursue only the objects for which its memorandum stated it was incorporated. Pre-CA 1989, therefore, a company could avoid performing its obligations under a contract which was outside the company's objects (an 'ultra vires' act). However, in *Rolled Steel Products (Holdings) Ltd v British Steel Corporation* [1986] Ch 246, it was confirmed that an ultra vires transaction was not void unless the contracting party had actual or constructive notice of the company's agents (ie, the directors) breaching their fiduciary duties (in which case the contracting party would be a constructive trustee for the company, and be liable to return any property it had received). The directors' breach of duty in allowing an ultra vires act could be ratified by the shareholders.

In the context of a facility agreement, a purpose clause stating that the loan was to be used 'for general corporate purposes' would allow a bank to assume that the purpose of exercising the borrowing power was intra vires. However, if a purpose clause were more specific, the bank may have been unable to assume the loan was within the borrower's objects, and there was a danger of the loan being void. (Note that, whilst all trading and commercial companies have an implied power to borrow (*Introductions Ltd v National Provincial Bank* [1970] Ch 199), this is an implied power not an implied object, and so generally it can be used only in pursuance of a purpose authorised by a company's objects.)

4.6.2.2   The position post-CA 1989

The CA 1989 attempted to consolidate the position at common law by substituting a new s 35(1) into the CA 1985, stating:

> The validity of an act done by a company shall not be called into question on the ground of lack of capacity by reason of anything in the company's memorandum.

(Equivalent language in the CA 2006 is not expected to come into force until late 2009.)

The intention was to remove the concept of ultra vires acts from the perspective of the company's creditors (the directors remained liable for any losses to the company due to the ultra vires act, unless ratified by two special resolutions – one ratifying the breach of duty, the other ratifying the loss). A person dealing with a company in good faith should not therefore be concerned with its constitution. The section does not, however, provide protection for a transaction which is invalid for other reasons (eg, illegality).

4.6.2.3   Conclusion

Whilst the CA 1989 appears to provide considerable protection for creditors with respect to a company's capacity, most practitioners remain cautious about relying on its provisions. In practice, a bank's solicitor should check the borrower's memorandum at an early stage. The memorandum should specifically 'authorise' the company's business activities, and most companies will include an express object in their memorandum allowing them to borrow. However, in the absence of clearly drafted clauses, the borrower should be required to alter its memorandum to include them (similarly, a company required to give guarantees or security should contain specific objects to that effect).

4.6.3   Authority

The second issue from a bank's perspective is to ensure that a person who acts to bind a corporate borrower has authority to do so, since agency law dictates that a principal will not be bound if an agent acts outside his authority. That authority may be actual or ostensible.

4.6.3.1   Actual authority

The articles of association of most companies provide for the powers of the company to be exercised at a meeting of the board of directors. It is also usual for the board to delegate their powers to a committee, or appoint an attorney to sign on their behalf. Prima facie, there may be several restrictions on this authority:

(a) The articles of association will often contain specific limitations on borrowing (although see CA 1985, s 35B, at **4.6.3.2**). These might restrict the amount of money which the company may borrow (often by reference to the net asset value of the company), or they may require a specific internal procedure to be followed before borrowing is sanctioned. Furthermore, some borrowers will be restricted under statute (eg, insurance companies).

(b)   It is not uncommon for directors to want to appoint an attorney to execute a document and to agree any 'eleventh hour' changes. However, most articles do not allow directors to delegate their powers to non-directors. Therefore, although a non-director can probably be empowered to execute a settled document, delegation of powers to agree substantial amendments may be ineffective (although see CA 1985, s 35A, at **4.6.3.2**).

(c)   An agent cannot have actual authority to bind a company to a transaction which is not for the purpose of, or reasonably incidental to, attaining or pursuing the company's objects (*Rolled Steel Products (Holdings) Ltd v British Steel Corporation* [1986] Ch 246, CA). See **Chapter 14**.

4.6.3.2   Ostensible (apparent) authority

The common law doctrine of ostensible authority implies, subject to certain limitations, authority on an agent which the agent appears to have because of his principal's representations, or because of his 'status'. However, any actual or constructive notice of limitations on the authority will restrict the ability to rely upon it. Furthermore, the scope of ostensible authority is by no means certain.

There are, nevertheless, a number of matters which might reassure a creditor as to an agent's actual or ostensible authority:

(a)   a trading company has an implied power to borrow money (*Introductions Ltd v National Provincial Bank* [1970] Ch 199);

(b)   English courts have, to date, taken a narrow view of what might be ultra vires when considering a contract between a company and a person who is not a member;

(c)   CA 1985, s 35A, which provides:

(1)   In favour of a person dealing with a company in good faith, the power of the board of directors to bind the company, or authorise others to do so, shall be deemed to be free of any limitation under the company's constitution.

(2)   For this purpose—

(a)   a person 'deals with' a company if he is party to any transaction or other act to which the company is a party;

(b)   a person shall not be regarded as acting in bad faith by reason only of his knowing that an act is beyond the powers of the directors under the company's constitution; and

(c)   a person shall be presumed to have acted in good faith unless the contrary is proved.

(3)   The references above to limitations on the directors' powers under the company's constitution include limitations deriving—

(a)   from a resolution of the company in general meeting or a meeting of any class of shareholders, or

(b)   from any agreement between the members of the company or of any class of shareholders.

(d)   CA 1985, s 35B, which provides:

A party to a transaction with a company is not bound to enquire as to whether it is permitted by the company's memorandum or as to any limitation on the powers of the board of directors to bind the company or authorise others to do so.

In other words, a corporate borrower cannot generally repudiate a transaction on the grounds that it is outside its objects.

4.6.3.3   Conclusion

Most practitioners are wary of relying on the possible 'lifeboats' outlined at **4.6.3.2**. Implied powers may be explicitly revoked, judicial interpretation is not a constant, ostensible authority has substantial limitations, and ss 35A and 35B of the CA 1985 depend on good faith and decisions being made through the board of directors.

The only sure way to avoid problems is to make certain that a company's agents are properly authorised to execute the facility agreement. The bank's solicitor should ensure that the borrower holds a board meeting which explicitly addresses the implications for the borrower of executing the facility agreement and any ancillary documentation, and authorising the borrower to execute all the documentation through specified agents (eg, the directors). The meeting must satisfy any conditions as to quorum, and certified copies of the minutes should be required as a condition precedent to utilisation (see **4.7**).

In addition, there are a number of institutions other than limited companies which may seek to borrow, such as partnerships, building societies or local authorities, all with different common law or statutory powers. A solicitor must therefore consider the legal status and nature of a borrower and then assess its legal capacity and what action is required to provide proper authority (local authorities have been particularly problematic, eg, *Crédit Suisse v Allerdale Borough Council* [1997] QB 306, where the local authority's guarantee was held void for being ultra vires).

4.6.4   Resulting trust

Another reason for including a purpose clause is an attempt to create a resulting trust if the purpose fails. For example, imagine a loan made specifically to fund a new factory for borrower B. After two months, B's orders suddenly dry up and it stops work on the factory. If the purpose of the loan was specified then, since that purpose has failed, any money which has been drawn down but remains unspent (and identifiable) will be held by B on resulting trust for the bank (*Barclays Bank Ltd v Quistclose Investments Ltd* [1970] AC 567). While B is solvent, the question of whether unspent monies are held on trust or in contract is largely irrelevant. On its insolvency, however, any money held on trust by B must be paid to the bank, irrespective of any claims by other creditors. If held under contract, the money would become an asset of B to be shared between its creditors in accordance with the liquidation process.

4.6.5   The bank's and borrower's perspectives

The purpose clause is designed to oblige the borrower to use the loan for the purpose stated, but it should also expressly absolve the bank from any liability to ensure that the funds are used in accordance with that purpose. This will avoid any claim by the borrower (or a guarantor of the loan) that the bank has consented to, or waived, any misuse of funds, or has a duty to ensure the money is properly applied.

The borrower's main concern is usually to ensure that the purpose clause is drafted widely enough to allow versatility in using the borrowed money and avoid any possibility that it might breach the clause. For example, the borrower will be responsible for paying all costs incurred in negotiating the loan. A borrower will usually want to ensure that the purpose clause is wide enough to allow him to pay these costs out of the money drawn under the loan.

4.7   Conditions precedent

4.7.1   Purpose

Conditions precedent (CPs) are, as their name suggests, specific conditions which a bank requires a borrower to fulfil before part or all of a facility agreement takes effect. The CPs provide tangible evidence that the representations and warranties (see **Chapter 5**) are met. The clause is usually found near the beginning of the loan facility, but if there are numerous CPs to satisfy, they may be listed in a schedule at the back of the agreement.

4.7.2   Condition precedent to ...?

Usually, the substantial parts of a loan document will come into effect as soon as it is executed by all the parties, but the borrower will not be able to utilise unless and until the CPs are satisfied. This has a number of advantages for the bank. First, the borrower is locked in to the main provisions of the agreement. This means the bank's fees are payable and remedies for default apply.

Secondly, the representations, warranties, undertakings, events of default and boiler plate (see **Chapters 5** to **9**) will all become operative as soon as the document is executed. This means the bank can begin monitoring the borrower, even whilst the borrower is trying to satisfy the CPs.

4.7.3   Watch out for ...

4.7.3.1   Time-limits

In many cases, the CPs will be satisfied by 'closing' (ie, the time the loan documentation is executed and goes 'live'). If a borrower believes it cannot satisfy one or more CPs it will have to ask the banks for a temporary or permanent waiver. Most of the CPs, aside from the legal opinions, are within the borrower's control and so it, through its solicitors, must collect the necessary paperwork and deliver it to the bank's solicitor before execution. In practice, however, the bank's solicitor also takes responsibility for ensuring that the CPs are either satisfied (or waived) and he may have to write a 'CP confirmation letter' to the agent confirming the position. If the loan is for a specific purpose, for example an acquisition, then timing of the CPs and first utilisation will almost certainly be tied in to the acquisition timetable.

4.7.3.2   Uncertainty

It is possible that a CP could be so vague as to make the agreement void for uncertainty. For example, a condition in a contract which stipulated that the sale was 'subject to the purchaser obtaining a satisfactory mortgage' was held to make the entire contract void in *Lee-Parker v Izett (No 2)* [1972] 2 All ER 800. It is, however, common to see wording requiring a CP document to be 'in form and substance satisfactory to the banks'. This is probably certain enough in legal terms, although it may trouble the borrower (see **4.7.6**).

4.7.4   Typical conditions precedent

Obviously the form of the CPs will depend entirely on the particular transaction, but a general purpose term loan is likely to require fewer CPs than a multi-currency term and RCF funding an acquisition. Many CPs to a facility agreement are fairly standard, however, and those most commonly seen are mentioned at **4.7.4.1**.

4.7.4.1 Documentary

Common CPs might include:

(a) current memorandum and articles of the borrower and any companies giving guarantees or security;

(b) a board resolution approving the terms and conditions of the facility agreement and authorising signatories (usually the directors);

(c) a list of names of authorised signatories, together with a specimen of their signatures;

(d) a shareholders' resolution from any guarantor, approving the guarantee (if there are any possible corporate benefit issues associated with it);

(e) legal opinions from the bank's lawyers confirming the validity of the agreement and effectiveness of any security (see **Chapter 16**);

(f) a comfort letter from the borrower's parent (see **13.2.2**);

(g) insurance policies (including any 'Keyman' insurance (see **7.6**));

(h) certificates of title for any properties;

(i) executed security documents, together with any documents of title (eg, share certificates) which those documents require;

(j) copies of any other related documents (eg, fee letters, hedging agreements, intercreditor, and of course the loan facility executed by all parties);

(k) management accounts;

(l) payment instructions notifying the bank where loan monies should be paid;

(m) any consents or licences which are necessary in connection with the purpose of the loan;

(n) an agreement for an agent for service of process to be appointed by a borrower which is domiciled abroad (see also **9.8**).

If a borrower does not want to provide an original document then a 'certified copy' might be sufficient. This is a copy which has been signed, usually by a director or secretary of the borrower, as a true copy of the original as at a given date. Clearly, certified copies of board minutes are acceptable; certified copies of share certificates are usually not. If the borrower is based overseas and original documents are likely to be in a language other than English, the facility agreement should require the borrower to provide translations.

4.7.4.2 Other

Most CPs entail providing documentary evidence. However, it will also be a condition of utilisation that no event of default is continuing (see **Chapter 8**) and CPs might include less tangible things such as obtaining a listing, being granted a licence, or obtaining competition clearance.

4.7.5 Conditions subsequent

In some transactions, notably acquisition finance bids which are required to happen quickly, some of the usual CPs are made 'conditions subsequent'. For example, the borrower may be required to give share security over its subsidiaries as a condition precedent, but the remaining security as a condition subsequent within, say, 90 days of utilisation.

4.7.6 CPs – the bank's perspective

A bank looks to the CPs, alongside the representations (see **Chapter 5**), to satisfy it of the borrower's position before any money is utilised. The bank simply lists what it requires. In a syndicated loan, the agent is sometimes given responsibility for receiving and checking the CPs. This is generally better for the borrower (see **4.7.6**), but, from the agent's point of view, greater discretion entails greater potential for liability to the other members of the syndicate.

4.7.7   CPs – the borrower's perspective

The borrower must approach a bank's shopping list of CPs with some caution. Can they be achieved within the required time? Even if the bank's time-limit appears generous there may be other pressures. A borrower which is seeking a listing or making a takeover bid for a listed company must demonstrate to the Listing Authority and Takeover Panel that it has sufficient money (known as 'certain funds').

The potentially problematic CPs for the borrower are those where a third party is involved. The form and availability of accountants' reports, licences and opinions should all be agreed early in the countdown to signing. There are solutions to most problems, provided they are addressed in good time: a bank may be less flexible if a problem is sprung on it at the last minute in what looks like tactical timing.

Another potential minefield for a borrower is wording, such as 'in form and substance satisfactory to the bank'. This gives a bank plenty of discretion to decide that something is not satisfactory and utilisation cannot be made. Wherever possible, an agreed form should be settled in advance, for example with respect to board minutes and legal opinions. These are sometimes appended in draft form in a schedule to the agreement, so that all parties know what is required. If a form cannot be agreed in advance, qualifying the bank's discretion with the word 'reasonable' gives a borrower some comfort.

Lastly, this is one area where the borrower in a syndicated loan might press for acceptance of documents to be in the discretion of the agent or, if not, a simple majority of the syndicate. The agent is likely to be the entity with which the borrower has the best relationship, and so may be more flexible. Majority decisions entail persuading a number of banks, but at least avoid dissenting minorities causing trouble.

4.8   Availability

4.8.1   Single utilisation loan

The availability or 'utilisation' clause deals with the mechanics of when and how the borrower can actually borrow money under the loan. A simple term loan might allow the money to be utilised in one amount on a specified day. The utilisation clause will essentially say: '... satisfy the CPs, repeat the representations, and so long as you are not in default we will comply with your utilisation request'.

4.8.2   Multiple utilisation loan

More sophisticated facilities might allow the borrower to utilise in a number of tranches (or 'loans') as and when required, up to the available amount. Tranches must be utilised within a 'commitment period' (see **3.2.2**). Revolving credit facilities offer even more flexibility, allowing repeated utilisation and repayment throughout the term of the facility. A bank will invariably charge a 'commitment fee' during any commitment period (see **9.5**). In either case, the availability clause must cater for multiple utilisation.

4.8.2.1　Notice of utilisation

A fundamental premise of syndicated facility mechanics is that banks will use the inter-bank market to fund large advances (sometimes known as 'matched funding') (see **4.9**). They will therefore usually require the borrower to give several business days' notice of utilisation. The number of days depends largely on the currency: in the London market, eurocurrencies (currencies held outside their country of origin – see **Chapter 17**) would technically require a minimum of two clear business days for the bank to fund, whereas domestic sterling, if available, could probably be funded on the day of request. In a syndicated loan, however, the banks will usually require notice no later than the third business day before the day of utilisation for eurocurrencies, or the first business day before for sterling (the extra time allows syndicate members to sub-participate the loan if required – see **Chapter 10**). Often the facility document will specify the latest time in a day when a request can be received (eg, 11 am). Money can always be made available more quickly, but at a cost. If the facility is a revolving one, where fees are usually higher to buy flexibility, the bank is more likely to accept a shorter notice period.

Some utilisation provisions require the borrower's request to be not more than a specified period (eg, two weeks) before the money is required. This is a purely practical point to avoid the situation, not unknown among sovereign borrowers, where a borrower puts in a request several years in advance!

Once a utilisation notice is given, a borrower is usually committed to taking the money requested. Once again, this is based on the assumption that banks will have matched funded a facility, and that 'funding loan' cannot be cancelled.

4.8.2.2　Representations and defaults

In its utilisation request, a borrower must confirm there is no current default (and that utilisation will not result in a default) (see **Chapter 8**). In a facility allowing multiple utilisations, those requirements must be complied with each time a utilisation is requested.

4.9　Interest

Banks have shareholders and must make profits in order to pay dividends. One source of profit is the interest a bank charges on its loans, and the following section examines how that interest is charged.

4.9.1　Floating rate loans

The vast majority of commercial loans will bear interest at a floating rate: the interest rate on the loan will vary periodically to reflect the cost to the bank of providing the money. The cost of providing the money depends on its source.

4.9.1.1　Base rate

Loans to individuals, small commercial loans and overdrafts will usually be funded from the money a bank holds for its depositors (eg, current accounts and certificates of deposit) and raises from other investors (eg, bond issues – see **Chapter 17**). The cost to the bank of funding these loans is essentially an amalgam of the amounts it must pay to attract the depositors and investors, together with certain associated costs of lending (see below and **9.3.2**). From those costs, the bank calculates its 'base rate' (eg, 5%) which acts as a yardstick from which it sets the interest rates on its smaller loans. A floating rate loan may, therefore, be set at, say, base rate plus 0.5%. This ensures that the bank maintains its margin of profit on the loan whatever its cost of funding, reflected in the base rate, might be.

4.9.1.2   LIBOR

In the case of large commercial loans, and loans in non-domestic currencies, a bank may not be able to fund the loan from its deposits and will instead borrow from another bank. This is known as 'interbank funding', or 'matched funding'. Interbank funding gives the loan market liquidity, providing quick and reliable money for banks which are short of funds to meet their lending commitments, and allowing banks with a surplus of funds to put them to work. The rate of interest which a bank demands on money it offers to other banks in the London markets is known as its London Interbank Offered Rate (LIBOR). A bank's LIBOR will vary depending on a number of factors, including:

(a)   the credit rating of the borrowing bank (banks with good credit ('prime banks') will command the lowest LIBOR);

(b)   the currency of the loan;

(c)   the length of the loan; and

(d)   the cost to the lending bank of the money it is prepared to lend (ie, how cheaply it can raise money itself).

LIBOR rates will fluctuate throughout each day (in contrast, base rates might be reset only every few months) and so any interest rates which are 'pegged' to LIBOR should specify the date and time at which the rate is to be taken (usually 11 am, when the interbank market is active). Note that references to 'LIBOR' often refer to the average rate compiled by the British Bankers Association (see **4.9.2.1**, 'Screen rate', below).

The London Interbank Bid Rate (LIBID) is the interest rate which banks are prepared to pay to borrow money in the inter-bank market (marginally below LIBOR); the London Interbank Mean Rate (LIMEAN) is the average of the bid and offered rate for a particular bank. Each major financial centre will have an interbank rate for borrowing particular currencies, for example MIBOR in Moscow, TIBOR in Tokyo, and HIBOR in Hong Kong.

4.9.2   Interest rate

The actual rate of interest which a borrower pays on a floating rate loan based on matched funding will be calculated on the basis of:

(a)   LIBOR (or other appropriate funding rate); plus

(b)   an amount known as the mandatory cost (also known as the 'mandatory liquid assets costs', 'reserve assets costs' or 'associated costs'), which is the cost of complying with supervisory charges (see **9.3.2**) (note that this cost is usually built into a bank's base rate); plus

(c)   the 'margin' (which is where the bank makes its profit) as recorded in the term sheet (and which includes regulatory capital 'maintenance' costs – see **9.3.3**).

4.9.2.1   Screen rate

If the loan is provided by a syndicate, each bank may have a slightly different LIBOR (depending on the bank's size and credit rating).

In order to simplify matters, most syndicated loans use an average rate, calculated and published by an information service. This is known as a 'screen rate', the most commonly used being an average rate compiled by the British Bankers Association ('BBA'). The BBA calculates its LIBOR rate (for sterling) by asking 16 prime banks to submit the rate at which they could borrow inter-bank funds, then discarding the four highest and four lowest rates and averaging the remaining eight. The European Central Bank also compiles an average rate for borrowing euros throughout Member States, known as 'EURIBOR'. EURIBOR is calculated by taking rates from 47 Europe-wide banks, discarding the highest and lowest 15%, and averaging the remainder.

All commercial banks will subscribe to screen-based information services such as Reuters or Bloomberg, which publish BBA LIBOR and other screen rates.

4.9.2.2 Reference banks

An alternative to using a screen rate is to calculate the average LIBOR of a small group of 'reference banks'. The reference banks are usually chosen as representative of the range of banks within the syndicate, but they may not necessarily be participants. Their identity is clearly of great importance to a borrower: Barclays Bank is likely to have a lower LIBOR (because it can raise funds more cheaply) than Dry Gulch Bank Inc. The reference bank rate is often used as a fallback if the screen rate is unavailable.

4.9.2.3 Alternative rates: market disruption clause

In some circumstances the screen rate and reference bank rate may be unavailable (eg, through market disruption, or, more likely, where a rate is required for a 'non-standard' period). If a borrower is about to utilise, the facility agreement will usually prevent it from doing so until a rate can be set. If the loan has already been utilised the agreement will usually provide for a temporary alternative way to fix LIBOR. Typically it requires each syndicate bank to calculate its actual cost of funds. It is usually known as the 'increased costs clause' or 'market disruption clause' and will also apply if a certain percentage of the syndicate can demonstrate that the screen rate does not cover their cost of borrowing.

4.9.3 Interest periods

A simple loan might require a borrower to pay interest at regular intervals throughout the term of the loan. More sophisticated agreements will divide the life of each tranche into successive 'interest periods' of varying duration. Interest periods fulfil a number of different functions:

(a) The LIBOR rate is recalculated at the start of each interest period and applies for the duration of that interest period (hence the 'floating rate' loan is really a succession of different fixed rates).

(b) Interest is payable at the end of each interest period.

(c) The borrower can usually select the duration of each interest period, giving him some control over the rate he pays and timing of payment to match income.

(d) The chosen interest period will (theoretically at least) be mirrored by the bank's interbank loan (the borrower's choice is often limited to one, three or six months, since these are the most common interbank funding periods).

(e) Repayments (and prepayments) are required to coincide with the end of an interest period, when the bank will (theoretically) be repaying its interbank loan.

If the borrower prepays mid interest period, it will be charged 'break costs'. These are typically the difference between total interest the bank would have received to the end of the broken interest period, less the interest it can raise by lending the prepaid amount in the interbank market. Strong borrowers will argue they should not pay margin or mandatory cost for the remaining period but just the difference between the LIBOR on the loan and the current LIBOR (if less).

Banks move to pass on rising cost of funding

By Anousha Sakoui and Kathrin Hille

Bankers have started to invoke rights that allow them to pass the rising cost of their funding on to companies, threatening to create further pressure in a deteriorating economic climate.

The controversial move comes as questions continue to surround the accuracy of Libor as a true measure of bank funding costs.

One of the world's largest electronics contract manufacturers is one of the first examples to emerge.

Taiwan's Hon Hai, whose Foxconn unit is one of the world's biggest contract makers of mobile phones, said a consortium of global and local lenders had more than doubled the interest spread on a $1.035bn loan owing to a rise in the banks' own borrowing costs.

'The lenders invoked the market disruption clause,' said Edmund Ding, Hon Hai spokesman. 'This happened because global interbank lending rates spiked following Lehman's breakdown just as our loans were being rolled over.' Mr Ding said the uncertainties were likely to force companies to adjust the way they borrow.

Most loan financings carry a 'market disruption clause', which allows lenders to switch the rate at which they lend to a company from a Libor-based price to a level that represents their true cost of funds. Depending on the deal, it requires the approval of at least a third of the syndicate and also requires banks to disclose what they believe their own cost of funding to be - something they have hitherto been reluctant to do.

A potential headache for banks is that many such facilities will have been agreed before the recent worsening in credit conditions at a fixed rate over Libor - a rate that may now be lower than a bank's all-in cost of funding that facility. Before triggering such clauses banks have to weigh the risk of upsetting clients that may take business elsewhere.

The British Bankers Association said on Monday it would delay the publication of a report on governance and scrutiny of Libor, the rate at which banks lend to each other, because of the market turmoil. It believes banks should not invoke 'market disruption clauses' as

this may exacerbate already difficult market conditions. The BBA does not believe conditions are extreme enough to warrant such a move.

'We are hoping people will return to their senses and not invoke these clauses,' said Alex Merriman, executive director at the BBA.

The BBA said it hoped to publish the report as soon as possible but the delay further highlights the turmoil in the market and could raise further questions about Libor in the meantime.

It is unclear whether market disruption clauses have been invoked in the US and Europe. However, some bankers say a couple of European companies have drawn down backstop credit lines - facilities that act as rainy day accounts or overdrafts - in small amounts to test whether the banks will fund them. Doing so often irritates banks. Instead bankers say they have had increased requests from companies to set up new facilities at prevailing market rates, rather than draw down on backstop lines.

Source: *Financial Times*, 30 September 2008

4.9.4 Fixed rate interest

The inevitability of regular interest payments is only compounded for a borrower by the possibility that the rate may increase. For most borrowers this is a risk they must take; however, it is sometimes possible to negotiate a loan with a fixed rate of interest throughout its term. A fixed rate loan gives the borrower certainty, but it will not come cheap: the bank will probably still use matched funding to provide the loan, and so faces the risk that the borrowing rate might increase when it renews its interbank loan, reducing its margin (although, conversely, the bank takes all the benefit of any reduction in rates). The fixed rate offered to a borrower will always be substantially higher than the prevailing floating rate in order to compensate the bank for taking the risk of rate increases. Therefore, a borrower looking for medium- or long-term funds at a fixed rate might be better advised to use the capital markets (see **Part III**).

4.9.5 Apportionment: the 'day count fraction'

Interest rates are almost invariably quoted at an annual rate. However, interest payments are usually due several times a year (ie, at the end of each interest period). The bank and borrower must therefore agree the basis on which the annual interest will be apportioned between each interest period (known as the 'day count fraction'). In domestic sterling facility agreements, the traditional basis for calculating interest is known as '365/365': the annual interest rate is applied to the principal outstanding, and the result is multiplied by the actual number of days in the interest period and then divided by 365.

> Example
>
> If the annual rate of interest is 6%, and the principal outstanding is £200, then:
>
> Total interest due each year = £12
>
> In February (non-leap year) the interest due will be:
>
> $$\frac{(12 \times 28)}{365} = \text{approx. 92p}$$

Interest paid under this method will therefore reflect the exact number of days in the interest period (other debt instruments may use methods which 'approximate' periods, for example treating each month as exactly one-twelfth of a year – see **19.4.3**).

4.9.6 Ratchets

Some facility agreements provide for their margin to vary in accordance with the health of a borrower, which is measured through monitoring its financial ratios or credit rating (see **17.11**). These 'margin ratchets' are intended to reflect the variation in risk borne by the bank, and provide an incentive for the borrower to perform well. If the ratios worsen, the margin increases; if they improve, the margin falls and the loan is 'cheaper'.

4.9.7 Hedging

There are ways in which a borrower can reduce the impact of interest rate fluctuations without having to pay a high fixed rate. This is known as 'hedging' the risk. A bank will, for a fee, provide a loan at a floating interest rate, but with an upper limit, say, 12%. This is known as a 'cap'. Conversely, a bank will 'pay' a borrower (ie, reduce its fees) to agree a floating rate loan with a lower limit, such that the borrower will never pay less than, say, 7%. This is a 'floor'. It is also possible to set up a loan with both a cap and a floor, so that the interest rate fluctuates, but only within an agreed band. This arrangement is known as a 'collar' or 'cylinder'. Alternatively, a borrower may get a third party bank or financial institution to make one of these arrangements for it and enter into an exchange agreement, or 'swap'. All of these arrangements help to give the borrower certainty as to its commitments, which is useful for long-term business planning. In a leveraged finance where the debt is large and interest costs high, banks will insist that the borrower hedges a proportion of its floating rate interest to cap its liability. The hedge is usually provided by a syndicate bank (for a fee!).

4.9.8   Default interest

If a borrower fails to pay any sum due under a facility agreement, there will invariably be a provision for default interest. This will charge a rate of interest on any overdue amount (eg, interest, capital or fees) which is a fixed rate above the usual interest rate payable, ie:

(a)   LIBOR (at the rate applicable to each day the amount is overdue); plus

(b)   Mandatory Cost Rate; plus

(c)   the margin; plus

(d)   default interest of around 1%.

As long as the default interest rate can be justified as reasonable compensation for the bank having to deal with a loan in default, the clause should stand. If, however, the rate appears to be more by way of a threat to encourage non-default by the borrower, then it is in danger of offending the rules laid down for trading contracts in *Dunlop Pneumatic Tyre Co Ltd v New Garage & Motor Co Ltd* [1915] AC 79, and being declared void as a 'penalty'. (In *Lordsvale Finance plc v Bank of Zambia* [1996] QB 752, a 1% default interest rate was considered too 'modest' to be construed as a penalty.)

A bank will usually justify the additional rate as compensation for increased risk of lending to a defaulting borrower.

It should be noted that some jurisdictions do not permit interest to be charged on interest (eg, Islamic law prohibits interest) and that most solicitors will not opine on the validity of default interest (see **Chapter 16**).

4.9.9   Basis points

Traditionally, banks were able to charge a relatively large margin, which would usually be measured in minimum amounts of 0.5%. In the 1980s, however, borrowing became a 'buyer's market', as the number of products increased and world markets shrunk. Banks were forced to trim their margins and, as a result, a smaller measure was required. Margins are now measured in 'basis points'. One basis point (or 'bp') is 0.01%. Thus, 1% is 100 basis points. If LIBOR is running at 6%, then loan interest of 85 basis points above LIBOR is a rate of 6.85%. Sometimes (particularly in capital markets), 1% is referred to as one 'point', and a basis point is referred to as a 'tick'. Most loan documents will simply refer to percentages.

SYNDICATED LOANS By Simon Davies and Edward Luce

Margins start showing signs of improvement

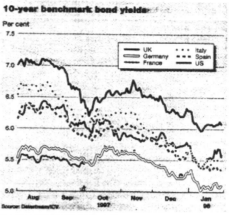

After four years of significant pricing declines, driven by substantial liquidity in the banking system and tough competition for mandates, the syndicated loan market is beginning to see improving margins.

Tim Elliot, a managing director at J. P. Morgan, argues: "The loan market has built up like a bubble over a long period of time, but the bubble has now burst. Other than perhaps the top quality sovereign niche, it is hard to argue that prices anywhere are not under upward pressure."

The most important factor behind the shift has been the crisis in east Asia, which has forced the Japanese banks to retrench substantially. Japan is estimated to represent between 10 and 15 per cent of the market for loans.

"The Japanese are practically nowhere to be seen," claimed one US banker. A Japanese banker said: "We are no longer in the position where we can undercut other banks on pricing."

There has also been pressure on European banks to improve returns on capital, which has removed some capacity from the loan market.

Investment bankers point to the forthcoming SFr4bn syndicated loan for Ciba Speciality Chemicals of Switzerland as a sign of changing market conditions.

Ciba, which is raising the cash to fund its £1.4bn acquisition of Allied Colloids, the UK company, is paying a significantly wider margin than on its last foray into the market in 1997.

According to an official at CSFB, arranger of the loan, Ciba will pay 18.75 basis points on the 364-day SFr2bn tranche and 22.5 basis points for the 18-month portion. This compares with a margin of nine basis points on the SFr1.5bn loan it took out last year.

"This is effectively a snapshot of what has happened to the market since then," said one banker. "But the pricing on the Ciba loan is fair pricing by any value."

According to a study by Merrill Lynch, if banks had bought bonds instead of taking a slice of sovereign and corporate loans to Turkey and Hungary last year, they would have made an average additional return of around 70 basis points and 112 basis points respectively. Also, they would have had a more liquid debt instrument. That is a lot to pay for ancillary business that may never come.

It is in emerging markets that the upswing in syndicated loan pricing has first been felt, and a number of offers have actually been pulled. The bond market responded aggressively to the Asian crisis, and the syndicated loan market is having to follow.

But even for the top notch corporate borrowers, spreads could start to widen. The $1bn revolving credit facility for Incentive, part of the Wallenberg family's corporate empire, is expected to give a pointer to market appetite, having been aggressively priced by lead arranger Deutsche Bank.

Most bankers expect to see gradual convergence between the syndicated loan and corporate bond markets. European economic and monetary union should help create a broad and liquid corporate bond market, against which loans can be more effectively benchmarked.

Moreover, the Loan Market Association is soon to produce its code of practice for the secondary trading of loans. Following the ICI and BAT Industries deals, Barclays Capital estimates that secondary loan trading amounted to $20bn last year, nearly double the figure for 1996.

Secondary market trading should also increase transparency in the market. The BAT Industries' jumbo $8bn syndicated loan has, for example, demonstrated how much the arrangers were paying for the relationship. In the secondary market, loans have been sold at 50 basis points below par, the breakeven point for co-lead arrangers.

This could add to the upward pressure on pricing. But despite the withdrawal of a number of the estimated 860 banks who participated in the $390bn euroloan market last year, many bankers expect further growth in volumes in 1998.

Mr Elliot said: "Volumes in Europe are all dependent on corporate and mergers and acquisitions activity. There is so much to happen in terms of industry consolidation and other structural change, that volumes should remain high."

NEW INTERNATIONAL BOND ISSUES

An illustration of market fluctuation from 1998.
Source: *Financial Times*.

4.10 Summary

This chapter has dealt with the following aspects of a facility agreement:

(1) Who? ... the parties to the agreement.
(2) When? ... the date, and the conditions precedent to be satisfied.
(3) What? ... the type of facility and the definitions clause.
(4) Why? ... the purpose of the facility, and the interest payable.
(5) Where? ... the availability of the facility.

Most of these provisions deal with the mechanics of lending. The conditions precedent and purpose clause give only a crude control over the borrower. The following four chapters, however, deal with the most important control aspects of a facility agreement (and thus often the most heavily negotiated), namely the representations, undertakings and events of default.

Brussels prepares for battle with London

Europe's challenge to the benchmark Libor rate could deprive the City of an important financial brand image, writes **Edward Luce**

Battle lines are being drawn for a fierce tussle between London and continental banks next January in the hitherto dry and uncontroversial world of money market reference rates.

Libor – the London Interbank Offered Rate – has for years been the undisputed benchmark for international transactions in most of the world's currencies. Of the important currencies, only the French franc and – in its domestic market – the Japanese yen could claim to have successful benchmarks that are calculated in their domestic capitals (Pibor and Tibor).

All this could be about to change. Europe's leading continental banks hope to take advantage of the UK's decision to opt out of the first wave of European monetary union to sponsor a rival benchmark rate of their own. The rate, which will be known as Euribor, will be launched on 4 January. At the same time, Libor's ecu rate will be converted into euros.

Given the political capital that has been invested in the success of Euribor (a number of European central banks have been campaigning behind the scenes for the adoption of the bench-mark), the battle is an important one. Is Euribor likely to topple Libor? And if so, would the adoption of Euribor harm London's position as the leading financial centre in Europe?

Market players appear to be split on which rate is likely to succeed. Broadly speaking, Libor, which is determined on a daily basis by the British Bankers' Association, has incumbency on its side. As the reference rate for most floating rate dollar and D-Mark transactions (and a host of less important currencies) the London rate has little to prove.

The rate is based on daily quotes from 16 international banks, with the highest and lowest four being eliminated, and is almost universally accepted. No one disputes Libor's accuracy. No other financial centre has attempted to compete with Libor except on its domestic currency.

Moreover, London is clearly the centre of offshore international finance, with the world's largest money and foreign exchange markets. This makes London the most liquid – and therefore the most price sensitive – financial centre in Europe and probably the world. Emu is unlikely to change this. Indeed,

judging by the recent hiring spree of US investment banks in London, Emu could even enhance London's primacy vis-a-vis Frankfurt and Paris.

Defenders of Libor also point to its relative simplicity. Unlike Euribor, which will be calculated from a panel of 57 (mostly European, banks) the BBA is under no political pressure to choose or omit certain banks. It simply chooses the 16 most creditworthy and internationally liquid banks in the relevant currency.

Euribor, on the other hand, will be based partly on a quota system, which means banks from every Emu member state must be included. Some believe this could lead to confusion, with banks based as far apart as Lisbon and Helsinki phoning in their daily quotes. Others say it will lower the average credit rating of the panel, thus producing a marginally higher reference rate than its competitor in London. Borrowers would then naturally choose to price offerings off the cheaper rate calculated in London.

Officials at the European Banking Federation in Brussels (the main sponsor of Euribor) reject these suggestions and point out that the highest and lowest 15 per cent of quotes will be eliminated, thus reducing the scope for volatility. Moreover, one of the effects of Emu will be to create a genuine cross-border

capital market in Europe that will make physical distance irrelevant. They also point out that a recent survey by Intercapital Data showed 70 per cent of European banks planned to adopt Euribor rather than Libor as their main reference rate.

Is it possible the two rates could co-exist, one for the offshore market the other for the onshore market? Few believe this is a long-term prospect. Given the possibility that the two rates could occasionally diverge, banks and corporations will be reluctant to duplicate back-office documentation by basing their transactions on both reference rates.

"With the year 2000 problem and the conversion to the euro, our technical staff have enough worries to start worrying about matching up alternative money market rates," said Edward Condon, head of derivatives at CSFB.

Bob Blower, banking markets manager at Reuters, predicts the market will quickly opt for one rate or the other. "It is too much of a back-office nightmare to keep both rates alive simultaneously," he said. "The tendency will be to opt for one rate and this will happen more quickly than people expect."

Given the pressure on European banks to adopt Euribor (not least the 57 that will make up the panel) many are betting that Euribor will eventually predomi-

nate. "Nothing has been put in writing but we have been told [by government officials] that we will not be popular if we continue to use Libor," said an official at a German bank. "European governments are setting great store in the prestige of Euribor."

Assuming – a big assumption – Euribor prevails, London would be affected on at least two fronts. First, it would give a competitive edge to the Deutsche Terminborse. Frankfurt's derivatives exchange, in its rivalry with Liffe, the London International Financial Futures and Options Exchange. Liffe plans to base its money market euro contracts on Libor. The DTB has somewhat nervously hedged its bets and plans to launch contracts based on both Euribor and Libor. Nevertheless, Liffe would be the clear loser if Libor was rejected as a benchmark.

Second, the loss of Libor would deprive London of an important brand image, at least in the euro-denominated markets. Whether this would have a tangible impact on the physical presence of money and capital market operations in London is unclear. Most believe the broader effects would be negligible. However, brand images are important. And if there was a tangible impact, it would almost certainly detract from London's competitive position.

An article speculating whether EURIBOR would replace LIBOR: in fact the two rates now happily coexist.
Source: *Financial Times.*

Chapter 5

Representations and Warranties

'Put all your eggs in one basket, and watch that basket!'

Mark Twain

5.1 Introduction

A bank will want to lend only if it is happy with the 'status quo' of a borrower. A facility agreement will therefore contain statements which the bank requires the borrower to make about various matters. These 'representations and warranties' (hereafter 'representations') are made on signing the facility agreement and usually repeated periodically thereafter. The first part of this chapter deals with these representations in the facility agreement. Representations and warranties under general contract law are discussed at **5.5**.

5.2 Representations and warranties in a facility agreement

5.2.1 Contractual remedies

Throughout the due diligence process (see **2.2**), the borrower will provide facts, records, forecasts, business plan, documents of title and other unpublished material (eg, management accounts). The most important pieces of information are effectively recorded in the facility agreement as representations, known colloquially as the 'reps and warranties'. The representations are simply statements of fact made by the borrower and, sometimes, by the guarantor(s) confirming their position.

The main reasons for including the borrower's statements in the facility agreement are to provide for a 'drawstop' and a specific contractual remedy in the event of their breach. Thus, the facility may be utilised only if the representations are true, and any money already utilised may become repayable if the representation becomes untrue (because the breach will be an event of default (see **Chapter 8**)). The borrower must therefore think long and hard before agreeing to the representations. A bank will also be entitled to various remedies under the law of contract in the event of misrepresentation or on the breach of a term, and these are examined in the second part of this chapter. However, these remedies are usually of secondary importance.

5.2.2 Examples of common representations

The representations should provide full disclosure of any circumstances which might affect the bank's decision to lend, and as such they will be tailored specifically to a particular borrower and particular loan; however, some of the areas commonly covered are outlined below.

5.2.2.1 'Legal' representations

The first group of representations (known as the 'legal' representations) relate to the validity of the borrower, any guarantor and the loan documentation.

Capacity

It might be thought that the question of whether a borrower has capacity to enter the agreement should be directed not to the borrower, but to its solicitors. Indeed, the borrower's capacity should be addressed in the bank's legal opinion (see **Chapter 16**). However, if the borrower turns out to have no capacity, suing a lawyer is of only limited comfort to the bank. A borrower must, therefore, usually declare that it has capacity to enter into the loan documents, and to perform its obligations thereunder. By making the borrower represent that it has capacity, any breach will allow the bank to refuse further advances and/or demand immediate repayment (known as 'accelerating' the loan). This is a recurring theme throughout the representations.

Status

A borrower is usually required to state that it is duly incorporated under the laws of its jurisdiction. In some jurisdictions (eg, the United States) the relevant authorities will produce 'certificates of good standing' which confirm that the corporate borrower has paid its taxes and filed documents. Reference should be made to these if appropriate.

Validity

Whenever a borrower is incorporated outside England and Wales, or there is any other 'international' element to the transaction, the bank will have concerns as to the validity of documents in other jurisdictions. The borrower will often be required to represent that the loan document is enforceable in the relevant jurisdiction and that the borrower does not have immunity to proceedings; that the performance of the borrower's obligations under the documents does not conflict with any laws or provisions; and that no deductions or withholding are required on payments under the loan (see also **9.3.4**). Other representations might include confirmation that the choice of English governing law and judgments will be recognised in the borrower's jurisdiction, and that no filing or taxation of the loan documentation is required. Lastly, there is usually a representation stating that the borrower has done everything necessary to ensure that the loan documents are legal, valid, binding and admissible in evidence in the relevant jurisdiction. Once again, the real value of these representations is to allow for withdrawal of the facility and/or repayment on default. The bank would therefore usually take a legal opinion on all these issues in addition to requiring the representation.

No resulting breach

A representation will usually be required to the effect that the execution and performance of the loan by the borrower will not result in the breach of any agreement to which the borrower is a party. This is primarily to rebut any claim in tort that the bank is guilty of 'procuring' the borrower to breach another contract (or 'interference with contractual relations'), which might give rise to damages or even to the facility agreement being declared illegal and the monies lent under it irrecoverable.

Ranking

The borrower is invariably asked to represent that any claims the bank may have under the loan documentation will rank at least pari passu (equally) with any other unsecured creditors, other than as a result of any preference through insolvency regulations (eg, for unpaid employees' wages). In fact this simply states the position under current English law, but if the representation is repeated it protects the bank (by becoming an event of default) if the law should change. In addition, some jurisdictions (eg, Spain) allow a borrower to favour some unsecured creditors over others (eg, by notarisation), and so it may be a provision that overseas syndicate members want to see in the facility (see also **7.6**).

5.2.2.2 'Commercial' representations

The second group of representations (known as the 'commercial' representations) relate to factual situations more specific to the borrower.

Litigation

It would clearly be disastrous for a bank if, shortly after execution of the facility agreement, the borrower had a crippling judgment given against it. A bank needs to know about any litigation (or similar proceedings), existing or threatened, in order to assess the risk and effect of an unfavourable judgment. The consequences may not just be a heavy fine; they might include loss of licences, bad publicity affecting trade, or cross defaults into other agreements.

The borrower might have a problem with an unqualified statement that it faces no current or threatened litigation, particularly if the statement is to be periodically repeated (see **5.2.4**). Most large companies (particularly those with a US presence) have a number of law suits in which they are involved at any one time. They may involve minimal amounts, they may be a 'try on' by a rival or creditor, or they may be started by the company itself to protect its intellectual property. The solution might be to use a disclosure letter (see **5.2.3**), though these are now uncommon, to include an element of de minimis or materiality (see **11.5.3** and **11.5.5**), to draft the representations to exclude frivolous and vexatious claims, or perhaps to use a combination of all the above.

Since 1 October 2007, the CA 2006 has made 'derivative actions' (ie, shareholders bringing claims against directors in the company's name) easier to bring, and so litigation representations are now likely to include claims against the borrower group's directors.

Winding-up proceedings

A bank will want to know that no insolvency proceedings in any form have been started or are threatened against the borrower. At first sight this might seem eminently reasonable. However, a creditor owed just £750 could theoretically commence liquidation proceedings over a disputed debt. The borrower should press for a de minimis provision and wording to exclude debts which it disputes in good faith, particularly if the representation is being repeated.

Other defaults

It is obviously of some concern to a bank if the borrower is in default under any other contract to which it is a party, and the borrower will invariably be asked to confirm that this is not the case (see also **8.3**).

Accounting principles

The bank will have closely reviewed the borrower's accounts as part of its due diligence procedures, and it will base lending decisions on the information they provide. Under UK GAAP (Generally Accepted Accounting Practice) it is quite legitimate for a company to use a variety of policies in compiling its accounts (see **6.9.2**), as long as they give a 'true and fair view' (CA 2006, s 400).

The borrower will therefore be required to represent that the original financial statements they provided to the bank were prepared in accordance with the relevant GAAP, consistently applied policies, and give a 'true and fair view' (or equivalent). The borrower will also give an undertaking to deliver future accounts on the same basis, but with a proviso to deal with any change in policies or practice (see **7.4.4.3**).

Information

The representations will usually include a general confirmation that all written information provided to the bank is complete and accurate, at least in all material respects. This may include both published and management accounts, business plans and group structures. In particular, the borrower will be required to confirm the accuracy of any information memorandum it may have prepared for the bank (see **3.3.4**).

Encumbrances

If a loan is to be secured over the borrower's assets, the priority and effectiveness of the bank's security will depend on any existing charges (see **Chapter 12**). It will therefore be of paramount importance that the bank knows exact details of any existing security. In practice, the bank's solicitor will have obtained a company search on the borrower and examined its register of mortgages and charges. In addition, the bank will usually require a representation by the borrower that there are no encumbrances other than those disclosed before execution (see **5.2.3**). A bank might also require a representation from the borrower that it has valid title, in its own name, to all property over which security is to be given.

Environmental

Environmental issues are of increasing concern to banks: quite apart from any civil liability (eg, adopting a nuisance), banks should be aware of increasingly tough legislation in this area. In particular, the Environmental Protection Act 1990 (EPA 1990), as amended by the Environment Act 1995, introduced a licensing system for specified 'polluting' processes, as well as powers to various bodies to enforce clean-up (or 'remediation') of polluted sites. On 1 April 2000, a regime for the clean-up of existing seriously contaminated sites became operational. Primary responsibility for remediation rests with the polluter, however 'innocent'. Owners or occupiers may be held liable if the person with primary responsibility cannot be found. This type of strict liability may mean expense and disruption for which a borrower has not budgeted, and which severely devalues the bank's main security. In the United States (where environmental legislation is more comprehensive than in the UK), lender liability is well established and a bank may find itself liable for clean-up costs.

It is increasingly common for a bank to require an expert's report on environmental issues before lending. The use of an 'environmental audit' will depend on the business of the borrower and the purpose of the loan. However, even if the borrower does not carry on a 'high risk' business, a bank will usually require it to represent that it is in compliance with all environmental laws and has obtained, and complies with, all environmental licences necessary for its business. This representation is usually subject to materiality.

MAC

One of the most important representations is the 'material adverse change' clause, often known as the 'MAC' representation. This provision addresses the problem that the written information provided to the bank (in particular any accounts) may be true when given, but may then change substantially before utilisation. The MAC clause is a representation that there has been no 'material adverse change' in, typically, the borrower's business, assets or financial condition (since the date of the latest accounts) and other written information provided to the bank. A bank often relies on the MAC representation to elicit information of any changes before the first utilisation, but then includes a specific event of default to deal with any later material adverse change (see **8.3**).

Catch all

From time to time, banks have asked for a representation that there is 'nothing the borrower has omitted to tell the banks that if it had told them they would not want to lend'! Most borrowers resist this on the basis that it is almost impossible for them to know if they have complied.

5.2.3 Disclosure letter

When a bank's solicitor is preparing the first draft of the representations, he will try to make them as wide as possible. For example, the borrower may be required to state that it has absolutely no encumbrances over its property. However, most borrowers will have encumbrances of some form, from time to time, albeit that they may be of no real significance to the bank. A would-be borrower is therefore forced to say that it cannot give the representation, the bank will ask why, and any encumbrance is revealed. The first objective of the representation has been achieved.

Assuming the bank is not unduly worried by the disclosed encumbrance, it could simply include it in the representation as a specific exception. An alternative solution, however, is to keep the representation 'clean' and use a separate document to deal with anything which would otherwise amount to a breach. This document is known as a 'disclosure letter'. The disclosure letter is essentially an agreed list of specific items which would ordinarily prevent a borrower from making a representation, but which the bank has agreed to waive. The representations in the loan document are then made subject to anything in the disclosure letter.

If a disclosure letter is used (they are now uncommon), the borrower should be wary of pegging a disclosure to one particular representation, because it may breach more than one. The disclosure should therefore be worded to modify all the reps and warranties. At the same time, the bank should be sure that the disclosure is a full and accurate one so that it can properly judge whether it may be waived. Using a disclosure letter to soften the representations is very effective when they are first given, but can lead to problems for the borrower if they are to be repeated (see **5.4**).

5.2.4 Repetition of representations

It should now be clear that the representations have three functions:

(a)   they provide, or induce, full disclosure of facts;

(b)   they prevent borrowing if they cannot be made without qualification (draw-stop); and

(c)   they allow specific action to be taken if untrue when made or repeated.

Representations and warranties are used in many other commercial agreements: the purchaser of a house, or a business, will want numerous representations from the vendor. Unlike many commercial agreements, however, a loan document provides for a continuing relationship, and a bank may therefore want the representations repeated from time to time. Since a representation can be made only as at a given date, the question arises as to when it should be repeated. Some agreements require the representations to be deemed repeated every day throughout the life of the loan (known as 'evergreening'). However, most facility agreements require the reps and warranties to be given on execution and then repeated immediately prior to each utilisation, and on the first day of each interest period (see **4.9**).

If the representations are deemed repeated, the loan document will often specifically state that they are to 'survive' the execution and first utilisation. Some agreements will require a certificate to be provided periodically, by an officer of the borrower, confirming that the representations are still correct (or that there has been no default). Both measures prevent a borrower from arguing that the representations were merely initial pre-conditions of lending. Furthermore, any claim for misrepresentation will depend on the innocent party showing reliance on the representation (see **5.5.1**). Reliance may be harder to prove on a deemed repetition, and so the additional emphasis provided by requiring a certificate or specifying repetition may be helpful.

Some practitioners believe that it is better not to deem someone to have made an incorrect statement and will instead use undertakings (**Chapter 6**) and events of default (**Chapter 8**) to allow the bank to respond to changes during the term of the loan.

5.3   Representations – the bank's perspective

There is an element of 'caveat emptor' which applies when a bank makes a loan: essentially, there is no common law obligation on a borrower to disclose information which might be pertinent to the bank's decision to lend. The representations will need careful drafting to achieve the required disclosure. Some reps and warranties are best cast in very wide terms, for example a representation that a borrower has 'no litigation, arbitration, or similar proceedings pending or threatened'. However, a representation that a borrower's accounts give 'a true and fair view' could benefit from being more specific.

Sometimes a borrower will ask to qualify its 'legal' representations by any qualifications used in the bank's legal opinions. This may be accepted for the 'binding obligation' and possibly 'governing law' representations, but a 'blanket' application is not appropriate or necessary. Remember, from the bank's perspective, the representations are about 'risk allocation', allowing them to take action if a situation is not what they had been led to believe.

5.4   Representations – the borrower's perspective

If a representation is untrue when made or repeated it will trigger an event of default, and therefore borrowers will want to negotiate wide margins for error. A repeated representation should avoid the need for an undertaking or an event of default on the same issue, but, at the very least, any concessions negotiated in drafting any equivalent or related events of default or undertakings (such as de minimis provisions) should be reflected in any representations which are to be repeated (see **5.2.4**). A borrower should never repeat a representation that there is no 'potential event of default' or equivalent, since that would turn a 'potential' into a 'full' default.

There is a particular danger for the borrower if the representations are to be deemed repeated. The bank will argue that when representations are first made, they should be tightly worded in order to flush out any problems (by way of a disclosure letter: see **5.2.3**). However, on repetition, the disclosure letter is ineffective against new breaches.

Example

A borrower is asked to sign a facility agreement which includes a representation that it is not involved in litigation or a dispute of any kind. However, the borrower has a small dispute currently running with a distributor in the United States. The bank suggests the representation remains, but that the borrower lists exact details of the dispute in a disclosure letter. The bank considers the letter and decides that the dispute is in fact trivial, and the loan may go ahead. The representation has therefore served its purpose by exposing the dispute, and allowing the bank to dismiss it as inconsequential to lending. If, however, the agreement provides that the representations are deemed repeated then any new dispute, even although it may be as inconsequential as the first, will cause a default. The disclosure letter is effective only in the first instance.

A borrower will sometimes ask for the representations to be qualified with, 'to the best of our knowledge and belief'. Whilst this might at first sight seem quite reasonable, it confounds the true purpose of the representations, which is to lay the risk of unknown problems on the borrower rather than the bank. The qualification is therefore acceptable to banks only in very limited circumstances (eg, with respect to knowledge of threatened legal proceedings or market information) and may carry the caveat 'after due and careful enquiry'.

Lastly, a borrower should be careful about any information it provides during negotiations. If the information is false, it may be liable for misrepresentation under general law in addition to any sanctions in the facility agreement (see **5.5**).

5.5 Representations in contract law

5.5.1 Representations

A representation is a statement of fact, made to induce the party to whom it is addressed to enter into a contract. The statement may be oral or written, and if it is drafted into the contract it also becomes a term of that contract. If the statement is untrue, it constitutes misrepresentation. The due diligence process (see **2.2**) will inevitably involve the borrower in making numerous representations. If a borrower makes a false statement during negotiations, when might it be actionable by the bank under the general law?

5.5.1.1 Misrepresentation Act 1967

The right to claim for contractual misrepresentation is governed by the Misrepresentation Act 1967 (as amended). A claim will be recognised only if the misrepresentation was of a material fact, was intended to induce a party to contract, and did induce the party to contract. The Act effectively places misrepresentations into two categories, one of which is sub-divided.

Fraudulent misrepresentation

A misrepresentation is fraudulent where it is made knowingly, or without any belief in its truth, or recklessly. The test is subjective, ie what did the maker truly believe?

Non-fraudulent misrepresentation

If the maker honestly believed the statement he made was true, the misrepresentation is not fraudulent. Non-fraudulent misrepresentation may be one of two types:

(a) *Negligent misrepresentation.* Negligent misrepresentation presumes that a representation was made negligently. The test here is objective, ie the 'reasonable man' type test.

(b) *Innocent misrepresentation.* If the maker can show that he had reasonable grounds to believe his statement was true, then s 2(1) says the misrepresentation will be innocent.

If the borrower makes a true statement but then learns before the loan document is executed that it has ceased to be true, it must notify the bank or it may be liable for misrepresentation.

5.5.1.2 Remedies for misrepresentation

The reason for categorising misrepresentation is that each category allows a slightly different remedy.

Rescission

Whatever form the misrepresentation takes, the innocent party has a prima facie right to rescind the contract he was induced to enter. Rescission aims to put the parties back into their pre-contractual position. The right to rescind may be lost in two particular circumstances.

First, s 2(2) of the Misrepresentation Act 1967 (as amended) gives a court the discretion to award damages instead of rescission in non-fraudulent cases. The court may exercise this discretion if it feels that the remedy of rescission is too drastic in the circumstances, particularly since the misrepresentation was not fraudulent. The court will lose this discretion if the right to rescind has been lost (see below).

Secondly, rescission is an equitable remedy and will not be available if, for example:

(a) it is impossible to restore the pre-contractual position;

(b) bona fide third party rights have been acquired;

(c) the innocent party, knowing of the misrepresentation, takes action affirming the agreement; or

(d) there is undue delay in seeking relief.

Damages

If the misrepresentation is innocent but not negligent, there is no right to damages. Damages may, however, be awarded in lieu of rescission as long as the right to rescind is not lost to an equitable bar (see above).

Negligent misrepresentation and fraudulent misrepresentation both entitle the innocent party to damages, under the Misrepresentation Act 1967, s 2(1) and the tort of deceit respectively. In both cases, however, any damages will be on a tortious basis and, therefore, a bank would get no compensation for loss of bargain or profit (see *Smith New Court Securities Ltd v Scrimgeour Vickers (Asset Management) Ltd* [1997] AC 254, HL, for a comprehensive guide to determining damages for fraudulent representation inducing a plaintiff to buy property).

5.5.1.3 *Hedley Byrne & Co Ltd v Heller & Partners Ltd* [1964] AC 465

There is a claim for negligent misstatement in the law of tort, based on the judgment in *Hedley Byrne v Heller*. This depends on there being a relationship between two parties that gives rise to a duty of care. This might occur, for example, if the borrower's in-house accountant provided information to a bank. The rule in *Hedley Byrne v Heller* is, however, eclipsed by the Misrepresentation Act 1967 in a situation of inducement to contract, because the onus of proof in the latter is more favourable to a claimant. The tortious claim is therefore of little relevance in the context of bank lending (other than in a claim for losses where a contract had never actually been signed).

5.5.2 Application to a facility agreement

Whilst the most important remedies for misleading and inaccurate information are built into the facility agreement, the general law of representations does have an application.

It should be clear by now that a borrower would be hard pressed not to make oral and written representations in the negotiations leading to executing a facility agreement. If any of those statements is untrue, the bank may have a claim for misrepresentation, which has the advantage over a simple event of default of applying even if the facility agreement is void.

5.6 Summary

The end product of a bank's due diligence process is the inclusion of representations, to be made by the borrower, in the loan document. The purpose of the representations is threefold. First, while the loan is being negotiated, they will force the borrower to disclose information and discuss problems. Secondly, after execution of the loan, the bank will not be obliged to lend unless the representations are (materially) correct. Lastly, once money has been lent, a breach of representation will allow the bank to pursue the remedies provided by the facility agreement, which ultimately includes demanding repayment (see **Chapter 8**).

Chapter 6

A Review of Company Accounts

'Fear is that little darkroom where negatives are developed.'

Michael Pritchard

6.1 Introduction

Chapter 4 considered some of the more important operative provisions at the beginning of a loan document. **Chapter 5** concentrated on how a bank gleans information concerning a borrower. This chapter 'steps back' from the loan document to provide a basic review of company accounts.

Most readers will now protest earnestly that they want to be lawyers, not accountants, which is why they are reading these pages in the first place. However, the most hotly negotiated area of a facility agreement, apart from the events of default, is the financial covenants. Whilst this is an area in which the commercial judgement of clients and expertise of accountants tend to outweigh any legal considerations, no banking solicitor can feel entirely comfortable producing a document where a whole section is beyond his comprehension. A basic grasp of company accounts is therefore essential. The following summary is not intended to be highly technical, specialised, or comprehensive, but a broad introduction.

The observations in this chapter are based on UK GAAP, a compilation of legislation, accounting standards and generally accepted practice. However, as part of the EU's Financial Services Action Plan, which aims to harmonise Europe's markets, most European listed companies must now publish *consolidated* accounts under International Financial Reporting Standards ('IFRS', but also known as International Accounting Standards or 'IAS') pursuant to Regulation (EC) No 1606/2002. Detailed coverage of IFRS is beyond this book, but a comparison of terminology and principles is made for key issues.

6.2 Financial statements

Why is a company required to produce accounts? The requirement was originally driven by the principle that members should know how the directors are running their company. Under ss 394–396 of the CA 2006, a company's directors must provide the following financial statements for its shareholders:

(a) a balance sheet (as at the last day of the company's accounting period); and

(b)   a profit and loss account,

and, under UK GAAP, a cash flow statement (see **6.6**).

These statements must be delivered to members (and registered at the Companies Registry) once a year, and so are often known as 'annual accounts'. Under s 442 of the CA 2006, they must be produced no later than nine months (or six months for public companies – four months if listed on the London Stock Exchange – see the Disclosure and Transparency Rules, DTR 4.1.3) after the end of the company's financial year, accompanied by a directors' report and an auditor's report (see **6.5**). Parent companies must produce group accounts: a consolidated balance sheet and consolidated profit and loss account (see **6.6**).

Although originally intended to keep members informed, the annual accounts are also an essential reference for potential lenders to, and would-be investors in, a company. What information do these financial statements provide?

6.3   The balance sheet

6.3.1   What does it show?

The first point to realise is that, in broad terms, a company will raise money to fund its business from two sources:

(a)   lenders (including, for these purposes, anyone allowing the company credit, ie time to pay a debt); and

(b)   shareholders:

    (i)   from money they paid for shares, and/or

    (ii)   from profits made by the company, which directors retain to invest in the company instead of distributing to the shareholders.

It follows that, once a company has paid back all its debts to the lenders, anything which remains represents money put in by the shareholders, and so it belongs to them. This can be expressed as:

$$\text{Assets} - \text{Liabilities} = \text{Shareholders' Funds}$$

To calculate what their share in the company is worth, therefore, the shareholders need to know exactly what assets their company owns, and how much money it owes. This is what a balance sheet shows. A balance sheet is written as a vertical list, and so the equation becomes:

ASSETS

less

LIABILITIES

=

SHAREHOLDERS' FUNDS

This is why a balance sheet will always balance. If a company's assets decrease in value there will be less money left for shareholders once the liabilities are paid off; thus the shareholders' funds will reduce, balancing the equation. The top half of a balance sheet will always equal the bottom half.

If a small company were to list its assets and liabilities, it might look something like this:

Example 1

Balance sheet as at 31 December 2008

	£	£	£
ASSETS			
Word processors	1,000		
Money at bank	600		
Delivery van	3,500		
Warehouse	8,000		
Money owed by customers	350		
Unsold stock	3,000		
Petty cash	175		
Goodwill	1,500		
TOTAL		18,125	
	£	£	£
LIABILITIES			
Long-term loan	6,000		
Overdraft	460		
Money owed to creditors	1,150		
TOTAL		7,610	
TOTAL OF ASSETS LESS LIABILITIES			10,515
CAPITAL AND RESERVES			
Called-up capital			5,500
Share premium account			1,500
Profit and loss account (reserves)			3,515
TOTAL			10,515

6.3.2 Grouping of assets and liabilities

The example at **6.3.1** is essentially correct, but in practice the published accounts will show assets and liabilities in groups, and list a total value for that group, rather than list them individually. The groups will usually be as follows.

6.3.2.1 Fixed assets

Fixed assets (known as 'non-current assets' under IFRS) are assets a company intends to retain on a fairly permanent basis. In the example at **6.3.1** this will include the word processors, the van, and the warehouse. Essentially, these are assets which the company needs to run its business. They may not be easily or quickly realisable. Fixed assets are sub-divided into 'tangible' (such as those listed above), 'intangible' (such as patents, copyrights or goodwill) and 'investments' (such as long-term shareholdings in other companies).

6.3.2.2 Current assets

Current assets are cash and other assets which a company expects to turn into cash in the ordinary course of its business (usually within 12 months). It is these liquid assets that the company intends to use to pay its short-term liabilities. The current assets therefore form part of the company's 'working capital', essential for maintaining its liquidity (see **3.2.1**). Current assets will include any stock which the company holds, money owed by customers (debtors) and any cash. Current assets are usually listed in order of permanence.

6.3.2.3   Current liabilities

Current liabilities are liabilities which the company must pay within 12 months of the balance sheet date. They are usually labelled in a balance sheet as 'Creditors: amounts falling due within one year'. They will include most trade creditors and any short-term loans, including any overdraft facility and any repayments of long-term loans falling due (see **3.2.1**). Current liabilities would also include any dividend declared but unpaid (eg, because it is awaiting shareholder approval).

6.3.2.4   Deferred liabilities

Deferred liabilities are liabilities which the company need not settle until more than 12 months after the balance sheet date. They are usually labelled as 'Creditors: amounts falling due after more than one year'. They will include long-term loans and possibly certain tax bills.

6.3.3   Bank's balance sheet

The majority of assets on the balance sheet of a commercial bank will be loans it has made to customers and other banks. Conversely, its key liabilities will be deposits by customers and other banks. A summarised balance sheet for the Tokai Bank Ltd is set out below by way of illustration.

THE TOKAI BANK, LTD.

21-24, Nishiki 3-chome, Naka-ku, Nagoya 460, Japan

BALANCE SHEET
March 31, 1995

Assets	(hundred million yen)
Cash and due from banks	34,312
Call loans	2,831
Bills purchased	417
Commercial paper and other debt purchased	1,451
Trading account securities	1,429
Money held in trust	2,917
Securities	39,741
Loans and bills discounted	196,900
Foreign exchanges	3,194
Other assets	7,300
Premises and equipment	1,703
Customers' liabilities for acceptances and guarantees	16,406
Total assets	**308,605**

Liabilities	
Deposits	203,613
Certificates of deposit	17,091
Call money	30,055
Bills sold	5,209
Borrowed money	13,544
Foreign exchanges	466
Convertible bonds	278
Other liabilities	8,148
Reserve for possible loan losses	3,088
Reserve for retirement allowances	357
Other reserves	127
Reserve for price fluctuation of national government bonds	31
Reserve for losses on trading account securities	95
Reserve for contingent liabilities from broking of futures transactions	0
Reserve for securities transaction liabilities	0
Acceptances and guarantees	16,406
Total liabilities	**298,386**

Stockholders' Equity	
Common stock	3,119
Legal reserve	2,909
Earned surplus	4,190
Net income	209
Total stockholders' equity	**10,219**
Total liabilities and stockholders' equity	**308,605**

STATEMENT OF INCOME
April 1, 1994—March 31, 1995

Income	(hundred million yen)
Income	**14,634**
Interest income	12,623
Interest on loans and discounts	7,308
Interest and dividends on securities	1,426
Fees and commissions	549
Other operating income	717
Other income	744
Expenses	**14,338**
Interest expenses	9,601
Interest on deposits	4,758
Fees and commissions	152
Other operating expenses	418
General and administrative expenses	2,377
Other expenses	1,789
Income before income taxes and others	296
Extraordinary profit	19
Extraordinary losses	39
Income before income taxes	276
Provision for income taxes	66
Net income	**209**
Retained earnings brought forward from previous year	113
Cash dividends	86
Addition to legal reserve	17
Total unappropriated retained earnings	220

Notes: 1. Accumulated depreciation of premises and equipment: ¥1,728 hundred million
2. Net income per share: ¥10.34
3. All amounts are rounded down to the nearest hundred million
4. Tokai Bank's fiscal 1994 annual report will be available for perusal at the Bank's London Branch (One Exchange Square EC2A 2EH) from August.

An example of a bank balance sheet.

6.3.4   Ordering of assets and liabilities

Rather than simply listing the groups of assets and then subtracting all the liabilities (as in Example 1 at **6.3.1**), a balance sheet re-orders these items slightly. First, it will show the total value of fixed assets. It will then show current assets less current liabilities. The resulting figure shows the 'Net current assets'. This provides an indication of whether the company can cover short-term liabilities with its current assets.

The net current assets figure is then added to the fixed assets to show all the company's assets less its current liabilities. Finally, the long-term liabilities are listed and then subtracted from the above figure to give a total value for the company once all its liabilities have been paid. This is the amount which belongs to the shareholders, and would be returned to them if the company was wound up at that point. Thus the re-written balance sheet from Example 1 would look like this:

Example 2

Balance sheet as at 31 December 2008

	£	£	£
FIXED ASSETS			
Tangible assets	12,500		
Intangible assets	1,500		
CURRENT ASSETS			14,000
Stock	3,000		
Debtors	350		
Cash at bank and in hand	775		
		4,125	
LESS CREDITORS: amounts falling due within one year			
Trade creditors	1,150		
Bank overdraft	460		
		1,610	
NET CURRENT ASSETS			2,515
TOTAL ASSETS LESS CURRENT			16,515
LIABILITIES			
LESS CREDITORS: amounts falling due after more than one year			
Borrowings			6,000
NET ASSETS			10,515
CAPITAL AND RESERVES			
Called-up capital			5,500
Share premium			1,500
Profit and loss account			3,515
			10,515

Some balance sheets will present the equation in a different order:

Assets = Shareholders' funds (ie capital and reserves) plus liabilities

This is the format required under IFRS.

6.3.5   Capital and reserves

As explained at **6.3.4**, the top part of the balance sheet calculates a figure representing all the company's assets less all the debts it owes (in Example 2, that figure is £10,515). These are the 'shareholders' funds' referred to at **6.3.1** – the amount which would be paid back to shareholders if the company were wound up. The bottom part of the balance sheet, headed 'Capital and reserves', takes the figure representing shareholders' funds and shows how it is comprised.

6.3.5.1   Share capital

This is the total amount of money which shareholders have invested in the company through buying shares. It is divided into:

(a)   called-up share capital, ie the nominal value of the shares which has either been paid by the shareholders, or called to be paid ('nominal' or 'par' value is the value attributed to shares when they are first issued, usually £1); and

(b)   share premium, ie any amount paid for the issued shares over and above their nominal value.

6.3.5.2   Profit and loss account

This is profit which directors have, over time, retained in the company instead of distributing it (as dividends). The profit and loss account is part of a company's 'reserves' (see also revaluation reserve at **6.3.7**). The amount shown at the profit and loss account on the balance sheet is calculated under a separate financial statement, called the 'profit and loss account' (see **6.4**). These amounts are not represented by money held in an account or by specific assets; they are simply retained value in the company.

6.3.6   Restrictions on disposal of assets

One of the reasons for splitting the shareholders' funds into categories showing their origins is that there is statutory control over the value of assets which must remain in a company to meet creditors' claims. Essentially, ss 135–141 of the CA 1985 (from 1 October 2008, ss 641–653 of the CA 2006) prohibit a company from returning the money paid for its shares to the shareholders (other than under very restricted circumstances), theoretically maintaining a minimum value of assets in the company to meet the demands of creditors. The amounts of paid-up share capital and premium are shown separately because the restrictions on disposing of assets representing the value of the latter are slightly less than for the former.

Example 3

The rules outlined above can be illustrated using the figures from Example 2 (see **6.3.4**). On the current figures, the company may pay up to £3,515 to its shareholders because this figure simply represents profits that the directors decided not to distribute at an earlier date. However, the company must keep sufficient assets so that (once all its liabilities are paid off) there is £7,000 worth of assets remaining. Of that £7,000, however, £1,500 is share premium. In limited circumstances, for example funding scrip issues (effectively turning premium into share capital), or writing off expenses of issuing shares (instead of reducing the profit and loss account), assets representing that premium may be disposed of and, in the second example, the value of the company's assets may be reduced to £5,500.

Thus the different categories into which the capital and reserves are divided show the value of assets which cannot be returned to shareholders ('non-distributable' reserves) and the value which may be disposed of freely, or under restricted circumstances.

6.3.7   Miscellaneous

Having reviewed the fundamental aspects of the balance sheet, there are a number of other matters which commonly occur, and which may be conveniently dealt with at this point.

6.3.7.1   Revaluation

Tangible assets are initially recorded on the company's balance sheet at cost. In time, that value is likely to become inaccurate because the assets have depreciated (see **6.3.7.2**) or appreciated. If its tangible fixed assets have appreciated, a company is permitted, but not required, to revalue them at market value in the balance sheet. Upward revaluation on the balance sheet increases the net assets figure. This in turn means the shareholders' funds will increase, which must be shown under the capital and reserves. The increase cannot be included in the profit and loss reserve in the balance sheet, however, because it is only an estimation of the asset's extra worth. It is shown as an entry labelled 'revaluation reserve', which indicates that it is not yet an amount of shareholders' funds which may be distributed.

The main advantage of revaluation to a company is that a higher net asset value usually increases borrowing power and improves the debt to equity ratio (see **7.4.3**). Any charge to depreciation will be based on the increased asset value.

6.3.7.2   Depreciation

Whilst upward revaluation is optional, UK GAAP requires that all fixed assets which have a limited useful economic life must be depreciated. The exact method of depreciation, as well as the estimation of useful economic life, are decisions for the company (although fundamentally covered by FRS 15 – see **6.9.2**). The effect of depreciation is to reduce the net recorded value of the asset shown on the balance sheet. Charging depreciation will therefore reduce profits in the profit and loss account (see **6.4**), which in turn reduces the profit and loss figure in the balance sheet.

6.3.7.3   Provisions

Provisions are amounts which are set aside out of a company's profits to cover expected liabilities or expenses. Provisions will commonly be made for deferred tax, pension costs and structural changes. They will appear in the balance sheet as a form of liability, usually as 'provisions for liabilities and charges'. Provisions will reduce the profits in the profit and loss account (see **6.4**), which in turn reduces the profit and loss figure in the balance sheet.

6.3.8   'Snapshot'

The balance sheet is always given 'as at' a certain day. This is because a list of everything owned, and everything owed, can be accurate only at one given moment in time: the list will change each time an asset is disposed of, or a new liability incurred. The balance sheet is therefore often said to provide a 'snapshot' of the company's assets.

6.3.9   IFRS

IFRS also requires a balance sheet to be drawn up with concepts similar to UK GAAP, although assets and liabilities are divided into 'current' and 'non-current', and assets must be recorded at 'fair value'.

6.4   Profit and loss account

6.4.1   Introduction

The profit and loss figure on a balance sheet has already been explained at **6.3.5**. Essentially, it shows profit that a company has made but which the directors have not distributed to the shareholders. This figure is a rolling total of retained profit (less any losses) from year to year. A shareholder could compare a profit and loss figure with the previous year to find any increase or decrease in the total. However, a shareholder really needs a breakdown to show exactly how the company made a profit, or loss, in a particular year. This gives rise to the second financial statement required by the CA 2006, the 'profit and loss account'.

Already the potential for confusion seems rife. The expression 'profit and loss account' could refer to the entry on a balance sheet, or to a whole financial statement. The context will usually clarify the situation. For brevity, the profit and loss accounting statement is referred to in the remainder of this chapter as the P&L account.

6.4.2   Period of a P&L account

Whilst the balance sheet is an inventory of assets and liabilities, and so has to be made at a specific date, the profit or loss that a company makes must be calculated over a specific period. The P&L account required by the CA 2006 calculates the profit, or loss, made over a period (generally 12 months) ending with the date of the balance sheet. There is, however, nothing to prevent a company's directors from drawing up a P&L account for a different period (see **6.5**).

6.4.3   Structure of a P&L account

The P&L account might be more accurately named the 'profit or loss' account, because it shows whether a company has made a profit or a loss over a period. The calculation is very straightforward: income less expenses. The income shown in a P&L account is income generated by the company's business activities, and does not include its share capital or loan monies. The expenses shown are expenses of a 'revenue' nature (ie, day-to-day costs of running the business), and do not include 'capital' expenses (such as plant and machinery) which are shown as fixed assets in the balance sheet.

In order to analyse a company's profit or loss, it is convenient to consider its trading in two stages:

(a)   The profit made on buying-in or manufacturing, and then selling the products of the business. This is essentially the money a company raises by selling its products over a period (its 'turnover'), less the price it paid for them. If the company manufactures its products, then the direct costs of producing the products as well as the cost of the raw materials must be deducted from turnover. This figure is known as the 'gross profit'. If a company is making a loss at this stage it is in serious trouble.

(b)   From gross profit, a company must then deduct all the general overheads of running the business, for example advertising costs, administration expenses, etc. This will produce a figure known as the 'net profit'.

The structure of a P&L account reflects the two stages outlined above. It will consist of:

(a) *Trading (or manufacturing) account.* The first few lines of the P&L account, which calculate gross profit. The calculation is usually shown in more detail, particularly in the case of a manufacturing account, in a separate financial statement as part of the management accounts (see **6.8**); and

(b) *Profit and loss account.* The main part of the P&L account showing the general expenses of the business to be deducted from gross profit to produce the net profit.

Example 4

Profit and loss account for the year ended 31 December 2008

	£	£	£
Turnover	110,000		
Cost of sales	58,000		
Gross profit		52,000	
ADMINISTRATION			
Salaries	31,000		
Stationery	240		
Telephone	930		
Electricity	576		
Auditors	325		
General Expenses	925		
	33,996		
SALES			
Advertising	4,300		
Carriage	1,105		
	5,405		
FINANCIAL			
Interest	1,670		
Professional fees	215		
Bad debts	350		
Depreciation	645		
	2,880		
TOTAL EXPENSES		42,281	
NET PROFIT on ordinary activities before TAXATION		9,719	
TAXATION		2,517	
PROFIT on ordinary activities after TAXATION		7,202	
Extraordinary items		2,405	
		4,797	
Dividends			3,000
Retained profit for the year			1,797
Retained profit brought forward			1,718
Retained profit carried forward			3,515

6.4.4   Points to note on the P&L account

6.4.4.1   Turnover

Turnover is the total amount of money the business has taken from sales over the previous 12 months.

6.4.4.2   Cost of sales

Cost of sales is the basic cost to the company of buying the products which were sold during the year. To calculate the cost of the stock which was sold, the account will add the cost of stock held at the start of the year (opening stock) to the cost of stock acquired during the year, and then subtract any stock unsold at the end of the year (closing stock). For example, a company starts the year with stock costing £1,000, spends another £4,500 buying stock during the year, but has stock costing £2,300 left at the end of the year. The total cost of stock held *during* the year is:

$$£1,000 + £4,500 = £5,500.$$

However, the cost of stock *remaining* is £2,300. That means stock costing £5,500 – £2,300 = £3,200 was sold during the year.

If the business makes the products which it sells, the 'cost of sales' becomes 'cost of manufacture'. If the company is in the service industry, a similar calculation will be required to ascertain the cost of providing the service.

6.4.4.3   Net profit

In the P&L account, 'net profit' is gross profit less all expenses of the business. In one sense, this is a true measure of the profit the directors have managed to make for the year. The more efficiently the business is run, the lower expenses will be and the higher the net profit figure. Whilst tax deductions are still to be shown, those are effectively beyond the directors' control.

6.4.4.4   'Extraordinary' and 'exceptional' items

Under SSAP 6 (see **6.9.2.1** for SSAPs), the P&L account had to reveal any 'extraordinary' and 'exceptional' items. 'Extraordinary' items were those outside the ordinary activities of the company and not expected to recur regularly or frequently; 'exceptional' items were those within the ordinary activities of the company which had to be disclosed as a separate item, due to their size or occurrence, to maintain a 'true and fair view' (see **6.5**). However, SSAP 6 has been superseded by FRS 3, and whilst the definitions of 'extraordinary' and 'exceptional' items remain largely the same, their interpretation has changed. Most items will now fall within the definition of 'ordinary' activities or 'exceptional' items, and the term 'extraordinary' items is practically redundant. Examples of 'exceptional' items include reorganisation costs, the disposal of a subsidiary, and profits or losses on disposal of material fixed assets.

6.4.4.5   Dividends and retained profit

Once any tax, extraordinary or exceptional items have been deducted from the net profit, there will be a final figure representing a profit or a loss. This is the actual amount of money made (or lost) from the company's trading throughout the year. If the figure shows a profit, the directors must decide whether it should be used to pay a dividend to the shareholders, or retained in the company as investment.

The P&L account also shows a figure for 'retained profit carried forward'. This is the total of any profit which has been retained throughout the company's life, less any losses which have been absorbed. When this total is added to the profit (or absorbs the loss) for the year of the P&L account, the result is the figure appearing as the 'profit and loss account' at the bottom of a balance sheet (see **6.3.5**). It is the total retained profit as at the date of the balance sheet.

6.4.5   IFRS

Under IFRS the P&L account is known as an 'income statement'. IFRS does not have the definitions 'extraordinary' or 'exceptional', but does require 'material items' (of income or expense) to be shown on a separate line of the income statement in order to draw attention to them.

6.5   Directors' report, auditor's report, and notes to the accounts

The CA 2006 (s 415) requires the directors of a company to include a report with the annual accounts. This normally appears before the balance sheet and P&L account. There are prescribed items to be summarised in the directors' report, although they are usually dealt with in minimal detail. These items include the principal activities of the company, any changes in the business through the year, any anticipated changes in the business, recommended dividends, charitable and political donations, the directors' names and any interests they have in the company's shares or debentures.

Annual accounts will require certification by the company's auditors. This appears as a report to the members immediately after the directors' report. If the auditors are satisfied with the accounts (they will want to see more than just the profit and loss account and balance sheet – eg, a cash flow statement and statement of gains and losses) their report will be very brief and their opinion for a UK listed company might typically be worded:

> In our opinion the financial statements give a true and fair view of the state of affairs of the Company at … (date of balance sheet) … and of the profit and cash flows of the Company for the financial year then ended and the financial statements and part of the directors' remuneration report to be audited have been properly prepared in accordance with the Companies Act 2006.

If the auditors are not happy with some aspect of the accounts, they must 'qualify' their report by clearly stating any problems they have discovered. Any such qualification is potentially damaging to a company because it will suggest the financial statements are not reliable. A bank may insist that a material qualification to the accounts will trigger an event of default (see **8.3**).

Finally, the accounts will invariably include notes, cross-referring to a numbering system against certain entries in the P&L account and balance sheet, which give additional information on some items.

6.6   Cash flow statements

As well as Companies Act requirements to produce a balance sheet and P&L account, FRS 1 (Revised 1996) requires companies to produce a cash flow statement. Essentially, a cash flow statement will show the source of cash coming into a business, and the destination of cash going out, over a period (typically the accounting year). The cash flow statement is created by taking the net profit figure from the P&L account and adjusting it by adding back any non-cash deductions and then taking account of any other cash movements not reflected in that net profit figure. For example, the P&L account will have deducted depreciation on fixed assets to calculate the net profit figure. However, depreciation does not represent real cash spent, and so that amount will be added back to the net profit figure. Once all other items of cash inflow or outflow are included (that were not included in calculating the net profit figure), the end result shows whether the company generated more cash than it spent over the period, or vice versa. Lenders usually prefer using the cash flow statement to set financial covenants because it is a much better indicator of the company's 'health' than net profit which is subject to accounting fictions such as accruals and non-cash elements.

An IFRS-based cash flow statement should be near identical to the UK GAAP version.

6.7 Consolidated accounts

When a company has one or more 'subsidiary undertakings', it must produce combined accounts for itself and its subsidiaries, known as 'consolidated accounts' (or 'group accounts'). Essentially, under s 1162 of the CA 2006, a 'subsidiary undertaking' is a company (or partnership, or unincorporated association) in which the parent:

(a)   has a majority of the voting rights; or

(b)   is a member and has the right to appoint or remove a majority of its board of directors; or

(c)   has the right to exercise a dominant influence:

    (i)   by virtue of provisions in the undertaking's memorandum or articles, or

    (ii)   by virtue of a control contract; or

(d)   is a member, and controls a majority of the voting rights through an agreement with other members; and

(e)   an undertaking is a parent undertaking in relation to another undertaking, a subsidiary undertaking, if:

    (i)   it has power to exercise or actually exercises a dominant influence or control over it, or

    (ii)   it is managed on a unified basis with the subsidiary undertaking.

The requirement for consolidated accounts is based on the premise that a parent company's business is likely to be closely linked with that of any subsidiary undertaking. The shareholders of the parent should therefore be provided with financial information on the whole group.

A subsidiary undertaking must continue to produce its own balance sheet and profit and loss account. A parent producing consolidated accounts must produce its own balance sheet, but is not obliged to (and usually will not) publish its own profit and loss account.

Consolidated accounts are usually produced by the parent company's directors to the same year end as the parent's accounts, and comprise a consolidated balance sheet and profit and loss account. The parent and subsidiary undertakings must also reveal each other's identity in the notes to their individual accounts. The exemption from producing accounts which applies to small and medium-sized companies (see **6.9.1**) also applies to the obligation to produce consolidated accounts.

From 2005, European listed companies must produce their consolidated accounts in accordance with IFRS (see **6.9.4** for more detail).

6.8 Management accounts

The balance sheet and P&L account are useful for shareholders to review how their company has been run over the past 12 months. They also provide very useful information about a company to potential investors, and to both potential and existing lenders. They do, however, have two main drawbacks. The first drawback is that they are produced only once a year and up to nine months after the year end (for private companies); the second is that they do not have to be very detailed. These drawbacks can both be overcome by the use of management accounts.

Management accounts are financial summaries produced from time to time by a company's directors. They may be a breakdown of figures within the balance sheet and P&L accounts (eg, a manufacturing account), they may be financial projections, or they may be an interim balance sheet or P&L account drawn up over a period of one month or more. The board will use the management accounts to monitor the business through its financial year, and help it to make changes and predictions. They may, for example, use them to decide whether to declare an interim dividend.

Unlike final accounts, management accounts do not have to be shown to the shareholders, or lodged at the Companies Registry. Whether a bank has sight of management accounts will depend on the size of the borrower and its relationship with the bank. A borrower will usually be reluctant to provide management accounts: the detail they provide makes them very sensitive, since they may expose information which is hidden behind the broad approach of the published accounts. Any disclosure will often be subject to a confidentiality undertaking.

6.9 Accounting regulations

Having reviewed the basic form of company accounts, this chapter concludes with a summary of the regulations which govern them.

There are three main sources of UK regulation affecting company accounts:

(a)   the Companies Act 2006;

(b)   SSAPs and FRSs; and

(c)   the UKLA's 'Listing Rules'.

Together with accepted accounting practices, these form 'UK GAAP' (Generally Accepted Accounting Practice). In addition, there is recent European legislation which will have an effect on the consolidated accounts of a listed European company from 2005.

6.9.1 Companies Act 2006

The CA 2006 requires the directors of every company to produce a balance sheet and P&L account for each financial year (ss 394–396). It also requires a directors' report (s 415) and auditors' report (s 495) to accompany the accounts (see also **6.5**). The Act then provides a range of rules relating to the content of those accounts, and the format in which they must be presented.

The CA 2006 also requires copies of the accounts and reports to be:

(a) sent to every member, debenture holder, and anyone entitled to receive notice of general meetings (s 423). This must be done at least 21 days before (b) below;

(b) laid before the company at a general meeting (unless, in the case of a private company, this requirement is dispensed with by elective resolution); and

(c) delivered to the Registrar of Companies, for publication.

The requirements at (b) and (c) must both be satisfied within nine months of the financial year end in the case of a private company, and within six months if a public company (four months if a UK listed company).

From 1 April 2008, the CA 2006 also requires quoted companies to publish their annual accounts and reports on a website (s 430).

6.9.1.1 'Small' and 'medium-sized' companies

Delivering accounts

In the case of 'small' and 'medium-sized' companies, the requirement to deliver accounts to the Registrar is modified. 'Medium-sized' companies may provide the Registrar with an abbreviated P&L account. 'Small' companies need not provide the Registrar with a P&L account, and may send an abbreviated balance sheet. They may also have a reduced directors' report. The parameters for qualifying as a 'small or medium-sized' company (which is estimated to include around 90% of British companies) are currently (CA 2006, s 382):

		'Small'	'Medium'
1.	'Turnover' not more than	£6.5m	£25.9m*
2.	'Balance sheet total' not more than	£3.26m	£12.9m*
3.	Average employees not more than	50	250

*net of group transactions

Any two criteria must be satisfied.

Auditing requirements

'Small' companies can also qualify for full or partial exemptions from auditing their accounts under the Companies Act 2006. Under s 477, a company is totally exempt from auditing its accounts in a given financial year if:

(a) it qualifies as a 'small' company for that year under s 382 of the CA 2006;

(b) its 'turnover' for that year does not exceed £6.5m; and

(c) its 'balance sheet total' for that year does not exceed £3.26m.

In addition, under s 482, a company which is a 'non-profit-making' company may enjoy exemption provided it is subject to a form of 'public' audit.

(Certain types of company are excluded from these exemptions, for example public companies, banking or insurance companies, and any company which is a parent company or subsidiary undertaking.)

6.9.1.2 True and fair view

There is a fundamental requirement under the CA 2006 that the accounts should provide a 'true and fair view'. This principle overrides all others. It is primarily the directors' responsibility to ensure that the accounts give a true and fair view, although it must also be addressed in the auditor's report (see **6.5**). Under IFRS, the equivalent concept is 'fair presentation'.

6.9.2 SSAPs and FRSs

6.9.2.1 Harmonisation

Whilst the CA 1985 provides some regulation as to the content and format of company accounts, it still leaves companies with a wide choice in compiling the detail of their accounts. Apart from any other considerations, this makes comparison between companies' results very difficult. In order to overcome this problem, the largest accounting bodies decided to create a number of statements for particular areas of accounting which outlined the basis on which their members would prepare company accounts. This process began in 1971, and resulted in 'Statements of Standard Accounting Practice', or 'SSAPs', issued by the 'Accounting Standards Committee'. In 1990, the body producing these statements became the 'Accounting Standards Board', and produced statements known as 'Financial Reporting Standards', or 'FRSs'. The original SSAPs still exist, but are gradually being updated or replaced by FRSs. Any new statements are FRSs.

6.9.2.2 Legal effect

A number of the SSAPs were considered so fundamental that they were given statutory effect by the Companies Acts. However, the SSAPs and FRSs do not generally have any authority other than with accountancy bodies requiring their members to follow them. Since every company must have its accounts audited, the auditor will be forced to record any variation from the SSAPs or FRSs in his report. Effectively, this ensures that a company usually follows the statements, with any deviation being made known. In the international arena, the equivalents are 'International Accounting Standards' (or 'IAS'), originally created as an academic exercise to provide 'globally' applicable accounting standards, now being gradually replaced by IFRS.

6.9.3 The Listing, Disclosure and Transparency Rules

The UKLA's Listing, Disclosure and Transparency Rules impose some additional accounting requirements on London-listed companies. First, the Listing Rules require listed companies to prepare their annual report and accounts in accordance with the company's national law and in all material respects with national accounting standards or IFRS (LR 9.8.2R).

LR 9.8.4 outlines the information to be included in the listed company's annual report and accounts. DTR 4.1 requires the annual report to be published within four months of the financial year end. DTR 4.2 requires a half-yearly (unaudited) financial report to be published no later than two months after the period to which it relates.

6.9.4 Summary accounts

Lastly, s 426 of the CA 2006 allows a listed company to substitute a summary of its full annual accounts for sending to consenting members. This is to avoid the expense of sending a full account, but the proviso is that the members retain the right to receive the full accounts on request.

6.10 Summary

(1)   The balance sheet lists all a company's assets, and deducts all its liabilities. The value then remaining belongs to the shareholders. The assets and liabilities fluctuate, and so the calculation can be made only for a particular day (a 'snapshot'), usually the company's year end.

(2)   The P&L account shows a company's income over the 12 months immediately before the balance sheet date. It then subtracts all expenses of the business over that period to show the profit or loss the company has made. That figure is then combined with any previous retained profit and the total is the 'profit and loss' figure at the bottom of the balance sheet, ie the total retained profit.

(3)   The balance sheet and P&L account must be prepared annually by the directors in order to show the shareholders how their company has been run. They are also deposited at the Companies Registry and are an invaluable source of information for lenders and creditors. The most useful analysis of company accounts comes from comparison with previous years and with results for similar businesses (see also **7.4.4**).

Chapter 7

Undertakings

> 'Why didst thou promise such a beauteous day,
> And make me travel forth without my cloak
> To let base clouds o'ertake me in my way,
> Hiding thy bravery in their rotten smoke?'
>
> William Shakespeare

7.1 Introduction

Representations are about information: undertakings are about control. The greater the control a bank has over a borrower, the better it can safeguard the money it has lent. Undertakings are one of the main provisions in a facility agreement which help a bank to monitor and control a borrower once the agreement is executed. As with representations and events of default, they may apply not just to the borrower, but also to other members of the borrower's group and to any guarantors.

7.2 What is an undertaking?

7.2.1 Form and purpose

In a facility agreement, an undertaking (also known as a 'covenant') is simply a promise given by the borrower to the bank. It may involve a promise to do (or not to do) something, or to procure that something is (or is not) done by a third party within the borrower's control.

The purpose of the undertakings in a facility agreement is to protect the loan monies, as far as possible, by controlling the assets and activities of the borrower and, sometimes, group companies. Control is achieved using up to three different categories of undertaking:

(a) *Financial covenants* – traditionally known as financial *covenants* (not *undertakings*), these are financial targets which the borrower is required to meet during the life of the loan relating to profit, generation of cash or net worth. They are designed to check adherence to (and so are set with reference to) the borrower's projected performance under its business plan (see **Chapter 8**).

(b) *Information undertakings* – these are promises to provide the banks with information with which they can check the borrower's compliance with the provisions of the facility agreement.

(c)   *General undertakings* – these are designed to control the business in general terms by, for example, prohibiting disposals, maintaining insurance and not diversifying from the key business.

These groups are examined more closely at **7.3–7.5** below.

An undertaking will require a borrower to meet certain standards (primarily financial) and to supply the bank with specific information in order to test those standards. Thus the undertakings allow the bank to monitor a borrower's status.

The undertakings are given 'teeth' by making their breach an event of default (see **Chapter 8**). The bank will then have an opportunity, amongst other things, to cancel its commitment and demand repayment.

7.2.2   Undertaking or representation?

There is an overlap between undertakings and the representations dealt with in **Chapter 5**. Certain points may be covered using either type of clause.

Example 1

A (repeated) representation such as:

'There are no encumbrances over the borrower's property'

may be recast as an undertaking:

'The borrower will ensure at all times that there are no encumbrances over its property'.

Example 2

An undertaking such as:

'The borrower will ensure it retains a majority shareholding in X Co'

may be recast as a (repeated) representation:

'The borrower has a majority shareholding in X Co'.

The choice of whether to use a repeated representation or an undertaking will often depend on the drafting preference of the solicitor. In either case, the likely result of a breach is an event of default. However, some practitioners feel uncomfortable with deeming a borrower to repeat representations, and then relying on a deemed misrepresentation to call a default. They prefer to ask a borrower to confirm the position at signing and at the same time promise (undertake) that it will maintain the position throughout the term of the loan. Once that promise has been given, it will survive for the life of the loan, and will be a default if broken at any time during that period.

Note also that using a representation followed by an undertaking allows a strict initial test (the representation) followed by a more relaxed test (the undertaking) going forward. This ensures the banks elicit maximum information initially, but avoid a 'hair trigger' once the money has been lent.

In addition, a breach of a representation may give remedies under the Misrepresentation Act 1967 (see **5.5.1**), whereas a breach of an undertaking may give remedies of specific performance or an injunction (although note that specific performance is a discretionary remedy, and the courts will not order specific performance where damages are an adequate remedy (almost always the case for a facility agreement), and are particularly averse to granting specific performance of loan contracts).

7.3 Financial covenants

7.3.1 What are financial covenants?

Maintenance covenants

The majority of financial covenants are financial targets which a borrower undertakes to meet, usually set by reference to the directors' projected performance. These are sometimes known as 'maintenance covenants' and the result of not meeting the targets (as for most undertakings) is usually that the borrower is in default of the facility agreement.

Incurrence covenants

Less common, in the London market at least, are 'incurrence covenants'. These set a financial target which a borrower must meet if it wants to do certain things, typically disposing of large assets or making dividend payments. Incurrence covenants are predominantly found in US high yield financing.

There are three main areas which may be monitored through maintenance-style financial covenants.

7.3.1.1 Liquidity

A bank will always be concerned about a borrower's ability to service a loan once it has been made. This will entail making regular interest payments, and possibly periodic capital repayments (although many loans are repaid by the borrower 'refinancing', ie arranging a replacement loan or other form of borrowing to repay the original loan when it matures). Quite apart from servicing the loan, the bank will also want to know that the borrower can meet its other financial obligations. This is not simply a question of ensuring that a company has more assets than liabilities; many companies get into difficulties because their money is tied up in assets which they cannot realise quickly. A bank will therefore want to satisfy itself that a borrower is generating sufficient cash to meet its liabilities.

7.3.1.2 General risk

Connected to liquidity is a bank's need to assess the long-term risk of a borrower getting into financial difficulty. This is rather wider than the simple question of liquidity. A bank's commitment to a loan is based on the borrower's situation when the facility agreement is signed. Compliance with the financial covenants will show that the borrower's business is being run in a prudent manner; breach of the financial covenants will warn of any deterioration.

7.3.1.3 Management

The financial covenants will also ensure that the borrower's managers demonstrate a degree of financial discipline and planning. Some facility agreements will use financial covenants with upper, as well as lower, limits to provide an incentive. If the borrower breaches the lower limit, it will be in default; but if it can attain the upper one, it will be rewarded with lower interest rates (known as a 'margin ratchet').

It is key to note that all three areas of maintenance covenants measure the *past* performance of the borrower, and so demonstrate whether it is meeting profit and liquidity targets it predicted at the outset of the loan (see **7.4.4**).

7.3.2 Form of financial covenants: limits and ratios

Some financial covenants simply set a financial limit which a borrower must attain, eg, net worth of at least £50 million. However, the most common type of financial covenants compares two figures obtained from the borrower's accounts. For example, comparing the level of debt to the amount of equity to determine 'gearing'; comparing cash flow to debt service to help determine liquidity. These comparisons are expressed as ratios, and set as limitations. For example, a borrower may promise to ensure that the ratio of debt to equity does not exceed 1:1. It may also have to ensure the ratio of current assets to current liabilities is not less than, say, 1.25:1.

7.3.3 Examples of financial covenants

7.3.3.1 Limits

The following financial covenants may be set as minimum or maximum financial limits with which the borrower must comply.

Minimum net worth

A minimum net worth financial covenant aims to ensure the company maintains a minimum value of assets in the business. The definition of 'net worth' will vary slightly between agreements, but is intended to represent the difference between the borrower's assets (at their value in the latest accounts) and the borrower's liabilities. The starting point is therefore the paid-up share capital of the borrower together with any reserves (essentially the 'shareholders' funds' in the balance sheet (see **6.3.1**)).

If a bank has to look to a borrower's fixed assets to repay the loan, the borrower is almost certainly in severe financial difficulty and will probably be wound up. Most calculations of 'net worth' will therefore exclude any assets which may have little or no value if the borrower is in liquidation (these will generally be the so-called 'intangible assets'). The definition of 'net worth' is therefore likely to be headed 'tangible net worth' and (if otherwise included) exclude the following:

(a) *Goodwill.* Goodwill is the difference between the current book value of the assets of a company which could be sold off separately (its 'separable assets'), and the value of the company if it were to be sold as a whole. Under UK GAAP, only goodwill which has been 'acquired' when buying another company may be shown on a company's balance sheet (FRS 10). Since a business that is not trading successfully will probably be worth little more than the value of its tangible assets (unless there are particular items such as a brand name which can be identified and sold off separately), goodwill is usually excluded from the calculation.

(b) *Capitalised research and development costs.* Research and development costs are usually entered as an expense in the P&L account for the year in which the expense was incurred. However, SSAP 13 allows these costs to be lumped together (capitalised) and treated as an asset in the balance sheet, if, amongst other things, it is reasonably certain that they will be recovered once the product to which they relate is developed. As the product makes profits they should be set against the capitalised research and development costs. In this way, the costs are spread over a period as a form of accrual (see **6.3.8**). Most definitions of 'net worth' will require any costs capitalised in this way to be excluded because they do not represent a tangible asset.

(c)   *Patents, copyrights, concessions, licences, etc.* Patents, copyrights and similar assets are likely to be excluded from a definition of 'net worth' because of their intangible nature.

(d)   *Payments on account.* Payments on account, where a borrower has received money in advance of providing any product or service, are also usually excluded from the net worth calculation since they would have to be repaid if the borrower did not perform.

(e)   *Unaudited revaluation.* If the borrower has written up the value of fixed assets (eg, freehold or leasehold property) after the date of the last audited balance sheet, the increase may not be permitted to count towards 'net worth' until it is confirmed by the auditors. This is to avoid the borrower over-inflating the value in order to meet its financial covenants.

(f)   *Tax provisions.* Any provisions for the payment of anticipated tax liability (see **6.3.7**) would usually be added back (ie, increasing net worth).

Capital expenditure

This financial covenant is common in leveraged deals and puts a limit on the amount the borrower can spend on 'long-term' assets of the business (ie 'capital expenditure') over a given period. The aim of this covenant is to limit expansion of the business and help retain cash to service the debt. This covenant is known colloquially as the 'capex' covenant.

Borrowing

A bank will want to limit a borrower's exposure to other creditors, and this may be achieved through a financial covenant capping total borrowings. A borrower may ask for the cap to be linked to its tangible net worth, so that it remains relevant in the context of the borrower's size (and it then becomes a gearing ratio). Since there are many different ways for a corporate borrower to raise money, the definition of 'borrowings' (or 'financial indebtedness') must be fairly sophisticated. The following transactions are likely to be included in the definition because their commercial effect is similar to borrowing:

(a)   *Finance leases and instalment credit agreements.* Some leasing arrangements are structured to finance the use of the leased asset by one lessee (known as 'finance leases'). The lessee will usually be required, over the life of the lease, to pay instalments to the lessor equivalent to the full value of the leased asset together with a return on the capital value. The lessee is usually responsible for maintaining the asset, and early termination of the lease will incur a heavy penalty. The effect of these leases is very similar to borrowing a capital sum and paying it back in instalments (SSAP 21 actually requires the asset and capitalised obligation of 'finance leases' to be recorded in the lessee's balance sheet). Finance leases are used to fund assets such as computer hardware or heavy machinery, and frequently feature in aircraft financing.

Other types of agreements under which the borrower is effectively given credit and repays capital by instalments will also be defined as 'borrowing'. The most common example is a hire purchase agreement.

(b)   *Deferred purchase agreements.* Deferred purchase agreements allow for the purchase price of an asset or services to remain outstanding for a period of time, and will usually be defined as 'borrowings'.

(c)   *Capital instruments.* Capital instruments, for example bonds, notes and commercial paper, are borrowing methods explained in **Part III** of this book.

(d) *Guarantees and indemnities.* Where the borrower has given a financial guarantee, indemnity or any other form of financial assurance in respect of any transaction, that will usually be included as 'borrowing'.

Since the 'borrowings' definition might also be used in the negative pledge (see **7.6.2.1**) and the cross-default clause (see **8.3**), the borrower will want it to be as narrow as possible. In particular, it should avoid any borrowing made in order to refinance existing debt being double-counted, so long as the two amounts only co-exist for a short time.

7.3.3.2 Ratios

There are no 'rules' for computing ratios; however, there is little point in comparing figures which have no logical connection. For example, comparing a company's fixed assets to its share premium would produce a ratio, but a fairly meaningless one. The more common ratios used by banks are set out below.

Financial gearing and leverage ratios

The terms 'gearing' and 'leverage' tend to be used interchangeably in practice, but technically they are different: 'gearing' compares debt to net worth, whereas 'leverage' compares debt to profit (EBIT or EBITDA – see below).

Consolidated [Net] Debt : EBITDA

'Consolidated' simply refers to the group accounts as opposed to the parent company accounts.

'Debt' will not usually include trade creditors, but otherwise will probably follow the definition of 'borrowing' outlined above. The ratio is commonly calculated using total debt less any cash in the company (on the basis that cash is 'unused' debt), known as 'net debt'.

In a 'leveraged' deal such as an acquisitions finance, the leverage ratio may be as high as nine or 10 to one.

Current ratio and acid test ratio

Whilst the debt–equity ratio provides a broad measure of a borrower's ultimate ability to meet all its obligations, it gives no indication of day-to-day liquidity. The current ratio provides a simple but crude measure of a company's immediate liquidity, which can be tested directly from a company's balance sheet.

Current ratio = Current assets : Current liabilities

Current assets are, by definition, cash and other assets which a company expects to convert into cash in the near future. They will provide the cash to meet the company's current liabilities (ie, those due within 12 months), giving a broad indication of whether the company has short-term liquidity. A ratio of less than 1 might suggest that the business is overtrading, but it is important to view this in the context of the industry concerned.

The current ratio is very unsophisticated. For example, the current assets may be largely made up of stock and work in progress. This may, respectively, be unsaleable at balance sheet prices, or incomplete within the year. A slightly more sensitive assessment of liquidity may be obtained from the 'acid test ratio', or 'quick ratio'. This disregards the value of any stock:

Acid test ratio = Current assets less stocks : Creditors due within 1 year

Even the acid test ratio provides only a very broad indication of liquidity and banks tend to prefer the tests relating to cash flow outlined below.

Interest cover

Allied to liquidity, but of direct interest to the bank, is a borrower's ability to service the interest payments (and related changes) on its loans and other fund raising. Many facility agreements will contain an 'interest cover' financial covenant, such as:

Interest cover = Profit before interest payable and tax : Finance Charges

The ratio gives some indication of the ease with which a borrower met costs and how much profit was left to invest elsewhere in the business, and eventually repay the loan capital.

The amount of earnings (or 'profit') made before deducting interest payable and tax is known as 'EBIT' (or 'PBIT'). As an obvious measure of the 'success' of a business it will frequently be used in financial ratios and usually be defined to exclude exceptional and extraordinary items (see **6.4.4**). 'Profit' is not a true reflection of actual 'cash' available to the business, and sometimes a figure representing actual cash flow will be used instead of EBIT (when the covenant is known as the 'debt service' ratio).

Fixed charge cover ratio

A 'fixed charge cover ratio' compares EBITDA (earnings before interest, tax, depreciation and amortisation) to key expenses the business must pay ('fixed charges'). The obvious expense the bank will want to monitor is any payment due under the facility. Other 'fixed charges' commonly tested against earnings include rent or lease payments where these are a significant regular expense to the company.

Seton purchase raises gearing

By Motoko Rich

Seton Healthcare, the medical products and sports equipment group, has acquired Simpla Plastics, the private incontinence product maker, for £20m in cash.

The acquisition, funded by debt, pushes gearing up to 100 per cent, although interest cover remains above 10 times, according to Mr Iain Cater, the chief executive.

He added that the group was comfortable with higher gearing as long as interest cover was more than 7 times.

The group said the payment would be raised or lowered by up to £1m depending on the extent to which net assets were more or less than £3m.

Seton has had two rights issues since December to fund acquisitions and reduce debt.

Simpla, which is the UK market leader for urinary incontinence bags, represents a new therapeutic area for Seton.

Mr Cater said the group would close down Simpla's administrative site in Cardiff, making about 30 people redundant. The manufacturing site in Scunthorpe, which employes 126 people, would be maintained.

An exceptional cost of £750,000 relating to the integration of the business would be included in the group's 1995 results.

Mr Cater said that excluding this charge, the acquisition would be earnings enhancing immediately.

An example of financial covenants in practice.
Source: *Financial Times*.

7.3.4   Using financial ratios

7.3.4.1   Defining terms

Accounting is certainly more akin to an art than a science. The CA 2006, SSAPs and FRSs allow the format and content of financial statements to vary widely between companies (see **6.9**). The financial covenants should, therefore, be carefully drafted so that they relate to the particular format used by the borrower, and the values required can be read from the financial statements.

Any terminology should be specifically defined to avoid ambiguity. For example, does 'Profit before income and tax' mean consolidated profit of the group or just the parent, and should extraordinary items be included?

7.3.4.2   Information for testing

Under the CA 2006, all companies must produce some form of year end accounts, while (London) listed companies must also produce 'interims' – an unaudited report on their activities and profit and loss for the first six months of their financial year. These will provide figures with which a bank can test the financial covenants it has set for the borrower. However, even interims would provide a test of the financial covenants only twice a year, and a breach could be undiscovered for many months. If a bank wants to test a borrower's compliance more frequently than twice a year, what figures can it use? (Note that whilst banks will usually have a right to request financial information at any time (see **7.5**), they will not usually do so without suspicion that the borrower is in trouble.)

The directors of most companies produce their own set of accounts, which are more detailed than those published under Companies Act requirements. These 'management accounts' (see also **6.8**) will be produced at regular periods throughout the financial year (although they are not published). They will often include predictions as to future trends in the company's business, as well as historic performance figures. The accounts are a mine of information to a bank, and will provide figures with which to test financial covenants; however, a borrower will not always be prepared to release them (a bank will usually insist on seeing management accounts of small borrowers, or in a 'rescue' situation). If a borrower is in a 'workout' situation (ie, it is being refinanced), a bank may insist not only that it sees the management accounts, but also that they are produced more frequently than usual, say once every month (most companies produce quarterly management accounts), to allow for more regular testing.

7.3.4.3   Changes to GAAP and accounting policies

A bank will want to ensure that each new set of financial statements delivered by the borrower adopts the same accounting policies and practice used for the accounts the borrower originally supplied and on which the financial covenants were based. However, GAAP evolves from time to time and borrowers may legitimately wish to modify the policies they apply, for example with respect to depreciation. The usual solution to this problem is to allow the borrower to modify policies and follow changes to GAAP as long as its auditors provide a description of changes necessary to re-cast the new financial statements as if written under the original policies and practice. This allows the bank still to check compliance with the financial covenants, and is known as a 'frozen GAAP' provision.

7.3.4.4   Historic or predictive?

Financial covenants are completely objective, and the question of compliance can (given sufficient accurate information) be answered precisely. It is important to understand, however, that the information on which financial covenants are tested is historic: they can therefore only show whether a borrower was in breach of a financial covenant during the period to which the particular accounts apply, which usually ended several months before. Between testing dates, all the bank can do is ask for financial information (see **7.5**) and try to ascertain whether the borrower will breach the covenant when next tested – not an easy task. Financial covenants are most useful, therefore, as an indication of whether a borrower is performing in accordance with the directors' projections given in their business plan.

A bank can also draft the financial covenants so that they change throughout the life of the loan. Thus a bank can set financial covenants to reflect what it wants to happen, or thinks should happen if the business is properly run. For example, a bank may be happy that a borrower initially has a ratio of debt to equity of 2:1, but will set financial covenants which require the ratio to be reduced to 1.5:1 after two years. Effectively, this means that a borrower must use profits to reduce debt, or (subject to any restriction in its loan facility) raise more share capital. Lastly, it is important to realise that the number and type of financial covenants will depend on the transaction: a working capital loan to a FTSE 250 company may have none; a loan financing a highly leveraged acquisition or management buy-out may have five or six.

PowerGen agrees terms for loan

By Antonia Sharpe

PowerGen, the UK electricity generator which has made an agreed £1.95bn bid for Midlands Electricity, the regional electricity company, will pay between 17.5 basis points and 22.5 basis points above the London interbank offered rate (Libor) when it draws on its £2.55bn acquisition facility.

The margin on the two-tranche facility will depend on the net gearing ratio of the combined group, according to PowerGen's offer document.

Tranche A. of £1.75bn, is a five-year term loan which can be drawn down over a nine-month period subject to Power-Gen making the offer and it becoming unconditional.

Tranche B. of £800m. is a five-year multi-currency revolving credit facility available for purchases of Midlands shares and for refinancing.

● A $500m five-year revolving credit facility for **KLM**, the Dutch airline, has been over-subscribed, with more than 30 banks joining the transaction. KLM is now considering the size of the facility, which is due to be signed towards the end of this month.

● A £700m credit facility for **BTR**, the UK industrial group, was also oversubscribed but the borrower has decided not to increase the amount.

An example of a ratcheting margin by reference to gearing.
Source: *Financial Times.*

7.3.4.5   Equity cure

Traditionally, borrowers could not cure a breach of a financial covenant: it was seen as a 'mathematical' test to be met at a given time, and failure to do so would require a waiver to avoid default. However, strong equity sponsors in acquisition financings have negotiated the right to inject cash into a borrower to help it meet its financial covenants. This right is known as 'equity cure' and usually works either:

(a)   by reducing debt (the bank's preference), either by actual prepayment or by leaving the money in an account which reduces 'net debt'; or

(b)   by treating the new cash as if it is profit made by the borrower (ie, increasing the borrower's EBITDA). Equity sponsors prefer this method because the ratio works for them: they need inject less cash to get the same result as in method (a).

7.4 Information undertakings

The effectiveness of most provisions in the facility agreement will depend on the bank receiving a regular supply of information from the borrower. The nature and extent of the information undertakings will depend on the type and size of loan, but might include those discussed below.

Syndicated facilities will require sufficient copies of any information to be delivered to the agent to supply the syndicate banks.

7.4.1 Financial information

The bank will require financial information to monitor the borrower's financial wellbeing and to check for any breach of the financial covenants. The main sources (not all of which are always required) are as follows:

(a)   Year end accounts (and interims, or possibly even pro forma quarterlies, if appropriate), including consolidated accounts if the borrower has subsidiary undertakings (see **6.6**).

(b)   Management accounts, which might include cash flow statements, income statements and a cash flow forecast. The frequency with which the management accounts are required will vary, but in extreme situations it might be as often as each month, with an overview every quarter. The bank will also want an undertaking specifying that the accounting principles used to prepare the management accounts are consistent with those used in the year end accounts.

(c)   A forecast of the borrower's performance, usually in the form of projected balance sheet, P&L account and cash flow statements for the financial year ahead. Sometimes a commentary of the borrower's actual performance as against its forecast performance is also required.

(d)   An annual certificate, signed by the borrower's auditors, which shows compliance with all the financial covenants at the borrower's year end.

(e)   A 'sweep-up' provision requiring the borrower to provide any other information within its control, which relates to the financial condition or operation of the borrower, and which the bank requests. A bank would not usually use such a right unless it suspected the borrower might be in breach.

7.4.2 Shareholder documents

A bank may ask for copies of all information sent to the borrower's shareholders, although a borrower might feel that this smacks of a 'trawling' process. A compromise might be to send the bank any information which the borrower is required, by statute, to send to its shareholders. This 'filter' should ensure the bank receives only the relatively important information.

7.4.3 'Know Your Customer'

Recent drives to combat money laundering have seen tighter monitoring of banks' clients, a process referred to as 'Know Your Customer' or 'KYC'. An undertaking to supply any information reasonably requested by any lender in order to fulfil KYC obligations is now standard. Lenders will give a similar undertaking to each other.

7.4.4 Insurance

Most banks will require a borrower to maintain adequate insurance for its major assets, even if the loan is unsecured. As a check to ensure the policies are renewed, a bank may include an undertaking requiring the borrower to produce an annual schedule of insurances maintained. A periodic certification by one of the borrower's directors that the schedule is correct, the premiums have been paid, and there have been no substantial claims, is also usually required.

7.4.5 Notification of default

There will invariably be an undertaking requiring the borrower to notify the bank if it defaults under the loan. The undertaking may also require the borrower to notify the bank of any 'potential' events of default that might occur (note that failure to notify would therefore cause a default, even if the potential event of default itself has been, or might be, cured (see **8.6**)). The definition of 'potential event of default' is therefore critical, because it determines the sensitivity of the undertaking.

The undertaking will sometimes require a 'certificate of compliance' to be given by the directors at the bank's request, confirming that there has been no default or potential event of default. In particular, this might include a requirement for the directors to supply computations sufficient to demonstrate compliance with the financial covenants.

7.5 General undertakings

The final set of undertakings comprises those under which the borrower promises to do, or not to do, something. The aim of these positive (or 'affirmative') and negative undertakings is usually to preserve the borrower's assets, and to ensure there is not a fundamental change in the business on which the bank assessed its lending risk.

Once again, the exact form of these 'general' undertakings depends on the circumstances of each particular loan. However, it is possible to identify a number that are commonly used.

7.5.1 Positive undertakings

Positive undertakings require some sort of positive action by the borrower, or by an entity within the borrower's control.

7.5.1.1 Insurance

The bank will usually require the borrower to keep all its major assets insured. This may be because the bank holds some form of security over the assets, but it also avoids the borrower losing assets which it cannot replace, with a subsequent loss of income. In the case of very small borrowers, or in an acquisition finance, the borrower will sometimes employ one or more managers who the bank sees as crucial to the ongoing success of the business. In such a situation, the bank may make it a condition of lending that the borrower obtains, and maintains, 'Keyman' insurance over the life of these individuals. If the insured should die, a lump sum will be paid to the borrower, which will bolster the borrower through a potentially difficult time and help to fund a replacement for the 'key' man.

7.5.1.2 Consents, licences and laws

An undertaking will also usually be included requiring the borrower to ensure that it obtains all necessary consents, authorisations and licences to perform its obligations under the loan document. Similarly, a borrower must invariably undertake to comply with all laws if failure to do so might have a 'material adverse effect' (usually a defined term). Compliance with environmental laws is often covered in some detail in a separate undertaking.

7.5.1.3 Access to information and assistance

Very occasionally, an undertaking is included which requires a borrower to give the bank access to its books and records. The bank may also require the right to inspect the borrower's assets. In either case the borrower will want reasonable notice, and availability restricted to within office hours.

If the loan is to be syndicated after utilisation, the bank will want an undertaking requiring the borrower to assist in syndication. This may involve creating a document, not unlike a prospectus or offering circular, which provides financial and commercial details of the borrower and its business plans. This 'information memorandum' will be used to help sell the loan to other banks. The borrower may also be asked to attend presentations and meetings with potential syndicate members. Once again, this is an obligation that could be quite onerous, and the borrower will want to be bound only by 'reasonable' requests for help.

7.5.2 Negative undertakings

Negative undertakings prohibit the borrower from doing something, or require the borrower to ensure something is not done by an entity within the borrower's control.

7.5.2.1 Negative pledge

One of the most important negative undertakings is the so-called 'negative pledge'. This is an undertaking by the borrower not to create any security (other than to the bank) over its assets. Where the bank is unsecured, the purpose of this clause is self-evident. However, even if the bank has taken security, it may insist on a negative pledge to help protect its floating charge security (see **13.3**). Furthermore, a secured creditor is more able to pursue a debtor's assets than an unsecured creditor, and so the former may be more willing, or more able, to precipitate any action.

A borrower may want certain exceptions 'carved out' of the negative pledge, for example:

(a)   security that might be necessary under equipment leasing, or hire purchase arrangements. Control on this type of transaction should be achieved through specific undertakings if necessary;

(b)   liens arising under the common law, statute, and in the ordinary course of business. A trading company has little control over these occurring (eg, an asset which is retained by a third party until payment for services). The bank may want to restrict any carve-out to allow liens only on amounts overdue for a maximum of, say, 30 days;

(c)   cash collateralisation (ie depositing money by way of security) that may be necessary as part of the borrower's business arrangements;

(d)   security which the borrower acquires through purchasing an asset or business over which the security already exists;

(e)   netting or 'set-off' arrangements between group companies, and any cash management arrangements with clearing banks;

(f)   retention of title clauses, allowing a creditor to recover assets from the borrower. If this carve-out is permitted, it should usually only be on the basis that the clause is not registered as a charge;

(g)   project finance, in which a borrower is lent money to finance a specific project, for example a factory. Banks to a project finance will want security over the asset being funded, but since that will not impinge on the existing assets of the borrower, there is an argument that it should be outside the negative pledge.

Sometimes the negative pledge contains wording which attempts to create security for the bank automatically in the event that the undertaking is breached. This provides that, if the borrower gives security to a third party (so breaching the negative pledge), it is deemed to create equal security for the bank, at the same time and over the same assets. There are some doubts as to whether this type of provision is effective under English law, the fundamental problem being that the new security would probably fail for lack of registration.

7.5.2.2   Pari passu ranking

The negative pledge clause will often be accompanied by an undertaking under which the borrower is to ensure that:

> The claims of the bank rank at least pari passu with the claims of all other present or future unsecured and subordinated creditors, except for those preferred by bankruptcy, insolvency, liquidation or other similar laws.

Whilst the negative pledge ensures that the bank's right to repayment is not subordinated to secured creditors, a 'pari passu' undertaking tries to ensure that the bank is not subordinated to unsecured creditors. In fact, drafting this as an undertaking (ie, a promise to do it) arguably looks a little awkward, and some practitioners prefer to use a repeated representation or event of default instead (see **5.2.2**).

7.5.2.3   Disposals and acquisitions

Any substantial disposal of fixed assets may affect the borrower's ability to carry on making money to service the loan (it might also be an indication of cash flow problems). A bank will usually, therefore, restrict, if not prohibit, the disposal of fixed assets.

The undertaking preventing disposals must be carefully drafted to allow the borrower to continue its normal trade. Obviously, the clause should not prevent the sale of stock, nor the replacement or disposal of obsolete assets, in the ordinary course of business, though disposals of shares, cash or land may require the bank's consent. It may also allow disposals at arm's length up to a maximum value, or be tied in to mandatory prepayment (see **9.2.3**).

A bank will have similar concerns with a borrower making substantial acquisitions: it will not want to risk the borrower buying a 'lemon', or trying to change its business. To prevent these, the financial covenants might limit the borrower's capital expenditure over the term of the loan.

A vigorous price war is gathering momentum in the increasingly cut-throat world of UK corporate banking.

After three years when lenders held the balance of power, blue-chip companies have been exploiting a sea-change in market conditions to push down the cost of borrowing and secure other important concessions in the terms and conditions attached to their loans and credit facilities.

"The pendulum has swung back in favour of the borrowers," says Mr Gerald Leahy, director-general of the Association of Corporate Treasurers, whose 2,000 members include corporate treasurers and finance directors at the UK's 100 biggest companies.

The concern now is that the pendulum may be starting to swing too far the other way, increasing the danger that banks may engage in reckless lending, which could put the domestic banking system under pressure.

Trends in the UK market are of international concern because London is the centre of the international syndicated loans market, used to raise cash by European governments and big international companies. Syndicated loans enable banks to contribute to part of a loan, thereby avoiding too large a commitment to any one customer.

More than 400 UK and foreign banks at present operate in the syndicated loans market. They are having to undercut each other in order to win business. Finance directors at big companies, especially those which had to dance to the tune of their bankers in the early 1990s when lending margins were comparatively wide, are determined to make the most of having the upper hand once again.

The present price war, which began to take root about a year ago, has sent lending margins tumbling to their lowest levels since 1986. A company with a single-A credit rating can now expect to pay less than 20 basis points over the rate at which banks lend to each other, which is currently about 6¾ per cent. This compares with a margin of 35 basis points at the beginning of the year. Each basis point equals one-hundredth of a percentage point.

Falling margins have not, on the whole, prompted banks to pull in their horns and stop lending to large companies, however.

More than $190bn worth of

UK banks' lending margins are shrinking as competition intensifies, says **Antonia Sharpe**

A shift in the balance of power

financing has been raised through syndicated loans so far this year, according to Euromoney Loanware, a specialist service which monitors activity in the international loans market. If banks continue to lend at this pace, volume will far outstrip the $280bn raised last year, which was itself the highest level since 1989.

The main reason banks remain willing to lend in spite of the unfavourable market conditions is that they regard loans as merely one aspect of their relationship with their most important corporate clients.

Says one banker: "If a bank is making millions of pounds by carrying out foreign exchange or money market transactions for a client, it will not fight too much when that client wants to shave a few more basis points off the interest rate on a loan."

Says another: "If you don't do the deal, there will be 10 other banks knocking on the borrower's door to replace you."

On the demand side, meanwhile, many companies – particularly those based in the UK – are still reluctant to countenance new loans on the grounds that they are not confident enough in the strength of the economy.

Many bankers say that most loans arranged in recent months are rather refinancings of loans which borrowers took out two years ago when margins were much higher. National Power and PowerGen, the electricity generators, BTR, the conglomerate, and BAA, the airport management group, are among blue-chip companies which have recently refinanced existing loans at much reduced rates of interest.

Many companies are also using their strong bargaining position to chip away at the terms and conditions which banks attach to loans. These so-called "covenants" are often based on a company's financial ratios; for example, many companies have pledged that the ratio of their debt against

UK loans: a borrower's market

Average margins
Including facility fees for single A credits in the euromarket
(Margins in basis points)

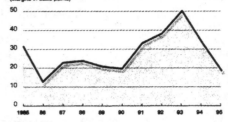

Volume of international loans (signed loans only)
$bn

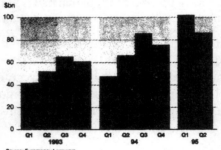

Source: Euromoney Loanware

equity will not breach a certain limit.

Covenants are not popular with corporate treasurers because, many argue, they limit companies' flexibility and give the banks too much of a say in how they are run. "In essence, covenants restrict a company's freedom of actions," says Mr Richard Desmond, corporate treasurer at BAT Industries, the financial services and tobacco group.

Mr Desmond argues that it is perfectly legitimate for companies to negotiate with their bankers on covenants when arranging the terms of a loan. "A company has a responsibility to its shareholders to get the best possible deal, even in loan documentation," he says.

Banks are reluctant to

weaken covenants, however, because, they say, they would then have fewer ways of knowing if a borrower was getting into difficulty. Mr Stan Hurn, head of syndicated loans at HSBC Holdings, believes that covenants which are applied intelligently are useful for both lender and borrower.

"These measures are designed to ensure the well-being of the borrower," says Mr Hurn. "If you do not have appropriate covenants, you are less likely to be able to get into early discussion to sort out the problem."

But the argument that covenants act as an early warning mechanism cuts little ice with many companies. Mr Nicholas Rose, financial controller at Grand Metropolitan, the big UK food and drinks group,

argues that, if a bank had a close relationship with its borrower, it would soon know that something was wrong.

GrandMet recently persuaded its bankers to remove the so-called "material adverse change" clause from its loan facilities. Such clauses allow banks to call in the loans if an unforeseen event, such as a major industrial accident, weakens the financial situation of the borrower.

In recent months, some banks have also agreed to remove the so-called "negative pledge" clauses in a number of loan agreements. These clauses prevent borrowers with unsecured loans from granting security to other lenders.

Some bankers are concerned that the way in which companies are using their present position of strength to erode covenants is damaging the close relationships banks have traditionally enjoyed with their large corporate customers. "We are now seeing structures which are further confirmation of the breakdown of good and durable bank-borrower relationships," according to Mr Peter Lucas, head of corporate banking at Sanwa Bank in London.

The erosion of covenants is also causing concern at the Bank of England. In its annual banking act report, published in May, the Bank described the loosening of loan covenants as "a worrying development".

"In the long run, banks will lose out if they allow lending standards to slip and properly worded covenants have an important role to play in ensuring that high standards are maintained," the Bank said.

It also suggested that competition to lend to large companies had forced down lending margins to the point where banks might not be charging enough to compensate for the risks they are taking.

Although the Bank is in favour of close relationships between banks and their clients, it is anxious that companies do not manipulate the relationship to such a degree that banks are no longer earning a reasonable rate of return.

The Bank hopes that by firing this warning shot across the bows of the banks, it will encourage them to stop and think before they make further, potentially dangerous, concessions to their clients' demands. Present market trends, however, suggest that this may be a forlorn hope.

An example of how markets fluctuate (from 1995).
Source: *Financial Times*.

7.5.2.4   Lending

Allowing a borrower to lend carries risk of non-repayment, and so a depletion of assets. The borrower will probably have to give an undertaking not to lend, other than in the ordinary course of its business (eg, trade credit) or within the group of companies 'controlled' by the facility agreement and any security.

7.5.2.5   Shares and dividends

With some small borrowers (and leveraged facilities) a bank may require an undertaking from the borrower not to make any distributions to its shareholders without the bank's consent. This is to avoid any money leaving the company, particularly as an interim dividend, before the bank is satisfied that the loan can be serviced. The bank may agree that the undertaking will not apply to the borrower's subsidiaries, since that would prevent profits being hived-up to the borrower to help it meet its obligations (sometimes known as 'dividend stripping').

Care must be taken if the borrower has issued any preference shares. Under the borrower's articles of association, these shares might provide the holder with a fixed rate of dividend which must be paid if the company's profits reach a pre-ordained amount. The undertaking should take account of any such obligations on the borrower to avoid inducing a breach of contract. Lastly, if the borrower has subsidiaries, then the bank may require that the borrower undertakes not to allow those subsidiaries to issue shares to third parties. This will prevent dilution of the borrower's holding, with the subsequent reduction in value.

7.5.2.6   Auditors

The bank may require a borrower to undertake that it will only appoint auditors whose size and status are satisfactory to the bank, although this clause is now rare.

7.6   Undertakings – the bank's perspective

The decision to include a particular undertaking, and the level at which an undertaking is set, will be taken in light of a number of factors:

(a)   *The identity of the borrower.* Larger borrowers (eg, those within the FTSE 250) will generally have more power to negotiate which undertakings they will accept, and what information they will provide. These borrowers are perceived as being low risk and so banks will happily lend to them. Similarly, a borrower which has an established relationship with its bank may face less stringent undertakings.

(b)   *The type of loan.* Plain vanilla loans used for general corporate purposes will require only standard undertakings. More complex facilities, and those designed for specific purposes such as a project finance or acquisition finance, will require more specific undertakings. Overdraft facilities will not usually require any undertakings or financial covenants since they are on demand.

(c)   *Market conditions.* Probably the most important factor with regard to setting undertakings and financial covenants is the current market practice. If there is a surplus of money in the loan market, the banks will be aware that a borrower may have other lenders to which it can turn. (See the article on p 92.)

When drafting undertakings for a bank (and advising on their enforcement), a solicitor should be aware of the provisions relating to 'shadow directorship' in the CA 2006, IA 1986, CDDA 1986 and FSMA 2000. A 'shadow director' is, in broad terms, a person in accordance with whose directions or instructions the directors of the company are accustomed to act (the definition is almost identical in all four statutes – see ss 251, 251, 22 and 417 respectively), with an exception for professional advisers. If a bank uses the undertakings in its facility agreement to force a borrower to take certain action, it seems possible that the bank might be a 'shadow director'. The time of greatest risk is usually when a borrower is in financial difficulties: in an attempt to preserve its assets, a bank may be tempted to persuade the borrower's directors to take certain action under threat of enforcement of security, or even liquidation.

In *Re A Company (No 005009 of 1987)* [1989] BCLC 324, a company was allegedly managed in accordance with the bank's suggestions under threat of the bank otherwise appointing an administrative receiver. The judge held that this was arguably a case of shadow directorship, although the allegation was in fact dropped later in the case. In a more recent case *Re PFTZM Ltd* [1995] BCC 280, a company which could not meet its obligations under a secured loan was subject to weekly management meetings with the lending bank's staff in order to monitor the business. It was held that the bank was not acting as a shadow director, but simply trying 'to rescue what they could out of the company using their undoubted rights as secured creditors'.

The implications of being a shadow director include taking on the duties and responsibilities of an executive director (in so far as common law rules or equitable principles apply – see CA 2006, ss 170–177). Perhaps more seriously from a bank's perspective, a shadow director may be held liable for wrongful trading under IA 1986, s 214(7), and may have to contribute to a company's assets on its liquidation. This is of particular concern to a bank involved in a workout or refinancing. Lastly, the provisions of the FSMA 2000 will apply equally to shadow directors as to executive directors (s 417).

7.7 Undertakings – the borrower's perspective

A borrower is unlikely to be able to negotiate a loan that is 'undertaking free'. However, it is important to all parties that the facility agreement (in particular, a long-term loan) is workable in practice. One potential problem of which a borrower should be wary is historic breaches. Financial covenants can be tested only against historical data (see **7.3.4.4**), which means that a breach could occur on the basis of the information against which the ratio is being tested and yet, against more current figures, it may have been corrected. The wording of the financial covenants is very important here. A borrower will not want to be defaulted if the breach has occurred but since been remedied: a bank will be reluctant to give up a chance to review its position.

Another problem for a borrower might be the administrative burden that undertakings entail. In particular, the provision of financial projections and management accounts can be very time-consuming if they are not already part of the directors' remit. Furthermore, any failure to provide information on time may result in default, even if the information itself was satisfactory. The borrower's solicitor will therefore need to ensure that the undertakings are not too tight. Any time-limits for producing information, or for achieving a target, must be attainable. Requests for information should be 'reasonable' requests wherever possible. The borrower should also try to negotiate cure periods for as many breaches as possible (see **8.3** and **8.7**).

Covenants in spotlight as banks reduce 'headroom' on company debt

By Anousha Sakoui

Mark Pain describes it as one of the most difficult periods of his 25-year career - involving round-the-clock work at an incredible intensity.

The finance director of Barratt Developments is referring to four months spent renegotiating the housebuilder's finances, at a time when the UK property market had nosedived.

It is an experience being lived by a growing number of companies having to face the fact that they can no longer refinance themselves out of trouble, unlike previous years, when debt financing was abundant and on easy terms.

"This is a turbulent river and we have crossed it, but there are still some on the other side," says Mr Pain.

Many companies are already in talks with lenders to ease debt terms, in particular waiving or resetting so-called covenants as earnings deteriorate.

The bad news is that banks have cut the margin for error they allow companies on meeting financial targets linked to earnings or other measures of ability to pay debt.

This so-called "headroom" has shrunk in bank lending terms this year by a third to about 20 per cent, according to research from analysts at Deloitte.

Covenants are financial ratios or limits that provide lenders with red flags warning of any sign that a company may start to struggle to meet debt repayments.

Advisers say more companies are struggling to meet these financing terms. Mike Duncan, chairman of the global banking practice at Allen & Overy, the law firm, believes this will worsen by the end of the year.

Barratt agreed with lenders to reset covenants, including swapping its interest cover-based covenant with a cash-flow covenant, highlighting banks' growing focus on the ability of companies to generate cash as they try to ride through the next few years, rather than profitability.

Barratt also had its leverage covenant and minimum tangible net worth covenants relaxed, which would allow it to make writedowns on its land bank.

Other covenants in the spotlight are based on the size of the loan relative to the value of the assets. Property companies are at risk of breaching these triggers as real estate prices plunge.

Mr Duncan says banks seem relatively relaxed about breaches for good quality commercial assets that still pay interest, but he expects them to be worried if rental income falls.

Banks balance the need to set these covenants tight enough to keep a grip on performance but loose enough to avoid breaches. Mr Duncan says initial breaches are more likely to be waived and covenants reset for a fee. A second breach is more of an issue

This year banks have, unsurprisingly, increased the covenants they place on loan financings, reversing the pre-credit crunch trend of ever-loosening terms.

Once a company realises it is close to breaching, or has breached, tests it is thrown into talks with banks in an attempt to get waivers.

In the Barratt example, the board was taken aback by a big drop in orders in the first week of April. Concerned about a £400m debt refinancing due in 12 months, Mr Pain started talking to banks. As the sector remained under pressure into May, stress tests of finances started to indicate it could struggle to meet covenants.

The process can be fraught. After a series of meetings with banks and private placement noteholders, which had the same covenants as its bank debt, Mr Pain finalised the creditor sign-off on a restructuring of its finances mere hours before a trading update to the market early last month.

For banks, though, the growing concern is that many existing financings carry so few, or such loose, covenants that by the time a company is forced into talks it will be too late.

Because covenants and the negotiations around them are carried out behind closed doors, the scale of the problem is hidden. Some believe the number of companies struggling with covenants could be double what has been reported in the press.

Covenant measures

* **Leverage** - a measure of borrowings relative to earnings. For an investment grade company, debt divided by earnings before interest, tax, depreciation and amortisation (Ebitda) typically has to be kept below 3.5-3.75. For a leveraged buy-out for example, with more speculative grade debt, it can be much higher

* **Interest cover** - the ratio of interest cost to earnings before interest and tax. Generally set at about 3:1-3.5:1 for an investment grade company. Ensures that profitability is enough to ensure a company can meet interest payments

* **Capex** - places a restriction on the amount a company can spend on capital expenditure over a period of time. More common in buy-out financing

* **Debt service or cash flow** - monitors that a company has enough cash to cover both principal and interest repayments on debt. More common in buy-out financing

* **Tangible net worth** - measures the value of a company's tangible assets

An example of renegotiating breached covenants.
Source: *Financial Times*.

Chapter 8

Events of Default

'How realistic is it that a pretty incoherent group of banks will put its client under at the first hurdle?'

Sir Alastair Morton, Co-chairman of Eurotunnel *(Financial Times*, 2 June 1995)

8.1 Introduction

The events of default dictate the circumstances in which a bank can terminate its loan early or take other action to reduce risk. Because of this, they will be among the most heavily negotiated clauses in the whole agreement. The events of default also dovetail with many other operative parts of a facility agreement.

8.2 Why have events of default?

If one party breaches the provisions of an agreement, an 'injured' party may seek a remedy for breach of contract. The type of remedy available under general law will depend on the type of term that has been breached:

(a) *Conditions.* Conditions are terms which are fundamental to a contract. Breach of a condition may allow the injured party to terminate the contract and claim damages, or to affirm the contract and claim damages.

(b) *Warranties.* Warranties are terms which are not considered fundamental to the contract (see also **5.5.2**). Breach of a warranty will not allow the injured party to terminate the contract, but merely to claim damages for any loss arising from the breach.

(c) *Intermediate (or innominate) terms.* Intermediate terms are a creature of judicial invention created to bridge the gap between conditions and warranties. They will usually be terms which are capable of being breached either in a trivial, or in a fundamental way. The remedy available on the breach of an intermediate term will be either damages, or damages and termination, depending on the effect of the breach on the contract.

In addition, if a party to the agreement makes a false representation to induce the other party to contract, the remedies for misrepresentation may be available (see **Chapter 5**).

However, if a borrower breaches a term of the facility agreement or is guilty of misrepresentation, a bank will not want to rely on common law or statutory remedies. If the breach is serious, a bank must be able to take immediate action.

Events of default are events, specified in the facility agreement, which provide the bank with a contractual right to terminate the loan, cancel any commitment and to demand repayment for all outstanding principal and interest (known as 'acceleration').

8.3   Common events of default

In common with most of the other operative provisions, the events of default will be tailored to meet the requirements of each particular loan, bank and borrower. There are, however, certain events of default which will appear in most facility agreements, and these are explained below.

8.3.1   Late payment

Banks are highly sensitive about punctual payment by the borrower, primarily because they themselves will usually have borrowed to fund the loan (the bank will therefore have its own loan to service, matched with the income stream from its loan to the borrower – see **4.9**). Even if the bank has funded a loan from its own resources, it may conduct other business on the basis that the loan will be repaid on time and that it can re-invest the repayment. In either case, therefore, a bank will require default interest to be paid on the overdue amount (see **4.9**). There is usually also a general requirement to indemnify the bank against any costs associated with a default.

A further concern for the bank is that since a borrower's payment commitments are established in the facility agreement, those commitments should be accounted for in the borrower's projected cash flow requirements. A missed payment probably means a missed budget and may signal serious cash flow problems.

The inclusion of a default for late payment will be non-negotiable, and will usually cover late payment of any amount due under the agreement, including fees and expenses, as well as interest and repayments of principal. However, a borrower may argue, not unconvincingly, that accidental errors do occur. Furthermore, technical problems may also unavoidably delay payments, especially where financing is cross-border, or in a foreign currency. If, therefore, late payment is due to an administrative error or for technical reasons, a bank will sometimes allow a borrower two or three further days in which to make payment (known as a 'cure period' or 'grace period'). The bank may, however, limit the errors to those of third parties and not the borrower. A bank's solicitor should ensure that any default interest and indemnity provisions are drafted so that they will run from the date when the payment is overdue, and not from the end of any grace period. A borrower may ask that any grace period should run only from when the bank notifies the borrower in writing that it has not received payment, though this is very rarely conceded.

Default for late payment is the most important event of default. The other events of default effectively play a 'supporting role': they are simply trying to predict situations which may lead to late payment, thus allowing early action by the bank.

8.3.2   Representations and warranties

A bank will always want the option to call a default if one of the written representations proves to have been incorrect or misleading when made. The problem with this default is that it is often drafted very widely. A typical clause might provide for default if:

> ... any representation, warranty or other statement made or repeated in, or in connection with, this agreement, or any document connected with this agreement, is incorrect or misleading when made, or repeated.

Thus, the default will cover statements made in connection with the document, as well as within the reps and warranties clauses. This might include anything from the inflated valuation of an important asset, to a mistake in the accounting reference date of a minor subsidiary.

A bank will therefore often concede some softening of this event of default. Usually this takes the form of a requirement for either the misstatement, or its consequences, to be 'material' or have a 'material adverse effect' (see also **11.5.3**). However, a bank will not want to start arguing over the meaning of 'material' at a time when it may want to pull the facility: it may insist that it will be the judge of 'materiality'.

8.3.3 Undertakings

A breach of undertaking will be expressed as an explicit event of default in much the same way, and for the same reasons, as a breach of a representation. It is not uncommon to see a grace period in this event of default, and sometimes a materiality qualification too.

8.3.4 Financial covenants

As mentioned at **7.3.4.5**, some equity sponsors in acquisition financings have negotiated 'equity cure' rights to avoid a default on breach of a financial covenant. A further concession demanded by strong borrowers is the so-called 'Mulligan' provisions. This works either:

(a) to prevent the bank calling an event of default unless the borrower breaches a financial covenant on two consecutive testing dates (this is a 'true' Mulligan); or

(b) to allow the bank to call a default on the first breach of a financial covenant, but to lose that right (if it has not yet called a default) if the borrower meets the financial covenant on the subsequent test date (arguably not a true Mulligan and probably reflecting the commercial position in any event).

The term 'Mulligan' originates from a golfing expression, meaning a player is allowed a second tee shot without penalty.

8.3.5 Cross default

Cross default is a key event of default, and one which will be heavily negotiated. Imagine that a borrower defaults under another contract (ie, other than the facility agreement). The other party to that contract may be in a very strong position to force terms on the borrower. These might include extra payment, additional security, or some other form of preferential treatment. The borrower may have done nothing to trigger a default of the facility agreement, and so the bank would have to sit and watch its position being eroded. A cross default clause operates by automatically defaulting the borrower under the loan in the event that it defaults under certain other types of agreement (see also **5.2.2**). This ensures that the bank is also in a position to 'influence' the borrower and, if necessary, to protect its position by accelerating the loan. A cross default clause also effectively gives a bank the benefit of the default provisions in other agreements to which the borrower is a party.

Because of the 'domino' effect which a cross default might have, it is usually limited by:

(a)   being confined to defaults which occur under other documents providing 'financial indebtedness' (eg, loans, bonds, notes, acceptance credits, finance leases, guarantees, etc – see also **7.3.3**); and

(b)   including a threshold amount below which the default will not apply (a 'de minimis').

Other aspects that might be negotiated include the following:

(a)   A borrower will often argue that the cross default should operate only if the other default will have a material effect on its ability to perform its obligations under the facility agreement.

(b)   A cross default might be set to trigger at different points in the initial default, for example if:

(i)   the borrower simply fails to pay an amount due under another agreement; or

(ii)   the creditor under another agreement obtains a right to demand early repayment; or

(iii)   the creditor under another agreement actually exercises a right to demand early repayment (known as a 'cross acceleration' clause).

A borrower would prefer option (iii).

(c)   There may be particular contracts which a borrower will want to carve out from the cross default. One example is a swaps contract (see **Glossary**), where the borrower may be obliged to pay out to a counterparty not because of a default, but due to interest or currency rate movements.

(d)   Sometimes a borrower will ask for a carve-out (ie, an exception) for any defaults with respect to unpaid debts which the borrower is disputing in good faith. This is, however, strongly resisted by most banks. Pure debt disputes are seldom bona fides. Furthermore, a bank will not want to be arguing whether or not a dispute is in 'good faith' at a time when it might want to accelerate the loan. A bank will want a position where it can default the borrower if necessary, and the borrower will have to prove a dispute is in good faith to earn a waiver.

One issue for a bank is the evidential problem of finding out when a borrower has defaulted under another agreement. If a borrower knows that a default in another agreement will cross default into its loan then it has little incentive to reveal the first default. The fact that this in itself may cause the borrower to breach its representations when they are repeated is of little consequence; the bank will still be no wiser, and the borrower has simply defaulted twice instead of once. Furthermore, a bank is subject to an implied duty of confidentiality with regard to a customer's affairs (see *Tournier v National Provincial and Union Bank of England* [1924] 1 KB 461). This limits the availability of any information about defaulting borrowers 'in the marketplace'. A bank will therefore have to resort to its knowledge of the borrower's obligations under other agreements (through initial due diligence and subsequent information covenants), and its monitoring of the borrower's financial position.

8.3.6   Cross default into subsidiaries

If the borrower is part of a group, a bank will often want the cross default provision to extend to a default by any other companies in the group. A bank will argue that financial difficulties in a subsidiary will usually have an effect on the parent because of intra-group guarantees and letters of support. Furthermore, a bank will argue that a parent should not let a subsidiary default without good reason: if there is good reason then the event of default can be waived. However, a borrower will usually persuade a bank to limit any cross default into its 'material' or 'principal' subsidiaries from time to time.

8.3.7 Change of business

The type of business in which a borrower is involved plays a large part in the bank's initial risk assessment when agreeing to lend. A change in that business would entail a change in risk, and so be unacceptable to the bank without its consent. It will therefore usually be an event of default if the borrower makes any material change to its business, ceases to carry on any material part of its business, or disposes of a material part of its business ('material' may be defined, eg, with reference to net worth). The point at which outsourcing would trigger a 'change of business' is open to some debate.

8.3.8 Change of control

There are several reasons why a bank will be concerned about any change in control of the borrower. First, the parent of a borrowing subsidiary might have provided support which may be lost. Secondly, a bank may have a particular relationship with a parent which has been influential in its decision to lend to a subsidiary. Thirdly, a bank's original credit assessment (see 2.2.1) may have been based on the group structure to which the borrower then belonged.

A change of control provision requires careful structuring. It might simply refer to any change in the shareholders, or include a change to the board of directors. Will a change of control occur if the original parent retains over 50%, or must it retain at least 75%? Some borrowers may actually welcome such a restriction as an obstacle to a hostile takeover (a 'poison pill').

8.3.9 Insolvency and related proceedings

The insolvency of a borrower will, without question, be an event of default. Any negotiation of this clause will simply relate to the timing of default. From a bank's perspective, an event of default should give it the ability to take action at the first sign of any problem. If a bank holds security, it will at least want the option to enforce it as early as possible to optimise its position with regard to other creditors and to preserve the borrower's assets. Typical triggers for this event of default are: 'inability to pay debts as they fall due', 'assets worth less than liabilities', 'ceasing to make payments on debts', 'negotiating with creditors to reschedule debts' and 'declaration of a debt moratorium'.

If provisions make reference to the definition of inability to pay debts at IA 1986, s 123, borrowers will want to carve out s 123(2), since it is very wide.

In addition to insolvency itself, there will also be triggers related to insolvency *proceedings*. Typically this will include any corporate action, legal proceedings or other procedure or step (these last two being particularly important since the Enterprise Act 2002 introduced out of court appointment of an administrator) taken in relation to, for example:

(a)   a moratorium, winding-up, dissolution, administration, reorganisation or arrangement with a creditor;

(b)   the appointment of a liquidator, receiver, administrator, administrative receiver or similar; or

(c)   the enforcement of any security over the borrower's assets.

From a borrower's perspective, once the bank 'pulls the plug' its problems are likely to get worse, especially if it is subject to cross default clauses in other documents. Ideally, therefore, a borrower wants any event of default to trigger as late as possible. A borrower might argue, therefore, that a creditor might 'take steps' to appoint an administrator as a method of forcing payment which the borrower disputes. It will typically ask for a remedy period, a carve-out for debts that are genuinely disputed (although see comments at **8.3.5** above), or even a default limited to the actual appointment of an administrator, receiver or similar officer.

8.3.10　Proceedings

If a borrower becomes involved in any litigation, arbitration or similar proceedings, the bank will usually want the ability to call a default. A borrower will argue that this default should not be absolute but should be subject to a de minimis figure (see **11.5.5**). A bank may even agree to a higher de minimis for proceedings which are vexatious, or are contested by the borrower in good faith. An alternative for the borrower is to draft the event of default so that it is only triggered by proceedings which will (the bank will want 'might') have a material adverse effect on the borrower's ability to perform its obligations under the loan.

8.3.11　Unlawful performance

A bank will invariably want to call a default if it becomes unlawful for a borrower to continue to perform its obligations under a facility agreement. The bank could not risk encouraging a borrower to break the law, and so the only option is to accelerate the loan. Similarly, a bank may also want an event of default if the borrower should lose any consents or authorisations necessary for it to perform its obligations under the loan. The borrower will want to introduce some element of materiality into both these clauses. A borrower may also argue that this should not be included as a default, since it has no control over the law, and ask instead for a provision for early termination for illegality.

8.3.12　General default

A provision will often be included in a facility agreement which makes it an event of default if the borrower fails to comply with any 'other obligations' (ie, other than representations and undertakings) under the facility agreement. This clause will invariably be drafted with a relatively long 'cure period' of perhaps 30 days. Specific events of default, which aim to pick up all the fundamental situations in which the bank may want to terminate the loan, will still stand, but the general default clause will 'sweep up' any minor defaults and make them actionable by the bank if the borrower cannot cure them.

8.3.13　Material adverse change

The material adverse change event of default, known colloquially as the 'MAC' clause (see **5.2.2.2**), also acts as a 'sweep up' provision. It allows a bank to call a default if there is a material adverse change in the borrower's position or circumstances which might prevent it from complying with any provisions of the facility agreement. If a MAC clause is included, it is always heavily negotiated. The potential breadth of this event of default means that many borrowers will try to exclude it, arguing that a detailed facility agreement which contains a raft of undertakings, financial covenants and events of default should not require such a 'catch all' provision. If a MAC clause is included (some banks' lending policies may require it), a borrower will want the 'circumstances' to be such that they 'will' make the borrower fail to comply with a 'material' obligation. The bank will want 'circumstances' that 'may', 'in the bank's opinion', cause the borrower to fail to comply with 'any obligation' under the loan.

There is a view that, as long as the borrower demonstrates that it can comply with all its obligations under the agreement (particularly any financial covenants – see 7.3), it would be difficult for a bank to argue that any material change had been 'adverse'.

MAC clauses are not commonly used to default a borrower (in recessionary times, this may change); however, in *BNP Paribas v Yukos Oil Company* [2005] EWHC 1321 (Ch), the court upheld the validity of accelerating a loan based on a MAC event of default (it must be said the facts allowed a very clear argument for a MAC). A bank must be very sure of its case to use the MAC clause to demand repayment; but may be more willing to use it as a 'draw-stop' (ie to prevent new borrowing). The most common use for the MAC, however, is to threaten possible default and thereby persuade a borrower to start a dialogue with the bank (see 8.5 below).

8.3.14 Qualified accounts

In leveraged transactions it is not uncommon for a bank to include an event of default which is triggered if the borrower's accounts are qualified by the auditors (see 6.5). A borrower will want to limit any default to a qualification which has a material adverse effect on its ability to perform its obligations under the loan facility.

8.3.15 Repudiation

Most facility agreements will make any actual, or attempted, repudiation of the facility agreement by the borrower an event of default, a provision that will probably be resisted on principle by borrowers with a strong bargaining position.

8.4 Events of default and other clauses

One of the problems with events of default, which is often overlooked, is ensuring that they dovetail with other provisions of the facility agreement, particularly any repeated representations and any undertakings.

For example, a borrower might have fiercely negotiated the event of default relating to litigation, to carve-out any proceedings against it which it contests in good faith and which represent claims for less than £10,000. However, the facility agreement may also contain a representation, deemed repeated every quarter, in which the borrower must confirm that it is not involved in litigation of any kind. If a small piece of litigation starts, say for £2,000, it will not directly trigger the litigation event of default, but it will mean that the borrower is unable to repeat the representation. If a representation cannot be repeated, it will be an event of default. The solution is to ensure that any carve-outs in the events of default are mirrored in the representations, warranties and undertakings, as appropriate.

Any representation to be repeated must therefore be treated as if it were an event of default, and enjoy the necessary carve-outs. Remember that a disclosure letter works to circumvent stringent representations with respect to breaches existing only when the letter is accepted (see also 5.2.3).

8.5 Action on default

If an event of default occurs, a bank will want a number of different options, which might include:

(a)   cancelling any undrawn commitments if part of the loan has not been utilised; and/or

(b)   putting all or part of the facility 'on demand', and taking over the selection of interest periods (see **4.9**); and/or

(c)   demanding immediate repayment of part or all outstanding capital and interest, as well as any cash collateral for contingent liabilities (eg, bills of exchange or letters of credit); and/or

(d)   enforcing any security it holds.

The bank may choose not to exercise any of these options. It may feel that the event of default is not serious enough to terminate the loan, but that it justifies demanding additional fees from the borrower. Alternatively, the bank may use the default as an opportunity to insist that the borrower gets 'around the table' with the bank to discuss its business plans.

A bank will usually want these remedies available 'on or at any time after an Event of Default has occurred ...'. A borrower may want to add 'unless such event of default is remedied'; however, this should be resisted. If a borrower can unilaterally cure an event of default, he will have little incentive to disclose it. Furthermore, what constitutes a 'cure' of some defaults is not straightforward, and any ambiguity usually favours the borrower. Banks might argue, therefore, that an event of default can be 'waived' but never 'cured' (although see **8.6** below).

In the case of a syndicated loan, the agent will often be given discretion as to what action to take on an event of default, but with an overriding obligation to act in accordance with any instructions of the majority banks (either in number or value). Giving the agent this autonomy allows a faster response in time-critical situations, but at the price for the agent of taking on potential liability for wrong decisions (through action or inaction). Clearly, a borrower would want the most considered response possible, and so it may prefer that any default decision (and decisions in relation to a particular event of default) is taken by the entire syndicate, or a large majority of them.

If the loan is terminated and all outstanding amounts are immediately repayable, then 'default interest' will apply until the amounts are settled in full (see **4.9**).

8.6   Potential events of default and grace periods

As described above, some events of default will include a 'grace period' (or 'cure period'), whereby the borrower is given a time period in which to remedy a 'default'. During this time, there is not a full event of default but simply a 'potential event of default'. A typical definition might be:

> ... an event which with the lapse of time, or giving of notice under the agreement, might constitute an event of default.

However, unless and until the default is remedied, the bank will not want to lend 'new' money to the borrower; thus, while a potential event of default is running, a bank's commitment to lend new money is suspended. This gives rise to a potential problem for a borrower under an RCF if a roll-over happens to fall within a grace period. A provision suspending further commitment will allow the bank to refuse to roll-over (ie, the borrower must repay the amount, but cannot then re-borrow). Roll-overs are therefore specifically allowed during a potential event of default. A borrower must usually undertake to tell the bank as soon as it is aware of any potential event of default.

Lastly, a borrower should never agree to give a repeating representation that there are no *potential* events of default, since if there are any the borrower will be unable to make the representation, which is, in itself, an event of default (effectively creating an event of default out of a potential event of default).

8.7 LMA definition

The Loan Market Association (LMA) facility agreements use the term 'event of default' in the traditional sense. However, they do not use the term 'potential event of default': they use the term 'default' to encompass both an 'event of default' and the equivalent of a 'potential event of default'. Thus the expression 'default which is not an event of default' is their rather convoluted way of expressing the equivalent concept of a 'potential event of default'.

8.8 Events of default – the bank's perspective

A bank will generally consider demanding early repayment of a loan as a 'last resort': recovering capital will usually involve selling assets, and this might mean winding up part or all of the borrower's business. However, the threat of recalling a loan can be used as a very potent negotiating tool. If a default occurs, the borrower is effectively at the bank's mercy, and the 'price' of not recalling the loan might be increased fees, a greater margin, tighter financial covenants or renegotiation of other terms. Any changes will be justified as consideration for the bank agreeing to continue despite the 'risk' of ignoring the default.

A borrower will sometimes argue that it should not be defaulted on the basis of events which are beyond its control, for example, a change in the law. Any such argument will be strongly resisted by the bank, because events of default are not based on 'fault' but on risk: they are situations in which a bank feels that the borrower's ability to perform the facility agreement may be compromised, and therefore it should have the right to terminate the facility agreement or take other appropriate action (see **8.5**).

Events of default do present some risk to the bank. The bank must ensure that it is justified in calling an event of default. Withdrawing a loan facility is likely to destroy a borrower's business, not least because of cross-default into other agreements. If a bank wrongly calls an event of default it may be sued by the borrower for breach of contract or in tort. In the recent case of *Concord Trust v The Law Debenture Trust Corporation plc* [2005] UKHL 27, the House of Lords ruled that the wrongful calling of an event of default was not a breach of contract, but simply an ineffective action. However, the *Concord* decision was given in the context of default under a bond; it would not apply to a loan facility which was not fully utilised and where calling the default prevents further borrowing (see also **19.2.4.4**). Because of the consequences of calling a default, a bank will want the events of default drafted as clearly as possible (see also **Chapter 11**).

8.9 Events of default – the borrower's perspective

The borrower must obviously be very cautious when agreeing to the events of default. To some extent, the events of default are intended to control how the borrower runs its business and what it does with the loan monies. If they are drafted too tightly, however, they will strangle the business.

Any breadth in the wording of the events of default will work for the borrower not just because it provides leeway, but also because a bank will be cautious about 'grey areas'. It is also true that a bank will not usually withdraw a loan without considerable provocation.

Wickes reaches deal on bank loans

By Andrew Taylor and Jim Kelly

Banks have renegotiated loan facilities made to Wickes, the troubled DIY retailer which last week warned that it had overstated profits due to accounting irregularities.

A syndicate of 11 banks and Trade Indemnity, the credit insurer, announced yesterday they had agreed to replace an £18m facility. Two other loan facilities for £50m and £30m have been capped, preventing Wickes from drawing further funds.

The deal will the ease worries of suppliers concerned about Wickes' ability to meet its obligations after lines of credit were temporarily frozen by the banks pending clarification of its financial position.

Barclays, which is leading the syndicate, said yesterday: "We believe that Wickes' problems can be resolved in the near future." It said bankers and accountants had worked over the weekend to "assess the cash flow position of Wickes' core UK operation".

Mr Michael von Brentano, who was appointed chairman of Wickes following the resignation of Mr Henry Sweetbaum, said: "We have made it plain that the accounting issues which have been uncovered should not detract from the fact that our operating businesses are sound."

Latest estimates suggest that Wickes' operating profits of £36.7m may have been overstated by £20m-£25m last year.

It is thought that the company, which normally pays suppliers at the start of each month, was fac-

ing a technical breach of its loan covenants. It was able to give the banks sufficient reassurance to allow loans to be renegotiated. The new £18m facility is thought to carry a higher interest rate than under the old agreement.

The company has said it will not pay its 1.5p final dividend, which had been due to be sent to shareholders today, because of uncertainty about its operating profits.

Price Waterhouse and Linklaters & Paines have been instructed to investigate the cir-

cumstances giving rise to the inaccuracies in Wickes' accounts, as well as the group's financial condition.

The inquiry is concentrating on the accounting treatment of rebates paid to Wickes by suppliers. In some instances, benefits to cover several years of trading were brought forward and included in a single year's profits.

The investigation is unlikely to be sufficiently advanced to allow the suspension of Wickes' shares to be lifted this week.

An example of loan agreement terms renegotiated after an event of default.
Source: *Financial Times.*

Chapter 9

Boiler Plate, Mechanics and Miscellaneous Clauses

'The fox knows a little about many things. The hedgehog knows only one thing, but it is a very big thing.'

Isaiah Berlin, Philosopher

9.1 Introduction

The preceding chapters have reviewed the main provisions of a loan facility in the order in which they will most usually be found in the agreement. Initial operative clauses will usually be followed by representations and warranties, undertakings and events of default (the only logic to this order is a vague chronology). The last three areas will be the most heavily negotiated, and unique to each facility agreement. In contrast, the remaining provisions are often seen as rather 'unglamorous', using standard clauses, and of minor consequence. The colloquial title for these clauses, the 'boiler plate', is far from inspiring, and many of them are in the back end of the document. Yet these provisions control some important areas: they seem unimportant only until something goes wrong. This chapter looks at the main 'boiler plate' clauses and funding mechanics, as well as at one or two miscellaneous items.

9.2 Repayment, prepayment and cancellation

The following clauses are part of the mechanics of funding and settlement ('funding mechanics').

9.2.1 Repayment

The repayment clause is arguably the most important provision in the agreement. As part of the funding mechanics, it will appear before the representations, undertakings and events of default. The form of repayment will depend on the type of facility: if the loan is to be amortised, tables listing the amount to be repaid on specific dates are usually attached as schedules to the agreement.

9.2.2 Prepayment

Some loans will allow (and in certain circumstances require) a borrower to repay capital before the dates envisaged by the facility agreement. This is known as 'prepayment'. Without some form of contractual provision, a borrower probably has no right to prepay a loan. From a borrower's perspective, the ability to pay down the loan as soon as spare capital is available will save interest payments. Furthermore, rates of both interest and margins will fluctuate: if there is a sustained downward movement, borrowers may refinance existing loans (either with their existing bank or a new one) part way through their term. A bank is usually happy for the borrower to prepay, but there are a number of points which the bank's solicitor will want to ensure are covered, and these are mentioned below.

9.2.2.1   Broken funding

As explained at **4.9**, many large commercial loans will be funded by interbank lending ('matched funding'). If a borrower prepays part of the loan, the bank may be left to service an interbank loan without an equivalent interest stream from the borrower. Alternatively, the bank would have to terminate the interbank loan early and incur breakage fees (there is usually no provision for prepayment in interbank borrowing).

Facility agreements will therefore usually include an indemnity under which the borrower must reimburse the bank for any loss or liability it incurs as a result of prepayment (a 'break costs' clause – see **4.9.3**). Break costs will be avoided if the borrower can ensure that any prepayment is always made at the end of an interest period.

9.2.2.2   Administration expenses

Sometimes a bank will want to charge a fee for prepayment (or a 'prepayment premium/penalty') to cover any extra administration costs, particularly in the case of an agent taking prepayment on behalf of a syndicate.

9.2.2.3   Order of application

In amortised loans, banks traditionally resist treating a partial prepayment as an early settlement of the next repayment amount due. This is primarily because the bank will want a borrower to continue to demonstrate the financial control necessary to maintain the steady repayment regime envisaged by the facility agreement. A bank may insist that any prepayment is treated as satisfying the final repayment obligations first (ie, prepayment will be applied against repayment obligations in inverse order of maturity), or else that the prepayment is spread across all the scheduled repayment amounts, reducing each one rateably. Taking the prepayment off the 'back end' of the loan reduces the life of the loan, which in turn reduces the bank's risk; using the rateable approach reduces exposure but maintains the relationship.

Strong borrowers will be allowed to apply any prepayment as they choose.

9.2.2.4   Preference

If a corporate borrower is insolvent when it makes a prepayment, there is a danger that the prepayment might be a preference under IA 1986, s 239. The bank could be required to repay any such 'preferred' prepayment to the insolvent company. A prepayment might also be a preference if it causes the borrower to become insolvent within six months of being made (or within 24 months if bank and borrower are 'connected', eg if the bank were a shadow director, or the two entities were under common control).

This might cause the bank a problem in two situations. If the bank's security is poorly drafted, the borrower (or its administrator, or receiver) might be able to claim that the secured debt is simply the amount of the outstanding loan when the borrower became insolvent. Any prepayment which has to be repaid as a preference will then become unsecured debt. Similarly, if the loan is fully repaid and the borrower becomes insolvent within six (or 24) months of a prepayment, the security might have fallen away and will no longer be available to secure a prepayment which has to be repaid as a preference. To avoid this, a bank might try to negotiate the right to retain security for a period after a prepayment (although often this is impractical and more a theoretical risk than a real one).

9.2.3   Mandatory prepayment

Some loans will actually *require* a borrower to prepay the loan in certain circumstances. This is known as 'mandatory prepayment', or sometimes as 'cash recapture' and can serve as an alternative to an event of default in some cases (with the advantage that it will not trigger a cross-default). Mandatory prepayment might be required where, for example:

(a)   the borrower disposes of certain fundamental assets other than in the ordinary course of business;

(b)   the borrower receives insurance monies for an asset which it is not replacing;

(c)   the borrower generates more profit (or, more accurately, cash) than it is deemed to require;

(d)   the loan is to fund an acquisition, for which the purchase price is subsequently readjusted downwards;

(e)   the borrower subsequently raises funds through an issue of shares or debt securities;

(f)   there is a change of control in the borrower (eg flotation).

The most important point for the borrower is to ensure that any mandatory prepayment provisions will leave it with sufficient working capital.

A mandatory prepayment regime will also be imposed if a bank is prohibited from participating in the loan, or from giving effect to its obligations under the loan document, because to do so becomes 'illegal' due to any law, regulation or directive. For example, the EU, US or both currently impose some degree of financial sanctions against Iran, Syria and Zimbabwe ('illegality' will not include a bank's internal policy changes which happen to conflict with the loan).

9.2.4   Cancellation

If a loan provides a commitment period over which the borrower is allowed to utilise the facility (see **4.8.2** and **3.2.2**), the bank will almost certainly charge a fee for making the facility available during that period (known as a 'commitment fee' (see **9.5**)). However, a borrower may realise part way through the commitment period that it will not require the full amount of the available facility. Many loans allow the borrower to cancel any available amounts during the commitment period and so save on commitment fees (although sometimes a bank will charge cancellation fees!). The advantage to the bank is that it can use the cancelled commitments for other lending. A syndicate of banks will therefore want any cancellation to reduce their commitments rateably. A borrower must be sure that any cancellation fee is not prohibitive and that cancellation is available in the smallest multiples possible in order to give maximum flexibility.

Commitments may be mandatorily cancelled if there is an event of default during the commitment period, and will be automatically cancelled to the extent they are undrawn at the end of the commitment period.

The following clauses are usually considered part of the 'boiler plate'.

9.3   Increased costs

The interest rate charged by a bank on a loan is calculated by adding a margin to its estimated costs of lending (see **4.9**). If the costs associated with making the loan rise unexpectedly, the bank's profit may suffer. It is important, therefore, that a bank provides for the possibility of an increase. What are the costs of lending, and how will a bank deal with any increase?

9.3.1   Funding rate

At **4.9.2**, the calculation of a bank's interest rate was expressed as:

(a)   funding rate (usually LIBOR); plus

(b)   mandatory costs; plus

(c)   margin (which includes capital adequacy costs).

The 'funding rate' was explained at **4.9**, and accounts for a bank's major cost when making a loan. If a bank makes a loan with a floating rate of interest, any fluctuation in the funding rate is automatically passed on to the borrower at the start of each new interest period. If the loan is at a fixed rate, the bank cannot directly pass on any fluctuation, and so it tries to ensure that the rate is high enough to cover any likely rise in funding rates during the term of the loan.

9.3.2   Mandatory costs

The Bank of England, in common with central banks in many jurisdictions, requires 'authorised deposit taking institutions' (ie, banks) to place non-interest bearing deposits with it (known as 'mandatory costs', 'mandatory liquid asset costs', 'cash ratio deposits', 'associated costs' or 'reserve asset costs'). The income from investing these deposits is used to help fund the Bank of England residual supervisory role (some central banks also use the deposits to help control money supply). The amount of the deposit is calculated as a percentage of a bank's 'eligible liabilities' (essentially *sterling* deposits made with that bank).

Since 1 June 1998, when the Financial Services Authority (FSA) took over most of its supervisory role, the Bank of England has lowered its required deposit to 0.11% of average eligible liabilities over £500 million (with the first £500 million of eligible liabilities escaping charge). This reflects the Bank's reduced supervisory workload. However, the FSA introduced its own fee structure (not a deposit) to help fund its function, which is charged both on sterling and non-sterling deposits.

The FSA fee applies (in its own words) 'in feeblocks, each of which applies to a different sector of the financial services industry, and aims to recover our cost of regulating each sector'.

The main fees for the deposit accepting activity of banks are based on 'modified eligible liabilities' (MELs – broadly all sterling deposits plus one-third of the sterling equivalent of non-sterling deposits) and current rates (to March 2009) are as follows:

£ million of MELs	Flat Fee (£)
0–0.5	160 (minimum fee)
>0.5–2	540
>2–10	690

	Additional Fee (£/£m or part £m of MELs)
>10–200	24.72
>200–2,000	24.69
>2,000–10,000	24.61
>10,000–20,000	24.43
>20,000	24.26

Both the Bank of England deposits and the FSA fee are a cost of raising money, which a bank will pass on to the borrower as 'mandatory costs'. It is quite common to see a formula attached as a schedule to the loan that calculates the proportion of the cost to be passed to the borrower. For sterling, the formula will look something like this:

$$\frac{AB + C\,(B - D) + E \times 0.01}{100 - (A + C)}\ \% \text{ per annum}$$

The formula will automatically pass any increase in mandatory costs to the borrower.

9.3.3 Capital adequacy/regulatory capital

Chapter 1 explained that banks are financial intermediaries which lend money lent to them by depositors, investors and by other banks in the interbank market.

If a major borrower was unable to repay its loan, or if the bank made large trading losses, the bank might be unable to repay a depositor or service its own interest obligations. The scenario of a defaulting borrower causing this 'illiquidity' is so serious that there is international agreement to require banks to maintain minimum 'capital' which may be offset against losses. This is known as a bank's 'regulatory capital ratio', explained in more detail below, and another factor which will add to the cost of making a loan.

9.3.3.1 Origins of regulatory capital – the Basel Committee

In the mid-1980s, a group of 12 nations set up a committee to discuss creating a joint policy on regulatory capital (those involved were Luxembourg plus the 'G10' – the self-styled 'group of ten most advanced economic nations', which actually number 11!). After several years the so-called 'Basel Committee' (they met in Basel, home to the Bank for International Settlements) came up with some 'Proposals for the International Convergence of Capital Measurement and Capital Standards'. Those proposals (known as the 'Basel Capital Accord') were adopted by all major banking jurisdictions. More recently, a second, more sophisticated version of the Basel regime has been adopted by most jurisdictions (the US being a notable exception). This new regime, commonly known as 'Basel II', was fully implemented in the UK from January 2008.

9.3.3.2 Basic proposition: assets backed by capital

The key proposition underpinning Basel I (and indeed Basel II) is that a bank needs to recover its assets to repay its depositors: if there is a risk that an asset cannot be recovered in full, it must be backed by 'capital' to create a 'buffer'. This capital buffer is known as 'regulatory capital'. The starting point for the amount of regulatory capital a bank must hold is 8% of the value of each asset: so making a £100 loan would require a bank to have £8 of capital. However, the risk of a particular loan (or other asset) not being recovered will vary and so assets are 'risk weighted' to calculate whether more or less than 8% capital should be held.

9.3.3.3 Risk weightings

Basel II has introduced a more sophisticated regime for risk weighting assets. A bank can either use the 'standardised approach' or the 'internal ratings based approach' ('IRB').

Under the standardised approach, the Basel II regulations provide a table of risk weightings to be applied to assets. For loan assets, the table looks to the credit rating of the borrower. For example, a loan to a company with an AAA rating would be risk weighted 20% (meaning 20% of £8, ie £1.60, of capital is needed to back a £100 loan). Risk weighting for a borrower with a BB rating would be 100% (£8) and, if rated B, 150% (so that £12 regulatory capital would be needed for a £100 loan). See **17.11** for more detail on credit rating.

The IRB approach actually has two versions, 'foundation' and 'advanced'. Both allow a bank to use their own (FSA approved) model to calculate the risk of recovery of different assets. The foundation version relies in part on the FSA's risk assessment figures to populate the model, whereas the advanced approach allows a bank to use its own figures for the calculation. Large banks will usually use the IRB advanced approach to calculate their regulatory capital requirement.

9.3.3.4 Types of capital

So, a bank will use either the standardised or an IRB approach to calculate the amount of regulatory capital it requires. This then begs the question, 'what is capital'? The first notion to disabuse is that it is cash in an account: in fact, regulatory capital is made up of most assets a company holds from time to time. Basel II splits capital into three types: 'Tier 1, 2 and 3 capital'.

Tier 1 capital includes ordinary share capital, verified net profits and certain reserves (the idea is that these represent assets in the bank which are permanent, able to absorb losses, rank behind depositors, and do not carry an unavoidable maintenance cost such as interest or compulsory dividends).

Tier 2 capital has less 'permanence' than Tier 1 and/or may incur fixed costs, and includes cumulative perpetual shares, subordinated debt and revaluation reserves.

Tier 3 capital is the least 'stable' of all, for example short-term subordinated loans or non-verified profits.

It should be noted that Tier 1 capital may be further classified as 'core' and 'innovative', and Tier 2 may be 'upper' or 'lower'; there are limits on how much regulatory capital can be made up of each type. For example, at least half a bank's regulatory capital must be core Tier 1 capital, and Tier 3 capital can only be used to cover limited regulatory capital requirements.

9.3.3.5 Provision for changes in regulatory capital

The requirement to maintain capital to back most loans effectively makes lending more expensive. This cost is passed to a borrower through a bank's margin. However, if a regulator were to decide that capital adequacy ratios for its jurisdiction (or a particular bank perceived to be 'higher risk') should actually be at 12%, or that the definition of Tier 1 capital should be narrower, a bank must be able to pass this extra cost on to the borrower. The increased costs clause will therefore include a provision to pass increased capital adequacy costs to the borrower.

9.3.4 Withholding tax

9.3.4.1 What is withholding tax?

Under the Income Tax Act 2007 (ITA 2007), there are certain circumstances in which a person paying interest must deduct tax from the payment before it is made. This is known as 'withholding tax' or 'deduction at source', and (like the more familiar PAYE) it is a tax imposed on the recipient of the payment but collected from the payer, providing a very efficient mechanism for tax collection. The withheld tax is either sent to HM Revenue and Customs, or it may sometimes be netted off against any tax credit of the withholding party. Withholding tax does not apply to repayments of principal, nor on repayment of the discount element of a loan issued at a discount.

9.3.4.2 Withholding tax and banks

The section of the ITA 2007 which is of primary concern to a bank receiving interest payments is s 879. Under s 879, interest payments may be subject to UK withholding tax at a rate of 20% if they have a 'UK source'. Various factors will determine whether interest has a 'UK source', including the borrower being a UK resident, a loan being secured on assets in the UK, and payments being made from or through the UK.

There are, however, several exceptions to s 879 of particular relevance to commercial loans.

'Short' interest

Essentially, s 879 applies only to what is known as 'annual' or 'yearly' interest (as referred to in s 874). There is no statutory definition for s 879 interest, but case law suggests that it is interest payable under a debt which is capable of having, and is intended to have, a term of at least 12 months. Interest on a debt for less than 12 months, known as 'short' interest, will not therefore be subject to withholding tax. This may be relevant for '364 day' facilities (see **3.2.4**) and bridging loans.

Some types of loan will be difficult to classify under this definition, for example, a loan which matures after six months but which may be rolled over by the borrower. HM Revenue and Customs therefore has some discretion, and may apply a 'hindsight test' which allows it to re-classify the type of interest once a loan has been running for a time. There is clear authority for the importance of intention (see Lord Denning MR in *Corinthian Securities v Cato* [1970] 1 QB 377). Paradoxically, the classification of 'annual' or 'short' interest depends only on the term (or intended term) of the loan, and has nothing to do with when the interest is actually paid.

Interest subject to corporation tax

Withholding tax will not apply to interest paid 'on an advance from a bank (as defined in ITA 2007, s 991) if, at the time when the payment is made, the person beneficially entitled to the interest is within the charge to corporation tax as respects the interest' (ITA 2007, s 879).

The requirement therefore has two elements to be satisfied before interest can be paid gross:

(a)   interest must be paid on an advance from a *bank* (essentially, an institution authorised as a deposit-taking institution under the Financial Services and Markets Act 2000); and

(b)   the person entitled to the interest is within the scope of *corporation tax* (at the time the interest is paid, and with respect to the interest).

Similarly, s 930 of the ITA 2007 exempts interest paid by a company if the payer reasonably believes that the beneficial owner of the interest is subject to UK corporation tax.

Interest paid by a bank

Section 878 of the ITA 2007 exempts interest paid by a bank in the ordinary course of its banking business.

The implications of withholding tax are discussed at **10.6**. If s 879 of the ITA 2007 applies, it imposes an obligation to withhold tax on anyone 'by or through whom' the payment is made. A syndicated loan will usually require the borrower to make interest payments to one of the banks as agent for the others (see **3.3.2**). When an agent bank pays the other syndicate members their share of the interest, it is someone 'through whom' the interest is paid. Will the agent be forced to deduct withholding tax a second time as it passes through its hands? Remarkably, the ITA 2007 is silent on this point. In practice, however, the view is that the 'double hit' will not occur, and this is supported by judicial authority (on the ICTA 1988, predecessor to the ITA 2007) in *Grosvenor Place Estates v Roberts* (1960) 39 TC 433.

Double tax treaties

A bank can also avoid UK withholding tax if the interest is paid to a person resident overseas in a jurisdiction which enjoys a double tax treaty with the UK. The provisions and application of these treaties are complex, but in brief they may provide for most or all of the tax on interest payments to be levied in the country of the recipient. The country of the payer does not therefore tax the payment. UK treaties with the USA and many European countries provide for no tax to be collected in the payer's country. Treaties with Japan and Australia reduce the amount of tax which must be withheld rather than extinguish completely.

The residence of a bank that is not lending out of a UK facility office is therefore of great importance to a borrower. If it is resident outside the UK and not in a jurisdiction which has a double tax treaty with the UK, the borrower may have to withhold tax and so suffer the grossing-up provisions (see **9.3.4.3**).

9.3.4.3   Provision for change in withholding tax – 'grossing-up'

Many banks will benefit from the exceptions under the ITA 2007, and will not suffer deduction of tax from interest payments. Furthermore, a borrower will usually be required to give a representation that all payments to be made under the loan will be free of any deductions. However, a bank will want to provide for any change in the situation, or for any unforeseen withholding tax, particularly if a loan has a non-UK element when interest might be paid from non-UK sources and be subject to withholding tax imposed by other jurisdictions. One solution is to provide for an indemnity from the borrower, under which it agrees to pay any withholding tax itself whilst paying the full amount due under the loan to the bank. However, in many jurisdictions the indemnity will not work, because the withholding tax will be levied on the amount indemnified.

A facility agreement will therefore usually include a 'grossing-up clause', requiring all payments to be made 'free and clear' of withholding tax. If a deduction is required by law, the borrower will be obliged to gross up the payment so that the bank receives the full amount due after deduction of any tax. Often this is achieved by providing that:

> ... the borrower will pay an amount such that after deduction of any withholding tax it will leave the sum of ...

Example

A UK borrower has to make an interest payment of £1,000. The bank receiving payment is not a UK corporation tax paying 'section 349 bank', nor subject to a relevant double tax treaty, and the payment will be subject to withholding tax, currently at 20%. This would mean the bank receives only 80% of £1,000, or £800. If the loan contains a 'grossing-up' provision, then the borrower must pay the bank an amount (X) sufficient to ensure that £1,000 remains after deducting 20% tax.

Thus 80% (or $^4/_5$) of X = 1,000

$X = 1,000 \times {}^5/_4$

X = £1,250

The borrower must make a payment of £1,250, of which £250 (20%) goes to the Revenue, and £1,000 to the bank.

Borrowers should ensure that the gross-up provisions only apply to banks that were exempt from withholding tax when they joined the syndicate. The borrower then only takes the risk of a change in tax law.

9.3.4.4 Tax credits

Withholding tax is simply a method of collecting tax on interest payments. If UK tax is withheld by a UK borrower, a UK bank can offset the tax against its corporation tax liability, and so the net result for a bank is simply a cash flow disadvantage. A borrower might then ask why it should be forced to gross-up interest payments when the bank can simply claim back any withheld interest. Once again, the gross-up provisions are a product of the way in which a bank is likely to fund the loan. When a bank borrows in the interbank market, any interest payments will not be subject to withholding tax (ICTA 1988, s 349(3)). If the borrower's interest payments attract withholding tax, it will cause a shortfall in the money the bank requires to service its own funding. The grossing-up provision avoids any problem by ensuring that the interest received from the borrower is always the same amount. It should not be thought, however, that banks simply rely on a gross-up clause without giving withholding tax a second thought. A bank will strive to ensure that all payments are free of withholding (and will usually want this specified in a legal opinion (see **16.5**)) since, if gross-up provisions apply, they will be costly for the borrower and will simply deplete the resources available to service the loan.

The effect of a gross-up clause can be very unjust to the borrower. The examples below show the potential cost to the borrower and benefit to the bank that a gross-up clause can bring. Imagine the situation with a Hungarian borrower, where, as in the first example, there is no withholding tax imposed on interest payments by the Hungarian tax authorities.

Example 1: no withholding tax

Borrower pays:	Bank receives:
£900 to bank	£900
	pays UK corporation tax (say 25%) = £225
	Net amount = £675.

Now imagine that the Hungarian tax authorities impose a 25% withholding tax on all interest payments made by their resident corporates. However, under a tax treaty between the UK and Hungary, the bank can claim a tax credit in the UK for the tax withheld in Hungary.

Example 2: withholding tax at 25%, but no gross-up provision in loan

Borrower pays:	Bank receives:
£900	£675
(ie £675 to bank,	plus tax credit for £225
and £225 to Hungarian	satisfying UK corporation tax
tax authorities)	Net amount = £675

Example 3: withholding tax at 25%, with gross-up provision in loan

Borrower pays:	Bank receives:
£1,200	£900
(ie £900 to bank,	plus tax credit for £300
and £300 to Hungarian	satisfying UK corporation tax
tax authorities)	Net amount = £900

With a gross-up provision and tax credit available, the bank stands to receive its margin and have its tax paid by way of the tax credit (this is why most facility agreements require the borrower to provide Revenue receipts for any tax deduction they make). The borrower, meantime, has had to pay 33% more interest. Some borrowers will demand that they are reimbursed for the extra cost of grossing-up if the bank receives any tax credit. Banks will want to resist a borrower's request for reimbursement on the basis that it is often logistically very difficult to allocate a tax credit to a particular borrower, and a bank will also have an innate reluctance to reveal details of its finances to a borrower.

9.3.4.5   Other taxes

The borrower will usually be required to indemnify the bank against liability for any other taxes (apart from corporation tax in its jurisdiction of residence or the jurisdiction in which its relevant 'facility office' is located) which might be imposed on the bank after payment has been made.

9.3.5   Right to prepay

If the cost of the loan does increase, and a bank chooses to claim under one of the clauses outlined above, it is usual to give the borrower a right to prepay the loan. Whilst this might not always be practical for the borrower, it can be valuable in the case of a syndicated loan where one bank is subject to increased costs imposed in its own jurisdiction. In this case, the borrower usually has the option of just prepaying that one bank's commitment.

9.4   Costs and expenses

A bank will usually require a borrower to pay for the 'incidental' costs it incurs in setting-up and running the loan. These might include any costs in connection with the following:

(a)   The negotiation, preparation and execution of the loan document, any security documentation, and any supplemental documents.

(b)   The registration of the loan and ancillary documents, including any stamp duty or similar tax. In the UK, a straightforward facility agreement is not currently subject to stamp duty, although a nominal fixed duty is levied on instruments transferring property by way of security (eg, shares). The Stamp Act 1891 (SA 1891), on which the present system is based, does not actually state who is accountable for the duty, and the main sanction for non-payment is that the unstamped document will not be admissible in evidence in civil proceedings (SA 1891, s 14(1)). Many jurisdictions have much higher duties, particularly with regard to security documentation.

(c)   The preservation and enforcement of the bank's rights under the loan and ancillary documents. This may also include the costs of investigating any potential, or actual, event of default it believes may have occurred.

9.4.1   Expenses – the bank's perspective

The bank should include expense provisions in the mandate letter (or separate fee letter) (see **2.4.5**). In a syndicated loan, the arranger/agent will bear more expense than the other banks, since it will have taken the most active role in negotiating the loan and is the point of contact between the borrower and the syndicate. An agent will therefore want a provision requiring the other banks to indemnify it, in the proportion of their contributions to the facility, in the event that the borrower does not reimburse its expenses.

9.4.2   Expenses – the borrower's perspective

A borrower will not want to provide a 'blank cheque' for the bank to spend on expenses. The best control it can probably hope to get is an obligation to repay only those expenses which the bank has 'reasonably incurred', with a requirement for the bank to produce full details of any amounts claimed.

9.5   Fees

9.5.1   Types of fee

In addition to paying interest and reimbursing certain of a bank's expenses, a borrower will also have to pay fees to the bank. The type of fees payable will depend on the nature of the facility. Fees are 'justified' as compensation for additional work or responsibility, and the widest range is found in syndicated facilities where the banks are required to take on a number of roles. A bank's fees can provide it with a very lucrative source of income (the bonus of the account officer responsible for a loan is often linked to the size of the fee). Common examples include the following.

9.5.1.1   Front end fees

Front end fees are usually paid shortly after signing or are recovered by withholding part of the initial utilisation. The bank in a bilateral loan may charge a 'front end fee' (also known as a 'facility' fee) in return for the initial work it must do to put the loan together (eg, due diligence and negotiation). It may be a lump sum, or be calculated as a percentage of the loan.

In a syndicated loan there may be several 'front end fees': the arranging bank is responsible for the initial work in constructing the facility, taking a leading role in due diligence and negotiation, and also for putting together the syndicate. The arranger's front end fee is usually larger than in a bilateral loan, and is known as the 'arrangement fee'. The arranger may have to use part of this fee in offering a 'participation fee' to attract other banks to the syndicate. The amount of management fees remaining once the arranger has paid any participation fees is traditionally known as the 'praecipium'.

9.5.1.2 Underwriting fee

A syndicated loan may involve a small initial group of banks who intend other banks to join the syndicate and take some or all of their commitment, but who agree to provide the entire loan between them if necessary. These initial banks underwrite the syndication, taking the risk that they may have to provide a larger part of the facility than they would want. Risk has its price, and the borrower will pay for this use of the underwriting bank's balance sheet by way of an underwriting fee (calculated as a percentage of the underwritten sum).

9.5.1.3 Commitment fee

The various costs that a bank must factor into pricing a loan were considered at **9.3**. They included a provision for regulatory capital which, essentially, requires a bank to back its lending with capital. The cost of meeting these requirements is covered by the margin a bank charges. However, regulatory capital provisions also apply, albeit on a reduced scale, to money which a bank is committed to lend but is as yet unutilised. A fee is therefore charged on any committed but undrawn money to cover the related regulatory capital costs. This 'commitment fee' is usually between 25% and 50% of the margin, and is charged in both bilateral and syndicated facilities on any unutilised (and uncancelled) commitment. The commitment fee is often drafted to run from signature of the facility agreement, even if the borrower has not yet satisfied the conditions precedent.

Some documents use a 'facility fee'. This is payable on both unutilised amounts (replacing a commitment fee) and utilised amounts, but with margin on utilised amounts reduced to compensate.

9.5.1.4 Agent's fee

A bank which takes on an agency role (eg, administrative or security agent – see **3.3.2**) will demand a fee to compensate for the extra responsibilities involved.

9.5.1.5 Cancellation fee

Some facilities are put in place but are never used. A common example is acquisition financing, where a company needs funding to bid for a target company. If the bid fails, the loan will never be utilised. If this is likely, the banks will usually incorporate a cancellation fee in the facility agreement (also known as a 'drop dead fee').

9.5.1.6 Utilisation fee

Facilities that are intended to be used only rarely, or not at all (eg, standby or swing-line facilities) may carry a utilisation fee. The utilisation fee will apply if the facility is used regularly, or borrowing under it exceeds a minimum amount.

9.5.2 Fee letter

A bank will usually want the details of its fees to be put in a letter separate from the loan facility (other than, usually, the commitment fee). The 'fee letter' provides confidentiality from syndicate members, other borrowers and the market generally.

The facility agreement should refer to the fee letter, and when the fees are payable, in order that non-payment carries the remedies of default under the facility.

An agent bank should also ensure that the facility agreement specifically refers to the fees payable to it to avoid any argument that its fee letter arrangement with the borrower is a secret profit in breach of its fiduciary duties. Likewise, any individual fee to an agent should be expressed as payable to the bank individually, to demonstrate it is not a fee to be distributed among the banks in an agency role. Conversely, the facility agreement should specify when a fee is to be paid to the agent or lead manager to be split amongst the syndicate.

9.6 Remedies, waivers, partial invalidity and amendments

9.6.1 Remedies and waivers

Most facility agreements will contain a boiler plate clause along the following lines:

> The rights and remedies of the Bank under this agreement:
> (i)   shall not be waived by any failure, or delay, in their exercise;
> (ii)   are cumulative, and shall not exclude or restrict its rights and remedies under any other agreement or the general law; and
> (iii)   may be exercised in whole, in part, and as often as necessary.

The first part of the clause attempts to preclude certain common law doctrines. Most importantly, an unreasonable delay in exercising a right can lead to the right being withdrawn under the doctrine of 'laches'. A bank might also be 'estopped' from exercising a right that it appears by conduct to have abandoned.

Sub-clause (ii) provides, first, that if the bank has more than one right or remedy under the agreement, it is not confined to using only one of them. This sub-clause also tries to avoid any merger of rights between, say, the facility agreement and a security document (there is authority that a superior security right will merge with an inferior one and the latter is effectively lost). Lastly, the sub-clause avoids any suggestion that the rights under the agreement should replace any rights under general law. Sub-clause (iii) tries to avoid an argument that, in exercising any rights or remedies, the bank has only 'one bite at the cherry'.

The effectiveness of any of these clauses cannot be guaranteed, and the best advice to a bank is usually to act quickly and decisively, and to keep the borrower informed of any action it takes.

9.6.2 Partial invalidity

There is a danger, albeit remote, that an illegal or invalid clause might make an entire agreement unenforceable. The following type of clause is therefore commonly included in a facility agreement:

> If any provision of this agreement is prohibited, unenforceable, void or invalid, that shall not invalidate, or otherwise affect the enforceability of, the remaining provisions hereof.

This type of clause tries to enhance the possibility of a court severing an invalid section, allowing the other provisions to stand. Under English law there are two underlying principles in relation to severance:

(a)   a court will not construct a new contract: any severance must leave the original contract standing and not alter its basic scope or intention; and

(b)   a court will not sever if to do so is against public policy.

In *Goldsoll v Goldman* [1915] 1 Ch 292, the court formulated the 'blue pencil test': a provision may be severed only if it is possible to do so simply by 'running a blue pencil' through the invalid provisions. Whether or not the type of damage-limitation clause outlined above has any influence on a court's willingness to sever is open to debate.

9.6.3   Amendments and waivers

Under English contract law, no alterations to the provisions of an executed document will be effective without the agreement of all the parties. It is not difficult to imagine the logistical problems this might cause with a syndicated loan of 30 banks. In addition, a requirement for unanimity can result in the 'tail wagging the dog', since even banks with the smallest commitment will have a right of veto over a waiver or amendment. Most syndicated facilities will therefore allow amendments and waivers to most of their clauses to be agreed by a majority of the syndicate. 'Majority' will usually be defined as banks with more than $66\frac{2}{3}\%$ (sometimes 50%) of either:

(a)   commitments to lend (if the facility is unutilised); or

(b)   actual money borrowed (once any utilisation has occurred).

The rational for switching to (b) is that once any banks are actually lending, they should get the voting power rather than those who are committed but have not actually lent (eg because they are providing an RCF which has remained unutilised).

There are two provisions related to amendments and waivers that have become common in leveraged deals during the recent 'borrowers' market':

(a)   '*Yank the bank*' – this colloquial term refers to a clause allowing the borrower to take a bank out of the syndicate if the bank votes against an amendment or waiver which a requisite majority of banks voted to allow. Usually, the dissenting bank can be removed only if the borrower can find another lender to take the commitment, but sometimes the borrower is allowed to prepay the dissenting bank's commitment.

(b)   '*Use or lose*' – another colloquial term, a 'use or lose' (also known as 'snooze and lose') provision says that if a bank does not vote on an amendment or waiver decision within a given time (eg, 10 days) then that bank's commitment is disregarded in calculating whether the borrower gets the required majority.

Whilst these clauses are borrower friendly, they are also popular with agents since they help with 'syndicate management'.

9.7   Force majeure

There will be circumstances in which the parties to an agreement consider that performance of their obligations is, through no fault of any party, no longer possible. A 'force majeure' clause attempts to define those circumstances. Those that spring immediately to mind are usually natural disasters and war, but it might be any circumstance which the parties could neither foresee nor prevent. The clause might provide that the obligations under the contract be suspended until the circumstances have passed, or that the contract be immediately terminated. In either case, however, there will not usually be sanctions on either party since, by definition, there is no blame.

Most facility agreements do not include a specific force majeure clause but rely instead on provisions for increased costs (see **9.3**), illegality (see **9.2.3**), and material adverse change provisions (see **5.2.2** and **8.3**).

9.8 Governing law and jurisdiction

In some Middle Eastern countries, the evidence of a woman is worth only half the evidence of a man. In the USA, juries rather than judges will usually decide the level of a plaintiff's damages. Clearly, it is crucial to the parties to know and, if possible, control the law and jurisdiction which will apply on enforcement of a facility agreement. Normal conflict of law rules apply to facility agreements as in the case of any other commercial contract.

It is important to recognise two separate issues: the governing law of a document is a quite different matter to the jurisdiction where a disputed document will be judged. If English courts have jurisdiction, they will rule on an agreement governed by Icelandic law: they must simply apply Icelandic law principles rather than English law principles.

9.8.1 Governing law

9.8.1.1 Common law rules

In English common law, the governing law of a contract (also known as its 'proper law') will determine issues which include the validity of the original document and any amendments (eg, sufficiency of consideration), interpretation of clauses and remoteness of any damages. The parties are free to choose the governing law provided their choice is bona fide and legal, and not contrary to public policy (see *Vita Food Products Inc v Unus Shipping Co Ltd (in Liquidation)* [1939] AC 277). However, for most contracts, including facility agreements, the common law rules have been largely superseded by statute.

9.8.1.2 Contracts (Applicable Law) Act 1990

Most EC countries are signatories to the Rome Convention on the Law Applicable to Contracts 1980, implemented in England and Wales by the Contracts (Applicable Law) Act 1990. This will apply to most types of contract (but not bills of exchange or promissory notes) being settled by the court of a signatory. The Convention allows complete freedom to choose the governing law of a contract (either expressly or impliedly), although the public policy, and certain 'mandatory rules' (eg, competition law, consumer protection) of the jurisdiction in which a dispute is heard, may supersede the governing law if necessary. If the choice of governing law is not express or reasonably certain, a court will attempt to identify the country with which the contract is 'most closely connected'.

9.8.1.3 Rome II Regulation

From 11 January 2009 (probably with retrospective effect to 20 August 2007) the Rome II Regulation will be applied in English courts. Rome II allows parties to choose the governing law of non-contractual obligations (eg, claims in tort). The choice will be upheld if: the claim falls within Rome II (some claims are excluded, eg those arising from voluntary trusts); the context is a commercial activity; and the choice of law was freely negotiated. In addition, if all the elements of a claim are outside the UK, non-English law provisions may still apply in limited circumstances.

9.8.1.4   Factors affecting choice

The party most likely to sue under a facility agreement is the bank, and so it is the bank which decides the governing law. It may choose the law of its own country, because it is familiar and accessible. Alternatively, it might consider using the law of the borrower's country, because that is where the contract will need to be enforced, and is probably the location of most of the borrower's assets. However, many overseas banks choose English law to govern loan documents because it is relatively sophisticated and stable, the legislation processes are (relatively) predictable, and it is considered 'creditor friendly'.

The jurisdiction in which the assets are situated will normally provide the governing law for any security documentation over those assets.

If the parties do not choose a governing law, the English courts will first look for any implied choice: the choice of jurisdiction will often be a strong influence. If no implied choice is evident, the courts will take a pragmatic view and look to factors such as nationality or residence of the parties, the currency of the loan contract and the place of execution or performance of the agreement. The issues of contractual capacity and authorisation of a party (see **4.6.2**) are determined by the law where it is domiciled.

9.8.2   Jurisdiction

From March 2002 a new EU Regulation on Jurisdiction (Regulation 44/2001 (often known as 'Brussels II')) came into force. There are now four regimes which might be relevant: the Regulation, the Brussels Convention on Jurisdiction and Enforcement of Judgments in Civil and Commercial Matters 1968 (still applicable to Denmark), the Lugano Convention on Jurisdiction and Enforcement of Judgments in Civil and Commercial Matters 1988 (applicable to Iceland, Norway, Poland and Switzerland) and 'domestic' English law.

Which regime applies needs to be considered in relation to each party to an agreement. However, the Brussels and Lugano Conventions are the strictest regimes and so compliance with those is the safest position (they were the principal regimes before the Regulation and so jurisdiction clauses can remain largely unchanged). Essentially, the Conventions provide that a person should be sued in the jurisdiction of his domicile. There are, however, some important exceptions to this rule. In particular, contracting parties are free to choose the jurisdiction in which they wish to enforce their document.

In cases not covered by the Regulation or Conventions, the English courts will apply traditional rules. Essentially, the court will have jurisdiction if:

(a)   a company has a place of business in England, or has registered process agents at Companies House (see below) and is served with a claim form in England;

(b)   a company submits to the jurisdiction of the English courts; or

(c)   the English court gives authority to serve a claim form on an overseas company.

Similar considerations will apply to choosing jurisdiction as when choosing governing law. A bank might want to take advice from a solicitor as to which forum is likely to be quickest, or may be most sympathetic to its case (frequently, a clause will specify several jurisdictions in which any proceedings might be brought). The court which is given jurisdiction will enforce the agreement under the chosen governing law on the basis of evidence from local experts. It should be borne in mind that this is likely substantially to inflate any enforcement costs.

If a borrower is not incorporated in the chosen jurisdiction(s), the facility agreement should appoint 'process agents' in that jurisdiction(s) to accept service of any proceedings on the borrower's behalf. Using process agents gives a certain address for service and will avoid a bank having to apply to court for leave to serve a foreign corporation. Several companies offer process agents services (for a fee), for example The Law Debenture Trust Corporation plc in the UK, and CT Corporation System in New York. Subsidiaries of the borrower are sometimes used as process agents, but this runs the risk that the subsidiary might be dissolved or sold. Using Consuls or Ambassadors is not a good idea either, in case they claim immunity to proceedings!

It is an ironic fact that the provisions for the governing law and jurisdiction are invariably the very last clauses in a document and yet they are the very first things a draftsman should consider. More than one solicitor has forgotten to look at the back of the agreement he has been given to review until late in the day, only to discover that he is reviewing a document governed by the tribal law of Uzbekistan.

9.8.3 Agent for service of process

If any of the obligors in the facility is not an English registered company and does not have a branch or other place of business in Great Britain, the service of any English court documents on that obligor would require service 'out of jurisdiction' – a time consuming process when time is of the essence. Fortunately, r 6.15 of the Civil Procedure Rules 1998 allows parties to use any contractually agreed method of service instead of serving out of jurisdiction:

(1) Where—
(a) a contract contains a term providing that, in the event of a claim being issued in relation to the contract, the claim form may be served by a method specified in the contract; and
(b) a claim form containing only a claim in respect of that contract is issued,

the claim form shall, subject to paragraph (2), be deemed to be served on the defendant if it is served by a method specified in the contract.

The usual 'contractually agreed method' is to appoint a conveniently located third party to receive documents on the obligors' behalf, known as an 'agent for service of process'. Note that this is different to a 'process agent' who is someone appointed to *serve* court documents.

9.9 Miscellaneous

9.9.1 Inter-bank provisions

A syndicated facility agreement will contain a section dealing with the relationship between the various syndicate banks, appointing the agent bank(s) and specifying their powers to act on behalf of the other banks. It will usually contain provisions on matters such as monitoring defaults, liability for actions and information, resignation of agent banks, and indemnities. It will also deal with sharing of money in the event that some banks receive payment, or recover money, from a borrower and others do not. All of these matters need careful consideration by banks, borrowers and their solicitors.

9.9.2 Set-off

A facility agreement will usually contain a specific authority from the borrower giving the bank a right (but not an obligation) to set off credit balances in favour of the borrower against any amounts due but unpaid (see **13.5**). The borrower will be prohibited from exercising set-off.

9.9.3 Illegality

A bank will always want the ability to terminate the loan if it becomes 'illegal' for it to perform its obligations under the agreement (see also **9.2.3**). If a contract is illegal when entered into, it will not be enforceable. Similarly, if the performance of a contract becomes illegal after execution, a party which continues to perform the contract will generally be unable to enforce the contract. Without an express clause providing for repayment it might prove very difficult for a bank to be repaid in these circumstances.

A borrower might try to mitigate this clause by placing an obligation on the bank to avoid illegality wherever possible. For example, this might involve booking the loan to a facility office in another jurisdiction, or assigning the loan (see **Chapter 10**) to a bank unaffected by the illegality.

9.9.4 Notices

The boiler plate will contain the provisions under which a borrower and bank give notice to each other. Mundane as this might appear, it can be very important, since many of the rights under the document cannot be exercised without notice. Communications must be written, and sent either:

(a)   by post. Banks will sometimes want a notice sent to the borrower to be deemed to arrive a certain number of days after posting, but will never accept a reciprocal arrangement. Always beware of deemed receipt: it has led to litigation in times of postal strikes (see *Bradman v Trinity Estates plc* [1989] BCLC 757); or

(b)   by fax. Fax is almost instantaneous, but the problem is knowing whether it has been received: there is little that can be done if a borrower, suspicious of bad news, simply turns off his fax machine.

A third option, telex, used to be common but is now rarely seen, reflecting its lack of use for modem communication. Perhaps surprisingly, e-mail has yet to be widely adopted as an acceptable medium for notices between bank and borrower, although posting information on a web page (eg, accounts) may be allowed in some circumstances.

9.10 Schedules

The schedules appear at the very end of a document, after all the operative provisions but before the execution clause. They attach lists of information which could be included in the operative provisions but which would make them rather clumsy, for example, banks' commitments, condition precedent documents, repayment dates and amounts, as well as the mandatory costs formula. The schedules may also contain any agreed drafts of the documents required under the loan, such as utilisation requests, transfer certificates (see **Chapter 10**), confidentiality undertaking and the form of any guarantee (if not built into the facility itself) and/or security to be provided, or sometimes the terms on which security will be given ('security principles').

9.11 Execution

Where a syndicated loan requires a party to perform several defined roles, it is conventional for a bank to execute separately for each of those roles. For example, a bank would sign three times if it were a participating bank, the administrative agent and the security agent. Note that from 15 September 2005, the Regulatory Reform (Execution of Deeds and Documents) Order 2005 is in force. The Order requires that if a director is signing a document as director for more than one company (quite common for large groups), he must sign separately for each company.

If the loan involves a large syndicate, it may not be possible to find a date on which all the members are available to attend a signing meeting. There are three possible solutions:

(a)   the documents can be sent to each signatory in turn. This can be a rather cumbersome process, however, and may stretch the execution over several days;

(b)   the absent party can appoint someone to sign on its behalf under a power of attorney, which should be created by a deed. Section 7(1) of the Powers of Attorney Act 1971 (as amended) allows an attorney to sign in his own name, or that of the principal. The borrower's solicitor should check the power of attorney document for expiry, powers, and any conditions or limitations, before accepting an attorney's signature; or

(c)   the document can be executed in counterparts. This allows identical copies of the document to be signed simultaneously in as many different locations as necessary. Usually, the document is e-mailed to parties who print it, sign it and send it back. The signing will usually be confirmed by an e-mailed pdf or fax of the signature page. The arranger's solicitor will then be responsible for collecting the different copies and producing a 'conformed copy' (see **Glossary**). If executing in counterparts, beware:

   (i)   the boiler plate should contain a clause allowing counterpart execution, and deeming all counterparts taken together to constitute one document;

   (ii)   print sizes are different in the US and the UK, and so the same document will be different lengths when printed, and the execution pages will carry different page numbers. This can look 'odd' when collating the originals: solutions include sending documents by pdf, or removing the numbers from execution pages; and

   (iii)   sending documents in pdf format also has the advantage that parties cannot change them before execution.

9.12 Further reading

Penn, Shea and Arora, *The Law Relating to Domestic Banking* (Banking Law vol 1) (2nd edn, Sweet & Maxwell, 2000).

Penn, Shea and Arora, *The Law and Practice of International Banking* (Banking Law vol 2) (2nd edn, Sweet & Maxwell, 2000).

Chapter 10

Novation, Assignment and Sub-participation

'The only permanent thing is change.'

Heraclitus

10.1 Introduction

Glance at a bank's balance sheet and it will contain the usual list of assets you might expect to find in a company: buildings, office equipment, and perhaps a few safes. The big difference is a large entry in the current assets under 'loans' (see 'Tokai Bank' balance sheet at **6.3.3**). As with other assets, a bank spends money to acquire loans, and they in turn produce money for the bank. However, once a bank has made a loan it might not keep it until it matures.

In one sense, a bank may use its loans like fixed assets: 'purchase' them, keep them for a time to earn an income, and then dispose of them. This chapter examines how banks dispose of their loans: an exercise known as 'asset sales'.

10.2 Why sell a loan?

Since the main purpose of a bank is to lend money, it might seem strange that it would want to dispose of its loans, but there are a number of common reasons for doing so.

10.2.1 Realising capital

A bank may want to realise some of the capital it has tied up in long-term loans in order to improve its liquidity. This would allow it to take advantage of any new lending opportunities which give a better return. Alternatively, a bank might decide to concentrate on a particular market and to sell any loans that do not 'fit the bill'.

10.2.2 Risk management

A bank may decide that its loan portfolio has become distorted. Too much emphasis on one type of loan or one type of borrower carries risk, and a bank may sell some existing loans to allow it to make others.

10.2.3 Balance sheet

A bank's ability to lend is subject to internal and external requirements to retain a percentage of its capital as cover for its loans ('regulatory capital' – see **9.3.3**). If a bank's capital is entirely allocated, it cannot participate in new loans (unless they carry a zero risk weighting), no matter how attractive or lucrative they might seem. Therefore, unless the bank can raise more capital, it must sell some existing loans to release capital for backing new ones.

10.2.4 Profit

A bank may see an opportunity to make some short-term profit by selling a loan. For example, if interest rates start to fall, an existing fixed interest loan might become very marketable.

10.2.5 Prestige

A bank will sometimes want an initial involvement in a facility because it is particularly high profile or important, for example the London 2012 Olympics financing. It may, however, choose to sell some or all of its share of the loan once it has derived any benefit to its market profile. Some forms of asset sale will allow a bank to keep its name to a loan but to lay off the lending risk.

10.2.6 Syndication

A bank will sometimes provide the full amount of a loan but bring in other banks to form a syndicate 'post-closing'. This 'postponement' of syndication allows large loans to be made quickly.

10.3 Moving rights and obligations

Before looking at how a bank might sell its assets, it is necessary briefly to consider the legal analysis of transferring a contractual role to another party. Most contracts operate by giving rights and obligations (liabilities) to each party. One party's rights will usually constitute another party's obligations. Under most facility agreements, a bank's fundamental obligation is to lend money (the borrower has a right to borrow), whilst its fundamental rights are usually to receive interest and eventual return of capital (the borrower is obliged to service and repay the loan). There are many other rights and obligations in a facility agreement, and since facility agreements are primarily designed to protect the bank, most rights are in favour of the bank and most obligations rest on the borrower.

In order to sell an asset, a bank must dispose of both its rights and its obligations, and this is where problems might arise. Under English law, rights under a contract (other than very personal rights) can be transferred at the instigation of the party entitled to them: contractual obligations can be moved only with the consent of the party to whom the obligation is owed. In other words, a borrower must agree to any change in a bank's obligations.

The rule is intended to prevent a party being prejudiced by the change in identity of an obligor. This can be illustrated by a simple example. Imagine that you lend your neighbour £500 on the understanding that she will pay you back in two weeks' time. You have known her for three years, she has a very well-paid job, and you obviously know where she lives. The chances of your neighbour fulfilling her obligation to pay back the money are good. Two weeks later your neighbour politely informs you that she had decided to lend the £500 to her brother who is a student in Spain, and so the obligation to repay you now rests with him. Not only have your chances of repayment probably fallen, but enforcing the obligation to repay has become much more difficult. It should now be clear why obligations cannot be transferred without the consent of the party to whom they are owed: you remain entitled to demand repayment of the £500 from your neighbour.

10.4 Selling assets

10.4.1 Summary

A bank can dispose of an asset in several different ways with different consequences. The most common methods are:

(a) novation;

(b) legal ('statutory' or 'disclosed') assignment;

(these two methods both result in the selling bank disposing of the asset completely)

(c) equitable (or 'undisclosed') assignment;

(d) sub-participation;

(e) risk participation.

(Using any of these last three methods will entail the selling bank retaining some involvement in the asset.)

On examining all of these methods in more detail, it is important to keep in mind that the basic aim of a bank in selling an asset is to remove the risk associated with it.

10.4.2 Novation

10.4.2.1 What is novation?

The only way in which a party can effectively 'transfer' all its rights and obligations under a contract is with the consent of all the parties involved. This type of transaction is known as a 'novation', a term with its origins in Roman law. Novation involves one party's rights and obligations under a contract being cancelled and discharged, whilst a third party assumes identical new rights and obligations in their place. Novating a facility agreement simply means that a new bank is put in place of the old one. This is set out in simplified terms in the figure below.

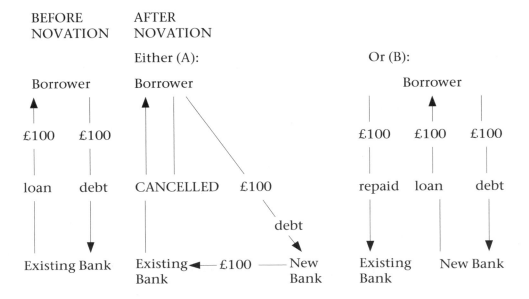

In method (A), the existing bank takes £100 from the new bank in return for releasing its rights and obligations under the loan (including its right to receive £100 repayment from the borrower). The new bank assumes identical rights and obligations with respect to the borrower as applied to the existing bank. This method is often contemplated in the original loan documentation, allowing the new bank to step into the facility agreement in place of the existing bank.

Method (B) has the same result as method (A), but it is achieved by the borrower effectively repaying the loan to the existing bank using a new loan from the new bank. This method will usually entail new loan documentation.

In strict legal terms, a novation does not transfer rights and liabilities: it cancels an existing contract and replaces it with another. The borrower's promise to perform its obligations in favour of a new bank is consideration for the existing bank releasing the old debt.

10.4.2.2   Advantages of novation

The main advantages in disposing of a loan by way of novation are as follows.

Moving obligations

Novation is the only proven method of moving contractual obligations as well as rights. In particular, this allows the existing bank to dispose of a loan which has an unutilised commitment (eg, under an RCF). Conversely, the new bank achieves a relationship with the borrower as if it were a party to the facility agreement.

Risk transfer

Novation can fully remove a loan (including any undrawn commitments) from the existing bank's balance sheet and so exclude it from any regulatory capital requirements.

Easy syndication

If the original facility agreement includes transfer certificates (see **10.4.2.3**), the existing (and any subsequent) bank can take on a large commitment without the delay of putting an underwriting syndicate together, knowing that it will easily be able to sell all or part of its commitment.

10.4.2.3   Disadvantages of novation

The main disadvantages of novating rights and obligations under a facility agreement are as follows.

Consent

The consent of all the parties involved in the original loan document is required, including any parties which have guaranteed the borrower's performance under the original facility agreement. This puts a great deal of power in the borrower's hands. Even if all parties are agreeable to a novation, a syndicated loan will present the logistical problems involved in organising the borrower, any obligors, and all the syndicate members to sign the document necessary to effect a novation.

One neat solution to the problem of consent, found predominantly in syndicated loans, is the use of 'transfer certificates'. The facility agreement will contain a clause under which the parties agree in advance that a bank may dispose of (by novation) any or all of its commitment. This is effectively an open offer to take a loan. To accept the offer, a new bank (together with the existing bank), must simply execute a transfer certificate. A pro-forma certificate will usually be included as one of the schedules to the facility agreement. Transfer certificates can be used to dispose of all or part of both a bank's participation and/or its commitment. A transfer certificate is not, however, a debt instrument (it does not contain evidence of debt), and so the new bank will have to sue on the original facility agreement in the event of any problems.

A similar system to the transfer certificate is the transferable loan certificate (TLC). The only significant difference is that the TLC operates through the agent bank issuing certificates and keeping a register of transfers. The TLC was originally devised to avoid stamp duties which are no longer in force, and so it is now relatively uncommon.

Secured loans

Since novation replaces existing obligations with new ones, it probably restarts the time periods ('hardening periods') during which the security might be set aside as a transaction at an undervalue, or preferred transaction, under the IA 1986, ss 238–241. The time-limits for any floating charge being avoided under the IA 1986, s 245 might also be restarted (see **14.9** – although the likelihood of a liquidator using any of these provisions against a novation must be small). The other danger of security being re-dated to the time of each novation is that it might lose its priority over other security (see **14.3**). The favoured way to resolve these potential problems (in common law jurisdictions at least) is to appoint a security trustee to hold any security granted under the loan on trust for the banks. The banks participating in (or committed to) the facility will be beneficiaries of the security under the trust and may vary from time to time whilst the security remains. If the relevant jurisdiction does not recognise trusts, a 'parallel debt' structure might be used.

Disclosure

For obvious reasons, it is difficult to hide the identity of a transferee bank using novation.

10.4.3   Legal assignment

10.4.3.1   What is legal assignment?

Assignment is simply the transfer of rights. The Law of Property Act 1925 (LPA 1925), s 136 provides that a legal assignment of all debts and other choses in action (ie, rights enforceable by legal action rather than possession) must be:

(a)   in writing and signed by the assignor;

(b)   absolute (ie, unconditional); and

(c)   notified in writing to any person(s) against whom the assignor could enforce the assigned rights.

In order to be 'absolute' in the context of loan transfers, an assignment must transfer the whole of the debt owed to the existing bank (see *Walter and Sullivan Ltd v Murphy (J) and Sons Ltd* [1955] 2 QB 584) (and cannot be 'by way of charge') (see **12.6**). If any one of the conditions for legal assignment is not fulfilled, the assignment will be an equitable one (see **10.4.4**). Legal assignments are also known as 'statutory assignments', or 'disclosed assignments'.

It is generally accepted that an assignment can only transfer rights and not obligations. The figure below shows an assignment in simplified terms.

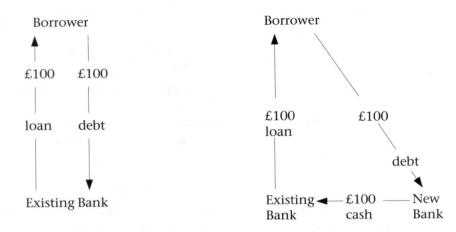

In the context of a facility agreement, a legal assignment will transfer to the new bank all the existing bank's rights under the facility agreement, the right to sue the borrower (and any guarantor), and the right to discharge the assigned debt. Any obligations of the bank can be transferred only if the borrower consents (ie by 'novation' – see **10.4.2**).

The assignment of some contracts is governed by legislation other than the LPA 1925. Of particular relevance in a banking context are bills of exchange and promissory notes (assignment of which is regulated under the Bills of Exchange Act 1882), and shares in registered companies, the rights under which are transferred in accordance with the CA 2006.

10.4.3.2　Advantages of legal assignment

Rights transferred

Subject to any restrictions in the loan facility and the 'disadvantages' discussed at **10.4.3.3**, legal assignment is an effective method of transferring rights under a facility agreement without requiring the borrower's consent.

Borrower's payments

On receiving notice of an assignment, the borrower is obliged to pay any monies due under the assigned loan to the new bank.

Secured loan

Any security, or a bank's rights as beneficiary of any security sharing agreement, may usually be assigned along with the debt.

10.4.3.3　Disadvantages of legal assignment

Obligations not transferred

An assignment cannot transfer the assignor's obligations. The main consequence of this rule is that the existing bank cannot assign any undrawn commitments without the borrower's consent. In addition, any obligations the existing bank owes to its fellow syndicate members will not be transferred. Some facility documents therefore contain a proviso that an assignment will be effective only if the new bank gives an undertaking to perform the existing bank's obligations towards other syndicate banks. Others go further by purporting to assign the existing bank's rights and require the new bank to assume *all* the existing bank's obligations (including lending commitment to the borrower).

Rights not transferred

The rights under a contract can be assigned without consent only in 'cases where it can make no difference to the person on whom the obligation lies to which of two persons he is to discharge it' (*Tolhurst v Associated Portland Cement Manufacturers (1900) Ltd* [1902] 2 KB 660). The test is an objective one and so, for example, the character of an assignee will be ignored. In a banking context, there is a danger that any indemnity provisions for increased costs (see **9.3**) might be unassignable without consent because they are 'personal' (eg, they may vary substantially with the jurisdiction of a bank). The standard transfer provision will require the borrower's consent but specify that it must not be unreasonably withheld or delayed. It will probably specify that consent cannot be withheld solely because it may increase mandatory cost, and may be deemed given if the borrower falls to reply within a given period (usually five days).

Restrictions in facility agreement

It is quite common for a borrower to require a restriction in the facility agreement preventing a bank assigning any or all of its participation without the borrower's consent. This is because the identity of its bank is usually of considerable importance to a borrower.

Risk transfer

The FSA imposes a number of requirements in order that a legal assignment is fully effective in removing a loan from a bank's balance sheet for regulatory capital purposes. The most important of these requirements is that the borrower must not exercise any rights of set-off (see **13.5**) against the original bank. To avoid a bank being forced to seek a borrower's confirmation at the time of assignment, the facility agreement may contain an undertaking by the borrower not to set-off. Any undrawn commitments will be transferred only if the borrower consents (ie, by novation – see **10.4.2**).

10.4.3.4 'Subject to equities'

Any assignment will be subject to 'equities' relating to the assigned debt and arising *before* the debtor is notified of the assignment. 'Equities' are remedies or defences which a borrower might have against the existing bank, most commonly rights of set-off and counterclaim. In other words, any remedies or defences the borrower has against the existing bank in relation to the assigned debt, and which arise before the borrower has notice of assignment, can also be used against the new bank.

10.4.3.5 Transferable loan instruments

Transferable loan instruments (TLIs) are simply a structured method of assigning a fully drawn commitment. They allow a bank to convert the repayment instalments due to it into debt instruments which mirror the terms of the facility agreement. These can be assigned by the new bank and existing bank executing a transfer instrument. In a syndicated facility, the agent bank will usually keep a register of any commitments which are transferred.

The TLI (like any assignment) will transfer only rights and not obligations. Since the TLIs are debt instruments (ie, they evidence debt), they can be sued on by the buying bank without resort to the original facility agreement. The disadvantage of this is that the TLI is a 'debenture', which can cause problems under the FSMA 2000 (see **10.7**).

10.4.4   Equitable assignment

An assignment which does not meet any one (or more) of the provisions required for legal assignment under the LPA 1925, s 136 will (as long as there is an intention to assign) be an equitable assignment.

10.4.4.1   Differences between legal and equitable assignments

As a purely procedural matter, an equitable assignee (ie, the new bank) must join the assignor (the existing bank) in any action on the debt (*Three Rivers DC v Bank of England* [1995] 4 All ER 312). However, significant differences between legal and equitable assignments arise only if the obligor (ie, in the case of loan transfers, the borrower) is not given notice of an assignment (see **10.4.4.3**).

10.4.4.2   Advantages of equitable assignments

Partial assignment and non-disclosure

If a bank wants to assign part of an outstanding loan, it must use an equitable assignment. Likewise, if a bank wants to assign an outstanding loan without disclosing the identity of the new bank to the borrower, it must use an equitable assignment.

In all other material respects, equitable assignments share the advantages of legal assignments (see **10.4.3.2**).

10.4.4.3   Disadvantages of equitable assignments

Payments

If the equitable assignment is not notified to the borrower, it will not know the identity of the bank to which its debt has been assigned, and it is entitled to continue making payments through the existing bank. In some circumstances, this may be an advantage to the existing bank: some assignments allow the assignor to retain a percentage of the interest paid on the assigned loan. In that situation, the existing bank will be happy to receive payments from which it can skim its entitlement.

However, the new bank buying a non-disclosed assignment must rely on the borrower to pay its money, and on the existing bank to pass it on. It is therefore taking a double credit risk. Furthermore, if the borrower should become insolvent the new bank might have the near impossible task of tracing any monies which the existing bank received from the borrower but did not pass on.

Subject to equities

If the equitable assignment is unnotified, a new bank will be subject to all 'equities' (eg, mutual rights of set-off) which arise between the existing bank and the borrower, even *after* the loan is assigned (until notification of assignment).

Risk transfer

As with legal assignments, the FSA has imposed conditions on the effective transfer of a loan from a bank's balance sheet by equitable assignment. Essentially, these conditions mirror those involved for legal assignment (see **10.4.3.3**), but also entail the existing bank protecting itself against any risk of pressure from a borrower (eg, to refinance) which is unaware of the assignment.

In all other material respects, equitable assignments share the disadvantages of legal assignments.

10.4.4.4   Form of notice of assignment

The rights of a bank taking an assignment depend almost entirely on whether notice is given to the borrower. In light of the issues outlined above, a notice of assignment (legal or equitable) should require a borrower to confirm:

(a)   the amount of the existing bank's debt;

(b)   that it has no rights of set-off or counter-claim against the existing bank;

(c)   that it has no notice of other assignments of the same debt;

(d)   the facility agreement has not been varied; and

(e)   that it will pay amounts due and payable under the underlying contract to the new bank's order.

10.4.5   Sub-participation

10.4.5.1   What is sub-participation?

The main reason why a bank is interested in novation and assignment is that they both enable it to remove loans from its balance sheet. There is, however, a way to achieve the same objective whilst leaving the original loan in place, known as 'sub-participation' (or sometimes 'funded participation' (to differentiate from 'risk participation' – see **10.4.6**) or simply 'participation', although this is confusing because it is also the label for a bank's share of a loan).

Sub-participation (which has no technical legal meaning) is an arrangement under which an existing bank matches part or all of its loan to a borrower with a deposit it takes from a new bank (the 'sub-participant'). So far, this sounds like the inter-bank funding described at **4.9**. However, in a sub-participation the new bank agrees that its deposit will be serviced and repaid only when the borrower services and repays the loan from the existing bank. The sub-participant has effectively taken on the risk of the first loan: if the borrower fails to make a payment due under its loan from the existing bank, the existing bank will not have to pay the new bank. This is set out in simplified form in the figure below.

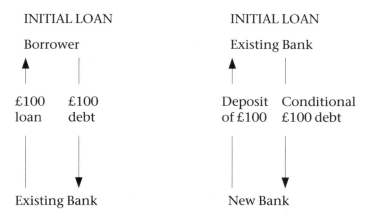

The existing bank's obligations to the new (sub-participant) bank match, and are conditional upon, the borrower's obligations to the existing bank.

There are two aspects to sub-participation which it is important to appreciate at this stage. First, the transaction does not involve any transfer of rights or obligations: the existing bank's contractual relationship with the borrower is unaffected. Secondly, since the sub-participation agreement is an entirely separate contract to the initial facility agreement, the new (sub-participant) bank will not have any rights directly against the borrower. This is known as a 'non-recourse' transaction. Any security provided by the borrower will remain with the existing bank.

10.4.5.2   Advantages of sub-participation

Risk transfer

Sub-participation will effectively remove a loan from inclusion in the existing bank's regulatory capital requirements, other than in respect of undrawn commitments (see **10.4.5.3**). The existing bank should ensure that any sub-participation agreement requires the new (sub-participant) bank to be subject to the terms of any re-financing of the borrower. Failure to do this will risk jeopardising an effective transfer of risk.

Consent

Unless there is a prohibition in the original facility agreement (which is unlikely), an existing bank may sub-participate without the consent of the borrower. The only problem the existing bank might face is in providing information about the borrower to a new bank, since all banks owe a duty of confidentiality to their clients (set out in *Tournier v National Provincial and Union Bank of England* [1924] 1 KB 461). An existing bank intending to sub-participate will therefore want to include a clause in the original facility agreement allowing it to release information about both the borrower and the loan, without a breach of duty.

Non-disclosure

An existing bank does not have to disclose a sub-participation to the borrower (unless it has a confidentiality issue – see above), and most sub-participations will be 'silent'. The advantage to both existing bank and borrower is that the relationship between them is maintained despite the risk being laid off.

10.4.5.3   Disadvantages of sub-participation

Sub-participant's credit risk

A new (sub-participant) bank must take a credit risk on both the existing bank and the borrower. If the borrower goes into liquidation, the new bank receives only what the existing bank can reclaim (because of the non-recourse nature); and if the existing bank goes into liquidation, the new bank will usually have to claim as an unsecured creditor. This double risk will be reflected in the new bank's fees for sub-participation.

Risk transfer

Funded sub-participation may not be fully effective to off-load the (entire) risk of undrawn commitments if it simply results in the existing bank taking a risk on the new bank instead of the borrower. The sub-participation agreement must ensure that the existing bank is put in funds in time to meet the borrower's demands for utilisation in order effectively to remove the risk.

10.4.6   Risk participation

Risk participation is a form of participation which acts like a guarantee. The risk participant bank will not immediately place any money with the existing bank, but will agree (for a fee) to put the existing bank in funds in certain circumstances (typically on any payment default by the borrower). Risk participation might be provided by a new bank as an interim measure before it takes full transfer of a loan.

A more common use for risk participation is to cover so-called 'unfunded' assets (ie, assets under which an existing bank has a potential outlay such as guarantees, letters of credit or swaps). If the existing bank's customer fails to meet its reimbursement obligations under these products, the new bank will put the existing bank in funds.

10.5   Global Transfer Agreement

Sometimes a deal requires a large amount of simultaneous transfers, for example if a small number of banks initially underwrite the loan but then transfer to several dozen new banks after the closing. To avoid preparing a large number of transfer certificates, a Global Transfer Agreement may be used. This is simply a new contract which amends (and restates) the facility agreement to add a new schedule of commitments. The logistical advantages are obvious, though it is very transparent: all banks will see who else is lending and the 'level' of their commitment, and this will not suit all deals.

10.6   Type of assets sold

Originally, the main market for asset sales was for so-called 'distressed debt' (also known as 'impaired debt'). Distressed debt is corporate debt which a bank is prepared to sell at a price below the amount outstanding, usually because it believes the debt may be repaid late, or repaid only in part. Sales of distressed debt are typically from a syndicated loan, and may be one or more banks selling part or all of their commitments. The selling bank will free the distressed debt from its balance sheet, and avoid the time-consuming process of restructuring the debt. The buying bank takes the seller's entitlement to full repayment for a fraction of that amount. Therefore, whilst the buyer takes the risk of non-repayment, if the borrower makes a recovery his reward will be high.

At the end of 1996, however, a number of banks formed the 'Loan Market Association' (LMA), intending to enhance trading in (primarily) performing loans. The LMA, which now has a very substantial membership, has produced standardised documentation, settlement procedures, and agreed a code of practice for market activity, all of which has helped create a more active and efficient secondary market.

10.7   Tax implications

Detailed analysis of the tax implications of asset sales is beyond the scope of this book. Briefly, there are usually two main types of tax which might affect asset sales: stamp duty (or stamp duty reserve tax (SDRT) payable on some undocumented transactions) and withholding tax.

Sub-participation does not involve any transfer of rights, and so will not attract stamp duty. Novation will not usually involve a transfer of property for stamp duty purposes and so will not normally attract the tax. If, however, the asset has rights other than those normally associated with a debt (eg, rights to acquire property) stamp duty or SDRT may apply. Assignment may prima facie attract stamp duty or SDRT; however, exemptions for transfer of loan capital (Finance Act 1986, ss 79(4) and 99(5)(a)) can often be used to avoid any duty.

In all asset sales between banks, and involving a UK resident/domiciled borrower, the relevance of withholding tax on interest payments will depend largely on whether the exemption under s 879 of the ITA 2007 applies (see **9.3.4**). The s 879 exemption will apply to loans which have been assigned as long as the advance was initially made by a 'bank' and the assignee is beneficially entitled to the interest and within the charge to UK incorporation tax at the time interest is paid. If the loan is novated (see **10.4.2**), however, this probably creates a new advance and so must be made to a 'bank' to ensure s 879 still applies.

10.8   Financial Services and Markets Act implications

Section 19 of the FSMA 2000 provides that:

> No person may carry on a regulated activity in the United Kingdom or purport to do so unless he is an authorised person or an exempt person.

This 'general prohibition' may impinge on some asset sales.

The only certain way for a bank to avoid the implications of the FSMA 2000 when selling participations, is probably to ensure that it is authorised to do so under the Act.

10.9   Borrower transfers

Facility agreements will invariably prohibit a borrower from transferring any of its rights or obligations under the agreement without consent from the bank(s).

10.10   Other jurisdictions

If a borrower (or any other obligor, such as a guarantor) is registered or domiciled in a jurisdiction other than England and Wales, there may be issues of local law which impinge on asset sales. Generally, sub-participations are unlikely to face problems because they use a contractual agreement completely outside the loan document and which will not affect the borrower. Novations and assignments may require consents of, or notices to, local regulatory bodies (or to the borrower) before being recognised. The golden rule is to get advice from a 'local' lawyer.

10.11   Securitisation

Sometimes a bank will want to sell not just one or two loans at a time but a whole group of loans together. Securitisation is a technique which allows banks to 'sell' a large portfolio of loans (or other income-producing assets), thereby freeing up capital to re-invest. In very basic terms, securitisation involves the owner of a pool of assets (the 'originator') transferring them to a specially formed company (a 'special purpose vehicle' or 'SPV'). The SPV funds its purchase of the assets by issuing debt securities (it is therefore known as the 'issuer'). Coupon and redemption of the debt securities are met with, and secured over, the asset pool.

10.12   Asset sales – the bank's perspective

Most banks will require the flexibility to sell a loan if they decide it is necessary or desirable. They will, however, usually be receptive to a borrower's feelings towards maintaining some form of lending relationship during the term of the loan and allow some restrictions (see **10.12** below). In current markets, many entities other than traditional banks are involved in buying loans on the secondary market. A bank's solicitor should therefore ensure the facility transfer language allows transfer not just to other banks but also to trusts, funds, or other entities engaged in buying loans. (Some facilities restrict transferees to other 'financial institutions': in *Argo Fund Ltd v Essar Steel Ltd* [2005] EWHC 600 (Comm) the court gave a helpfully wide interpretation to the phrase 'financial institution'.)

10.13 Asset sales – the borrower's perspective

At first sight, the identity of the bank might appear to be of little importance to a borrower. After all, on novation, assignment and sub-participation the provisions of the facility agreement will apply to the existing bank(s) or any of their successors. However, whilst the provisions of the facility agreement will remain unchanged, some may affect the borrower more strictly (eg, the increased cost provisions). A borrower will usually enjoy a good relationship with its existing bank which it will be reluctant to lose. It might be a well-established relationship; a borrower might feel that the existing bank's involvement in due diligence and negotiating the loan give it a better insight into the borrower's business; a new bank might be less flexible.

It is unlikely that a bank will agree to a complete prohibition on asset sales in the facility agreement. And a prohibition is probably not in the borrower's best interest: it would severely limit the number of banks willing to participate in the loan at syndication, and therefore result in higher fees or margin.

It is therefore common to see the borrower's consent required for transfer, albeit not to be unreasonably withheld or delayed. Sometimes the agent will agree to maintain a minimum commitment, which gives the borrower the comfort of a continuing involvement by the existing bank.

Finally, the difficult credit conditions during 2008 have seen many loans trading at substantially less than their face value (below par). This has prompted borrowers to consider buying back portions of their own loan debt: buying the debt at a discount is a cheap way to prepay. Most loan agreements do not contemplate a borrower buying back, but there may be issues with prepayment restrictions, pro-rating sharing between lenders, restrictions on cash usage, and issues with novation. The LMA is planning to add specific mechanics to its facilities to deal with borrower debt buy-back.

10.14 Further reading

Penn, Shea and Arora, *The Law and Practice of International Banking* (Banking Law vol 2) (2nd edn, Sweet & Maxwell, 2000).

Fuller, *Corporate Borrowing Law and Practice* (2nd edn, Jordans).

Debt buy-back sparks loans policy revision

Martin Arnold and Anousha Sakoui

Phones 4U has bought back some of its debt and with it joined a growing legion of companies capitalising on record-low debt prices.

The UK mobile phone retailer, owned by Providence Equity Partners, has bought £25m ($45m) of its debt at about 75 per cent of face value, according to a person familiar with the company.

Providence has already invested $2.5bn (£1.4bn) buying debt in its own and other buy-out deals, and recently hired Thomas Gahan from Deutsche Bank in the US to head its new capital markets group.

The news follows an ever-increasing number of mainly private equity-backed companies and their shareholders buying up their own debt either as an investment or in an attempt to reduce leverage as they navigate the global financial crisis.

However, lenders are not always supportive. One concern is that these debt buy-backs could allow shareholders or the company to build a blocking stake in the debt and influence future debt renegotiations or even block lenders from enforcing a default.

In response, the Loan Market Association, a trade body representing lenders, has published revised loan documentation that includes the ability to prohibit borrowers from buying back debt and stop shareholders or their affiliates voting debt they have bought back in negotiations with lenders - in a bid to avoid conflicts of interest. Borrowers can be allowed to buy back debt under certain conditions.

These buy-backs can happen in different ways.

The first is for a private equity company to buy its portfolio company's debt through a special purpose vehicle it owns, then consolidate it with the rest of the group - either selling the vehicle to the business or contributing it as equity ñ reducing leverage.

Another way is for the private equity group to use its own fund or a separate debt fund to buy the debt for investment purposes.

However, private equity groups with separate debt funds, such as KKR and Permira, say they have solid Chinese walls between their credit and buy-out teams.

Amadeus, the BC Partners and Cinven-owned travel IT company, has asked lenders' consent before doing a buy-back and has been negotiating the terms of it - a process investors generally prefer.

After discussion with lenders, the company has limited the size of the debt buy-back to €320m (£254m) and agreed not to vote in lender negotiations, according to a person familiar with the company.

Blackstone's German plastic film producer Klöckner Pentaplast has also been buying back debt, helping it reduce leverage. Earlier this year, it bought back about €25m of mezzanine, or subordinated, debt at about 20 to 30 per cent of face value, but has bought more since.

However, in spite of concerns, some banks may ultimately see these moves as a way to reduce the risk of a debt restructuring.

"Banks don't really want to end up owning the equity in these companies, so there is an alignment of interest between the debt and equity," said Peter Combe, chief executive of Permira Debt Managers, the €800m debt fund set up by the UK private equity group last year.

Source: *Financial Times*, 30 September 2008

Chapter 11

Drafting Tips

> 'I am a bear of very little brain, and long words bother me.'
>
> Pooh Bear, in *Winnie-the-Pooh* by AA Milne

11.1 Introduction

Probably the hardest task of a banking solicitor is drafting the documentation. Having identified the issues which affect his client and having negotiated those issues (usually at some length), the solicitor must return to his office and create a document to reflect what the parties have agreed.

Most solicitor's firms have a house style of drafting documents to which they encourage adherence, and never was there a truer application of the old adage 'one man's meat is another man's poison'. Furthermore, like most skills, drafting legal documents is best learnt and perfected through practice. The aim of this chapter, therefore, is not to produce a set of drafting rules, but rather to highlight some of the issues and techniques which commonly arise in the context of drafting loan documentation.

11.2 Creating the document

In order to put the techniques explained below into context, it is important to appreciate the way in which a facility agreement is created. Since a written facility agreement is primarily used to benefit the bank (see **3.6**), the drafting of the document starts and remains in the control of the bank's solicitor (although in some acquisition financings, where the equity sponsor has drafted the term sheet, it may also draft the loan). The bank's solicitor will produce a first draft from the term sheet (see **2.3.2**), which will then be sent to all parties for comment. The borrower and his solicitor are likely to have a number of clauses which they want deleted or varied, and will annotate the first draft accordingly (this is usually the only time when the borrower's solicitor does any substantial drafting). Once the marked-up draft has been seen by all parties, a conference call or (more rarely) meeting is arranged to discuss the points that it raises. There then ensues a series of e-mail exchanges, telephone calls or meetings which will attempt to resolve all the issues, with the bank's solicitor periodically producing amended drafts of the agreement to reflect substantial changes.

The burden of drafting which the bank's solicitor must shoulder is partly offset by the fact that in creating the document he knows what he has, and has not, included. The borrower's solicitor must not only review the provisions that are in the draft agreement, but also identify any points which should be included for his client's protection but which are not. It is worth noting that the LMA (see **10.5**) has produced a series of widely-used term and revolving facilities which have been 'blessed' by both the LMA members and the Association of Corporate Treasurers (ACT – akin to a representative body for borrowers). These are intended to provide conformity to the market and a first draft which eliminates some basic negotiation.

11.3   The aims of drafting

There are a number of aims to bear in mind when creating or amending a facility agreement.

11.3.1   Certainty

The primary reason for having a written facility agreement is to create certainty between the parties. The document must be drafted to reflect what has been agreed. Furthermore, it is important that the document achieves what it is intended to achieve. If, for example, a document is intended to create a first ranking security interest, it will have failed if the interest created is a subordinated one.

Certainty may also help to avoid litigation. In a case before the House of Lords (reviewing the interpretation of a guarantee), Lord Jauncey said:

> I find great difficulty in understanding the desire of commercial men to embody so simple an obligation in a document which is quite unnecessarily lengthy, which obfuscates its true purpose and which is likely to give rise to unnecessary arguments and litigation as to its meaning. (*Trafalgar House Construction (Regions) Ltd v General Surety & Guarantee Co Ltd* [1995] 3 WLR 204)

11.3.2   Ambiguity

Despite the requirement for certainty discussed at **11.3.1**, there are circumstances in which a party will want some ambiguity drafted into the facility agreement, for example, a requirement for 'reasonableness' when the bank exercises a right (see **11.5.6**). Any uncertainty will usually work in favour of the borrower and against the bank.

11.3.3   A workable document

There are two elements to a document being 'workable'. First, it must be reasonably user-friendly from the parties' point of view. A borrower in particular will not be happy with drafting which can only be understood by a banking solicitor or a rocket scientist. The borrower must be able to refer to the document from time to time in order to check what it can and cannot do. Whilst many facility agreements are long and complicated, the language need not be: the best documents are those which have simple language and are easily understood.

Attention to detail can also improve a document from the client's point of view. For example, putting a meaningful heading to each main clause and including a list of clauses at the front of the document is very helpful. When referring to a clause number, it is good practice to add the heading of the clause as well as the number. For example, 'subject to clause 16 (permitted disposals) the borrower may...'.

Secondly, the drafting must work in practice as well as in theory. For example, it is of little use drafting a clause which provides for interest payment dates to fall on a certain date each month if it does not also provide for what happens when that day is not a 'business day' when bank and borrower are open.

11.4 Templates and precedents

At some stage, most legal drafting will rely on the use of templates and/or precedents. Most firms have a set of template documents on their word-processing system which have been compiled over some years and which represent their most commonly used documents (eg, term loans, RCFs, guarantees and debentures). These templates can be used as a starting point for the bank's solicitor to create the first draft of the facility agreement. If the document to be drafted does not have a template, it is common practice to cannibalise precedent documents, ie those drafted for previous transactions, making alterations as required. The use of templates and precedents not only avoids 're-inventing the wheel', it also helps to maintain the house style of a particular firm.

There are two potential pitfalls in using precedents: first, failing to ensure conformity of terminology (for example, a precedent clause might define the borrower as 'the Borrower', whereas the document which is being created might use 'the Company'); secondly, precedents are negotiated documents, meaning standard clauses may have been changed or removed.

11.5 Drafting techniques

Precedents are particularly useful for boiler plate clauses, since these often require minimal alteration between documents. However, those clauses which are likely to require heavy negotiation (eg, representations, undertakings and events of default) are also likely to need substantial re-drafting. This section outlines some of the more common drafting techniques which can be used to achieve a compromise in these clauses.

11.5.1 Clause construction

When drafting a clause from scratch which must incorporate a right or obligation (eg, undertakings), it is worth remembering a principle of clause construction devised by George Coode, and outlined in *Skills for Lawyers*. In 1843, Coode suggested the following order for clause construction:

(1) Refer to any exceptions first: eg 'Subject to ...'.

(2) Next, set out the circumstances or conditions upon which the legal right or obligation depends, using the present tense: eg 'If X does [...] and Y does [...]'.

(3) Next, set out the right or obligation using the active and avoiding the passive: eg 'X must do 1, 2, 3, 4 and 5'.

(4) Finally, put the provision into paragraphs and give it a heading.

For example, a provision that the borrower can draw money only if the conditions precedent have been satisfied, notice has been given in the required form, and no event of default has occurred, might be drafted as:

> 4.1   Availability of loan
>
> Subject to no event of default having occurred under clause 7, if the Borrower:
>
> (a)   satisfies all the conditions precedent listed in clause 3; and
>
> (b)   delivers to the Agent a notice of utilisation in accordance with clause 9;
>
> the Banks will make available to the Borrower a term loan facility up to a maximum amount of £10,000,000 (ten million pounds).

The advantage of using this technique is that any provisos to the right (or obligation) created by the clause are clearly stated in the first part of the clause. However, many banking documents will not conform to this style. It is quite common to see the phrases 'subject to' or 'provided that' in the middle of a clause. For example:

> The Banks will make available to the Borrower a term loan facility up to a maximum amount of £10,000,000 (ten million pounds) provided that no event of default has occurred under clause 7, the Borrower has satisfied all conditions precedent ...

11.5.2   Qualifying an obligation

Many obligations will be drafted as absolute. For example, an undertaking might provide: 'the borrower will not change the date of its financial year end without the bank's consent'. It would not be appropriate to draft this as 'the borrower will use its best endeavours not to change its financial year end without the bank's consent'.

However, a borrower will sometimes argue that it is inappropriate to make an obligation absolute. For example, 'the borrower will ensure that none of its subsidiaries is declared insolvent', might be drafted as 'the borrower will use its best endeavours to ensure that none of its subsidiaries is declared insolvent'.

If the borrower must rely on a third party then 'best endeavours' will again sometimes be used, for example, 'the borrower will use its best endeavours to obtain planning permission for the proposed warehouse ...'.

What does 'best endeavours' (sometimes phrased as 'best efforts') mean? In *IBM United Kingdom Ltd v Rockware Glass Ltd* [1980] FSR 335, the Court of Appeal decided that the:

> ... covenantors are bound to take all those steps in their power which are capable of producing the desired result, namely, the obtaining of planning permission, being steps which a prudent, determined and reasonable owner, acting in his own interests and desiring to achieve that result, would take.

Best endeavours may require incurring expense, though not to the 'ruination of the company'.

It has been held that an undertaking to use 'best endeavours' to procure a shareholders' vote does not oblige a director to go so far as to give the shareholders bad advice (see *Rackham v Peek Foods Ltd* [1990] BCLC 895).

An undertaking to use '*all* reasonable endeavours' is probably the same as 'best endeavours' (see *Rhodia International Holdings v Huntsman International LLC* [2007] All ER (D) 264).

A borrower (or bank) will sometimes argue that it should be required to use only 'reasonable endeavours', or 'take all reasonable steps'. This is a less onerous provision than 'best endeavours', and probably allows the borrower to take more commercial factors into consideration and to take account of any financial outlay that might be involved (see *Yewbelle v London Green Developments Ltd* [2006] All ER (D) 122). Furthermore, the test of 'reasonable endeavours' is more likely to be subjective (ie, what is reasonable for that borrower) than the test for 'best endeavours'. Once an obligation ceases to be absolute, there will always be an element of uncertainty as to its application. There has been an insufficient number of this type of clause subject to judicial scrutiny to say with any certainty what would be required to satisfy a requirement for 'best' or 'reasonable' endeavours. The party subject to a qualified obligation will therefore gain not just because the obligation is no longer absolute, but also because the obligation is no longer clear.

A bank's primary obligation to the borrower under a facility agreement is its commitment to lend. Ancillary obligations will usually include an undertaking to minimise costs in providing the loan. For example, a bank might undertake to mitigate the effect of its lending becoming illegal (see **9.9**). However, it will invariably qualify this obligation so that it need only use 'reasonable efforts' and only for a limited period (such as 10 working days). 'Reasonable efforts' might involve assigning the loan to another bank at a discount, but would certainly not involve relocating its head office in another jurisdiction, or restructuring its lending at a massive cost (this is an area in which the bank benefits from uncertainty). The bank's solicitor will also attempt to ensure that his client has an indemnity from the borrower in respect of any expense or loss the bank might incur in fulfilling the obligation.

11.5.3   Materiality

It is often the case that a borrower will not object to a clause (eg, an event of default) in principle, but finds that it is too tightly drafted. A common compromise for this sort of provision is to qualify the clause with 'materiality'. For example, an absolute provision under which the borrower will be defaulted in the event that it 'is in breach of any licence necessary for operation of its business' has no regard to the varying scale and consequences of any breach. A provision which defaults the borrower only in the event of a breach which 'may have a material adverse effect on its ability to perform its obligations under the facility agreement' is far more palatable for the borrower. A material adverse change clause is an obvious example of the use of 'materiality' (see **5.2.2** and **8.3**).

Unfortunately, any clause which calls for a judgment may hold some danger for a bank. What does 'material' mean in the context of 'a material adverse effect'? A bank will be wary of calling a default only later to be proven to have acted negligently (see **8.8**). This is another case of uncertainty acting in the borrower's favour. The best solution from the bank's point of view is to define 'material'. However, quantifying 'material' might be very complicated, or even impossible. The next best solution for a bank is to be specifically entitled to make the decision as to what is 'material'. Thus wording such as 'material in the opinion of the bank' will avoid any argument. In a syndicated loan, the agent bank might prefer any discretion with respect to important decisions (eg, events of default) to be exercised by a 'majority' of the banks rather than the agent (see **9.6.3**). This may delay the process, but it relieves the agent of a difficult responsibility.

11.5.4   'Would' or 'might'

Some clauses (eg, certain events of default) will be drafted so that they are triggered by events which 'might' have particular consequences. For example, a borrower could be asked to give a representation that it:

> ... is not subject to any litigation, arbitration, or similar proceedings which might affect its ability to perform its obligations under the facility agreement.

From the borrower's point of view, this is clearly preferable to providing an absolute warranty that it is not subject to any such proceedings whatsoever. However, it is arguable that almost anything 'might' occur: the Earth might be overrun by aliens. A borrower will sometimes argue, therefore, that the word 'might' should be replaced by the word 'will' or 'would'. This can give a bank problems. To be certain that something will cause something else can be very difficult. The parties will usually agree to some form of compromise, such as 'is reasonably likely to ...', or 'will in the bank's opinion'.

11.5.5   De minimis

De minimis non curat lex is the general legal principle that some breaches of duty or mistakes are too trivial to attract a legal remedy. In common parlance a 'de minimis provision' is one which excludes minor breaches of a term. It is another technique for softening the effect of a provision but, unlike some of the methods (eg, materiality) outlined above, without the risk for the bank of creating uncertainty. For example, a cross default clause (see **8.3.5**) might provide for a default '... if the Borrower fails to pay any indebtedness when it falls due'. This would mean the borrower could be defaulted for failing to pay the milk bill on time. A de minimis provision might add '... if the Borrower fails to pay any indebtedness in a principal amount exceeding £50,000'.

The level at which a de minimis is set is crucial; it must allow the borrower sufficient 'leeway' to run its day-to-day business, whilst not being so high as to prevent the provision which it modifies from operating effectively. The level of the de minimis provision will therefore largely depend on the nature of a borrower's business. For example, the US$6 billion RCF arranged for Canada by Citicorp (see 'tombstones' at **3.3.3**) is likely to have a cross default clause with a de minimis provision of several hundred thousand dollars. One problem with de minimis provisions is that they can allow a multitude of minor breaches, which might together be as 'harmful' as a large breach. To overcome this problem, some de minimis provisions will set an aggregate outstanding maximum.

11.5.6   Reasonableness

The effect of most provisions can be altered substantially simply by inserting the word 'reasonable'. For example:

(a)   in the bank's reasonable opinion;

(b)   take all reasonable steps;

(c)   reasonably likely to have an effect;

(d)   use reasonable endeavours;

(e)   consent not to be unreasonably withheld.

This is a powerful tool for the borrower to reduce the severity of a provision. The real value for a borrower is the difficulty for the bank in making an objective decision about what is 'reasonable' in a given situation. Once again, the word introduces uncertainty into a provision, which will make a bank hesitate before calling a default.

11.6   Key words

Some of the words and phrases which occur in many loan documents, and which can cause some confusion, are explained below.

11.6.1   'Subsidiary'

It is quite common for a bank to require a parent company to guarantee any loans it has made to the parent's subsidiaries (and occasionally vice versa) (see **13.2**). Such 'cross guarantees' effectively breach the companies' status as separate legal entities vis-à-vis each other. Furthermore, a parent company may simply be a 'holding company', with most of the group's business being run through its subsidiaries and with no substantial assets of its own other than shareholdings. For these reasons many of the undertakings and events of default in a facility agreement may be drafted to take account of, or apply to, other companies in the borrower's group. The definition of 'subsidiary' in the facility agreement is therefore very important. Most agreements will usually refer to one of the two definitions in the CA 2006.

The CA 2006 uses two different concepts of 'subsidiary'.

11.6.1.1 Section 1159

For a company to be its subsidiary, the 'parent' company must:

(a)   hold a majority of the voting rights which can be exercised at a general meeting of the 'subsidiary'; or

(b)   be a member of the 'subsidiary' and have the right to appoint or remove its directors who together control more than half the voting rights at board meetings; or

(c)   be a member of the 'subsidiary' and control, pursuant to an agreement with other shareholders, a majority of the voting rights which can be exercised at a general meeting of the 'subsidiary'; or

(d)   be a holding company of another subsidiary which is itself the holding company of the 'subsidiary'.

In determining the voting rights, etc, of the 'holding company', the voting rights of its subsidiaries and certain nominees and trustees are taken into account.

11.6.1.2 Section 1162 and Sch 7

Section 1162 and Sch 7 provide a definition used in the CA 2006 in relation to financial statements (see full explanation at **6.6**). The important difference from s 1159 is the concept of 'subsidiary undertaking', whereby the ability to exercise a 'dominant influence' over a company (or partnership, or other unincorporated association) makes it a 'subsidiary undertaking' for accounting purposes. This might include joint-venture arrangements which a company would not usually consider to be a subsidiary.

A bank will always want as much control over the borrower as possible and so it will favour a wide definition of subsidiary in the facility agreement, usually the definition under s 1162 of the CA 2006. It is probably best to set out the definition in the loan document, rather than simply refer to the section number, in order to avoid any problems if the statutory definition is amended after the agreement is executed.

If a borrower is part of a large group of companies, it might ask that the provisions in the facility agreement only apply to its 'material subsidiaries' (ie, those worth over a certain amount). Subsidiaries may grow in size and importance, and so the bank will want the definition to embrace 'material subsidiaries from time to time', to catch any non-material subsidiary which becomes 'material' at a future date.

The concept of 'subsidiary' varies widely internationally. The Japanese can define a shareholding of just 5% as creating a subsidiary. It is therefore very important when dealing with foreign borrowers or foreign banks to be quite clear as to the scope of the 'subsidiary' definition.

11.6.2   Notwithstanding

'Notwithstanding' is most remarkable for the fact that it is one word and not three! It means 'in spite of', and so pushes aside the clause(s) to which it refers. For example: 'Notwithstanding the prohibition in clause 29 (giving security), the Borrower may provide a guarantee', means the borrower can give a guarantee whatever clause 29 might say.

The opposite effect can be achieved with the phrase 'Subject to...'. For example, 'Subject to the prohibition in clause 29 (giving security), the Borrower may provide a guarantee', means the borrower can give a guarantee only if clause 29 does not prevent it from doing so.

11.6.3   Definitions

Since, by its very nature, a definition will be repeated frequently throughout a document, it is particularly important to ensure that it is correct. Some of the points to watch out for include the following.

11.6.3.1   'Means' or 'includes'

Using the word 'means' will give a precise definition and avoid uncertainty. For example, '"Security" means a fixed charge or a floating charge'.

However, using the word 'includes' makes the definition much broader and less certain. For example, '"Security" includes a fixed charge or a floating charge'.

Imagine a facility agreement incorporating a negative pledge which prohibits the borrower from giving any 'security'. Under the first definition, the borrower could be safely advised that giving a guarantee would not breach the agreement, but not under the second definition. This is an example of drafting which is deliberately imprecise in order to benefit the bank: a precise definition of 'security' carries a risk that the bank might not think of everything to be included, and it may not cover new products.

11.6.3.2   Law of Property Act 1925, s 61 and the Interpretation Act 1978

Section 61 of the LPA 1925 applies, amongst other things, to all deeds and contracts made after 1925 and, unless the context otherwise requires, will deem:

(a)   'month' to mean a calendar month;
(b)   'person' to include a corporation;
(c)   the singular to include the plural (and vice versa);
(d)   the masculine to include the feminine (and vice versa).

Under the Interpretation Act 1978, any reference to statutory provisions in a document will be deemed (subject to contrary intention) to be a reference to those provisions as amended or re-enacted from time to time. Curiously, but perhaps because most solicitors are cautious by training, many commercial documents explicitly state the provisions deemed by these two statutes. However, sometimes the 1978 Act provision is excluded to avoid amended legislation from bringing new meaning to a document (eg, if the definition of 'subsidiary' in the CA 2006 was changed under new legislation).

11.6.3.3   Eiusdem generis rule

The eiusdem generis rule of interpretation means that where general words follow a list of specific words, they are taken to be limited to categories of the same kind as the specific words. If a definition or other clause includes a list which is intended to be non-exclusive, the eiusdem generis rule can be avoided by the use of words such as 'whatsoever' to emphasise generality.

11.7 Time computations

Time-limits are a crucial element in facility agreements. Most notice provisions and certain events of default will revolve around timing. Provisions dealing with timing will require careful drafting, and may be subject to certain statutory implied terms.

Unless specified otherwise, reference to a 'month' will mean a calendar month (LPA 1925, s 61). Furthermore, unless there is a contrary intention, the courts are likely to hold that:

(a)   the day on which an event occurs is not included when calculating a period which runs from the occurrence of that event (*Lester v Garland* (1808) 15 Ves 248). For example, the calculation of a period '21 days after giving notice', will not include the day on which notice is given (unless wording such as 'including' or 'commencing on' is used);

(b)   the period of a 'month' (or 'months') will end on the day which has the same date in the subsequent month (see *Dodds v Walker* [1981] 2 All ER 609). For example, two months from 20 March will be 20 May. If this rule would not yield a date (eg, one month from 31 August), the period is taken to end on the last day of the month in which it expires (eg, 30 September). The period will end at midnight on the appropriate day;

(c)   if a period is stated as 'not less than 3 months nor more than 6 months', the rule outlined in (b) above will apply. For example, if a notice is to be given 'not more than 3 months nor less than 2 months before cancellation', then cancellation on 30 November may be notified from 31 August to 30 September (inclusive);

(d)   notice of 'at least' or 'no fewer than' 21 days will usually exclude the day on which notice is given and the day on which it expires. The same effect is obtained by the expression '21 clear days';

(e)   'day' is a calendar day (ie, including all holidays, and not just a 'business day').

These implied rules will probably reflect the parties' intentions in most cases. However, since they are particularly critical in loan documents, timing provisions should be very specific. For example, a period of time should specify whether it is to include the day on which it begins or ends. A period should be stated as '21 clear days' if that is what is intended. Most documents will also specify that time-limits or payment dates will always end by close of business on a 'business day' (usually defined as a day on which banks are generally open for business in London). If the end of a particular period will not fall on a 'business day', provision should be made for it to be deemed as falling on the 'business day' which immediately precedes it, or next follows it, as required. Loans which involve funding in currencies other than sterling will have to source those currencies in their country of origin (eg, a bank in London providing a US$ loan will have to borrow the dollars in, say, New York). This means that the 'business day' definition in the loan should specify that funds can be drawn only on a day on which both London and New York are open for business.

Repayment dates are usually contained in a schedule to the document, which specifies the exact date and time by which the money is to be received.

Part II
SECURED LENDING

Chapter 12

Common Forms of Security

'Protection is not a principle, but an expedient.'

Benjamin Disraeli

12.1 Introduction

What would you do if someone failed to repay money you had lent him? Your options might range from forgiving the debt to threatening bankruptcy, but ultimately your only effective sanction is probably to sue him for the unpaid amount. Litigation has its drawbacks: it is usually expensive, protracted, and obtaining enforcement of a judgment may take too long to be effective. Furthermore, if you have to litigate to recover a straightforward debt claim, it probably means the debtor cannot pay because he is insolvent. His assets must almost certainly be shared with other creditors, and the bottom line is that you will probably recover only part of the money due to you.

Taking security as a bank is all about increasing the likelihood of getting repaid. There are many ways to achieve this, but most rely on giving a bank direct recourse to a borrower's property in the event of the borrower's default. This will usually avoid the need for litigation, may ensure priority over other creditors, and will almost certainly hasten recovery of the debt. This chapter provides an introduction to some of the more common types of security, **Chapter 13** looks at 'quasi-security', **Chapter 14** develops some of the issues which can arise on taking security and **Chapter 15** briefly examines a typical security document.

Whilst security might be used to support almost any type of obligation, the following four chapters concentrate on security for loan transactions. For the sake of continuity, therefore, the text will generally refer to the giver of the security as the 'borrower', and the holder of the benefit of the security as the 'bank'.

12.2 Categorising security

Security arrangements are sometimes categorised into 'consensual' (ie, agreed between the parties) and 'non-consensual' (ie, arising at law). It is probably more helpful, however, to categorise the main types of loan security according to their effect, that is:

(a)   security which merely gives the bank rights over an asset (eg, fixed or floating charge – see **12.3**);

(b)   security under which 'ownership' (ie, legal or equitable title: see below) in the secured asset is transferred to the bank (eg, a mortgage – see **12.4**); and

(c)   security under which the bank has actual (or 'constructive') possession of the secured asset (eg, pledge or lien – see **12.5**).

Each of these categories is examined below. At this stage, however, it is worth clarifying some terminology. In everyday language, the words 'ownership' and 'possession' are virtually interchangeable. However, in the context of security interests, the two terms have distinct meanings: 'ownership' means having title to an asset (legal or equitable); and 'possession' means having physical possession of an asset. These are the meanings attributed to 'ownership' and 'possession' in this book.

12.3   Giving rights over assets

The cornerstone of most loan security will be the charge. Charges may be 'fixed' or 'floating' and are always 'equitable' (other than the 'charge by deed expressed to be by way of legal mortgage' (LPA 1925, s 87) which is arguably not a true 'charge' anyway – see **12.4** – and other statutory charges, which are rarely seen).

12.3.1   Fixed charges conferring rights not possession

Probably the best way to ensure that a secured asset is available to meet unpaid monies is to take possession of it (known as a 'pledge' – see **12.5.1**). This will prevent the borrower disposing of the asset, or diminishing its value in any way. Consider, however, some typical assets of a trading company: machinery, vans, office equipment and premises. Giving a bank physical possession of those assets would simply prevent the borrower from running its business. If it is impractical, or impossible, for a bank to take possession of an asset, an alternative is to give it rights over the asset which:

(a)   prohibit the borrower from disposing of the asset without permission;

(b)   attempt to maintain the asset's value whilst it is in the borrower's hands; and

(c)   allow the bank recourse to the asset in the event of the borrower's default under the loan.

This is the aim of a fixed charge.

A fixed charge does not immediately transfer ownership or possession, but allows a borrower to use the charged assets (subject to conditions designed to maintain their value, and a prohibition on disposal) unless and until any 'enforcement event' occurs as specified in the charge document. On an 'enforcement event', the bank may require the borrower to sell the asset, or the bank may take possession of, and sell, the asset, or appoint a receiver to do the same (this carries less risk for the bank since the receiver acts as the borrower's agent). The fixed charge simply gives the bank a claim over the proceeds of a sale of the charged assets in priority to other creditors. If the borrower sells an asset subject to a fixed charge, the rights created by the charge usually remain with the asset.

Some security documents will refer to fixed charges as 'specific equitable charges'.

12.3.2   Floating charges

By their very nature, and because of the rights they provide to both parties, floating charges are more complicated than fixed charges.

12.3.2.1   What is a floating charge?

There will be certain of a borrower's assets for which a fixed charge is not an appropriate form of security. For example, any stock in trade subject to a fixed charge could not be sold without the bank's consent. This might not be a problem if the borrower is a boat-builder selling two or three boats a year. Consider, however, the problems that would be caused by taking a fixed charge over the stock in a sweet shop: clearly, it would be unworkable. The unsuitability of a fixed charge to secure assets which a borrower might want to deal with quickly and at some unspecified future date (ie, the borrower's current assets – see **6.3.2**), led to the development, from the late 19th century, of the floating charge.

A floating charge secures a group of assets which may fluctuate from time to time. The assets secured by a floating charge are identified generically, for example a borrower's 'trading stock' or its 'undertaking and assets' (fixed charges may also use generic descriptions, or alternatively refer to individual assets). Unlike a fixed charge, a floating charge specifically allows the borrower to deal with the charged assets in the ordinary course of business (which is very widely construed). This allows a borrower to sell its stock and dispose of its other current assets so that it may continue trading and make money which (in theory at least) it will eventually use to repay the secured loan. Conversely, any assets which are acquired after the floating charge is formed but which fall within the identified group will be subject to the charge.

The freedom to deal with assets, which is the very advantage of the floating charge, does give rise to a very important question: what is to stop a borrower from disposing of all its current assets, leaving the floating charge 'empty'? This is, in fact, a very real problem, and is one reason why a bank prefers to take a fixed charge over an asset whenever possible. The problem is minimised, however, through the concept of 'crystallisation'.

12.3.2.2   Crystallisation

Each floating charge document will incorporate a mechanism through which the borrower's freedom to deal with the assets over which it floats can be frozen. This is known as 'crystallisation'. On the occurrence of certain events (see below), the floating charge will effectively become a fixed charge with respect to any of the assets over which it previously 'floated', and which remain in the borrower's ownership. The borrower will then be unable to dispose of those remaining assets without the bank's consent. Most charges provide for crystallisation to be simultaneously effective over all the assets secured by the charge. There is, however, no reason why a floating charge should not be partially crystallised (ie, preventing only a selection of the secured assets being dealt with) as long as the charge document specifically provides the power to do so.

The effectiveness of this mechanism is entirely dependent on the sensitivity of the trigger for crystallisation. There are two ways in which crystallisation might occur: under common law, or under the terms of the document creating the charge.

Crystallisation under common law

Case law has established a number of events which will cause a floating charge to crystallise, all of which are triggered by a cessation of the business as a going concern, or by a prohibition on the borrower using its charged assets:

(a)   *The borrower's liquidation.* Crystallisation will occur when a winding-up order is made (including a voluntary winding-up, even if merely for reorganisation), but not simply when a petition to wind up is presented.

(b)   *An administrative receiver, or receiver, is appointed by the bank.* If the bank appoints a receiver or an administrative receiver, this implies that the borrower's authority to deal with the asset has been withdrawn and thus it will crystallise a floating charge. There is authority that a floating charge will not be crystallised (under common law) merely by the crystallisation of another floating charge (since it does not necessarily signify the end of trading). The making of an administration order which is not intended to prevent the borrower continuing to run as a going concern will probably not crystallise a floating charge at common law.

(c)   *The borrower ceases to carry on business.* A floating charge will crystallise if the borrower ceases trading for any reason (including where the borrower has disposed of its assets to such an extent that it can no longer carry on its business).

(d)   *Intervention by the bank.* Most forms of intervention by a bank which prevent a borrower dealing with its charged assets will cause crystallisation at common law.

Under the charge document

Crystallisation will also occur in any of the circumstances agreed contractually between the borrower and bank in the charge document. These are important to alleviate any uncertainty about crystallisation at common law. These will usually consist of an immediate right to crystallise the floating charge at any time by giving notice to the borrower (a borrower may request the proviso 'if the bank reasonably believes the secured assets are in jeopardy...', etc), and a number of specified events which will crystallise the charge without any action by the bank, for example the appointment of an administrator. This second group of events is often referred to as 'automatic crystallisation' (somewhat confusing, since the term might be thought more applicable to the common law situations which cause crystallisation, outlined above). A lender may sometimes be asked to provide a certificate of non-crystallisation (eg, to a purchaser of the borrower's assets).

12.3.2.3   Post-crystallisation

The most widely accepted legal analysis of a floating charge is that it creates an immediate security interest, but does not attach to any individual asset until crystallisation (in contrast to a fixed charge, which attaches immediately – ie, it encumbers the charged assets with the rights it creates). However, crystallisation does not, in itself, create a new charge to be registered under CA 1985, s 395 (*Re Manurewa Transport Ltd* [1971] NZLR 909). Some practitioners will, however, register a crystallisation as a new fixed charge (see **14.2**) on the basis that it provides notice to prospective purchasers and encumbrancers that the borrower has lost its authority to deal with the secured assets.

The charge document will contain the powers which can be exercised by the bank (see **Chapter 15**) and will invariably include the power to appoint a receiver to run the business and realise the charged assets. Crystallising a floating charge will create an effective stranglehold on a borrower: without the use of its current assets it cannot usually make any money. A bank will therefore not take crystallisation lightly, and frequently it is a precursor to the appointment of a receiver.

On crystallisation, a floating charge effectively will become a fixed charge. However, this 'fixed charge' will rank behind any fixed security created before it crystallised and will be subject to any third party rights of set-off (see **13.5**), including legal or equitable rights, which accrued prior to the crystallisation.

12.3.2.4 Weaknesses of a floating charge

The floating charge suffers from a number of weaknesses to which the fixed charge is immune.

Fixed charges and administrator's costs

A floating charge is vulnerable to later fixed charges, although this may be alleviated by a prohibition on creating further security (see **14.2.2** and **14.3**). Floating charges also rank behind the costs and expenses of an administrator appointed to the borrower; the administrator can use any of the floating charge assets to fund the administration costs.

In addition, from 6 April 2008, all liquidation expenses (other than litigation expenses) will have automatic priority over floating charge holders, and will be recoverable from the assets of the company (see the Insolvency (Amendment) Rules 2008 (SI 2008/737)).

Preferential creditors

Any proceeds realised from assets secured by a floating charge must be used to pay any 'preferential debts' of the company before meeting claims under the floating charge (IA 1986, s 40). 'Preferential debts' are defined at s 386, and specified fully in Sch 6 to the IA 1986, as modified from 15 September 2003 by the Enterprise Act 2002 (s 251). The main preferential debts are now limited amounts of outstanding employees' wages and pension scheme contributions. The preferential status previously accorded to 'Crown creditors' (eg, PAYE contributions, VAT, social security contributions, etc) was abolished by the Enterprise Act 2002. These now rank as unsecured creditors. However, the Act also provides for an amount of the company's property which would otherwise go to floating charge-holders (the 'prescribed part'), to be set aside to pay unsecured creditors. The amount of this 'fund' is determined by statutory instrument from time to time. It is currently 50% of the first £10,000 of the prescribed part and 20% thereafter, subject to a maximum amount of £600,000 (see IA 1986, s 176A).

Avoidance of floating charge

As well as the provisions concerning transactions at an undervalue and preferences (see **14.9**) which can apply to all forms of security, the IA 1986 provides for specific circumstances in which a floating charge can be set aside by the court on the application of a liquidator or administrator (s 245). The degree of vulnerability of a floating charge will depend on whether or not it is granted to a 'connected person'.

12.3.2.5 Charge to connected person

If a company grants a floating charge to a 'connected person' (this includes a director, his close relatives, his business partners and their close relatives – see s 249 of the IA 1986) then it might be set aside if it was granted within two years of the onset of a company's insolvency.

12.3.2.6   Charge to unconnected person

A floating charge granted to a person not 'connected' with the company might be set aside if it was given within 12 months of the onset of the company's insolvency, provided that the company was either insolvent when it gave the charge, or became insolvent as a result.

However, a floating charge will not be invalid in either case to the extent that it is in return for valuable consideration (ie, money, goods, services or the reduction of any debt) given on or after the creation of the charge. The underlying debt will remain unsecured if the floating charge is set aside.

The concept of a 'floating charge' is very much a product of the English legal system (and derivative systems) and so may not be recognised or have an equivalent in other jurisdictions.

12.4   Transfer of ownership

12.4.1   Mortgages

A fixed charge creates an encumbrance over assets, giving the holder priority over other creditors. An alternative way to provide security over assets is by transferring ownership (ie, legal or equitable title) to the bank, along with a right to sell on default and an obligation to re-transfer title on satisfaction of the debt. This form of security interest is known as a 'mortgage'. The transfer of title may enhance a bank's ability to realise the security if necessary, and in the meantime prevents a borrower from selling the secured assets. A mortgage can therefore be thought of as an 'enhanced' charge, since it gives rights over an asset which are backed with a transfer of legal or equitable title. As Professor Goode explained in *Legal Problems of Credit and Security*, '... a mortgage is a right of appropriation (= charge) plus a transfer of ownership ...'. Subject to contrary intention (and statutory restrictions in the case of land), a (legal) mortgage entitles the bank to take immediate possession of the mortgaged asset. However, possession is not required to perfect the security (it is 'non-possessory' security) and, for reasons of practicality, most banks will not take possession of mortgaged assets before default.

12.4.2   Mortgages over land

Almost any asset can be secured by way of a mortgage, although it is most commonly used to secure land, aircraft, ships and shares. Under the LPA 1925 (as amended by the Land Registration Act 2002), a legal mortgage over freehold or leasehold land can be created by way of 'a charge by deed expressed to be by way of legal mortgage' (LPA 1925, s 87). The terminology is not particularly helpful (it is not a 'true' charge, neither does it actually transfer legal title like most legal mortgages), but the net result is to provide the bank with rights equivalent to granting it a 3,000-year lease (or, for leasehold, a lease for one day less than the borrower's lease).

12.4.3   Legal and equitable mortgages

If a mortgage does not transfer *legal* title, it will be an equitable mortgage. Equitable mortgages can be created with less formality than their legal equivalent, and may result from any of the following, depending on the circumstances:

(a)   a written agreement by a borrower that the property is to be secured by way of equitable mortgage;

(b)   an agreement to provide a legal mortgage (once money has been lent, an agreement to provide a mortgage will take effect as an equitable mortgage); or

(c)   a mortgage over an equitable interest;

(d)   a mortgage over property not yet owned by the borrower; and

(e)   in the case of land, a deposit of title deeds or Land Certificate with the bank, together with written recognition of an equitable mortgage from the borrower (known as a 'memorandum of deposit') which must be under seal and contain a power of attorney to avoid any suggestion that the title documents have simply been deposited with the bank for safe keeping: see s 2 of the Law of Property (Miscellaneous Provisions) Act 1989; *United Bank of Kuwait v Sahib and Others* [1997] Ch 107.

The fundamental difference between equitable and legal security interests is that the former can be ignored by a bona fide purchaser (or 'security taker') for value of the legal title to an asset without notice (actual or constructive) of the equitable security. However, the 'disadvantage' is largely overcome if the equitable security is registered under CA 1985, ss 395–424 (see **14.2**), because this provides notice of the security to anyone searching, or who is deemed to search, the register. Lastly, an equitable mortgage may not benefit from the 'automatic' powers vested in legal mortgagees under LPA 1925, s 101, which include the power of sale (although these powers should be specifically given in the security document).

12.5   Giving physical possession

For the reasons of practicality explained at **12.3.1**, the most common forms of debt security are 'non-possessory': that is, the bank does not take immediate physical possession, but simply takes certain rights over the charged assets. However, there are circumstances in which a security interest involves possession of an asset from the outset.

12.5.1   Pledge

A pledge is a way of creating security by the actual (or constructive) delivery of a tangible movable asset to a creditor, to be held until the performance of an obligation (eg, repaying a debt). The bank will take possession while the borrower retains ownership. The best known example of a pledge is placing an article with a pawnbroker.

12.5.1.1   Rights of the pledgee

The security created by a pledge is essentially the possession of an asset. A pledged asset must therefore be 'delivered' by the borrower. This can be achieved by physical delivery, or by vesting control (sometimes known as 'constructive delivery' – eg, having the keys to a safe deposit box) with, in either case, an intention to create security. Some assets may be pledged by delivery of documents; however, the pledge will fail if the document does not effectively provide control. For example, simply holding the share certificate of a registered share does not give sufficient control (even if accompanied by a 'blank' stock transfer form) because the share certificate is not a document of title and it does not give the right to vote or receive dividends.

Since it does not transfer rights of ownership, a pledge will end as soon as the pledged asset is returned to the borrower. A pledge will confer certain implied rights, the most important of which is the right to sell the pledged assets to meet a defaulted debt.

12.5.1.2   Problems with taking a pledge

There are a number of practical difficulties with taking pledges. A bank will probably want to take a pledge only over valuable assets. This will lead to problems of keeping the pledged assets secure (imagine a pawnbroker taking a pledge over a Stradivarius violin) both on delivery to the bank and on return. Furthermore, the bank will probably be liable as bailee while it holds the pledged assets, and this may entail insurance costs.

A bank may not want to take a pledge of any negotiable instruments (see below, and **18.3.2**) for which it has notice of other parties' rights, since any enforcement may be jeopardised if the bank has notice of defects in title. The pledge of a negotiable instrument which carries the right to receive periodic payments will also entail the administrative problems of collection by the bank, either to be secured or passed back to the borrower.

There is no requirement for documenting a pledge. However, to avoid any argument that an asset has merely been deposited for safe-keeping, a 'letter of pledge' or 'memorandum of deposit' is usually provided by the borrower to evidence the terms of the pledge. One advantage of pledge security is that it does not require any form of registration: giving up possession is notice to third parties ('perfection').

12.5.1.3   What assets may be pledged?

A pledge involves the delivery of an asset into the possession of a creditor, therefore the asset must be capable of actual (or constructive) delivery. The most common types of asset to be pledged are therefore bearer instruments, such as bills of exchange, promissory notes and bearer bonds (see **18.2.2**). More substantial assets may be 'constructively pledged' by placing them in a location (eg, a warehouse) only accessible to the bank.

12.5.2   Lien

A lien is the right to retain possession of another person's property until he settles an obligation. The term 'lien' derives from the word 'ligamen', meaning 'binding'. Liens arise automatically under English law in certain types of commercial relationship. There are three main types of lien.

12.5.2.1   Common law (or particular) liens

A common law lien allows retention of the goods under which the debt arises. If, for example, a customer refuses to pay for his dry-cleaning, the cleaner has a right to retain the clothes in lieu of payment.

12.5.2.2   Statutory (or general) liens

Statutory liens allow certain persons to retain any goods in their possession against any obligation owed to them by the owner of those goods. Stockbrokers, bankers, solicitors and innkeepers all benefit from statutory liens, which arise by operation of law and without the need for any agreement.

Common law and statutory liens are both types of legal lien. Legal liens will usually require actual possession of the property which has been rightfully acquired. Unlike a mortgage or pledge, legal liens will not generally confer any right to sell the property. A banker's lien is an exception, however, allowing the retention and sale of any securities and cheques deposited by a customer.

12.5.2.3 Equitable liens

An equitable lien does not require possession of the property to which it attaches (usually land) and will give a right of sale through application to the court.

It is also possible for a lien to be created by contract. However, if the contract provided for any right of sale the 'lien' would be little different to a pledge.

12.6 Assignment

Chapter 10 explained how a bank wanting to sell a loan could transfer its rights under the facility agreement by way of assignment. Assignment may also be used to create a security interest over certain forms of asset.

The most common assets secured by assignment are a borrower's rights against a third party ('choses in action'), for example debts, and rights under various contracts. As with an assignment by way of sale, an assignment by way of security can be legal or equitable: it will be legal if it complies with s 136 of the LPA 1925 (a 'statutory assignment' – see **10.4.3**); otherwise it will be equitable (see **10.4.4**) (notice that assignment 'by way of charge' is expressly excluded from s 136 and so assigning rights by way of security will constitute a legal assignment only if it is an absolute assignment with a proviso for re-assignment on satisfaction of the secured obligation – ie, an assignment 'by way of legal mortgage'). Assignments by way of security will always include a provision (either explicit or implied) for reassignment on satisfaction of the debt. Priority between assignments depends on notice being given to the third party (see **14.3.3**).

12.7 Some terminology

Unfortunately, the area of loan security suffers more than its fair share of overlapping and interchangeable terminology. Documents and statutes use identical terms to describe entirely different things, and the legal meaning of terms is often subtly different to their colloquial meaning. Some of the terms which have multiple meanings are explained below.

12.7.1 Debenture

At common law, a 'debenture' is any document which a company issues to acknowledge, or create, a debt. In other words, a debenture is simply a document creating an 'IOU'.

But beware! In common banking parlance a 'debenture' is the name given to the document under which a borrower creates the security for a secured loan, usually incorporating fixed and floating charges along with other security interests (see **Chapter 15**).

12.7.2 Charge

A 'charge' is the appropriation of assets to the satisfaction of a debt. Strictly speaking, a charge does not transfer any ownership in property, but simply creates certain rights over it: in other words, it creates an equitable security interest. Used in this sense, there are only two forms of charge, fixed and floating (see **12.3**).

But beware! The term is used colloquially (even in statutes and case law) as a generic label for almost any type of security, including mortgages, liens and assignments.

12.7.3 Security/securities

The term 'security' refers to the provision of rights against a person's assets which are intended to enhance the probability of recovering a debt claim against him.

But beware! In common banking parlance the terms 'security', or 'securities' refer to the instrument (ie, the 'piece of paper') in which a borrower acknowledges debt, or to investments such as shares, debentures, stock, bonds, bills of exchange and other forms of tradeable debt (see **Part III**).

12.7.4 Statutory definitions

The confusion which can arise in terminology is illustrated by statutory definitions. In the LPA 1925, 'mortgage' is defined to include 'any charge or lien on any property for securing money or money's worth'. Under the IA 1986, 'security' means 'any mortgage, charge, lien or other security' (s 248(b)). In the CA 1985, 'charge' is generally used to mean 'any form of security interest over property'.

The statutory definitions are also often inclusive rather than specific. The 'moral' of this maze of terminology is that the label given to an instrument is not always a reliable indication of the type of security it provides; it is important to examine its substance.

12.8 Further reading

Ellinger and Lomnicka, *Modern Banking Law* (3rd edn, Clarendon Press, 2002).

Goode, *Commercial Law* (3rd edn, Penguin, 2004).

Goode, *Legal Problems of Credit and Security* (3rd edn, Sweet & Maxwell, 2003).

Fuller, *Corporate Borrowing: Law and Practice* (2nd edn, Jordans, 1999).

Chapter 13
Quasi-security

13.1 Introduction

Chapter 12 examined the most common methods by which a bank might take security in order to increase the likelihood of recovering a borrower's debt. However, there are various other ways a bank might choose to enhance its prospects of repayment, which are not strictly security interests because they do not create any rights 'in rem' (ie, rights over the asset). This chapter explains some of the more common types of 'quasi-security' before considering the main reasons for taking loan security.

13.2 Third party support – guarantees and comfort letters

A bank will frequently look for a third party willing to support the borrower's repayment obligations. The generic name usually given to such third parties (together with the borrower) is 'obligor', and the two most common forms of third party support are the guarantee (which may be secured on the guarantor's assets) and the comfort letter. Guarantors are sometimes known as 'sureties'.

13.2.1 Guarantees

13.2.1.1 What is a guarantee?

A guarantee is a form of undertaking by one party to answer for another party's liabilities, usually on its default. In the context of a loan, the guarantor will frequently be a company in the same group as the borrower. For example, a bank might make a loan conditional on receiving a guarantee of the borrower's obligations from its parent company. Furthermore, the company which has given the guarantee may be required to give security over its own assets to support its potential liability under the guarantee. As well as providing a second source of repayment, a guarantee from a parent company will help to ensure the support and supervision of the borrower by the parent.

13.2.1.2 Guarantees and indemnities

Before considering guarantees further, the strict legal differences between the terms 'guarantee' and 'indemnity' should be appreciated (although the guarantee document will usually purport to contract out of these limitations – see **13.2.1.3**).

A guarantee must support a primary liability between two parties other than the guarantor: the guarantee agreement will be a secondary contract and will not create a 'stand alone' obligation. In other words, the obligation under a guarantee will be entirely dependent on the guaranteed obligation (the main implications of which are explained at **13.2.1.3**).

An indemnity creates a binding obligation to indemnify a party for a specified loss which it may incur. The end result is almost identical to that of a guarantee, but unlike a guarantee, an indemnity creates a 'stand alone' (or primary) obligation which is independent of the liability or default of another party. Furthermore, unlike a guarantee (see **13.2.1.4**), an indemnity does not need to be in writing to be enforceable.

13.2.1.3   Legal implications of a guarantee

Once a contract is legally classified as a guarantee there are a number of consequences at common law (some of which the bank will want to vary), including the following.

General

(a)   Since the guarantee is a 'secondary' contract, the guarantor will not be liable unless the default and liability of the borrower is proven. Most banks will therefore require that the 'guarantee' is 'on demand': once the borrower defaults, the bank can immediately demand performance from the guarantor (ie, the bank does not need to prove the liability or default of the borrower – although, strictly, this creates an 'indemnity' rather than a guarantee).

(b)   As a consequence of the secondary nature of a guarantee, if the contract between bank and borrower (the primary contract) is void (or if the borrower's obligation is discharged) the guarantor's obligation will fall away. A bank will therefore usually include a provision that the guarantee survives failure of the underlying obligation, as well as an indemnity within the guarantee document in order to create a primary obligation on the 'guarantor' if the guarantee fails.

(c)   If the contract between bank and borrower is varied in any material way without the guarantor's consent, the guarantor is released from the guarantee (even if the variation was not prejudicial to the guarantor). Similarly, certain acts which might be prejudicial to the guarantor (eg, if the bank fails to register security for the debt) will void the guarantee. This issue commonly arises where the facility which the guarantee supports is to be increased. In *Triodos Bank v Ashley Charles Dobbs* [2005] EWCA Civ 630, the Court of Appeal considered a guarantee which purported to allow 'any amendments, variation, waiver or release of an obligation' by the borrower, without reference to the guarantor. The Court held that any amendment or variation must be 'within the general purview of the original guarantee' (a test adopted in *Trade Indemnity Co Ltd v Workington Harbour and Dock Board* [1937] AC 1). In *Triodos* the guarantee was held not to survive an increase of the underlying facility, in part because the facility was to be used for a different purpose. The fact that the guarantor *knew* of the amendments made no difference – he had to *consent* with a clear understanding of the facts. Banks should therefore be aware that even with 'saving language' designed to bolster a guarantee, it might be jeopardised by refinancing the underlying facility.

Guarantor's rights

(a) A guarantor may use most rights of set-off or counter-claim which the borrower has against the bank (and which arose before the borrower defaulted) to reduce its liability under the guarantee.

(b) Once it has paid out under the guarantee, a guarantor will be entitled to reimbursement from the borrower. This right will arise through an implied or actual indemnity between the borrower and guarantor

(c) The guarantor will also be entitled to any security the bank holds for the borrower's debt, under the doctrine of subrogation. Subrogation arises only once a guarantor has paid the full amount to which it is liable under the guarantee.

(d) If there is more than one guarantor of the debt, any guarantor that pays out will have a right to claim back a share of the payment from the co-guarantors (a right of 'contribution').

The problem with all these rights from a bank's perspective is that it may not want the guarantor to enforce them immediately (eg, if the subrogated security secures borrowings in addition to the guaranteed loan). The guarantee document should therefore postpone the rights until such time as the bank has been repaid in full and no longer requires the security. It will also want any obligation of contribution to be waived in respect of any subsidiary it wants to sell (eg, on enforcement of security).

13.2.1.4 General considerations for a bank's solicitor

In addition to the points mentioned above, a bank's solicitor should take account of the following:

(a) The governing law of a guarantee should, if possible, mirror that of the other loan documents as this will make enforcement easier.

(b) If the contract is legally a guarantee it must be evidenced in writing before it can be enforced (Statute of Frauds 1677, s 4). As with any other contract, a guarantee is enforceable only if it is given for consideration. In particular, there is a danger that a guarantee will be void for past consideration if it is pre-dated by the obligation it supports. The problem can be resolved by creating the guarantee document as a deed.

(c) A guarantee should be expressed as 'continuing' to avoid the rule in 'Clayton's case' (see **14.6**) and to help it to survive variations to the primary obligation (but see **13.2.1.3(c)**)

(d) The guarantee should provide that the bank's evidence of the borrower's liability is conclusive (at least in the first instance) to avoid any argument on enforcement.

(e) As with any other contract, a company must have the requisite power to enter into a guarantee, and its officers must be properly authorised. In particular, under the principle laid down in *Rolled Steel Products (Holdings) Ltd v British Steel Corporation* [1986] Ch 246, if a guarantee is not in the commercial interest of the guarantor the directors may be in breach of their fiduciary duties in proceeding with it: if a bank is aware that they are acting in breach of such duties it may not be able to rely on the guarantee.

(f) A guarantee is capable of being 'financial assistance' under the provisions of CA 1985, s 151 (see **14.12**).

13.2.1.5   Insolvency Act 1986

A guarantee is arguably capable of being a transaction at an undervalue (because, unlike a borrower granting security, it usually increases the guarantor's liabilities) and, in limited circumstances (eg, where the guarantor had previously only given third party security, with no guarantee), a preference, and so being set aside under IA 1986, ss 238 and 239 respectively (see **14.9**).

13.2.1.6   Counter-indemnity

A guarantor will usually want an express counter-indemnity from the borrower (ie, a contractual right to claim back any money it pays to the bank – see 'Guarantor's rights' at **13.2.1.3**).

13.2.1.7   Terminology

Terminology in this area is often used loosely. Watch out for documents referring to 'guarantees' which are actually warranties given by the borrower (see **5.2**). As mentioned at **13.2.1.2**, some 'guarantee' contracts are actually indemnities. The generic terms 'surety' and 'suretyship' are sometimes used; 'guarantor' and 'guarantee' should technically be used.

13.2.2   Comfort letters

Sometimes a parent company or other potential obligor will refuse to provide a guarantee. It may be contractually prevented from doing so (eg, by a negative pledge style undertaking; see **13.3**), or a company might not wish to create a contingency on its balance sheet. In such cases, the bank might demand a comfort letter from the company. Comfort letters (also known as 'support letters', or 'letters of intent') are usually given by a parent company in respect of a subsidiary. They range from a simple written acknowledgment of the fact that the subsidiary is undertaking the obligations created by the loan, to a statement of intention to maintain an interest in, and support for, a subsidiary, and to ensure it is capable of fulfilling those obligations (sometimes known as a 'keep-well' agreement).

Comfort letters are not normally intended to be legally binding but are used to reassure a bank that the parent company is aware of, and supports, its subsidiary's borrowing and other general or specific activities. They will require careful drafting. Statements of the comforter's 'intention' or 'policy' will not usually amount to an actionable undertaking. However, words such as 'guarantee' and 'undertake' may be binding. The general phrasing of comfort letters is usually deliberately vague so that the terms are not certain enough to be enforced under English contract law.

The test for determining whether a comfort letter has legal effect is to analyse it as though it were a contract. Was there offer and acceptance, intention to create legal relations and consideration? Did the issuer of the letter promise to do something? Has it failed to do that thing? Has the recipient of the letter suffered loss as a consequence of the failure? What is the measure of damages for the breach? In the seminal case of *Kleinwort Benson Ltd v Malaysia Mining Corpn* [1989] 1 All ER 785, a parent company's comfort letter stated: 'It is our policy to ensure that the business of [subsidiary] is at all times in a position to meet its liabilities to you under the above arrangements.' The Court of Appeal held this to be a statement of fact (ie, that this was the parent's policy) at the time rather than an undertaking actually to support the subsidiary going forward. However, the conclusion depended entirely on the facts – in this case, the parent had previously refused to give a guarantee or accept joint liability, which suggested that it did not intend the comfort letter to be binding. In contrast, the recent Australian case of *Gate Gourmet Australia (in liquidation) v Gate Gourmet Holding AG* [2004] NSWSC 149 found a 'comfort letter' to be legally binding. The key points were that the letter included technical language, was provided to reassure directors that their otherwise insolvent company could continue to trade, and made statements which were clearly promises, not just statements of fact.

In the case of *Re Atlantic Computers plc (in administration); National Australia Bank Ltd v Soden* [1995] BCC 696, it was held that the common intention of the parties to a comfort letter must be ascertained by reading it as a whole. The final paragraph of the letters in question, which asserted that they 'were not intended to be a guarantee' and that they were 'an expression of present intention by way of comfort only', was sufficient to show that they did not amount to a contractual promise.

A solicitor should be aware that even if the tests outlined above are not fulfilled, comfort letters may still be treated as binding in jurisdictions other than England and Wales.

13.3 Negative pledge

There is a sense in which a negative pledge provision (one which prohibits a borrower granting security to third parties – see **7.5.2.1**) provides a form of security, because it is arguably a restriction on how the borrower may use its assets. There is, however, little doubt that a negative pledge clause is not technically a security interest (although a negative pledge might provide a claim in tort for damages against a third party which induces a borrower to breach the prohibition, and there is an argument that the third party (which cannot benefit from its own wrongdoing) holds any security on trust for the negative pledge holder). The negative pledge is usually included on the Companies Act registration form (see **Chapter 14**). This will be a mandatory requirement when s 885(3) of the CA 2006 comes into force, currently scheduled for 1 October 2009.

13.4 Retention of title

Retention of title arrangements are dealt with in ***Business Law and Practice***. In essence, a retention of title clause allows a seller to retain legal title to goods which have been supplied to a buyer until the buyer settles its account. If payment is not forthcoming, the seller can recover the goods from the buyer. A retention of title clause therefore acts as a type of security interest for the seller. This is clearly not of any use to 'secure' a loan. However, the existence of such a clause may undermine a bank's security: if a borrower does not have beneficial ownership of an asset, it cannot usually grant security over it. Where the borrower's business makes it appropriate, a bank should consider requiring representations and/or warranties to the effect that the borrower is not party to any agreements which contain a retention of title clause.

A bank should also check if any assets which are in a borrower's possession are actually subject to a finance lease (see **Glossary**), in which case ownership of the leased asset technically remains with the finance company (although usually subject to contractual rights of the borrower).

13.5 Set-off

13.5.1 What is 'set-off'?

Imagine that you take a loan from your bank for £1,500. You also have a current account with that bank into which your salary of £1,100 per month is paid. The money in that current account is owed to you by the bank. If you default on the loan repayment the bank will not want to let you draw your salary from the current account and then have to make a demand against you for the £1,500. It would prefer to keep the £1,100 towards payment of the loan, and then demand the balance of £400. This is known as 'set-off'. It is not strictly a security interest (and not so registrable) but a right to set a debt owed by a creditor to a debtor against the debtor's debt, and so reduce or extinguish that debt.

13.5.2 When is set-off available?

The right of set-off is a complex area of law. In general terms, however, there are three ways in which a bank is *likely* to have a right of set-off against a borrower.

13.5.2.1 Equitable right of set-off

Broadly, a bank may set-off a liquidated debt owed to it by a borrower against a liquidated debt owed by it to that borrower.

13.5.2.2 Contractual set-off

Most security documents supporting a loan will enhance the equitable right of set-off by allowing the bank to set-off unliquidated (ie, contingent) claims.

13.5.2.3 Set-off on liquidation

Both equitable and contractual rights of set-off may be affected by the liquidation of a borrower when, in certain circumstances, r 4.90 of the Insolvency Rules 1986 (SI 1986/1925) provides for mandatory set-off. Basically, any 'mutual' credits, debts or dealings can be set off so long as the bank did not know of the petition for insolvency against the borrower when it gave credit. From 1 April 2005 the Insolvency (Amendment) Rules 2005 have rewritten r 4.90 and allowed set-off of contingent claims against a company.

There is a statutory right of set-off under the Statutes of Set-Off dating from the 1700s, but this is now of little real significance.

The right of set-off is particularly important if a debtor is in danger of becoming insolvent (but no petition has been lodged), since it allows access to the debtor's unsecured assets (ie, cash) without risk of being a transaction at an undervalue or a preference under IA 1986, ss 238 and 239.

13.5.3 Banker's right of combination

There is an implied right under common law which is peculiar to banks and which allows them, subject to contrary agreement, to combine two or more accounts of a borrower. If one account is in debit (ie, overdrawn), an account in credit can be used to 'repay' the overdraft. This is sometimes known as 'bankers' set-off', but is more correctly the right of 'combination'.

13.6   Why take security?

The introduction to **Chapter 12** stated that 'Taking security as a bank is all about increasing the likelihood of getting repaid'. There are a number of peripheral reasons for taking security.

13.6.1   Appointing an administrator or administrative receiver

If a bank wants to enforce security it will invariably do so through a third party, and usually when the borrower is, or is about to become, insolvent. Until recently, a bank with security (including a floating charge) over all (or substantially all) of the borrower's assets would usually appoint an administrative receiver with wide-ranging powers to manage the company and sell off assets to repay the bank. However, the Enterprise Act 2002 (EA 2002) has changed the insolvency landscape. To understand the current position, it is necessary briefly to consider two procedures both before and after the 2002 Act took effect.

13.6.1.1   Administration pre-Enterprise Act 2002

The administration procedure was introduced by the IA 1986. A court had to consider that one (or more) of four specific purposes would be achieved before making an administration order and appointing an administrator. The first, and key, purpose was to ensure 'the survival of the company, and the whole or any part of its undertaking, as a going concern'. To help achieve the purposes, an administrator was given wide powers to run the company and, crucially, a moratorium (or 'freeze') applied to the rights of all secured and unsecured creditors. This took effect immediately on presentation of the petition for administration.

The idea of a moratorium was unpopular with banks which, as the major creditors of a company, wanted the ability to enforce their security whenever they chose. They therefore lobbied for, and won, the right to block an administration order if they held security (which included a floating charge) over all, or substantially all, of a company's assets. This was achieved by appointing an administrative receiver under IA 1986 (s 9).

13.6.1.2   Administrative receivership pre-Enterprise Act 2002

An administrative receiver is defined in IA 1986, s 29(2), as:

(a)   a receiver or manager of the whole (or substantially the whole) of a company's property appointed by or on behalf of the holders of any debentures of the company secured by a charge which, as created, was a floating charge, or by such a charge and one or more other securities; or

(b)   a person who would be such a receiver or manager but for the appointment of some other person as the receiver of part of the company's property.

The term 'debenture' 'includes ... bonds and any other securities of a company ...' ('securities' is not defined).

Therefore, as long as a bank held security (which included a floating charge) over 'all or substantially all' of a borrower's assets, it could appoint an administrative receiver, with wide-ranging powers to manage the business and sell assets to repay the bank debt and, crucially, the power to block an administration order and moratorium. This was a critical part of a bank's security package, because it allowed the bank to take control if it wanted to realise its security.

13.6.1.3   Enterprise Act 2002

The EA 2002 is intended to assist small businesses and makes reforms to competition law, consumer protection law, personal bankruptcy law and corporate insolvency law. From 15 September 2003, the law relating to administration and administrative receivers has been significantly amended. The key changes to the position outlined above are explained below.

13.6.1.4   Administration post-Enterprise Act 2002

The four original purposes of administration are replaced by three new ones with more emphasis on corporate rescue. They essentially require the administrator to:

(a)   *attempt to rescue the company as a going concern* – if this is not reasonably practical, or would not produce the best result for the creditors as a whole;

(b)   *attempt to achieve a better result for creditors than if the company were wound up;* and (only if the administrator thinks the first two purposes are not reasonably practical)

(c)   *realise the company's property to distribute to secured or preferential creditors, so long as he does not unnecessarily harm the interests of the creditors as a whole.*

These purposes apply regardless of who appoints the administrator.

The appointment of an administrator has also been streamlined: as long as the company is or is likely to become insolvent, an administrator may be appointed:

(a)   by court order (as previously);

(b)   out of court by the holder of a 'qualifying floating charge'. This is essentially the same definition as under IA 1986, s 29(2) (see **13.7.2.2**), as long as the floating charge document also states that the EA 2002 applies to it, or it purports to allow the holder to appoint an administrator or administrative receiver; or

(c)   out of court by the company or its directors.

13.6.1.5   Administrative receivership post-Enterprise Act 2002

Perhaps the most significant change for banks is that the ability to appoint an administrative receiver, and so block an administration order, is abolished other than in limited circumstances. There are six 'exceptions' under which an administrative receiver *may* still be appointed: the 'capital market' exception, 'public–private partnership' exception, 'utilities' exception, 'project finance' exception, 'financial markets' exception and 'registered social landlord' exception. Suffice it to say these are intended to apply to 'specialised financing' and not to general commercial bank lending (see IA 1986, ss 72B–72G, inserted by EA 2002, s 250, for further details).

The EA 2002 does allow 'grand fathering'; in other words, if a bank was able to appoint an administrative receiver before the 2002 Act took effect (15 September 2003), it will retain the right (see IA 1986, s 72A, inserted by EA 2002, s 250).

In summary, where the bank holds a 'qualifying floating charge' created after 15 September 2003, but does not fall within one of the six exceptions, it will be permitted to appoint an administrator only to realise security on insolvency. The bank's administrator must consider the two prior purposes of administration before realising assets on the bank's behalf.

Further details on these procedures can be found in ***Business Law and Practice***.

13.6.2 Asset control and stability

The primary aim of due diligence (see **2.2**) is to ensure that a borrower is capable of servicing a loan out of cash flow. A bank does not want to resort to a borrower's assets for repayment if it can be avoided. Taking a fixed charge over a borrower's assets will prevent it from disposing of them in normal circumstances, and this will at least help to ensure that the fixed assets on which forecasts were based in the due diligence remain in the company. The security therefore helps to maintain the borrower's stability.

13.6.3 Management

There are a number of ways in which a security interest can provide some degree of control over the management of a borrower even before it is enforced. First, it may prevent other banks from providing finance to the borrower if there is insufficient value in the assets to support any further security, effectively giving the secured bank a monopoly over a company's borrowing. Secondly, a bank will sometimes require the directors of a small company to provide security for the company's loan, usually in the form of personal guarantees. This does not just provide another source of repayment should anything go wrong, it also serves to concentrate the minds of the directors when making decisions crucial to the business. A bank may require a parent to guarantee the borrowings of its subsidiary for similar reasons. Thirdly, a security interest will sometimes allow a bank the right to take part in management decisions if the borrower defaults, even if the security is not realised (although this is more usually dealt with in the loan document). Any substantial involvement by a bank in the management of a corporate borrower will carry the danger of shadow directorship and subsequent liability (see **7.6**), although this is probably less of a risk for banks than for others.

13.6.4 Costs

Chapter 9 explained the requirement of regulatory capital imposed by central banks. Secured loans will carry less risk for a bank than unsecured loans, and compliance with regulatory capital requirements will make some types of secured loan 'cheaper' than unsecured loans.

13.6.5 Miscellaneous

Some of the points made above may not be a bank's primary reasons for taking security but merely the welcome consequences of doing so. There are many other consequences which might benefit the secured bank. For example, if all a borrower's assets are secured, an unsecured creditor might be less likely to wind up the company in pursuance of the debt, since he may find nothing left for him. Security interests may also give a creditor the right to pursue assets 'illegally' sold to third parties, and sometimes the right to trace proceeds.

13.7 Security – the bank's perspective

It is important to understand that not all loans are secured: taking security is expensive and time-consuming, and not usually necessary unless the bank thinks there is a real risk of insolvency or a specific need to preserve assets. Investment grade loans are unsecured; highly leveraged loans almost always secured. Whilst enforcement of most types of security will be a last resort, until that time a secured bank has greater control over the borrower and greater leverage to get the borrower 'around the table' to talk if a problem should arise.

A bank's solicitor should check that the borrower and any other party providing security has capacity to do so (see also **4.6.2**). For example, the articles of some companies will allow them to provide a guarantee only if it is matched by an indemnity from the guaranteed party. A check should also be made that there is no existing negative pledge.

13.8   Security – the borrower's perspective

The borrower is invariably liable for all (reasonable) costs of providing security, which will include solicitors' fees, registration costs and, in some jurisdictions, notarial fees and stamp duty. As mentioned at **13.7** above, not all loans are secured, although more specialised lending for large assets (eg, for a ship or aircraft) or financing a project ('project finance') will always be secured over the asset or project in question. Leveraged loans are also secured, although borrowers have negotiated two 'concessions' in recent years. First, in most acquisition financings only share security is provided at 'closing' (ie, when the loan is available). The borrower is then given anything up to 120 days to provide the remaining asset security.

Secondly, it is now common to agree 'security principles' early in the negotiation. These are pre-agreed parameters for the type and extent of security to be given (particularly where multiple jurisdictions are involved), the costs that can be incurred, and any obligations on the borrower (eg, giving notice of an assignment).

13.9   Further reading

Ellinger and Lomnicka, *Modern Banking Law* (3rd edn, Clarendon Press, 2002).

Goode, *Commercial Law* (3rd edn, Penguin, 2004).

Goode, *Legal Problems of Credit and Security* (3rd edn, Sweet & Maxwell, 2003).

Penn, Shea and Arora, *The Law Relating to Domestic Banking* (Banking Law vol 1) (2nd edn, Sweet & Maxwell, 2000).

Chapter 14

Further Issues on Taking Security

'Borrow £1 million, and you are in trouble; borrow £1 billion, and the bank is in trouble.'

Old banking adage

14.1 Introduction

Professor Goode, in *Legal Problems of Credit and Security* (3rd edn, Sweet & Maxwell, 2003), has identified three distinct aspects of taking security:

(a) attachment: that is, creating a particular security interest such that it is valid against the debtor;

(b) perfection: that is, ensuring that the security interest is valid against third parties; and

(c) priority: that is, maintaining a claim on the secured assets in priority to other creditors.

The two previous chapters examined some of the most common forms of security and the way in which they take effect. This chapter looks at some of the issues associated with perfection and priority.

14.2 Perfection through registration

14.2.1 The purpose of registration

The point has already been made that the best way to secure an asset is to take possession of it (take a 'pledge'), and in most cases taking possession of an asset is sufficient to perfect a pledge. Practical considerations dictate, however, that the overwhelming majority of loan security is non-possessory. This gives rise to a problem: if a borrower retains the secured asset, what is to stop it, albeit fraudulently, selling or re-securing the asset to an unsuspecting third party? The problem is alleviated by a statutory requirement for the registration of security interests: placing the security contract on a public register creates a system of actual and deemed notice to third parties. When a registered company grants most forms of security it will be subject to registration requirements under the provisions of the CA 1985. In addition, the very nature of the secured asset may entail registration under a different statutory regime (see **14.2.3**).

14.2.2 Companies Act provisions

14.2.2.1 The regime

The CA 1985, ss 395–409 deal with registration of security in England and Wales. Most types of non-possessory security created over the property of a registered company must be notified to the Registrar of Companies to be included in a publicly accessible charges register.

In essence, the CA 1985 provides:

(a)   certain security will be void in some respects if not registered in time (s 395);

(b)   it is the company's duty to register security (s 399);

(c)   the Registrar of Companies must keep a register of security granted (s 401); and

(d)   a certificate of registration is conclusive evidence of good registration.

These provisions are worth examining in a little more detail.

14.2.2.2 What must be registered?

CA 1985, s 396

The following 'charges' ('charge' is defined to include 'mortgage') must be registered to ensure their validity (see s 396):

(a)   a charge securing an issue of 'debentures' (eg, bonds and other securities, but not a single bank debenture);

(b)   a charge on uncalled share capital;

(c)   a charge created or evidenced by an instrument which, if executed by an individual, would require registration as a bill of sale;

(d)   a charge on land or an interest in it (other than for rent);

(e)   a charge on book debts;

(f)   a floating charge;

(g)   a charge on unpaid calls for capital;

(h)   a charge on a ship (or any share in a ship), or aircraft; and

(i)   a charge on goodwill, or intellectual property (see s 396(3A)).

The list covers most types of non-possessory security interest that a company might grant. One notable exception is security over shares (note, however, that a floating charge over shares must be registered with the Registrar of Companies).

Bills of Sale Acts 1878 and 1882

The Bills of Sale Acts 1878 and 1882 impose registration requirements on security created by individuals. The Acts require most written, non-possessory charges given by an individual or a partnership over tangible property to be registered in prescribed form at the Supreme Court as a bill of sale (the Bills of Sale Acts require each charged asset to be identified in the register, which is the main reason why it is impracticable for individuals or partnerships to give floating charges). Furthermore, IA 1986, s 344 requires most forms of assignment of a trader's book debts to be registered as a bill of sale if they are to be valid against a trustee in bankruptcy. Under CA 1985, s 396(1)(c), therefore, virtually all non-possessory fixed charges (and mortgages) over chattels which are created by a company in writing, are registrable.

Overseas property

Under CA 1985, s 395, a company registered in England and Wales must register a 'charge' (falling within the s 396 categories) over any of its property, even if the property is situated, and the charge created, overseas.

Overseas companies

Under the CA 1985, s 409, the registration provisions will also apply to 'charges' created over property situated in England and Wales, by companies which are incorporated outside England and Wales, if those companies have an 'established place of business in England and Wales'. In *Slavenburg's Bank NV v Intercontinental National Resources Ltd* [1980] 1 All ER 955, it was held that 'having an established place of business in England and Wales' is tested on a factual basis and not, for example, on whether a company has registered an established place of business with the Registrar of Companies. This means it is near impossible to determine whether or not a particular company has an established place of business in England and Wales. *Slavenburg* also suggested that registration was required for assets outside England and Wales when such a charge was created but the asset subsequently brought in. As a result, it is customary to attempt registration of any 'charge' created by a foreign company with even a remote business connection with Great Britain. This is known as a 'Slavenburg' registration, and usually results in the application being recorded by the Registrar on a separate 'Slavenburg' register. This at least demonstrates an attempt to register which is the only option until s 409 is clarified (see **14.2.2.8**). This rule is due for amendment under the CA 2006 on 1 October 2009.

14.2.2.3   Who must effect registration?

The requirement to 'register' (actually a requirement to deliver 'prescribed particulars' together with the document creating the charge) is found at CA 1985, s 399(1):

> It is a company's duty to send to the Registrar of Companies for registration the particulars of every charge created by the company ... requiring registration under sections 395 to 398; but registration of any such charge may be effected on the application of any person interested in it.

In view of the effects of non-registration (see **14.2.2.6**), in practice the bank invariably takes responsibility for registering any security (usually through its solicitor). Recognition of this practical reality can be seen in the last part of s 399(1) above. A third party registering the charge is entitled to recover any registration fee from the company.

The duty under s 399 is to register every charge 'created by the company' (a phrase which is also used in s 395). This would mean that a company which acquires property already subject to a charge, would not be required to register the charge since it did not 'create' it. This loophole is closed by s 400, which specifically requires a company to register any pre-existing charges over property it acquires (although failure to do so does not lead to avoidance). The wording of s 399(1) provides a further argument against the need to register the crystallisation of a floating charge: even if crystallisation created a new charge, it would not have been 'created by the company' (see **12.3.2** for a reason to register a crystallisation).

An agreement to provide a legal mortgage at a future date (commonly found in fixed security documents) is registrable as an equitable mortgage.

14.2.2.4 How to register

Registration of a 'charge' is made using Form 395 (or Form 400 if acquired with property). The simplicity of the registration form masks the difficulties that can occur in its completion. The main problem is that the completed form must 'stand alone'. In other words, anyone inspecting the Companies Register must be able to understand fully the scope of the registered security without resorting to other documents. Thus, any definitions used when providing 'short particulars of the property charged' must be explained. Consider, for example, a charging clause which referred to the 'Charged Property'. The definition of this term would have to be included in the charging document (eg, 'all the property held by the Obligors'). But this in turn would mean that the term 'Obligors' would need to be defined, and so it goes on. An original copy of the charging document must be sent to the Registrar along with Form 395. The particulars must be received by the Registrar within 21 days after the date of the charge's creation (s 395).

If there is any defect with the application, it will be returned to the submitting party unregistered. The 21-day time-limit will, however, continue to run. This means that the solicitor must make certain that the application is without fault, or else submit it as soon as the security is created, or preferably both (there is a procedure under which the court may grant a time extension if, essentially, it is equitable to do so, or if late registration was accidental, or if it will not prejudice other creditors or the shareholders (s 404)).

A successful registration will result in the return of the original security document with a stamp signifying registration, as well as a certificate showing the date of registration. This certificate of registration is absolute proof that the security is properly registered under s 395. So strong is this 'proof' of registration that, where a solicitor had forgotten to register a 'charge' within 21 days of creation (making it prima facie void), but still obtained a certificate of registration some months later, the 'charge' could not be invalidated for late registration by a liquidator (*Re CL Nye Ltd* [1971] Ch 442, CA).

M

CHWP000

Please do not
write in
this margin

*Please complete
legibly, preferably
in black type, or
bold block lettering*

* insert full name
of Company

COMPANIES FORM No. 395

Particulars of a mortgage or charge

A fee of £10 is payable to Companies House in respect of each register entry for a mortgage or charge.

Pursuant to section 395 of the Companies Act 1985

395

To the Registrar of Companies
(Address overleaf - Note 6)

For official use

Company number

Name of company

*

Date of creation of the charge

Description of the instrument (if any) creating or evidencing the charge (note 2)

Amount secured by the mortgage or charge

Names and addresses of the mortgagees or persons entitled to the charge

Postcode

Presentor's name address and
reference (if any) :

For official Use
Mortgage Section

Post room

Time critical reference

Page 1

Short particulars of all the property mortgaged or charged

Particulars as to commission allowance or discount (note 3)

Signed   Date

On behalf of [company][mortgagee/chargee]†

Notes

1   The original instrument (if any) creating or evidencing the charge, together with these prescribed particulars correctly completed must be delivered to the Registrar of Companies within 21 days after the date of creation of the charge (section 395). If the property is situated and the charge was created outside the United Kingdom delivery to the Registrar must be effected within 21 days after the date on which the instrument could in due course of post, and if dispatched with due diligence, have been received in the United Kingdom (section 398). A copy of the instrument creating the charge will be accepted where the property charged is situated and the charge was created outside the United Kingdom (section 398) and in such cases the copy must be verified to be a correct copy either by the company or by the person who has delivered or sent the copy to the registrar. The verification must be signed by or on behalf of the person giving the verification and where this is given by a body corporate it must be signed by an officer of that body. A verified copy will also be accepted where section 398(4) applies (property situate in Scotland or Northern Ireland) and Form No. 398 is submitted.

2   A description of the instrument, eg "Trust Deed", "Debenture", "Mortgage", or "Legal charge", etc, as the case may be, should be given.

3   In this section there should be inserted the amount or rate per cent. of the commission, allowance or discount (if any) paid or made either directly or indirectly by the company to any person in consideration of his:
        (a) subscribing or agreeing to subscribe, whether absolutely or conditionally, or
        (b) procuring or agreeing to procure subscriptions, whether absolute or conditional,
for any of the debentures included in this return. The rate of interest payable under the terms of the debentures should not be entered.

4   If any of the spaces in this form provide insufficient space the particulars must be entered on the prescribed continuation sheet.

5   Cheques and Postal Orders are to be made payable to **Companies House**.

6   The address of the Registrar of Companies is:-

Companies House, Crown Way, Cardiff CF14 3UZ   Page 2

14.2.2.5 Effect of valid registration

Registration of a 'charge' perfects the security by providing notice of its existence to existing and subsequent charge-holders (the only significance of the date on the certificate of registration is to show the charge was registered within 21 days of its creation). Other than providing notice, registration does not create any priority (but failing to register may destroy priority). Priority between charges is outlined at **14.3**.

Whilst valid registration serves as notice of the existence of a particular security interest, it will not provide constructive notice of the *detailed provisions* (although the CA 1985, s 408 allows anyone searching the register to view the security document at the company's registered office). This is of little relevance to a fixed charge: once other creditors know of its existence, they are deemed to know that it will prevent any dealing with the charged asset free of the charge. Floating charges, however, suggest a freedom to deal with the charged assets. There is an argument that the negative pledges which will frequently accompany them may not be deemed 'known'; and without notice of the negative pledge, a subsequent bank could take security ranking ahead of the floating charge.

To help alleviate this problem, it is standard practice to register details of any restrictions in the security document (eg, a negative pledge) as 'short particulars' in Form 395. Alternatively, they may be included in a document under which they must be filed, such as a special or extraordinary resolution. This will provide actual notice to parties who do search the register. However, at best it will serve only as constructive notice to parties who would be expected to search the companies register (so that, for example, it would not be constructive notice for purchasers in the ordinary course of business). Some commentators believe that there can be constructive notice only of the particulars which the CA 1985 requires to be filed and not of particulars filed voluntarily (eg, a negative pledge). If this is true, the only solution would seem to be giving actual notice of any such provisions to existing creditors, which will, of course, be impracticable in the majority of cases.

On a practical note, registration provides an accessible and cheap (although not exhaustive) record of any security granted over a company's property. This is obviously helpful to potential creditors, but is also useful for actual or potential shareholders and investors.

It is important to be aware that whilst valid registration will prevent the security being void under the CA 1985, it will not cure a defect in the document itself. Thus even a properly registered document is open to challenge by the borrower (or a liquidator, administrator, etc) if it is incorrectly drafted.

14.2.2.6 Non-registration

The main consequences of non-registration are threefold:

(a)   Probably the most serious consequence of non-registration (from the bank's perspective at least) is invalidity against administrators and liquidators, and a loss of priority against other creditors of the borrower who subsequently acquire a security interest in the same property and have their security registered (this is the case even if the third party had notice of the prior 'charge' by other means) (s 395).

(b)   If a 'charge' is void for non-registration, the debt it secures becomes immediately payable under s 395(2). In other words, the secured loan becomes 'on demand'.

(c)   Since the duty to register a 'charge' is placed on the borrower, failing to register will result in a fine on the borrower and any defaulting officers (s 399(3)).

Non-registration will not invalidate the contractual rights which a security document creates between a bank and borrower.

14.2.2.7   Late or inaccurate registration

If the 21-day registration period is missed, or if the details provided in the application on Form 395 (or details on a memorandum of satisfaction) are wrong or incomplete, there is a possibility of rectifying the situation, but only through the court. The CA 1985, s 404 allows the court to order an extension of the 21-day time-limit, or to allow rectification of the register, as appropriate. The court must be satisfied that the mistake was 'accidental, or due to inadvertence or some other sufficient cause, or is not of a nature to prejudice the position of creditors or shareholders of the company, or that on other grounds it is just and equitable to grant relief'.

These provisions should not be seen as a panacea to general mistakes in registration. Not only is the remedy far from automatic, but there also is no certainty that a late registered or amended security will enjoy a 'backdated' perfection of its priority: it may be subject to security registered in the meantime.

14.2.2.8   Memorandum of satisfaction

At some point, all or part of the secured debt will be repaid, and the security will be wholly or partially released (however, a security document will sometimes allow the bank to retain the security for up to 12 months after repayment, as 'insurance' against the repayment being set aside under the provisions of the IA 1986 – see **14.9**). Alternatively, the secured property might be released to allow the disposal of a particular asset. In either case, the borrower should prepare a document evidencing the release (usually by way of deed) and a statutory declaration that the whole, or part, of the property has been released (Forms 403a and 403b respectively). The form is sent to the Registrar of Companies, who makes the appropriate note on the company's file (see below). Neither the Registrar's certificate of discharge nor the company's mortgage register is conclusive evidence of discharge and release.

Any entries made at Land Registry or the Land Charges Department should be removed once the secured loan is repaid.

14.2.2.9   Company's register

As well as registration at the Companies Registry, a registered company must keep a register of 'charges' over its property at its registered office (CA 1985, s 407). The register must be open for inspection to any creditor or member of the company and to the public (for a nominal fee prescribed under CA 1985). All companies must also keep a copy of any security document requiring registration under the Act (s 406) available for inspection by any creditor or member of the company (s 408).

14.2.2.10   Part 25 of the CA 2006

Part 25 of the CA 2006 ('Company Charges') is due to come into force on 1 October 2009. The 2006 Act largely restates the relevant provisions of the 1985 Act, but with a few minor amendments relating to overseas companies.

14.2.3 Registration requirements for specific assets

Brief mention must be made of certain registration requirements for specific assets sited in England or Wales, or registered under English law. The most notable statutory regimes for registration of non-possessory security are:

(a)   land – registered land (under the Land Registration Act 2002 (LRA 2002) and Land Registration Rules 2003, SI 2003/1417 (from 13 October 2003)) at District Land Registry; unregistered land (under Land Charges Act 1972 (LCA 1972)) at Land Charges Registry unless the bank takes title deeds (see **12.4**);

(b)   ships – (under the Merchant Shipping Act 1894) registered at the ship's port of registration;

(c)   aircraft – (under the Mortgaging of Aircraft Order 1972, SI 1972/1268) in the UK Aircraft Mortgage Register maintained by the Civil Aviation Authority; and

(d)   intellectual property, for example patents and copyrights – under various statutory provisions.

14.3 Priority of security

This is a complex area, and what follows is therefore a summary of the main rules.

14.3.1 Priority between charges and mortgages

Priority between charges is essentially determined as follows.

14.3.1.1 Between fixed charges and mortgages

Generally, fixed charges and mortgages rank in order of creation (provided they are properly registered). At common law, a legal mortgage will take priority over an existing equitable security interest, provided the legal mortgage was taken bona fide, for value and without notice of the prior equitable security. Registration in accordance with the CA 1985 (s 395) gives notice to anyone who has, or ought to have, searched the register, which will usually protect a prior registered equitable security.

14.3.1.2 Fixed and floating charges

A fixed charge (and a mortgage) will rank in priority to a floating charge. This is because a floating charge, ostensibly, allows the chargor to deal with the charged asset, and this will include granting security over it. However, this vulnerability may be avoided if the floating charge contains a negative pledge and the later fixed charge-holder has notice of the prohibition (constructive notice is probably achieved through registration – see **14.2.2.5**). (In the case of *Griffiths v Yorkshire Bank plc* [1994] 1 WLR 1427, the judge ruled that a negative pledge in a floating charge was not effective to prevent later security being created with priority, although details of the restriction were registered in the Companies Registry. This decision also seems to suggest that a crystallised floating charge might sometimes rank ahead of preferential creditors. However, both conclusions fly in the face of previously long-accepted principles and seem contrary to the CA 1985, and to the position apparently espoused in the CA 1989.)

Priority between floating charges is (subject to contrary agreement) governed by their time of creation (if properly registered): an earlier charge will take priority even if the later one has crystallised.

Remember that registration simply perfects a security and prevents it from being ignored by other creditors, purchasers, a liquidator or an administrator. The date of the charge from which priority can be calculated is not the date it is registered but the date it is created. This means that a search made on the day of registering a charge might not show a charge created within the last 21 days, which would have priority over a charge created more recently.

14.3.2   Security over land

The priority between interests in security over land is a complicated area. Of primary importance, however, is the priority between registered mortgages.

14.3.2.1   Registered land

Under the LRA 2002, s 48, priority between two registered mortgages will be determined by the date when they appear in the charges register. The date of their creation is irrelevant.

14.3.2.2   Unregistered land

Registration in the land charges register (under the LCA 1972) gives notice of a mortgage to third parties, and therefore priority is determined by the order of registration. If registrable mortgages are not registered they will usually be void against subsequent mortgagees for value. Equitable mortgages protected by the deposit of title deeds are not registrable, but will automatically take priority over any subsequent mortgages in most circumstances (unless a subsequent legal mortgagee acts on the basis of a reasonable explanation for the absence of the deeds).

14.3.3   Priority between assignments – the rule in *Dearle v Hall*

The case of *Dearle v Hall* (1828) 3 Russ 1 established a rule of priorities between assignments over choses in action. In order to ensure priority, notice of assignment must be given to the third party which owes the obligation. For example, if C is owed £1,000 by D, and C assigns the debt to its bank B as security for a loan, B can perfect the assignment by notifying D that his debt is assigned. However, if B fails to notify D, and C later assigns D's debt to E, then E's assignment will gain priority over B's if E notifies D first. The rule will not apply, however, where a subsequent assignee (ie, E) knows of the earlier assignment (ie, to B) when taking his assignment. Thus, registration of the security at the Companies Registry will usually defeat the rule.

14.4   Contractual subordination

14.4.1   Contractual priority arrangements

The previous section discussed the order of priority between various security interests and nothing can be done directly to vary that order. It is possible, however, for creditors to decide between themselves on the order in which they will benefit from claims against a defaulting debtor. Such priority arrangements are frequently used in large financings which involve several 'layers' of debt: if the borrower defaults, the order in which the banks will have their loans repaid is contractually prearranged. The document creating these rights is usually known as an 'intercreditor agreement', 'subordination agreement' or 'deed of priorities'. These are complex documents and the legal issues surrounding the effect and effectiveness of contractual subordination are unsettled. However, the key provisions are outlined below.

14.4.2 A typical arrangement

How do these subordination arrangements work? A typical intercreditor agreement will restrict its participants so that:

(a) the participating lenders are divided into an agreed order of priority for repayment of their credit. 'Senior creditors' enjoy top priority whilst 'subordinated creditors' rank below them. Subordinated creditors are further subdivided, for example 'mezzanine', 'high yield' and 'second lien', all of which enjoy different levels of priority among the subordinated group;

(b) no participating bank may enforce any security or otherwise proceed against the borrower without the agreement of the senior banks (or occasionally only with majority consent);

(c) when any security is enforced, or any money received after a specified event (eg, a potential default by the borrower), either:

(i) subordinated creditors agree contractually not to claim against the borrower until the senior creditors are repaid, thereby maximising the assets available to satisfy senior debt (usually known as 'contingent debt subordination'), or

(ii) subordinated creditors agree to hold any money they receive on trust for senior creditors (known as 'turnover' or 'trust' subordination). This is more robust than contingent debt subordination and maximises return in all circumstances. Some practitioners take the view that this type of subordination creates a proprietory interest over the debt which requires registration as a charge under the Companies Act 1985. However, the court in *SSSL Realisations Limited* [2004] EWHC (Ch) 1760 held that the turnover trust in that case did not create a charge: it did create a proprietory right, but since it was limited to the debt owed there was no charge over the 'junior' creditor's property.

(d) the pooled money will then be distributed in accordance with the agreement. Thus the 'senior' banks will be paid back first. Once they have been repaid in full, any remaining money will be used to repay the 'mezzanine' or subordinated creditors as appropriate.

Subordination occurs in other ways. For example, ordinary shareholders (equity) will be automatically subordinated to all other creditors (debt), because they cannot usually distribute the company's assets and realise their capital until all creditors of the company are repaid. Subordination between shareholders can be achieved by issuing preferential shares which carry rights to participate in the distribution of assets before other shareholders.

14.4.3 When is contractual subordination used?

Why would a bank agree to postpone its claim to, and even share its security with, other banks? The main incentive is that, generally, the greater the risk, the larger the share of the syndicate fees (or the greater the margin). Provided the borrower does not default, the subordinated banks will ultimately get a better return on their loans. All banks will want to diversify their lending to create a mixture of risk and, when a syndicate is formed, some banks will be looking to make less risky loans and will participate only as senior banks: other banks will accept subordinated positions because they can take more risk (see also **9.3.3**).

Contractual subordination might also be used where an unsecured bank requires any debts to a borrower's directors or parent company to be subordinated to its own. Alternatively, an existing bank might benefit by allowing new finance into the borrower to enhance the business. The only way to attract new finance might be to release some existing security, or to agree subordination to the new bank.

Subordination agreements are usually executed as deeds. The borrower need not be a party to the agreement unless it is necessary to bind him to the provisions.

14.5   Tacking

Tacking is the ability to secure new advances under existing security. It will depend on whether the secured asset is unregistered land, registered land or personalty.

14.5.1   Unregistered land

New advances relating to unregistered land can be 'tacked' onto an existing mortgage (or charge) under s 94 of the LPA 1925 if:

(a)   an arrangement has been made to that effect with the subsequent mortgagees; or

(b)   the mortgagee had no notice of subsequent mortgages when it made the new advance; or

(c)   where the mortgage imposes an obligation on the first mortgagee to make further advances.

14.5.2   Registered land

In the case of registered land, there are specific provisions brought in by the LRA 2002, s 49. In outline, these allow a mortgage (or charge) holder to tack if:

(a)   he has not received notice of the subsequent security; or

(b)   the new advance is under an obligation already on the register when the subsequent charge was created; or

(c)   the maximum amount of the first charge was agreed and on the register when the subsequent charge was created.

14.5.3   Personalty

Mortgaged/charged personalty is subject to the provisions of LPA 1925, s 94. Thus any actual or constructive notice of a subsequent mortgage/charge will end a prior mortgagee's/chargee's right to tack unless the conditions in (a) or (c) at **14.5.1** are fulfilled.

14.6   Ruling off accounts

When a borrower makes a payment to a bank, the borrower may (subject to any contrary agreement) instruct the bank as to which account it should be appropriated (although see the banker's right of combination at **13.5.3**), or which loan should be repaid (but see **9.2.2**). However, in the absence of instructions or specific agreement, the rule laid down in *Devaynes v Noble* (1816) 1 Mer 572 (known as 'Clayton's case') will apply. In a banking context the rule says that money paid to the bank will discharge the borrower's debt in the chronological order in which the debt was incurred. If this rule applied, there might be circumstances in which a bank would be disadvantaged, particularly if it was providing a secured revolving account (eg, an overdraft or RCF). This is best explained by way of example:

Example

Bank provides a secured RCF for Borrower. Borrower draws two tranches as follows:

1 January – £2,000

1 March – £4,000

On 1 February, Bank also provides Borrower with an unsecured overdraft of up to £5,000. On 1 April, Borrower makes a payment of £2,000 to Bank, with no instructions as to whether it should reduce the overdraft, the RCF, or be put into a new account. If there is no other agreement between them, the rule in Clayton's case means that the £2,000 will be treated as repaying the debt which was incurred earliest – it will reduce the secured RCF.

There are several reasons why this might disadvantage Bank:

(a)   If Borrower is in financial difficulty, Bank might prefer the £2,000 to reduce the unsecured overdraft rather than the RCF which has the benefit of security.

(b)   Even if the overdraft was secured, new security may be more vulnerable to being set aside than older 'hardened' security (see **14.9**): Bank may prefer newer secured loans to be repaid first.

(c)   Finally, if Bank learns that Borrower has organised a loan from another lender secured by second ranking security, in certain circumstances new advances would rank behind the second loan. Therefore, as the RCF was repaid and re-drawn, it would lose priority to the new loan.

To avoid problems (a) and (b), banks may insist that they can choose where payments are appropriated in some circumstances (eg, where payments are not received in full). The third problem is usually dealt with by allowing a bank to 'rule off' an account if it learns that a borrower has taken a second secured loan. This means that the original secured loan (which has priority to the new secured loan) is preserved ('ruled-off') and not treated as repaid by any amounts received from the borrower until the first bank can ensure that any new advances it makes will rank ahead. In addition, security should be specified as securing all amounts due from time to time from the borrower to the bank, and banks should include a negative pledge in their loan facility and debenture.

The rule in Clayton's case may also affect guarantees. Subject to contrary agreement, once a guaranteed liability has been fixed in value, any payment by the borrower to the bank will be deemed to reduce the guaranteed debt, placing any other debts which are outstanding beyond the guarantee. This can be avoided by specifying the guarantee to be 'continuing', or alternatively an 'all monies guarantee'.

14.7 Fixed or floating charge?

14.7.1 Which is preferable?

Chapter 12 outlined the main differences between fixed and floating charges. But which is preferable if the bank has a choice? The principal advantages of the floating charge are two-fold:

(a)   it allows the borrower to deal freely with the charged assets in the ordinary course of business; and

(b)   in restricted circumstances, it allows the bank to appoint an administrative receiver (see **13.7.2)**, who may manage the borrower's business, and also block an administration order (a floating charge taken primarily for this reason is known as a 'lightweight' or a 'phantom' floating charge). After changes made by the EA 2002, this is relevant only to 'specialised' financial structures (eg, project finance, housing finance and capital markets – see **13.7.2**).

The main disadvantages are:

(a)   a floating charge will be subordinated to any preferential creditors (see **12.3.2**);

(b)   a floating charge might be vulnerable to later fixed charges, even if it contains a negative pledge which is registered (see **14.3**);

(c)   a floating charge can be set aside under wider circumstances than a fixed charge (see **12.3.2**);

(d)   some of the proceeds which would otherwise be available to floating charge-holders may be allocated to unsecured creditors (see **12.3.2**).

The flexibility of the floating charge would almost certainly score points with a borrower and, arguably, the trading freedom it gives the borrower is also good for the bank. However, that freedom and the general vulnerability of the floating charge mean that it will always be second choice for the bank where a fixed charge is available. The protection of a fixed charge is more certain. Banks are inclined to take a floating charge where 'necessary' (eg, for stock), giving them the right to appoint an administrative receiver in some circumstances (see above), and to declare all other charges as fixed. However, as explained below, the nature of a charge is not determined by its label, but by its effect.

14.7.2   Recognising a floating charge

If the name of a charge is not conclusive proof of its nature, how is it determined as fixed or floating? The most commonly quoted description of a floating charge is that of Romer LJ in *Re Yorkshire Woolcombers Association Ltd* [1903] 2 Ch 284:

> I certainly do not intend to attempt to give an exact definition of the term 'floating charge', nor am I prepared to say that there will not be a floating charge within the meaning of the Companies Act 1900, which does not contain all the three characteristics that I am about to mention, but I certainly think that if a charge has the three characteristics that I am about to mention it is a floating charge. (1) If it is a charge on a class of assets of a company present and future; (2) If that class is one which, in the ordinary course of the business of the company, would be changing from time to time; and (3) If you find that by the charge it is contemplated that, until some future step is taken by or on behalf of those interested in the charge, the company may carry on its business in the ordinary way as far as concerns the particular class of assets I am dealing with.

Subsequent cases have emphasised the third characteristic identified by Romer LJ: the security must allow a company to deal with its assets in the ordinary course of business. Put another way, if a charge allows a borrower to deal with the charged assets without the bank's consent, it almost certainly will not be a fixed charge, even if it is called a 'fixed charge'. A fixed charge requires the bank to exhibit control over the charged asset (see also *Chalk v Kahn and Another* [2000] 2 BCLC 361).

14.8   Hardening periods

When new security is granted, there is often a reference made to its 'hardening period'. This refers to a period during which the security is vulnerable to provisions in the IA 1986 for setting aside certain transactions. The primary concerns are as follows.

14.8.1 Transactions at an undervalue (IA 1986, s 238)

An administrator or a liquidator can apply to court to set aside a transaction in which a company received either no consideration, or significantly less consideration than it provided (a 'transaction at an undervalue'), and which was entered into within two years of winding-up. The transaction must either have been made when the company was insolvent, or have resulted in the company's insolvency (this is presumed if with a connected person). Furthermore, if the directors can show the transaction was entered into in good faith, and with reasonable grounds to believe it would benefit the company, it cannot be set aside.

14.8.2 Preferences (IA 1986, s 239)

A 'preference' is a transaction in which a company intentionally benefits a creditor (or a surety or guarantor) by enhancing its position in the event that the company becomes insolvent. Providing new or enhanced security can be a preference. As under s 238, a transaction will be set aside only if it was made when the company was insolvent, or results in insolvency. A liquidator or an administrator can apply for a transaction to be set aside if it was made within six months of winding-up, although if the transaction was with a 'connected' person (this includes a director, his close relatives, his business partners and their close relatives – see s 249) the time-limit is extended to two years. A transaction will not be a preference unless the company was influenced by a desire to put the preferred person in a better position on winding-up (this is a rebuttable presumption in the case of a connected person). Granting security in an attempt to ensure 'survival' is therefore probably not a preference.

A director might also be warned that any involvement in an insolvent company giving a transaction at an undervalue or a preference may lead to his disqualification under the CDDA 1986.

14.8.3 Floating charges (IA 1986, s 245)

Floating charges can be set aside if not granted for valuable consideration, and if granted within a given period before the company's insolvency (see **12.3.2**).

14.8.4 Summary

The important periods for hardening of security are therefore six months, 12 months (setting aside a floating charge) and two years, depending on the circumstances.

14.9 Capacity

One of the first things that should be checked by the bank's (and strictly, the borrower's) solicitor is the capacity of a borrower to provide security (if lack of capacity is discovered early enough it can usually be rectified). The issues as to a company's capacity to give security are largely the same as those which apply to its capacity to borrow, discussed at **4.6.2**.

Trustees are something of a 'special case'. Most of their powers and limitations will be found in the deed creating the trust, which will need careful review. Under the Trustee Act 1925, s 16, trustees (including personal representatives) are given the power to grant security, provided that the borrowing is for the purposes of the trust and is authorised by the trust deed, or under general law. This power applies whatever the trust deed might provide, but does not apply to trustees of charitable property.

14.10 Corporate benefit

It is not uncommon for a bank to require additional security from a borrower's parent, subsidiary or sister company. This might be necessary to make up for a deficiency in the borrower's assets and reduce an otherwise unacceptable risk of lending. Alternatively, it might reduce the cost of the loan. However, it is necessary for a company providing a guarantee or indemnity to prove it derives sufficient 'corporate benefit' from granting the security. This stems from the duty a director owes to his company to act in good faith and in what he considers to be in the best interests of the company.

At first sight, it might seem difficult to justify a company giving security for another company's loan as being in its best interests. When can a director justify his company securing another's obligations? This is really a commercial question of substance: what are the benefits and risks of providing the security? In crude terms, the greater the risk, the more benefit the company must derive as a consequence thereof. A parent company might justify supporting a subsidiary because directly or indirectly it will normally receive dividends from its shareholding. A subsidiary securing its parent (eg, an 'up-stream' guarantee) could argue that the support from its parent (eg, financial, marketing, product development) provides sufficient corporate benefit. This argument is more tenuous if the company is a small fish in a large group pond, but can be strengthened by a down-stream support letter (see **13.2.2**).

If a company believes there is insufficient corporate benefit to provide security, there is authority to suggest that it may still be given, provided that:

(a)   the company's shareholders unanimously direct the security to be given; and

(b)   the company is not insolvent either at the time of giving the security, or immediately following the giving of the security.

14.11 Financial assistance

Under CA 1985, s 151, a company and any of its subsidiaries are generally prohibited from directly or indirectly providing financial assistance to any person in order to purchase that company's shares. The prohibition is absolute for public companies, although the prohibition on financial assistance for private companies is due to be abolished by the CA 2006 (unless the assistance is for acquisition of shares in their public holding company) on 1 October 2008.

14.12 Applicable law

The legal system which governs a security interest will dictate how the security will be perfected (eg, notice, registration, etc) and how it may be enforced. Under the provisions of English law (and most other jurisdictions) the legal system applicable to a security interest will depend on whether the secured assets are movable or immovable. Security over immovable assets will, for purely practical reasons, be governed by the legal system of the place where the assets are physically situated (known as the 'lex situs'). The most common types of immovable assets include land, buildings, and heavy plant and machinery.

Ascertaining the legal system applicable to tangible movable assets is slightly more complicated. Generally, the lex situs of the asset when the security is created will determine the validity of its creation and perfection. However, if the asset is moved into another jurisdiction then the rules of that legal system may supersede the original lex situs with regard to perfection and enforcement. Local lawyers must therefore be instructed to ensure that any necessary steps are taken to maintain the validity of the security. These issues are of particular importance for valuable assets which regularly move between jurisdictions, such as ships and aircraft.

Security over intangible assets (eg, debts) is usually subject to the governing law of the contract creating the asset, but the law of the place of performance of the asset (eg, where the debt is to be paid) is also relevant.

From 31 May 2002, the EU Insolvency Regulation (EUIR) came into force in all EU Member States except Denmark. The EUIR provides rules that dictate which system of insolvency law applies in a 'cross-border' insolvency situation: in other words, it resolves conflicts of law situations but does not change the substantive insolvency laws currently in existence.

Under the EUIR, the main insolvency proceedings will be opened in the jurisdiction of the entity's Centre of Main Interest (COMI). The rather vague definition of COMI is where an entity 'conducts the administration of his interests on a regular basis' (Preamble 13). More helpfully, there is a rebuttable presumption that the COMI is in the jurisdiction of an entity's registered office (Article 3(1)), although factors such as location of employees, head office, board meetings and where the company does most of its business can influence the COMI. There can only be one COMI, but it can change over time.

There are two main circumstances in which assets may be subject to insolvency proceedings in jurisdictions other than the COMI. First, assets outside the COMI which are subject to 'rights in rem' (broadly, security interests) are basically unaffected by the COMI proceedings. Secondly, supplemental proceedings may be brought in a jurisdiction where a company has an 'establishment'. An 'establishment' is defined, in best euro-speak, as 'any place of operations where the debtor carries out non-transitory economic activity with human means and goods' – in essence a branch. Any supplemental proceedings will only apply to assets within the jurisdiction of the establishment.

The EUIR applies to companies, partnerships and individuals with their COMI in an EU Member State (other than Denmark), but not to most regulated entities (eg, banks, insurance companies) which have separate regimes. Once the definitions have benefited from the clarity brought by litigation, the EUIR should prove a positive tool for banking lawyers assessing insolvency risk in a cross-border transaction.

14.13 UNCITRAL Model Law

In April 2006, the Cross Border Insolvency Regulations 2006 (SI 2006/1030) came into force in England and Wales. These Regulations implemented the main provisions of the 'Model Law' on Cross Border Insolvency devised by UNCITRAL (the United Nations Commission on International Trade Law). The Model Law aims to facilitate cross border insolvencies by providing a framework for dealing with problematic issues, for example where creditors, debtors and assets are located in different jurisdictions. Where the Model Law covers the same ground as the EUIR, then the EUIR takes precedence.

14.14 Other considerations on taking security

When a solicitor is advising on security issues, there are a number of peripheral points to be covered, including the following.

14.14.1 Prior security

Copies of any existing charges (and other security interests) should be checked to ascertain the extent of their influence, and also to check for negative pledges. A subordination agreement may be necessary (see **14.4**).

14.14.2 Notification requirements

It may be necessary to notify third parties such as licensing authorities and landlords.

14.14.3 Overseas registration

Security interests over property situated overseas may need to be registered in the jurisdiction in which it is situated as well as in this country: some property may be incapable of being the subject of security, and rules about enforcement and insolvency may be very different from those of English law. Local lawyers should be instructed.

14.15 Further reading

Ellinger and Lomnicka, *Modern Banking Law* (3rd edn, Clarendon Press, 2002).

Goode, *Commercial Law* (3rd edn, Penguin, 2004).

Goode, *Legal Problems of Credit and Security* (3rd edn, Sweet & Maxwell, 2003).

Penn, Shea and Arora, *The Law Relating to Domestic Banking* (Banking Law vol 1) (2nd edn, Sweet & Maxwell, 2000).

Chapter 15

Security Documentation – Debentures

15.1	Introduction	191
15.2	Structure of a typical debenture	191
15.3	Execution	197

> 'Men lend their money to traders on mortgages or consignments of goods because they suspect their circumstances and they will not run the risk of their general credit.'
>
> Lord Mansfield *(Foxcroft v Devonshire* (1760))

15.1 Introduction

In broad terms, a debenture is 'a document which either creates a debt or acknowledges it' (see *Levy v Abercorris Slate and Slab Co* (1887) 37 Ch D 260). The document creating security for a secured loan is commonly known as a 'mortgage debenture', or simply a 'debenture'. The label is slightly misleading: these documents will usually create charges as well as mortgages, and they are only created as 'debentures' for one particular reason (see **15.2.1**). This chapter briefly examines the typical structure of a mortgage debenture (hereinafter 'debenture').

15.2 Structure of a typical debenture

Most banks have their own short standard form debenture, consisting of two or three pages of closely typed terms which are not usually open to negotiation. They will use these debentures for creating security over small, straightforward loans. However, more complex secured loan facilities will require a longer and more sophisticated debenture, which is usually drafted by the bank's solicitor. The broad structure of most debentures is similar to other commercial documents: ie, date, title and parties; preamble; definitions; operative provisions; schedules; and execution. The main operative provisions are explained below.

15.2.1 Covenant to pay

The first clause in the operative part of a debenture is invariably the 'covenant to pay'. This clause acknowledges the debt obligation of the borrower to the bank (making the document a 'debenture' to comply with IA 1986, s 29(2) if it is able to appoint an administrative receiver – **13.7.2**). The covenant to pay may refer to a specific debt obligation, or to all debts between the bank and borrower, known as an 'all monies' clause (a debenture securing an overdraft facility will usually use an 'all monies clause'). A typical 'all monies' covenant to pay is:

> The Borrower agrees to discharge on demand, each and every liability which the Borrower may have to the Bank, whether under sole or joint liability, whether under this Debenture or otherwise, and whether as principal or surety, and to pay to the Bank every sum now or hereafter due, owing or incurred by the Borrower to the Bank in respect of such liabilities.

The phrase 'on demand' is intended to prevent the Limitation Act 1939 operating against the bank until it makes a demand. It does not, and should not, alter the payment obligations in any facility agreement which it secures (see *Cryne v Barclays Bank plc* [1987] BCLC 548 in which it was held that the words 'due, owing or incurred' meant that demand under the debenture could be made only when the loan was due under the facility agreement which it secured).

Some debentures refer to monies owing or incurred 'on any account whatsoever', but this wording may be inadvisable because there is a danger that it would not include certain types of obligation (eg, loan stock – see *Re Quest Cae Limited* [1985] BCLC 266).

15.2.2   Charging clause

The second clause in a debenture is usually the charging clause. This clause specifies which of the borrower's assets are charged to repay the debts acknowledged in the covenant to pay, as well as how each type of asset is secured. The following paragraphs examine some of the issues which arise with respect to charging particular assets.

15.2.2.1   Land

A debenture will usually secure leasehold and freehold land by way of a 'charge by way of legal mortgage' (see **12.4**). Details of any registered land which is to be secured will be included in a schedule to the debenture, so that the security can be registered at Land Registry under the LRA 2002 (the schedule will also usually list details of unregistered land for ease of reference). The terms of any leases to be secured should be checked to ensure they do not prohibit particular forms of security interest being granted over them (eg, a prohibition on assignment or sub-letting). Future acquired land cannot be secured by legal mortgage, and is therefore secured by an equitable mortgage over the property once acquired. (The borrower may then be required to give a legal mortgage – see **15.2.3**.)

Some practitioners put security over land in a separate 'stand-alone' document to avoid having to register and disclose 'incorporated documents' (eg, the facility agreement) under Land Registry, Rule 139.

15.2.2.2   Fixed plant and machinery

A mortgage of land will automatically secure any assets which are, or become, permanently fixed to the secured property (known as 'fixtures'), and it is not strictly necessary to list these individually. There may, however, be other assets which will not be 'fixtures' but are nevertheless fixed assets (eg, certain plant and machinery), and so the charging clause should specifically mention 'buildings, trade and other fixtures, and fixed plant and machinery' if these are to be secured.

15.2.2.3   Cash

There are circumstances in which a bank may want to take security over a cash deposit made with it. For example, the bank might have provided a performance guarantee in return for which it demands a cash deposit from the guaranteed party. The obvious way to secure the deposit is for the depositor to create a mortgage or charge over it in favour of the bank. However, in 1987, a controversial first instance decision by Millett J in *Re Charge Card Services* [1987] Ch 150 included the following statements (emphasis added):

> [a debt] ... cannot be made the subject of a *legal* or *equitable mortgage* in favour of the debtor, since this requires a conveyance or assignment by way of security, and this operates as a conditional release;

and

> a *charge* in favour of a debtor of his own indebtedness to the chargor is conceptually impossible.

In other words, a depositor could not *charge* or *mortgage* (ie, assign by way of security) its account with a bank *to that bank*. The argument for this proposition was based on the fact that an account is a debt owed by a bank to a depositor, and a debt is simply a right to sue the debtor for the amount owed. If that right were charged, or mortgaged, in favour of the debtor it would be giving the debtor the right to sue himself: this would simply cancel (or reduce) the debt. Millett J's judgment (at least with respect to the invalidity of a charge in these circumstances) was criticised by practitioners and legal commentators.

In October 1997, in *Morris v Agrichemicals Ltd* [1997] 3 WLR 909 (also known as 'BCCI No 8'), the House of Lords, led by Lord Hoffmann, declared that a *charge* in favour of a person over the benefit of a deposit made with that person, by another, is not a conceptual impossibility. It must be assumed, since Lord Hoffmann did not opine otherwise, that an assignment (by way of security) of the account to the bank remains ineffective.

How should a depositor provide a bank with security ('cash collateral') over a deposit (ie, an account) with that bank? It is important that the means of enforcing a cash collateral arrangement is by set-off – contractual set-off prior to winding-up, and mandatory set-off after winding-up (see **13.5**): any security granted over the account is intended to ensure that the money is in the account when the bank needs to set off. Therefore, the bank should usually require (assuming the depositor will not have unhindered access to the account – otherwise (b) will probably be a floating charge and (d) will not usually be appropriate):

(a) an express (contractual) right of set-off;

(b) a fixed charge over the account (assuming the depositor will not be allowed to withdraw any money without the bank's prior consent);

(c) a prohibition on the depositor assigning the account (to deal with the fact that a bona fide purchaser, for value, without notice could defeat the fixed charge); and

(d) if the depositor's obligation is contingent, a 'flawed asset' arrangement (that is, the deposit only becomes repayable at the same time that the depositor's debt becomes due and unpaid). This protects the account from a liquidator until the bank can exercise its rights of set-off.

Note that an assignment will usually be possible if security over an account is given to a security trustee or an agent bank on behalf of a syndicate, and that none of these issues will apply if a borrower gives security over accounts held with a third party bank.

15.2.2.4   Goodwill

The goodwill of a borrower is probably automatically secured as an inseparable part of the borrower's secured 'undertaking'. However, to avoid any uncertainty, a debenture will usually specifically secure the borrower's goodwill (as well as other intellectual property rights) by way of a fixed charge.

15.2.2.5 Book debts

Book debts (also known as 'receivables') are the monies owed to a borrower by its debtors, and a bank will want to secure them with a fixed charge or, for single large debts, possibly an assignment (see **12.6**). The fact that book debts are usually a valuable asset means there has been considerable litigation over what constitutes fixed security (remember, if security is deemed floating not fixed, it will increase the amount available to preferential creditors). Most cases suggest that book debts have two elements, the debt and the proceeds of the debt, and that a bank must show control over both elements to achieve fixed security over either (eg, *Re Brightlife* [1987] Ch 200; *Re Keenan Bros* [1986] BCLC 242). Taking control over the debt element is usually uncontroversial: the bank must prevent the borrower doing anything other than collecting in the debt (eg, not allowing any discounting, factoring or assigning of the debt). Controlling the proceeds, however, is more difficult, because the borrower usually needs access to them to run its business.

In the early 1990s there was a run of judgments which moved against the previous cases and was much more in favour of the banks. The leading case was *Re New Bullas Trading* [1994] 1 BCLC 485, where the Court of Appeal blessed a debenture allowing fixed security over the unrealised debt and floating security over the proceeds (the New Bullas debenture required the realised debts to be paid into a specified account and then released under the directions of the creditor (ie, fixed security), but with the proviso that an absence of creditor's directions would automatically release the account monies from the fixed charge into a floating charge).

Many debentures subsequently used the *New Bullas* approach; however, the decision was subject to judicial criticism (see *Re Westmaze Ltd* (1998) *The Times*, 15 July, *Chalk v Kahn and Another* [2000] 2 BCLC 361 and *Agnew and Another v Commissioner of Inland Revenue* [2001] UKPC 28, [2001] 3 WLR 454 ('*Brumark*')). Most recently, the House of Lords in *National Westminster Bank plc v Spectrum Plus Limited* [2005] UKHL 41 held that to create a fixed charge over book debts, the chargee must control both the debt and its proceeds; the exact degree of control required to avoid recharacterisation remains unclear. Furthermore, the Lords suggested that the same principles would apply to security over assets other than book debts. This has led to concern that security over shares, insurance policies and even land may be recharacterised if control is not taken over the proceeds of those assets.

In summary, while total control over both debt and proceeds will definitely give fixed security, such tight restrictions are usually commercially unworkable. The vexed question for practitioners, still unanswered by the courts, is how much control (if any) may be given to the borrower without fixed security being lost.

Take note that bank accounts may not be considered 'book debts' and so the charge should refer to them expressly if they are to be secured.

15.2.2.6 Shares

Shares may be in registered form (in which a register of legal owners is maintained by the company), in bearer form (where legal ownership is generally determined by possession of the share certificate, or, in English companies, by possession of a 'share warrant' – see CA 2006, s 779) or 'dematerialised' (where they are held and traded electronically – see below). There are two common ways in which security is taken over registered shares (for companies incorporated in England and Wales).

(a) Creating a legal mortgage by transferring the shares into the bank's name and issuing a new share certificate to that effect. (The disadvantage of this method is the administration and possible liabilities, and so many banks use a nominee to take the shares.) The debenture will allow the bank to sell the shares on default of the borrower and provide for re-transfer when the loan is repaid.

(b) Creating an equitable mortgage (or charge) by taking custody of the share certificate together with a stock transfer form executed by the borrower, but with the transferee's name and other details left blank. The security document should also contain a power of attorney allowing the bank to complete the stock transfer form and submit it, with the share certificates, to register a new owner (see **15.2.8**). The bank can then enforce the security by completing the transfer form with its own name, or that of any purchaser. The advantage of this method is that the bank does not have the 'inconvenience' of ownership pre-enforcement (eg, voting, passing dividend and shareholder information back to the borrower, etc) and does not run the risk of the company whose shares are secured becoming a subsidiary of the bank (before enforcement).

In either case, enforcement of the security will not require further involvement of the borrower. The bank's solicitor should ensure that the shares are fully paid up, that (in the case of (a) above) any stamp duty payable on the transfer form has been paid, and that there are no restrictions on transfer in the articles (eg, pre-emption rights). In the case of bearer shares, security is usually achieved simply by taking delivery of the share certificate and a memorandum of deposit (ie, a pledge). The matter is more complex if the shares are held in a depository or clearing system (see also **19.2.7**), or are traded on an electronic transfer system, and details are beyond the scope of this book.

15.2.2.7 Stock in trade and sundry assets

The main asset which is specifically subject to a floating charge is the borrower's stock in trade (see **12.3.2**). However, there will be other 'grey areas' where purported 'fixed charges' may not effectively secure assets (eg, book debts or insurance proceeds). Control might be demonstrated by requiring segregation of assets, restrictions on dealing with assets, or an obligation to account for any proceeds of disposal. There is, however, no absolute guarantee that these methods will be sufficient in all circumstances. Most debentures will therefore declare any assets within these 'grey areas' to be secured by a fixed charge, but then use a floating charge to secure any property not effectively secured by the fixed charge. The floating charge acts as a type of 'safety net'.

15.2.2.8 Choses in action

Various choses in action will be secured by way of legal or equitable assignment. These might include rental or leasing rights, debts, property rights, insurance proceeds, investments and any uncalled capital contributions on the borrower's shares. The assignment should be specified as subject to redemption to avoid any question of permanence which would attract stamp duty.

15.2.3 Perfection of security

A debenture will usually include an undertaking by the borrower to do anything necessary in order to perfect the security (this is sometimes known as a 'further assurance' clause). This might include execution of any documents required by the bank, the conversion of equitable mortgage to legal mortgage, the deposit of any documents of title, or even the provision of additional security to ensure that the bank obtains the full security anticipated in the debenture.

It is customary (though not a requirement of the regime) to include the further assurance clause in Form 395 for Companies Act registration (see **14.2.2.**)

15.2.4 Undertakings

Most debentures will contain a number of undertakings, the most common being:

(a)   a negative pledge. This may be included even if the facility agreement contains a negative pledge to help ensure registration at the Companies Registry (and therefore notification) of its terms;

(b)   an undertaking to execute, at the bank's request, a legal mortgage in place of an equitable one (ie, perfection of security);

(c)   an undertaking to provide the bank with any documents of title it might request;

(d)   an undertaking to repair and maintain land, and insure all assets, together with a power of attorney allowing the bank to do these things (and recover any expenses it incurs) if the borrower does not.

Care should be taken not to duplicate (except in the case of (a) above), or conflict with, similar clauses in any loan documentation.

15.2.5 Crystallisation clause

If it creates a floating charge, the debenture will specify when the floating charge crystallises (see **12.3.2**). This will usually be:

(a)   at any time the bank notifies the borrower in writing (although a borrower may resist the bank being able to crystallise the floating charge at will, and insist that it is linked to a default under the facility agreement, or at least a perception that the assets secured by the charge are in jeopardy); and

(b)   automatically on specified events, for example on any demand by the bank for repayment, on a petition for the winding-up of, or an administration order in relation to, the borrower, or if the borrower ceases to carry on a substantial part of its business.

15.2.6 Appointment of a receiver, administrator or administrative receiver

The bank will have a right (subject to contrary agreement) to immediate possession of any assets over which it has a legal mortgage. However, this right of possession does not extend to assets over which the bank has merely an equitable mortgage or charge. The debenture should therefore give the bank an express contractual right to take possession of the charged assets on specified 'enforcement events' (ie, events of default).

The bank should also be given the right, on an enforcement event, to appoint a receiver of the secured property, an administrator and, if permitted, an administrative receiver – see **13.7.2**. These individuals are licensed insolvency practitioners and are usually appointed as agents of the borrower, selling assets to meet the borrower's obligations to the lender, to avoid the bank being liable for any of their acts or omissions. The debenture will contain any powers the office-holder is to have beyond his normal statutory powers.

15.2.7 Collection of debts

A debenture will usually require the borrower to collect in any debts and claims of the business 'promptly', and to pay them into specified accounts (see **15.2.2.5**).

15.2.8 Power of attorney

A debenture will invariably provide the bank and any receiver it appoints with a power of attorney. This will allow the bank to carry out any of the borrower's obligations under the debenture which the borrower fails to honour, for example, conveying legal title for any assets over which it has only equitable security, or enforcing equitable security over shares (see **15.2.2**). The instrument creating a power of attorney must be executed as a deed and, provided it is also expressed to be 'irrevocable', it will survive the borrower's liquidation (Powers of Attorney Act 1971, s 4). Powers of attorney are strictly construed and therefore will need to be widely drafted to cover the bank's needs.

15.2.9 Redemption of the security

The debenture must provide for the release of the security once the secured obligations are satisfied. However, the bank may require the right to retain the security for a period of at least six months after satisfaction of the debt, in case the monies used to repay the loan are reclaimed by the courts as a preference (see **14.9**). There are no strict formalities for the discharge of security, other than for registered land for which the requisite form should be filed with the Registrar. The borrower will usually be made liable for any costs involved in discharging the security.

15.2.10 Administrative provisions

As with any other commercial agreement, a debenture will contain a number of boiler plate clauses concerning administrative matters, such as notice periods, interpretation, service of documents, and costs and expenses.

15.3 Execution

Debentures should be made by way of deed. Under the Law of Property (Miscellaneous Provisions) Act 1989, a document will not be a deed unless:

> it makes clear on its face that it is intended to be a deed ... whether by describing itself as a deed or expressing itself to be executed or signed as a deed or otherwise.

The introduction or execution (or preferably both) of a debenture should be drafted accordingly. A debenture should be created as a deed because:

(a)   it avoids any doubt as to sufficiency of consideration;

(b)   it is necessary because debentures invariably create a power of attorney (see the Power of Attorney Act 1971, s 1);

(c)   it is necessary if a debenture conveys or creates a legal estate in land (LPA 1925, s 52); and

(d)   it is necessary if the bank is to take powers under LPA 1925, s 101.

A debenture should also be expressed as being made by the borrower 'in favour of the bank' (rather than 'between' borrower and bank) to ensure that it can be enforced by a party other than the bank (eg, a receiver or attorney).

Note that, from 6 April 2008, a company can execute a deed by the signature of one director whose signature is witnessed (CA 2006, s 44).

Chapter 16

Legal Opinions

'The public buys its opinion as it buys its meat, or takes in its milk, on the principle that it is cheaper to do this than to keep a cow. So it is, but the milk is more likely to be watered.'

Samuel Butler

16.1 Introduction

Legal opinions were first introduced in the USA, where they were required by banks' auditors in order to confirm the enforceability of loan documentation inter-state. It is now usual for banks in the UK, making either substantial loans or capital market investments (see **Chapter 17**), to require a legal opinion. This chapter briefly explains the typical structure and content of a legal opinion relating to loan documentation.

16.2 What are legal opinions?

16.2.1 Purpose

Legal opinions relate only to matters of law and not to matters of fact. In a banking context, legal opinions will usually confirm that all the documents associated with the loan are legally valid and enforceable. The opinion will also highlight areas which may be problematic (eg, on enforcement), helping the bank to assess any associated risk. The opinion does not, however, provide a guarantee that the borrower will service or repay the loan, a confirmation of commercial efficacy for a transaction, or a complete risk assessment. In one sense, a legal opinion is simply a written statement by a solicitor that he has done his job properly.

16.2.2 Who provides the opinion?

The opinion is usually provided by the bank's solicitor (who will have created and negotiated the loan documentation) and is addressed to the bank. Generally, only an addressee may sue the solicitor if the opinion proves wrong, although the solicitor will owe a general responsibility to anyone he knows has relied on his advice. If the transaction involves a syndicate (or underwriters), the opinion may be addressed to the agent bank on their behalf, or be addressed to each of them individually (so that they can each sue on it individually).

A lawyer can only opine on the law of the jurisdiction in which he is qualified. Therefore, if an opinion is required on an overseas matter, it will be necessary to instruct local lawyers.

16.2.3   When are opinions used?

There are two situations in which legal opinions will almost always be required:

(a)   *Secured lending.* Where a bank takes security for a loan, it will usually want an opinion to confirm the priority and enforceability of the security, and to outline any risks associated with those issues.

(b)   *Overseas jurisdictions.* If a bank is providing money to a borrower incorporated outside England and Wales, or is taking security falling under an overseas jurisdiction (see **14.12**), it will invariably require a legal opinion from a local lawyer with respect to the enforceability, legality, priority, etc, of the relevant documents.

Banks will not usually require legal opinions for small, unsecured loan transactions: the fact that a bank's in-house legal department has 'signed off' on the loan may be sufficient for the bank's internal procedures. The more substantial the loan, the more likely it is that the bank will require an opinion. Even if the loan is a repeat of an earlier one, the bank may still require a new opinion (even if the opinion is identical to the previous one) in order to update its effect (see below).

A bank will usually make the delivery of a satisfactory legal opinion a condition precedent to the loan being drawn down (see **4.7.4**). If this is the case, a borrower ideally should insist that the bank and the opining solicitors agree the form of the opinion in advance of executing the facility agreement (it will then appear as a schedule to the facility agreement). Unfortunately, this does not always happen, and many 'eleventh hour' problems are due to disagreement over the content of legal opinions.

16.2.4   Form of the opinion

Legal opinions are invariably written in the form of a letter on the solicitor's headed notepaper, addressed to the bank and signed in the firm's name (it is common policy that only partners may sign legal opinions). The date of the letter is very important, since a legal opinion can be given only at a particular date, taking account of the law as it stands at that time.

Most legal opinions will follow a similar format:

(a)   preamble;

(b)   assumptions;

(c)   opinion; and

(d)   qualifications.

Some firms will put the assumptions and qualifications into a schedule in order to emphasise the actual 'opinion'.

More detail on each section is given below.

16.3   Preamble

The first section of the opinion will specify the addressees and then briefly outline the form of the loan transaction (eg, the parties, the type of loan, the maturity date, etc). The opinion will then usually provide two lists: the first will be a list of all the documents in respect of which the opinion is given (in addition to the facility agreement, this will normally include any security documents and guarantees); the second list will specify the documents which the solicitor has reviewed in order to give the opinion (which, in addition to the documents opined upon, will probably include board and shareholders' resolutions, memorandum and articles, security registration forms, etc).

Usually, the legal opinion will be delivered after the documents to which it refers have been executed. However, the timing of some transactions may make this impossible, and the opinion will need to refer to unexecuted documents. In this case, the opinion should be clear that it refers to a specific draft and assumes the executed document is unchanged from that draft.

Lastly, the preamble to the opinion will also contain a record of any searches (eg, at the Companies Registry and Companies Court) on which the opinion relies, together with the dates on which they are made.

16.4 Assumptions

All opinions will be based on certain assumptions of fact (remember, the opinion only addresses the law) which the opining solicitor must make. The most common assumptions include:

(a)   that all signatures appearing on the reviewed documents are genuine;

(b)   that the documents submitted to the solicitor as originals are authentic and complete;

(c)   that the documents submitted to the solicitor as copies are complete and conform to the original document (which was itself authentic);

(d)   that any resolutions were properly passed at quorate meetings which were duly convened and held;

(e)   that the documents on which the opinion relies (as listed) remain accurate;

(f)   if the opinion predates the execution of the documents on which it opines, that those documents are executed unchanged;

(g)   that any searches (see above) remain unchanged;

(h)   that (since the date of the relevant search) the companies to which the opinion relates have not become subject to any type of insolvency procedure;

(i)   that no foreign law would affect the conclusions reached in the opinion;

and, if the opinion covers security documents:

(j)   that the bank had no notice of any prohibition or restriction on creating the security, or notice of any other security in the same assets;

(k)   that immediately after providing any guarantee (or other security), each obligor was fully solvent, and that the provision of the guarantee (or security) was in good faith, for the benefit of the obligor and did not constitute financial assistance.

The assumptions will also often be followed by a list of limitations, for example that the opinion is based solely upon the law of England and Wales, that no opinion is expressed as to the title of any obligor with respect to the secured assets, and that no opinion is expressed as to matters of fact.

16.5 Opinion

At this point the actual opinion appears, usually in the form of a series of numbered statements. The actual opinion will be quite short by comparison with the overall length of the letter: the vast majority of the paragraphs are assumptions and qualifications. The exact form of a legal opinion will be a matter for negotiation between the bank and its solicitor. It might relate only to the borrower and the facility agreement, or it might include some or all of the obligors and other transaction documents. However, for a straightforward domestic loan facility, the matters which are most commonly opined upon (either by the bank's, or sometimes the borrower's, solicitors) are as follows:

(a)   That the borrower was properly incorporated and is not in liquidation. If the loan is secured, the bank might want this opinion to cover any main obligors. In the USA, it is common to opine that a company is of 'good standing', meaning it has paid all due taxes and other substantial levies necessary for it to continue in business; however, this phrase has no technical meaning in English law.

(b)   The borrower has the requisite power to enter into and perform the facility agreement, and has taken any action necessary to authorise execution of the facility agreement. The first part is essentially a statement that borrowing under the facility agreement is intra vires for the borrower. Once again, this will occasionally be worded to include main obligors, with respect to their security. The second part covers any procedural matters which were necessary, such as board meetings. The opinion will usually assume that the necessary procedures were validly performed.

(c)   The execution, delivery and performance of the facility agreement will not contravene English law, any regulation applicable to companies (incorporated in England and Wales), and will not violate any provision of the borrower's memorandum and articles. This is essentially a declaration that the facility agreement is not illegal, is properly constituted so as to bind the borrower, and would be upheld in the courts if sued upon (although the remedy cannot be predicted with any certainty). Under English contract law, an agreement which is illegal at the time it is formed will not be enforced by the court. One of the functions of the legal opinion, therefore, is to ensure the loan documents are not illegal ab initio. The consequences of a contract which becomes illegal after execution can be dealt with in the contract itself (see **9.9.3**).

(d)   Payments made by the borrower will not be subject to UK taxes (ie, withholding tax), and no taxes are payable on execution or registration of the facility agreement. The implications of withholding tax and grossing-up provisions are dealt with at **9.3.4**. The second part refers primarily to stamp duty (the result of non-payment being non-enforceability of the document on which the stamp duty is due).

(e)   All necessary registration, filings, licences and consents have been obtained in order to validate the loan document. Some jurisdictions may impose exchange controls or other requirements. Almost all jurisdictions will have a registration system for non-possessory security.

16.6 Qualifications

The statements made in a legal opinion will never be unequivocal. They will always be subject to a number of qualifications or provisos. In a similar way to the disclosures against warranties (see **5.2.4**), the qualifications to an opinion allow the opining solicitor to modify general declarations. The most common qualifications are as follows:

(a) The validity, performance and enforcement of the facility agreement may be affected by insolvency proceedings (and similar processes). The opinion may give particular examples, such as the powers of administrators and administrative receivers under IA 1986 (as modified by the EA 2002), and the provisions for setting aside transactions at an undervalue and preferences under IA 1986, s 423 and ss 238–239 respectively.

(b) Any declaration in the opinion that the facility agreement is enforceable must be read on the basis that equitable remedies are at the discretion of the court (eg, specific performance and injunctions are not usually available if damages would be an adequate alternative).

(c) A provision purporting to create a fixed charge may be construed as creating a floating charge (see **14.7**).

(d) The enforcement of some security rights is controlled by law. For example, a mortgagee has duties to both the borrower and any prior mortgagees.

(e) Any claims under the loan may be affected by lapse of time (ie, under the Limitation Acts), by any rights of set-off or counter-claim. Provisions in the facility agreement absolving the bank of liability for default may not be effective in court.

(f) The opinion can only take account of the law of England and Wales.

(g) A court may refuse to entertain proceedings if a claim has been, or is being, brought elsewhere.

(h) Certain specific provisions may not be upheld by a court, most notably default interest (which may be declared penal – see **4.9**), provisions for severability (see **9.6**), and provisions requiring a borrower to pay the costs of litigation on enforcement. Evidence which might be held as conclusive under the facility agreement will not necessarily be acceptable to a court.

16.7 Conclusion

The examples of matters opined upon, and the assumptions and qualifications given above are designed to provide an idea of the areas commonly covered. All of these will vary between transactions depending on the nature of the loan, the documents involved in the transaction, any international aspects of the deal and the requirements of the bank. The format of most legal opinions will, however, closely follow that outlined above.

Finally, on the basis that it is a necessary expense in providing the loan, it is invariably the borrower who must pay the solicitor's fees for producing any opinions.

16.8 Further reading

Penn, Shea and Arora, *The Law and Practice of International Banking* (Banking Law vol 2) (2nd edn, Sweet & Maxwell, 2000).

Part III
CAPITAL MARKETS

Chapter 17

Introduction to International Capital Markets

'When investing money, the amount of interest you want should depend on whether you want to eat well or sleep well.'

Wall Street dictum

17.1 Introduction

The preceding two parts of this book have dealt with aspects of raising finance by way of a commercial loan. In certain circumstances, however, entities with substantial borrowing requirements may turn to a different source of funds known as the 'capital markets'. This part of the book introduces the capital markets, the most common instruments that are used to raise finance on those markets, and the process of issuing one such instrument, the eurobond.

17.2 What is a capital market?

17.2.1 Investment capital

A capital market is not a marketplace in the sense of a physical place, such as a trading floor with people waving their arms and trading in securities. It refers instead to the vast amount of capital available from financial institutions, pension funds and investment funds (and a few high-net-worth individuals) which want to buy securities, either to hold as an investment or to trade. References to the 'market' are more accurately references to the borrowing requirements of potential issuers, and the funds available from investors. The 'size' of a market refers to the amount of funds available from the participants and the tradeability of the securities issued. An 'illiquid' market means that the participants are unwilling to buy new or trade in issued securities.

The international capital markets are subject to an even more confusing array of terminology than commercial bank lending. The terms used in this section of the book are given their most common meaning, but different participants in the capital markets may have different terminology for the same thing or process, and no terminology should be thought of as definitive (eg, strictly speaking, commercial bank lending is a 'capital market', but colloquially the phrase refers to debt and equity securities only).

17.2.2 Comparing debt securities to loan facilities

There are some fundamental differences between raising money through the capital markets and borrowing by way of a loan facility. The main differences include:

(a) In a capital markets issue a borrower traditionally issues a document (or documents) evidencing the debt obligation (known as 'debt securities' or 'instruments') in return for the money it receives from lenders. The borrower is therefore known as the 'issuer'.

(b) Whilst the vast majority of loan facilities are (at least initially) provided by banks, a wide variety of institutions 'lend' by purchasing securities on the capital markets. The lenders in the capital markets are known as 'investors' (although they are not just investors in the traditional sense of holding on to the investment until it matures, but also speculators who buy securities hoping to sell them at a profit prior to their maturity).

(c) Since the potential number of investors is far greater than lenders offering commercial loans, the amount of funds available to an issuer is potentially much larger. This wide investor base allows a borrower's debt (and therefore any risk) to be spread among numerous 'investors'. Furthermore, the capital costs associated with most commercial loan facilities (see **9.3.2** and **9.3.3**) will not apply to capital markets investors. These factors help reduce the cost of raising money on capital markets.

(d) **Chapter 10** explained how loan facilities can be sold, but despite the advent of the LMA most 'asset sales' have a limited market. In contrast, the capital markets are well established and geared towards the relatively quick and simple trading of debt. The ability to sell securities easily and quickly provides liquidity to the market: more investors are prepared to buy knowing that they can sell prior to maturity and realise their capital if necessary. The liquidity of the market means investors are prepared to accept lower yields, which reduces the cost of borrowing for the issuer.

(e) The more extensive market means that the size and maturities of the debt can be more varied than for most commercial loans. An investor can usually invest in smaller 'participations' in a capital markets issue than in a loan facility. Certain debt securities can be significantly longer term than commercial loans, for example 30-year Gilt-edged securities (government bonds).

(f) A listed eurobond issue inevitably involves 'publicity', whereas a syndicated loan can remain confidential (so, eg, takeover bids are sometimes financed through a commercial loan).

(g) Generally speaking, the undertakings and events of default in the terms and conditions of capital markets securities are less onerous and restrictive than in a facility agreement. There is no specific relationship bank monitoring compliance with wide-ranging financial covenants as there would be in a loan facility, although a trustee will have a basic role of overseeing standard undertakings (see **19.2.4**).

17.3 Domestic and euromarkets

Capital markets may be either 'domestic' markets, or 'euro' markets (also known as international markets).

17.3.1   Domestic markets

A 'domestic' market is the market in a currency in its country of origin. Raising sterling in the UK, euros in France or US dollars in the United States are all examples of using domestic markets. When currencies are raised in their domestic markets, they are usually subject to control by that country's central bank or relevant central monetary authority (eg, the FSA and the Bank of England in the UK, or the Securities Exchange Commission and Federal Reserve Bank in the USA). The largest domestic capital market is the USA.

17.3.2   Euromarkets

17.3.2.1   The meaning of 'euro'

'Euro' is a prefix used very frequently in capital markets terminology: there are 'eurobonds', 'euronotes' and 'eurocurrencies'. 'Euro' does not imply the involvement of European currencies, money deposited in Europe or, indeed, necessarily indicate any 'European' connection. The term 'euro' simply refers to a currency held outside the currency's country of origin. (Note that the 'euro' prefix is market jargon, but will not appear on the face of the instrument.)

17.3.2.2   Eurocurrencies

Imagine a large UK exporter, such as Jaguar cars, which receives several millions of US dollars every year in payment for the cars it sells in the USA. If Jaguar invests those dollars outside their country of origin (eg, in an issue of securities in the UK) they are 'eurodollars'. There is a large number of exporters in this country earning currencies from all over the world, as well as many financial institutions which find themselves holding foreign currencies as a result of various transactions (these are sometimes known colloquially as currencies 'on holiday'). In London, therefore, as in any financial centre of a country which has a modicum of international trade, there is ownership of a large pool of the most common foreign currencies. The organisations owning these currencies will invest them by lending them to other institutions which require dollars, yen, sterling, etc. This creates the eurocurrency market.

17.3.2.3   Eurosecurities

Securities issued to attract the pool of eurocurrencies are known as 'euro' securities or, sometimes, 'international securities'. For example, if Tesco plc issues dollar denominated bonds in London, they are 'eurobonds'. (Note, however, that a bond issued in London to raise sterling from *overseas* investors (rather than *domestic* investors) may also be regarded as a eurobond.) The two most common forms of securities found in the euromarkets are eurobonds (or euronotes) and medium term notes (see **17.6.1**). The euromarkets have 'globalised' the world's capital markets (they are often called the 'international markets'), providing an issuer with access to a much greater source of funds than in its domestic market alone. Any currency which is held outside its 'natural' country in sufficient quantity is likely to be targeted by the euromarkets.

17.3.2.4   Why use eurocurrencies?

Why should an issuer be particularly interested in the eurocurrency markets? What is wrong with borrowing dollars from US investors, or yen from the Japanese? Why do institutions keep foreign currency to invest instead of exchanging it for the currency of their own country? The answer to these questions lies within the origins of the euromarkets. In the late 1960s and early

1970s, the US Government put strict controls on interest rates and levied taxes on non-nationals issuing bonds in the USA (a form of exchange control). Investors avoided the interest rate restrictions by lending dollars outside the USA, and companies issued dollar denominated bonds outside the USA to avoid the US Government tax. The dollar and other euromarkets evolved, therefore, because they were immune to any domestic restrictions. Today, there are fewer domestic controls, and eurocurrencies are no longer 'refugees' from monetary restraints. However, having established an abundant (and therefore relatively cheap) source of funds, the euromarkets continue to flourish. Even if, for example, a borrower does not require koruna, it will often be cheaper, and easier, to issue koruna eurobonds and exchange the eurodollars into a currency it requires, than to borrow that currency direct.

Czech koruna broadens eurobond currency base

By Conner Middelmann

The Czech koruna is the latest newcomer to the growing range of currencies in which borrowers can tap the eurobond market, and observers say other eastern European currencies could lure borrowers in the coming months.

General Electric Credit Corporation last Friday inaugurated the Czech koruna sector with a Kc2bn ($76m) issue of 10.5 per cent three-year bonds via Merrill Lynch.

That issue was followed yesterday by Kc1.5bn of 10.625 per cent five-year bonds for the Nordic Investment Bank, via Bayerische Vereinsbank.

Both issues, which can be settled through Euroclear, are targeted largely at continental European retail investors keen on juicy yields and not particularly worried about currency risk, but also at institutional investors, some of whom are already involved in the domestic Czech bond market.

"Expectations of currency stability, as well as prospects for declining interest rates there, indicate that now is a good time to lock in high rates on triple-A rated paper," said a trader involved in the NIB deal.

From 1991 the Czech koruna has been pegged to a basket of currencies; since 1993 the bas-

ket has been 35 per cent US dollars and 65 per cent D-Marks.

On September 26, the Czech parliament passed a foreign exchange law enshrining full convertibility for current account transactions and significantly liberalising capital account transactions. This is likely to pave the way for OECD membership, which is expected to be announced by year-end.

"The convertibility of the currency has opened the eurobond market, and other issuers are now looking at this sector," said another trader.

Merrill Lynch, the US investment bank which has long been an active player in the domestic Czech market, is one of the entities rumoured to be planning a euro-koruna issue, as are some supranational borrowers, such as the European Investment Bank and the European Bank for Reconstruction and Development.

Among possible candidates for future euro-koruna issues are foreign companies seeking to fund their operations in the Czech Republic more cheaply than they can in the local banking system, says Mr Rupert Harrison, syndicate manager at Citibank.

Alternatively, he says, issuers with no natural need for koruna could swap it into

other currencies to obtain funds at advantageous rates.

Indeed, this is what attracted the NIB to the sector. "We tapped the market mainly for arbitrage reasons," says Mr Jan Lund Sorensen, the bank's funding officer, who declined to say how the proceeds were swapped.

"The NIB has always had an opportunistic way of approaching capital markets – it has moved very quickly into new markets which offer attractive funding." Moreover, issuing bonds in koruna has allowed the bank to diversify its funding base, he says.

However, dealers warn that the koruna swap market is quite illiquid and could limit arbitrage-driven deals. "You have to work very hard to bring counterparties together," says Mr Harrison at Citibank.

Other convertible currencies in the region, such as the Estonian kroon or the Latvian lat, are now being eyed as potential eurobond currencies and some foreign entities have already tapped these countries' domestic markets in unswapped transactions.

Finnish bank Postipankki and the NIB recently issued Estonian kroon bonds, and McDonalds Polska, the Polish subsidiary of the US fast-food chain, has just issued 14m zlotys of three-year bonds.

Source: *Financial Times*.

17.3.2.5 'Foreign' securities

A eurocurrency instrument taps into money which is held outside of its country of origin. This is not the same as tapping into money held outside the *issuer's* country. For example, if a German company issues sterling securities in Germany (or France, Switzerland, Japan, etc – ie anywhere outside the UK) it is a 'euro' issue, since it is aimed at sterling owned outside the UK. However, if a *non-British* company issues a sterling instrument (to 'domestic' investors) in the UK, this will raise currency in its country of origin, and so it is not a 'euro' issue but rather a 'foreign' issue. Foreign issues are known in the markets by highly colloquial names: an instrument issued by a non-British company in the UK to raise sterling from the UK domestic market is known as a 'bulldog'. Likewise, if a foreign company issues a dollar instrument in the US domestic market it is known as a 'yankee', and a yen instrument in Japan raising local yen is a 'samurai', etc.

17.4 Debt and equity securities

'Securities' were defined at **12.7** as instruments in which a borrower (or more accurately an 'issuer') acknowledges a debt or an investment. The best-known securities are probably shares in listed companies which are traded on the stock market. Raising finance through share issues (known as 'equity' securities, since they provide equity in the issuer) is the subject of *Public Companies and Equity Finance*. This book is primarily concerned with debt securities which, in legal terms, are more similar to a straightforward debt obligation under a loan than to a share (although certain equity linked securities (see **17.5.5**) initially have the characteristics of a debt obligation but may be exchanged or converted into equity securities). There are a number of important differences between debt and equity securities.

17.4.1 Equity securities (eg, ordinary shares)

In general terms:

(a)   they are essentially a non-returnable investment. An investor can realise its investment capital only by selling the shares or winding up the company;

(b)   an investor has no absolute right to receive a return on its investment (a 'dividend');

(c)   an investor will rank behind all other creditors of the company (ie, those owed 'debts') in the event of a winding-up;

(d)   an investor will take equity (a share) in the issuer, and is usually (although not always) given the power to vote on major issues at shareholders' meetings.

17.4.2 Debt securities (eg, bonds)

In general terms:

(a)   the investment will have a maturity date on which the issuer must redeem the security by repaying the investor. Most debt securities are tradeable on established markets, allowing an investor easily and quickly to realise the capital value of the instrument prior to its maturity;

(b)   under the terms and conditions of the security it holds, an investor will have the right to receive a regular return on its investment (an interest payment or 'coupon'), or the investment may be issued at a 'discount' to its face value on redemption at maturity (see below);

(c)   the investment may occasionally be secured, although it will more commonly be unsecured and rank behind all secured and preferred creditors and pari passu with all other unsecured creditors (but ahead of the equity investors) in the event of the winding-up of the issuer;

(d)   with the exception of equity linked securities where the original debt obligation may be exchanged for equity (see **17.5.5**), an investor does not take any equity in the issuer, or have any rights over the issuer other than basic rights to call an event of default if coupon or principal are not paid or undertakings (which are very basic) are breached.

The following section explains the characteristics of the most common debt security structures found in the capital markets.

17.5   Bonds and notes

A bond is a certificate of debt under which the issuer obligates itself to pay the principal to the bondholder on a specified date, usually (there is no hard and fast rule) three years or more after the date of issue.

The main characteristics of a bond are:

(a)   it is a debt obligation (although some bonds may have conversion rights into equity) made by way of a transferable instrument (see **18.3.1**) with a medium- or long-term maturity;

(b)   initially, it is sold by way of marketing to a wide number of investors through a syndicate of financial institutions, or it is sold to a small group of specifically targeted investors (known as a 'private placement');

(c)   it is a marketable instrument (ie, it has an established secondary market);

(d)   it may or may not be listed on a recognised stock exchange (see **21.8**);

(e)   it will bear interest (usually payable semi-annually), or be issued at a discount to its face value on redemption.

Until relatively recently, the term 'note' was reserved for securities with a short maturity (eg less than three years) or with a floating rate coupon: everything else was a 'bond'. However, the terms are now almost interchangeable and 'note' is probably used more commonly than 'bond'. Confusingly, there are no written rules; the cognoscenti just know which terms are used in the market. As a rule of thumb you should refer to:

(a)   'floating rate notes', not 'floating rate bonds' (see **17.5.2**);

(b)   a 'global note', rather than a 'global bond' (see **18.2.1**);

(c)   securities issued under a programme as 'notes', not 'bonds' (see **17.6**);

(d)   securities issued under a securitisation as 'notes', not 'bonds'.

If in doubt, use the term 'note' rather than 'bond'.

Bonds are probably the most widely used debt security on the capital markets. They can take a number of different forms, the most common of which are explained below.

17.5.1   Fixed rate bonds

Many bonds are issued on a 'fixed rate' basis. This means that the rate of interest (known as the 'coupon': see **17.5.4**) they yield for the investor is fixed at the time of issue and will not change during the life of the bond. The interest is usually payable annually (or semi-annually in the case of some 'emerging markets' issuers) in arrear, an infrequent return on investment compared with most loan facilities. The rate of interest will depend primarily on the market conditions prevailing at the time of issue, the credit rating of the issuer (see **17.11**), and the length of maturity of the bond. The starting point of the interest calculation will be based on the rate offered at that time on a government security (eg, a treasury bill) of similar maturity. A margin will be added to reflect the issuer's creditworthiness and the maturity of the bond (the longer the maturity, the higher the interest rate, since investors must wait longer for the return of their capital), and the composite rate is then shown on the bond as a single figure. Fixed interest bonds without any special features are known as 'straight bonds' or 'plain vanilla bonds'

WORLD BOND PRICES

GLOBAL INVESTMENT GRADE

Aug 18	Red date	Coupon	S&P* Rating	Moody's Rating	Bid price	Bid yield	Day's chge yield	Mth's chge yield	Spread vs Govts
US $									
KFW	10/04	3.75	AAA	Aaa	100.2100	1.73	+0.29	-0.16	+0.35
IBRD	01/05	4.00	AAA	Aaa	100.8400	1.77	-0.02	-0.50	+0.03
Ford Motor Cr	02/06	6.88	BBB-	A3	105.2700	3.10	-0.03	-0.38	+0.68
Walt Disney	03/06	6.75	BBB+	Baa1	105.1000	3.47	-0.06	+0.26	+1.06
Morgan Stanley	04/06	6.10	A+	Aa3	105.5000	2.66	+0.01	-0.34	+0.24
American Elec	05/06	6.13	BBB	Baa3	105.3150	2.94	-	-0.35	+0.53
FHLMC	07/06	5.50	AAA	Aaa	105.3700	2.59	-0.01	-0.37	+0.18
Canada	11/08	5.25	AAA	Aaa	107.1100	3.41	+0.02	-0.34	+0.01
Wal Mart	08/09	6.88	AAA	Aa2	113.0500	3.95	+0.02	-0.31	+0.55
Du Pont	10/09	6.88	AA-	Aa3	112.6600	4.12	-0.03	-0.13	+0.75
Phillips Petr	05/10	8.75	A-	A3	119.5100	4.83	-	+0.20	+1.34
Unilever	11/10	7.13	A+	A1	115.2900	4.29	+0.03	-0.29	+0.88
Bank America	01/11	7.40	A	A3	114.8100	4.69	-0.04	-0.12	+1.32
JP Morgan	02/11	6.75	A	A2	111.1600	4.72	+0.02	-0.28	+1.31
France Telecom	03/11	8.75	BBB	Baa3	118.2000	5.18	-0.03	-0.32	+1.78
FNMA	03/31	6.75	AAA	Aaa	116.6400	5.55	-	-0.21	+0.52
Goldman Sachs	11/14	5.50	A+	Aa3	97.0500	5.88	-	-	+1.12
Italy	09/23	6.88	AA	Aa2	117.3700	5.41	+0.03	-0.19	+0.37
Pacific Bell	03/26	7.13	A+	A1	108.5950	6.39	+0.03	-0.11	+1.35
Lockheed	12/29	8.50	BBB	Baa2	126.9360	6.35	-	-0.03	+1.14
Daimler Chrysler	01/31	8.50	BBB	A3	120.2300	6.83	+0.02	-0.34	+1.80
FHLMC	03/31	6.75	AAA	Aaa	116.6400	5.55	-	-0.21	+0.52
GE Capital	03/32	6.75	AAA	Aaa	111.7400	5.88	-0.01	-0.94	+0.85
Gen Motors	11/31	8.00	BBB	A3	103.7600	7.67	-0.01	-0.19	+2.63
€									
Ford Motor Cr	08/04	4.88	BBB-	A3	100.0000	-	-4.65	-2.70	-
Vodafone Fin	09/04	4.88	A	A2	100.1200	2.45	-0.18	-0.14	+0.38
Rabobank	10/04	4.75	AAA	Aaa	100.3500	2.14	-0.01	-0.11	+0.10
L Rentenbank	01/05	4.13	AAA	Aaa	100.7700	2.23	+0.02	-0.02	+0.13
BNG	04/05	5.00	AAA	Aaa	101.7600	2.30	+0.01	-0.08	+0.20
BASF	07/05	5.75	AA-	Aa3	103.0400	2.37	-0.01	-0.14	+0.16
Deutsche Telec	07/06	6.38	BBB+	Baa3	106.1500	2.96	-0.04	-0.17	+0.50
Eurohypo	02/07	4.00	AAA	Aaa	102.8630	2.77	-	-0.23	-0.05
Depfa Pfandrbnk	01/09	3.75	AAA	Aaa	101.7030	3.32	+0.01	-0.25	-0.04
Mannesman Fin	05/09	4.75	A	A2	104.6900	3.68	+0.02	-0.29	+0.29
Deutsche Fin	07/09	4.25	AA-	Aa3	103.1000	3.55	-	-0.29	+0.19
Repsol Int Fin	05/10	6.00	BBB	Baa2	109.3800	4.12	-0.01	-0.27	+0.61
Elec de France	10/10	5.75	AA-	Aaa	110.4100	3.82	-	-0.24	+0.15
HVB	09/11	5.00	n/a	Aa3	106.4710	3.93	+0.01	-0.24	+0.25
YEN									
Nippon Teleg	03/06	3.35	AA-	Aa2	105.0204	0.15	-0.02	-0.05	-
Tokyo Elec	11/06	2.80	AA-	Aa3	105.7281	0.26	-0.02	-0.05	-
Toyota Motor	06/08	0.75	AAA	Aaa	100.8000	0.54	-0.02	-0.09	+0.02
KFW Int Fin	03/10	1.75	AAA	Aaa	104.8800	0.85	-0.03	-0.15	-0.08
Chubu Elec	07/15	3.40	AA-	Aa3	116.3511	1.64	-0.03	-0.20	-
£									
Gen Elec Cap	05/05	5.75	AAA	Aaa	100.5100	4.95	-0.04	-0.09	-0.08
DaimlerChrysler	12/06	7.50	BBB	A3	103.9800	5.50	-0.06	-0.25	+0.68
Halifax	04/08	6.38	AA	Aa2	103.0800	5.33	-0.07	-0.23	+0.43
Boots	05/09	5.50	n/a	A1	99.4300	5.56	-0.02	-0.16	+0.63
France Telecom	03/11	8.25	BBB	Baa3	110.3400	6.30	-0.01	-0.22	+1.35

US $ denominated bonds NY latest; all other London closing. * Standard & Poor's.   Source: Reuters.

BENCHMARK GOVERNMENT BONDS

Aug 18	Red Date	Coupon	Bid Price	Bid Yield	Day chg yield	Wk chg yield	Month chg yld	Year chg yld
Australia	11/06	6.75	103.2110	5.20	-0.06	-0.06	-0.07	+0.35
	04/15	6.25	105.2330	5.59	-0.03	-0.01	-0.11	+0.12
Austria	07/06	5.88	106.1600	2.50	+0.01	-0.03	-0.23	-0.19
	07/14	4.30	101.2800	4.14	+0.02	-0.01	-0.21	-0.09
Belgium	09/05	4.75	102.7000	2.23	-	-0.03	-0.16	-0.49
	09/14	4.25	100.6750	4.17	+0.01	-0.01	-0.21	-0.08
Canada	06/06	3.00	100.0320	2.98	+0.01	+0.03	-0.23	-
	06/13	5.25	104.4570	4.63	+0.04	+0.04	-0.16	-0.19
Denmark	11/06	3.00	100.5400	2.74	-	-0.04	-0.22	-0.16
	11/15	4.00	96.1700	4.44	+0.02	-0.02	-0.22	+0.08
Finland	07/06	2.75	100.5100	2.46	-	-0.03	-0.22	-0.47
	07/15	4.25	100.5100	4.19	+0.02	-0.01	-0.20	-
France	07/06	4.50	103.6600	2.50	+0.01	-	-0.21	-0.11
	07/09	3.50	100.6000	3.36	+0.01	-0.02	-0.25	-0.15
	04/14	4.00	99.1600	4.11	+0.03	-	-0.20	-0.07
	04/35	4.75	99.6000	4.77	+0.01	-	-0.18	-0.11
Germany	06/06	2.75	100.5200	2.45	+0.01	-0.02	-0.23	-0.13
	04/09	3.25	99.8200	3.29	+0.02	-0.01	-0.25	-0.16
	07/14	4.25	101.3100	4.08	+0.01	-0.01	-0.21	-0.10
	07/34	4.75	100.0700	4.75	+0.02	+0.01	-0.17	-0.12
Greece	06/07	3.25	100.9760	2.87	-	-0.03	-0.23	-0.13
	05/14	4.50	101.7950	4.26	+0.01	-0.01	-0.22	-0.04
Ireland	10/07	4.25	104.0000	2.90	-	-0.03	-0.24	-0.44
	04/13	5.00	107.2950	3.98	+0.01	-0.02	-0.23	-0.20
Italy	09/06	2.75	100.3390	2.59	-	-0.02	-0.22	-0.06
	04/09	3.00	98.4600	3.39	+0.02	+0.14	-0.09	-0.07
	08/14	4.25	100.2100	4.27	+0.02	-0.01	-0.21	-0.05
	08/34	5.00	101.0100	5.00	+0.02	+0.01	-0.17	-0.08
Japan	09/06	3.20	106.2920	0.16	-0.01	-0.05	-0.05	-0.05
	09/09	1.80	105.3950	0.70	-0.03	-0.09	-0.14	+0.02
	06/14	1.90	102.8520	1.57	-0.03	-0.10	-0.21	+0.13
	06/24	2.40	103.2600	2.17	-0.04	-0.09	-0.21	+0.19
Netherlands	07/06	3.00	100.9100	2.54	+0.01	-0.03	-0.22	-0.14
	07/14	3.75	96.8500	4.14	+0.02	-0.01	-0.21	-0.06
New Zealand	02/06	6.50	100.4600	6.17	-0.04	-	+0.12	+0.89
	04/13	6.50	101.8700	6.22	-0.06	-0.01	+0.05	+0.32
Norway	05/09	5.50	108.1700	3.59	-0.05	+0.09	-0.24	+0.42
	05/15	5.00	105.2000	4.38	-0.03	+0.12	-0.18	-0.63
Portugal	07/06	3.00	100.8790	2.52	-	-0.03	-0.21	-0.21
	06/14	4.38	101.6200	4.17	+0.02	-0.01	-0.22	-0.12
Spain	10/06	4.80	104.6300	2.59	+0.01	-0.02	-0.22	-
	07/14	4.75	105.1850	4.10	+0.01	-0.01	-0.22	-0.10
Sweden	04/06	3.50	101.3030	2.68	-0.02	-0.04	-0.21	-0.97
	05/14	6.75	118.5950	4.36	-0.01	-0.03	-0.22	-0.39
Switzerland	04/06	4.50	105.5500	1.04	+0.02	+0.07	-0.18	+0.87
	01/14	4.25	113.4000	2.62	-0.04	-0.03	-0.20	-0.02
UK	12/05	8.50	104.6700	4.75	-0.02	-0.02	-0.08	+1.21
	12/09	5.75	103.7900	4.93	-0.02	-0.06	-0.18	+0.57
	09/14	5.00	100.3900	4.95	-0.01	-0.03	-0.18	+0.38
	06/32	4.25	93.2900	4.68	-0.02	-0.02	-0.18	-0.02
US	07/06	2.75	100.6406	2.41	-	-0.09	-0.28	+0.61
	08/09	3.50	100.4336	3.40	+0.01	-0.08	-0.33	+0.06
	08/14	4.25	100.1719	4.23	+0.02	-0.04	-0.26	-0.21
	02/31	5.38	104.9609	5.03	+0.02	-0.03	-0.19	-0.26

London close. New York closing.   Source: Reuters.
Yields: Local market standard Annualised yield basis. Yields shown for Italy exclude withholding tax at 12.5 per cent payable by non residents.

HIGH YIELD & EMERGING MARKET BONDS

Aug 18	Red date	Coupon	S&P* Rating	Moody's Rating	Bid price	Bid yield	Day's chge yield	Mth's chge yield	Spread vs US
HIGH YIELD: US$									
Tyumen Oil	11/07	11.00	BB-	n/a	111.5000	6.93	+0.12	-0.43	+4.12

17.5.2 Floating rate notes

Floating rate notes ('FRNs') pay interest which fluctuates in accordance with a variable benchmark rate, which (if it is issued in London) is usually the LIBOR (see **4.9**) for the currency in which the bond is issued. The interest rate payable on the FRN is the benchmark rate plus a margin (in a similar way to floating rate loan facilities – see **4.9**), for example US$ LIBOR plus 50 basis points (0.5%). The rate is recalculated each time the interest is paid in order to reflect the then current benchmark rate. FRNs will usually pay interest more frequently than fixed rate bonds (eg, quarterly) in order to reflect the changing market rate.

FRNs appeal to issuers such as financial institutions which lend at a floating rate and so want to borrow at a floating rate to achieve 'matched funding' (ie, when the interest rate falls, they will receive less money from their lending, but will also be paying less for their borrowing).

17.5.2.1 Reverse FRNs

Under a reverse FRN, the interest rate payable on the bond rises or falls in the opposite direction to a benchmark level of market interest rates. This type of bond might appeal to investors who believe that general interest rates are likely to fall from the current level and want to speculate. Alternatively, they may be used to hedge an exposure that an investor has in a particular currency.

17.5.3 Variable rate bonds

Some bonds have a rate of interest which varies throughout their term, although, unlike FRNs, the rate does not vary freely in accordance with an underlying benchmark. Under a variable rate bond, the variation of interest rates is restricted, or is designed to alter in accordance with a pre-determined schedule. This type of bond can be structured in a variety of ways.

17.5.3.1 'Step-up' or 'step-down' bonds

In a 'step-up' bond, the initial fixed interest rate moves up to another (pre-determined) fixed rate after a given time. For example, a 10-year bond with a fixed rate of 3% for the first five years and 5% for the remaining five years (there may be more than one step). In a 'step-down' bond, the interest rate reduces rather than increases.

17.5.3.2 Collars

A bond which is subject to a 'collar' is similar to an FRN in that its rate of interest will vary in accordance with a benchmark rate (eg, LIBOR); however, the rate of interest payable is subject to an upper a and lower limit. These limits are known as the 'cap' and 'floor' respectively, and turn the underlying FRN into a variable rate bond. The advantages of a collar are that it guarantees a minimum return for the investor, and a maximum outlay for the issuer.

17.5.4 Zero coupon bonds

Zero coupon bonds do not pay any interest. The term 'coupon' refers to the interest on a bond and is derived from the fact that interest on definitive bearer bonds is claimed by tearing off perforated coupons at the side of the bond instrument and presenting them for payment. It might be thought strange that any investor would purchase an instrument which bears no interest. However, the amount which the investor pays for a zero coupon bond on its issue is less than its face value (ie, the value printed on the bond) on redemption. The bond is said to be issued at a 'discount' (a bond issued at substantially less than its face value is known as a 'deep discount bond'). The investor's return is achieved on maturity, when the issuer will redeem the bond at its face value.

> #### Example
> Imagine that an instrument with a face value of $100, and a maturity of 12 months, is sold on issue at a discount of 10%, ie at $90. On maturity, one year later, the investor can claim $100 from the issuer. The investor will have made a return of $10 on a one-year investment of $90 – equivalent to an interest rate of a little over 11%.

The investor's return is represented by the difference between the cost of the bond at issue and its value when redeemed, spread over the term of the bond. There is therefore a gradual appreciation in the amount for which the bond might be sold as the date of maturity becomes closer. The investor can therefore make a partial return on its investment even if it sells the bond before it matures. The size of discount given on the issue of a zero coupon bond will reflect the return available to an investor purchasing interest-bearing bonds at the same time as the issue of the zero coupon bond (otherwise the bonds would not be attractive to investors). Furthermore, as interest rates fall, the price of a zero coupon bond already in issue will rise since the yield it offers to maturity can be lower yet still compete with equivalent interest-bearing bonds. Zero coupon bonds are usually favoured by investors who prefer to be taxed on a capital gain than on income.

17.5.5   Equity linked bonds

Although this section of the book is focusing on debt instruments, it is important to recognise that some bonds are linked to the equity (ie, the share capital) of the issuer. These are known as 'equity linked bonds' and they provide an investor with the opportunity to obtain some form of equity interest in the issuer (in which case the issuer must clearly be a company), or a related company. There are three main types of equity linked bond:

(a)   convertible bonds;

(b)   bonds with warrants; and

(c)   exchangeable bonds.

The typical characteristics of these instruments are explained below.

17.5.5.1   Convertible bonds

Convertible bonds provide the bondholder with an option to convert (or sometimes the issuer with an option to force conversion of) the bond into shares in the issuer, at some stage after issue. The bondholder's option to convert usually exists throughout the life of the bond. However, the bond may include a condition that the option is available only during a specific period, or expires after a given date.

Once a bondholder converts, the issuer will create new shares to be given in exchange for the bond, which is then redeemed in consideration for the issue of shares (thereby extinguishing the debt obligation of the issuer). The directors may therefore need to increase the authorised share capital (requiring shareholder authority – CA 1985, s 121(2)(a)); they will require authority to allot the new shares (either through shareholder approval, or under the articles of association – CA 1985, s 80); and, since the new shares are effectively issued for cash consideration, the existing shareholders may have pre-emption rights to be disapplied (under CA 1985, ss 89–95).

A convertible bond will also specify the 'conversion price'. This is the price at which the shares a bondholder receives in exchange for its bond will be valued upon conversion. For example, if the bondholder converts its convertible bonds with a total face value of $10,000 at a conversion price of $25 per share, it will receive 400 shares. The conversion price of the shares is invariably higher than their market value at the time the convertible bond is issued. The difference between the two is known as the 'conversion premium'.

The main attraction of convertible bonds from an investor's point of view is that they provide a potential high return with a limited risk. The bondholder may be happy simply to retain the steady fixed income from the unconverted bond (although this will usually be less than a similar non-convertible bond issued at the same time), particularly if the issuer appears to have a policy of not paying dividends. However, if the issuer performs well, the bondholder can take advantage of any resultant rise in its share price by exercising its conversion rights and selling some or all of the shares it has received on conversion.

From an issuer's perspective, the interest rate it must offer on a convertible bond will be less than an equivalent non-convertible bond, due to the added attraction of convertibility. The convertible bond also allows an issuer effectively to defer equity financing if it feels that its share price is currently undervalued and is therefore reluctant to raise equity finance at that time.

17.5.5.2 Bonds with warrants

Bonds with warrants are bonds which are issued as two securities: an interest-bearing security (the 'bond'), and an option to purchase shares in the issuer which can be exercised by the bondholder (the 'warrants'). The bond element will pay a fixed rate of interest and have a specified maturity, and will always remain as a debt obligation whether or not the warrants are exercised. The warrants provide the bondholder with a right to buy shares at a pre-determined price, either within a specified time period (a 'narrow exercise period', found in most European-style warrants), or at any time (a 'wide exercise period', found in US-style warrants).

The warrants are intended to provide an incentive for investors to purchase the bond and also allow the issuer to have a lower coupon (as for convertibles – see **17.5.5.1**). The warrants are detachable instruments, allowing a bondholder to trade them (as a right to buy shares in the issuer) separately from the bonds. Like convertible bonds, bonds with warrants are, to some degree, a speculative investment since the value of the right to take equity depends on the future market value of the issuer's shares.

17.5.5.3 Exchangeable bonds

Exchangeable bonds are similar in nature to convertible bonds, sharing the characteristics of an option to convert the debt into an equity interest. The difference is that the shares for which the bond can be exchanged are not shares in the issuer of the bonds but shares in a related company, such as a parent or subsidiary. Exchangeable bonds are less common than convertible bonds.

17.5.5.4 Conclusion

Equity linked bonds are debt instruments when they are issued and do not confer any 'shareholder' type rights on the investor until such time as the debt instrument converts or changes, in accordance with its terms and conditions, into some form of equity instrument.

17.6 Other debt securities

17.6.1 Medium term notes

Medium term notes (usually referred to as 'MTNs') are very similar in form to bonds or FRNs, other than the way in which they are issued. Bonds and FRNs are usually issued as a 'one off' issue for that issuer (a 'stand-alone' issue), for example 5,000 bonds at US$10,000 each, with a five-year maturity to raise US$50,000,000 for ABC Plc: MTNs, however, are issued in several series (ie, separate sets of issues) through a 'programme'. Essentially, an MTN programme involves the issuer and an arranger agreeing a set of legal documentation under which the issuer can issue notes of varying currencies and maturities (usually between one and 30 years), and bearing fixed, floating or variable rates of interest. The MTN programme may provide that the notes are issued in either bearer or registered form; and if in bearer form, they may be held as global notes or in definitive form (see **18.2**). The agreed documentation will specify the terms and conditions of any series of notes which are issued, as well as provide an information memorandum to be used for selling the notes to investors (this will need updating periodically). The programme will state an initial aggregate amount which it intends to raise through the series of issues.

The programme will also appoint a number of 'dealers', one of whom (although not always the same one) acts as a lead manager to each separate issue of notes. The advantage of an MTN programme is that it allows an issuer to issue a wide variety of notes at very short notice (since the majority of the necessary documentation is already in place).

17.6.2 Commercial paper

Commercial paper is a type of security providing issuers (which include large companies, banks and building societies) with short-term borrowing in the capital markets. It is issued through a programme, in a similar way to MTNs. An entity wishing to issue commercial paper must first find a bank willing to set up a programme for an agreed maximum amount of borrowing. The bank will then usually appoint a number of dealers, who will be responsible for finding buyers for the commercial paper in return for a commission. Commercial paper issues are not usually underwritten (ie, there is no guarantee that an issue will be sold), but conversely the issuer is not under any obligation to issue.

Commercial paper is usually unsecured, sold at a discount rather than being interest bearing (for withholding tax reasons), may be issued with varying maturities and is almost always in global form (see **18.2.2**). Commercial paper is usually available in various maturities of up to 365 days, although in practice, maturities will often be just one or two months. When the issuer wants to raise money, the dealers will sell the requisite amount of commercial paper under the programme (the dealers will sometimes suggest to the issuer that it is a good time to issue paper of a certain maturity under the programme). Whilst the programme specifies a maximum amount of paper which may be issued, it is a 'rolling' maximum limiting the amount which can be outstanding at any one time. The British Bankers' Association produces guidelines for the London Commercial paper market specifying standards which are a pre-requisite for issuing paper in the UK.

17.6.3 Certificates of deposit

Certificates of deposit (known as 'CDs') are quite literally certificates (ie, receipts) issued by a bank or building society in return for a deposit of money made with them in the form of a loan. They are negotiable instruments issued in bearer form. CDs issued and payable in the UK (known as 'London CDs') usually have a maturity of no more than five years and may bear interest (which is more common), or be issued at a discount. The advantage to a lender of investing spare cash in a CD is that it receives a very good rate of interest (because the loan is not repayable until the CD matures), but it can recover capital at any time by selling the CD in the market. The issuer, meanwhile, has the advantage of a deposit which it knows is not repayable until maturity. CDs are unsecured obligations and, like commercial paper, any issue, if it is intended to trade in the London market, is bound to follow British Bankers' Association guidelines.

Gilts back in favour with £3bn issue covered twice

**By James Harding
and Graham Bowley**

Just one month after the Bank of England's failure to find enough buyers at its monthly auction of UK government bonds, gilts yesterday were back in favour.

The September gilts auction was uncovered for the first time in its history, but yesterday's £3bn issue of 20-year gilts with an 8 per cent coupon was almost twice covered, the highest level of investor interest since November 1991.

Last month, investors stayed away, concerned by the high level of UK government borrowing and worried by the prospects for European monetary union, which had upset currency and bond markets all across Europe.

While those anxieties linger, investors at yesterday's auction were attracted by a few exceptionally positive features: the high yields currently offered by gilts, recent signs of a slowdown in the UK economy and the appeal of rarely-offered long-dated paper.

The day of the uncovered auction, gilts shed 1 point and since then have remained subdued. While German and US bonds have rallied over the past month, gilts have lagged, with the 10-year yield spread over German bunds widening to close to 190 basis points earlier this week.

After yesterday's auction, gilts rallied by more than 1 point and the yield spread over bunds narrowed to 174 points.

The strength of investor demand startled City analysts, who had held their breath ahead of the auction fearing another failure, which would have sent prices plummeting.

"There was a sizeable feeling of relief," said Mr Ian Shepherdson of HSBC Markets, a leading UK gilt-edged market-maker. "It has shown that the appetite for UK government paper is still there."

The Bank of England's auction of UK government bonds was almost twice subscribed yesterday, the highest level of investor interest in long-dated gilts for almost four years. The success was in sharp contrast to last month's auction, when for the first time the Bank of England failed to sell all the bonds it was offering for sale.

At the latest auction, domestic and overseas investors were reassured by signs of slowing UK economic growth and by the high yields currently offered by gilts. Investors placed bids worth £5.99bn for the £3bn of 20-year gilts issued. Institutional investors such as pension funds and insurance companies were large buyers, since long-dated bonds are particularly useful for matching their long-term liabilities.

The auction was covered 1.99 times, against an expected cover of around 1.5 times. The yield tail – the difference between the yield at the average price and the yield at the lowest price – was zero, showing that the Bank of England did not have to drop the price in order to sell all the gilts. See Lex

A Bank of England official said the result "demonstrates the auction process is working well and keeps the government's funding on track".

Analysts pointed to three reasons for the success.

First, gilts had fallen significantly since the last auction. Mr Peter Moore of AMP Asset Management said: "The market was looking very attractive, with a sizeable spread over German bunds and the lowest gilt prices since the Tory leadership crisis."

Second, the auction came against a background of slower economic growth. Gross domestic product figures released this week and a Confederation of British Industry survey of manufacturers both gave a downbeat view.

Third, the 20-year stock on offer appealed strongly to institutional investors, which can use it to match their long-term liabilities.

The government can always bank on a high level of interest in long bonds, said Citibank's Mr Neil Mackinnon: "There is a natural demand at the long end of the yield curve."

If that was not enough, after September's poor auction, this month the Bank undertook a concerted marketing campaign to ensure that all the gilts would be sold.

Regardless of the good reasons to buy UK gilts yesterday, the worries about higher public borrowing have not gone away. Mr Andrew Roberts of UBS said the government still had around £20bn to raise in its funding from a total requirement for the year of £35.2bn and Mr Sanjay Joshi of Daiwa in London said concern surrounding excessive government debt may continue to dog the market in the run-up to forthcoming auctions.

"Three or four years ago, we used to trade lower in the run-up to the T-bill auctions and then higher through the auction. Trading in the UK is now likely to follow a similar pattern," says Mr Joshi.

In the more immediate future, some analysts expect bonds to hold the gains.

However, dealers reported that a large proportion of the gilts sold yesterday were taken up by only a few market players – in particular, large US and German houses which bought for their own proprietary trading.

"A lot of the stock found its way into relatively few hands," said Mr Thomas O'Shea, economist at Yamaichi.

This, they suggested, could weigh on market sentiment as these houses begin to offload some of these holdings.

Source: *Financial Times*.

17.6.4 Bills of exchange

A bill of exchange was, originally, simply an instrument recognising a trade debt. Rather than demanding immediate payment for goods, a seller draws up a document under which the buyer of the goods promises to pay for them after a specified period, such as three months. This form of credit is a 'trade bill of exchange'. Trade bills of exchange may be sold, at a discount, in the capital markets. Whilst the seller gets slightly less money than if he had waited for the buyer to pay under the trade bill, he gets the money earlier. Some bills of exchange will have payment of the amount due under them guaranteed (or 'accepted') by a bank. These are known as 'bank bills' or 'accepted bills'. Because they carry less risk of non-repayment, accepted bills will be sold at a higher price (ie, less discount) than identical non-accepted trade bills.

Accepted bills also provide large companies with a form of very short-term finance. A company can establish an agreement with a bank allowing it to issue bills of exchange (up to an aggregate amount) which the bank will 'accept' (ie, undertake the payment obligations) in return for a fee. This is known as an 'acceptance credit facility': there is no underlying trade debt. The company can then sell the accepted bills to raise short-term money.

17.6.5 Treasury bills

Treasury bills are capital markets instruments which work in a similar way to bills of exchange and are used by governments for short-term borrowing in order to balance their cash flow. In London, the Government auctions treasury bills to banks and other financial institutions every Friday. The treasury bills do not bear interest, but are sold at a discount.

17.7 Primary and secondary markets

When a security is issued, it is offered on what is known as the 'primary market'. The primary market involves the sale of securities by an issuer to investors in order for the issuer to raise the money it requires. If the investor holds the security until it matures, the transaction will have been confined to the primary market. However, most investors will want the ability to sell a security before it matures, allowing them to realise its capital value early. This is known as the 'secondary market', in which investors and traders can buy and sell securities already in issue.

Certain investors will buy securities to hold as a 'long-term' investment, ie until the security matures. Other investors buy securities in order to 'play' the market, ie to sell them when their value rises. These investors may hold a selection (or 'book') of securities (in the same way as an equity investor holds a portfolio of shares in various companies), which they trade on the market (some financial institutions act as brokers, buying and selling securities on behalf of their client investors). These investors are generally known as 'traders'. An instrument with an established secondary market is usually known as a 'marketable instrument'.

Whilst an issuer usually has no direct part to play in it, the secondary market will have an effect on its ability to issue in the primary market. This is because one of the most important features of any security instrument, both at and after issue, is its marketability. Some of the factors affecting marketability include:

(a)   the identity of the issuer and its credit rating;

(b)   the type of security being issued;

(c)   the number of potential investors that can be offered the issue (ie, are there any regulatory or practical restrictions?).

Marketability may also be enhanced if the securities are listed on a regulated market. For example, many domestic and eurosecurities are listed on the London Stock Exchange which provides regulated information about the issuer (in the form of listing particulars). This encourages investors to take the securities on issue, and provides an indication of market interest and value of particular securities which is helpful in launching and pricing a new issue. Although the securities may be listed on a stock exchange, they may (particularly in the case of eurobonds) still be traded in the secondary market 'off exchange' (see **21.8.1**).

17.8   Clearing systems

17.8.1   What is a clearing system?

Some bonds will eventually be issued in a form (known as 'definitive' bearer form) in which the debt is represented by a paper certificate. Whilst this allows the bonds to be transferred easily, it also makes them vulnerable to theft or loss in the same way as bank notes. One way to minimise the risk involved with dealing in bearer bonds is to use a third party to hold the bond instruments securely and deal with any transfers (known as 'settlement' or 'clearing'). Specialised clearing systems therefore exist for the safekeeping and settlement, inter alia, of internationally traded debt securities. Using a clearing system avoids the need to handle bearer instruments that are being traded. There are a number of clearing systems worldwide which deal with the issue and transfer of bearer securities. However, in the international eurosecurities markets, there are two systems of paramount importance: the Euroclear system and the Clearstream Service which is part of the Deutsche Börse Group, commonly referred to as 'Euroclear' and 'Clearstream' (formerly known as 'Cedel').

Euroclear was created by Morgan Guaranty Trust Company of New York in 1968. It is now owned largely by 'user shareholders' with a core operation in Brussels and subsidiary operations in Paris, Amsterdam and London. Clearstream was created in 1970, operates primarily from Luxembourg and Frankfurt, and is now part of the Deutsche Börse Group.

17.8.2   Operation of the clearing systems

Euroclear and Clearstream are not confined to dealing with bonds. Both clearing systems will accept most common forms of securities which are actively traded in the international capital markets, for example bonds, notes, debenture stock, commercial paper, certain certificates of deposit (depending on their place of issue) and some types of shares. However, in order to explain the clearing systems' processes, this section concentrates on eurobond issues.

Euroclear and Clearstream operate in similar ways. Securities accepted by the clearing systems may be in definitive or global form (see **18.2.2**). The primary purpose of a clearing system is to avoid the physical handling of bearer instruments on issue and on subsequent trading. Therefore, the actual bond certificates (which may be in definitive bearer form or global form – see **18.2**) are invariably passed on to a bank known as a 'depositary' (see **19.2.7**) for safekeeping, and the clearing system works through a series of 'book entries' (akin to depositing cash with your bank and debiting your account to pay debts rather than withdrawing cash). In order to participate in a clearing system, an investor will have two accounts with the system (although some investors will use accounts held by their bank or broker who act as nominee for them):

(a)   a securities clearance account to and from which the securities are credited (the account does not usually allocate the holder specific bonds, ie the bonds in a particular issue are fungible); and

(b)   a cash account (like a current account) through which all payments from the sale or purchase of securities must pass.

Each issue of securities is allocated a unique code number, known as its ISIN (International Securities Identification Number), from which is derived the 'Common Code'. The Common Code is used as a label to identify the particular *issue* each time the clearing system is instructed to deal in securities, and it should not be mistaken for a security device, nor a way of identifying individual bonds within an issue (other issue identification numbers are sometimes seen, eg 'sedol' – used by the London Stock Exchange). If a bondholder wants to sell some bonds on the secondary market, it instructs the clearer, which reduces the seller's securities clearance account by the requisite number of securities and credits them to the securities clearance account of the purchaser. At the same time, the cash account of the purchaser is debited, and the cash account of the seller credited, to represent payment for the securities. Euroclear and Clearstream also allow trading between their two systems since each has securities and cash accounts with the other (this is known as the 'bridge').

Clearing systems have a function in both the primary and secondary markets. In the primary market, they will accept a new issue of bonds onto their systems, so long as it has complied with any regulations applicable to it (eg, selling restrictions – see **18.2.1**). On the closing date of a new issue, the requisite number of eurobonds will be credited to the securities clearance accounts of the syndicate members and can then be transferred to the accounts of the investors (see **21.10**).

The clearing systems also keep a record of interest payment dates and redemption dates for each issue, and will 'present' the securities for payment when appropriate. The bondholders therefore avoid the need to present the coupons or certificates themselves. The clearing systems will also act on investors' instructions with respect to any options or conversion rights which might be attached to the securities. The legal position of securities held in a clearing system is discussed in **Chapter 18**.

17.9 International Capital Markets Association

The International Capital Markets Association (ICMA) was formed in July 2005 by the merger of the International Primary Markets Association (IPMA) and the International Securities Markets Association (ISMA). ICMA is the association for financial institutions which play an active role, usually as managers underwriters and traders, in the eurobond primary and secondary markets. ICMA is a trade association, as opposed to a statutory body, created by participants in the international capital markets with a view to establishing recognised standards of market practice. Membership of ICMA brings a financial institution the status and recognition, from other institutions and issuers, necessary to take a major part in large euromarket deals. Members of ICMA include banks, members of recognised stock exchanges, licensed dealers in securities and affiliated organisations.

ICMA is a self-regulating body and the ultimate sanction for non-compliance with its recommendations is expulsion from the Association. In order to appreciate the gravity of expulsion, it is important to understand that the euromarket works with something of the aura of a 'members' club'. An institution which breaches ICMA rules will soon become known to other euromarket institutions, and they may become reluctant to deal with the offender. Persistent or serious breaches will eventually result in an offender being unable to raise a syndicate, and being left out of invitations to join other syndicates.

ICMA publishes, and periodically updates, recommendations to its members in relation to both debt and equity issues in the form of a handbook (non-members must comply with the recommendations if they hope to join the institution). The areas typically covered include the following:

(a)   The timing of a bond issue. In particular, ICMA regulates the time which must elapse between the various stages of the issuing process (eg, the minimum time which managers should be allowed to review documentation prepared by the lead manager – see **21.5**).

(b)   The minimum content of certain documents (eg, the invitation telex).

(c)   The timescale to be allowed for payment of fees and commissions to the managers.

These, and other ICMA regulations, are dealt with in more detail in **Chapter 19**, which explains the process of issuing a eurobond.

17.10   The issuers

The following types of entity use capital markets for raising money:

(a)   companies, including banks and financial institutions (recent examples include Volkswagen (€956m, average life 4.1 years), Nordic Investment Bank ($500m, due 2009), HBOS (£150m, due 2010);

(b)   governments/sovereign (ie, government-owned) entities (eg, Republic of Portugal (€3bn, due 2015), National Bank of Hungary (¥50bn, due 2009));

(c)   public authorities (eg, City of Berne (SFr 180m, due 2025);

(d)   supranationals (eg, the European Investment Bank (€75m, due 2030)).

Each entity will need the authority to issue bonds. English companies must be authorised in their memorandum and articles of association to issue debt securities; whilst governments and public bodies are likely to be authorised by statute or statutory instrument.

17.11   Credit rating

When an investor is deciding whether to purchase or make a particular investment, the most important factor affecting its decision is the risk of non-payment. The higher the risk that an issue may not be serviced or repaid, the greater the return an investor will demand. Some institutions, such as pension funds and investment funds, are limited by their constitution as to the risk they can take when investing their funds.

Investors in the international capital markets are particularly sensitive to risk, and most issuers and/or their individual debt security issues will therefore be given a credit rating. Official ratings for the euromarkets are provided by specialist independent rating organisations, the best known of which are the US firms, Moody's Investors Service, Standard and Poor's, and Fitch Ratings, Duff & Phelps. A credit rating is an opinion on the risk of default on payment, and will be based on a number of different factors, including an issuer's current financial statements, past and projected performance, management, market position and operating environment.

The ratings are split into two broad categories: 'investment grade' and 'speculative grade'. The range of Standard and Poor's long-term debt ratings (which are very similar to those used by Fitch), together with their brief explanation of each grade, are shown below.

Standard and Poor's ratings

AAA Highest rating, ability to repay interest and principal extremely strong.

AA   Very strong capacity to repay interest and principal.

A   Strong ability to pay, but somewhat susceptible to adverse economic conditions.

BBB Adequate capacity to repay debt, but more subject to bad economic conditions. Lowest investment-grade rating.

BB   Any debt rated this grade or below has significant speculative characteristics.

B   Has vulnerability to default but presently has the capacity to meet interest payments and principal repayments.

CCC Vulnerable to non-payment.

CC   Currently highly vulnerable to non-payment.

C   Typically in arrears on payment or liquidation petition filed, but payments still continuing.

D   Debt is in default.

Moody's ratings

Aaa Bonds of the best quality.

Aa

A

Baa Lowest form of investment grade.

Ba   Speculative elements.

B

Caa

Ca

C   Lowest rated class of bonds.

If a eurobond issue is to be individually rated, a rating will be assigned at launch of the issue (there is an appeals procedure for issuers who are unhappy with the proposed rating). The rating given to an issue is then periodically reviewed: if the risk has increased, the rating will fall (and vice versa). Ratings of issuers themselves are also periodically reviewed. A rating above the dotted line (ie, BBB or Baa) is known as 'investment grade', but anything below the line carries an increasing degree of speculation as to whether the issuer will be able to meet its obligations. To provide greater flexibility within their main gradings, Standard and Poor's may modify grades between AA to CCC by adding a + or – symbol to show relative standing within the main grade (eg, AA– or BBB+). Moody's achieve a similar effect by applying 'numerical modifiers', 1, 2, and 3 ('1' being better than '2', etc) to classifications between Aa and Caa inclusive (eg, A2 or Baa1).

Richard Lapper examines the downgrading of JP Morgan

The loss of an A shouldn't be the end of the world

J P Morgan's loss of its much vaunted triple A rating from Moody's, the US credit rating agency, is a blow to the pride of one of the world's biggest and most powerful banks.

Morgan was the last US bank to enjoy a top rating from Moody's as well as Standard & Poor's. The downgrading has raised few eyebrows, however, among bankers. In the immediate future, it seems likely to have only a minimal impact on the bank's business.

Moody's said the shift towards investment banking was responsible for the downgrade of Morgan's two US bank subsidiaries, Morgan Guaranty Trust Company and JP Morgan Delaware, to Aa1 from the top Aaa grade.

Earnings from capital markets activities such as equities and derivatives dealing are more volatile than those from corporate and retail banking, which Morgan has relied on. "The company's businesses are increasingly sensitive to the behaviour of global financial markets," Moody's said.

Yet Morgan is merely following industry trends. Over the past 10 years, competitive pressures have forced most of Morgan's international rivals in the same direction, leaving only a handful with triple A ratings from either Moody's, its biggest US rival, Standard & Poor's or IBCA, the London-based agency.

Morgan was one of a select band of blue chip institutions to enjoy a triple A rating from all three firms, sitting alongside Deutsche Bank, Union Bank of Switzerland, and Rabobank Nederland. The liabilities of four other German banks are guaranteed by their respective *länder*.

Since 1989, the average rating of the top 50 European banks has dropped by a notch from AA to AA-, according to S&P. Mr Barry Hancock, head of European financial institutions at S&P, expects the average to fall another notch before 2000.

The downgrade might be expected to have some impact on prof-itability. Banks with lower ratings generally find it more expensive to obtain credit lines in the interbank market. Bigger companies can sometimes be more reluctant to do business with them and strong ratings are frequently used by bank marketing departments to show their security. "In retail banking it is always an advantage, proof that your bank is a safe haven," says Mr Ian Linnell, analyst with S&P.

Most of all in the market for over-the-counter derivatives – in

CREME DE LA CREME

Banks with top credit ratings from IBCA, Moody's and S&P (by size)

1. Deutsche Bank
2. Union Bank of Switzerland
3. Bayerische Landesbank
4. Rabobank Nederland
5. Südwestdeutsche Landesbank
6. Landesbank Hessen-Thüringen
7. Landeskreditbank Baden-Württemberg

Source: Global Finance

which banks provide customised swaps and other deals for corporate customers and in which Morgan is a leading player – a triple A rating has been seen as a plus. In swaps transactions, especially longer dated currency and interest deals, which can cover a period of as much as 10 to 15 years, companies can assume significant exposures to their bank counterparties.

Since the early 1990s, a number of banks have set up special subsidiaries to handle derivatives transactions. These are "bankruptcy remote" – structured to give creditors a prior claim on assets in the event of the bank-ruptcy of the parent – and have been awarded triple A ratings by the agencies because they are relatively overcapitalised. "We certainly see a number of investment banks seeking to enhance their credit in this way," says Mr David Cannon, partner in Ernst & Young's international capital markets group in London. Yet he points out that most of the nine banks which formed such subsidiaries so far have lower ratings than Morgan. And although buyers – or "end users" in market jargon – might have insisted on a triple A rating for all deals five years ago, today they are more likely to be satisfied with a lower credit benchmark – AA or AA- from S&P or Aa2 or Aa3 from Moody's. "There were some people who had the triple A standard five years ago – I can't think of any today," one trader explained.

Dealers in the OTC market are also beginning to demand collateral from counterparties. So far this has been mainly restricted to deals between banks, but multilateral agencies are reported to have followed their example.

"The reality is there are so many ways that people come up with to modify credit risk through the use of collateral," points out Mr Paul Spraos, editor of Swaps Monitor, a specialist newsletter. Collateral arrangements are sometimes linked to the credit ratings of the parties involved, so that as its credits ratings fall a bank might be expected to place more collateral against its own exposure. Even so, Mr Spraos expects the impact on Morgan to be minimal. "I don't think it's that big a deal, although they may have to rewrite their publicity material."

Source: *Financial Times*.

S&P warns on revised capital adequacy rules

By Khozem Merchant

Standard & Poor's, the US credit rating agency, will warn today that proposals to improve international banking capital adequacy rules by the Basle committee of banking supervisors could lead to "perverse outcomes".

S&P's comments emerge in its first detailed response to the central bankers' recent paper on upgrading the 1988 accord on capital risk management.

The agency backs the Basle document but expresses caution in some key areas, notably preferential weightings for sovereigns.

"It is not clear why Basle chose to give sovereigns the best weighting and exercise little differentiation in the case of corporates. This is a concern," said Mike Destefano, managing director, S&P, and the author of the report.

"This lack of subtlety in ratings could have a powerful, adverse impact on the flow of funds."

S&P's paper is significant because the Basle proposal, published in June, controversially places greater reliance on external rating agencies.

At the heart of the Basle proposal is a more explicit linkage between the level of capital set aside for risky loans and a borrower's credit rating.

In the existing system the amount of capital set aside must equal at least 8 per cent of the bank's assets, weighted according to risk. For example, a mortgage is 50 per cent risk-weighted, requiring a provision of 4 per cent; a corporate is 100 per cent risk-weighted requiring a full provision of 8 per cent.

Critics have attacked the explicit linkage between capital set aside and the credit rating of a borrower. They say Basle hands too much power to rating agencies – which were widely criticised for failing to spot the onset of the Asian crisis in mid-1997 – without proposing how to regulate them.

S&P's paper, which is published today, endorses the Basle committee's call for greater bank disclosure, a more proactive regulatory stance and more explicit capital charges for interest rate and operating risk.

"If implemented in close to current form, the Basle proposal could lead to a strengthening of banks, especially in emerging markets," said Mr Destefano.

Besides co-opting rating agencies, the Basle committee identified two other ways of building on its framework for capital adequacy: allow banks to use their own internal credit scoring systems; and encourage the development of portfolio credit models.

S&P says the first option is impractical and would be limited to a small number of big banks. It would also be difficult for central bankers to compare different internal models. The second option it says is still in its infancy.

S&P also questions Basle's two methods of assessing banks.

The first, which "would discount the sovereign rating of the country in which a bank is located by one full grade", would penalise higher-rated banks, and help weaker ones.

The second option would be to use ratings on individual banks and give a 50 per cent weighting to unrated banks, which S&P says "at least has the merit of assessing banks individually".

S&P strongly rejects the idea of treating banks and securities houses on a par because the latter typically have higher risk commitments.

It says some of Basle's ideas might "introduce non-credit considerations into the weighting process", suggesting political interference. A case in point is leaving unchanged the rule whereby national authorities determine the weighting of local currency sovereign debt. Local currency defaults are rare, but as Russia's default on its domestic debt illustrated, the impact can be immense.

Source: *Financial Times*.

There is only a limited European market for bonds issued at below investment grade; indeed, the constitution of some types of financial institution will only allow them to invest in securities graded AA (or Aa) or above. Issues with a rating below 'Investment Grade' must try harder to attract investors, and so generally pay a higher coupon; hence, they are known as 'high yield' (or, in the 1980s, as 'junk bonds').

Credit ratings are not only available on fixed income securities: they are also provided for short-term investments, and even some syndicated loans.

17.12 Further reading

Valdez, *An Introduction to Global Financial Markets* (5th edn, Macmillan, 2006).

Chapter 18

The Forms and Legal Characteristics of a Bond

'Within three months – that's a month before this bond expires – I do expect
return of thrice three times the value of this bond.'

William Shakespeare, *The Merchant of Venice*

18.1 Introduction

Chapter 17 explained the concept of raising finance on the capital markets and
examined the characteristics and structures of various debt securities. The
remainder of this part of the book concentrates on bonds, since they are probably
the most common form of debt security issued on the capital markets. This
chapter explains the different forms which a bond may take during its life and
examines the legal characteristics of those forms.

18.2 The form of a bond

Most bonds will take a number of different forms from the time they are issued to
when they are redeemed. The usual forms are:

(a) temporary global form, followed by either:
    (i) permanent global form, or
    (ii) definitive form (which may be bearer or registered); or
(b) permanent global form from the outset.

18.2.1 Temporary global form

18.2.1.1 What is a temporary global note?

When a bond is first issued, it will almost certainly not be in the form of
certificates. The total debt obligation of the issuer will, instead, usually start life as
a single document known as a 'temporary global note'.

The temporary global note document is a wordprocessed document, prepared by
the lead manager's solicitor, and which represents all the bonds to be offered
under that particular issue. It will be executed by an authorised officer of the
issuer and 'authenticated' by the fiscal agent (or principal paying agent) (see **19.2**).
All the terms and conditions which apply to the bonds (see **19.4**) will be attached
to, or incorporated in, the temporary global note. The document will also have a
schedule attached to it on which the fiscal agent (or principal paying agent) can
record all exchanges of the temporary global note for definitive bonds, as well as
interest payments (if any) which are made during the life of the temporary global
note.

18.2.1.2   Why use a temporary global note?

As the name suggests, the temporary global note exists only for a short time. There are two reasons why bonds are initially issued as a single document in temporary global form.

Time constraints

Once an entity has decided to raise money through a bond issue, the process of issue will usually proceed relatively quickly. Many bond issues (in particular, eurobond issues) have a time scale of three to five weeks between launch (ie, when the offer is announced) and closing (ie, issue of the bonds). This timetable is primarily driven by market practice: issuing a bond is intended to be a relatively quick way for a borrower to raise finance, and the markets therefore have an expectation to fulfil (a short period between launch and issue also minimises the risk that the market moves and the price of the bonds becomes unattractive to potential investors). However, such a short timetable makes it difficult to complete the security printing and necessary 'authentication' of the certificates which represents the final definitive form of a bearer bond. Producing a temporary global note allows the issue to close, and be placed in a clearing system, before the final certificates are ready.

Selling restrictions

In order to understand the second reason for producing a bond in a temporary global form, it is necessary to appreciate the concept of 'selling restrictions'. Most jurisdictions impose restrictions on securities being offered or sold within that jurisdiction. Many of these restrictions are imposed on issues made to the public in order to protect unsophisticated investors. However, they may also be driven by policies of investment control or taxation (a detailed analysis of these restrictions is beyond the scope of this book).

In order to avoid contravening any restrictions which might apply to it, a bond will include contractual restrictions on the institutions selling the issue (the 'syndicate'). These are known as 'selling restrictions'. For example, the syndicate might be contractually prohibited from selling bonds to 'US persons' if this would require registration of the issue with the Securities Exchange Commission (an elaborate and costly procedure) (there are exceptions to these rules and procedures to follow in order to benefit from those exceptions, commonly known as 'safe harbours').

The most commonly applicable selling restrictions are those imposed under US tax and securities laws. Some of these require that definitive bonds cannot be delivered for a period (usually 40 days) after issue (known as a 'lock-up' period). More commonly, there will be a restricted period during which definitive bonds may be offered only to certain investors. In either case, the use of a temporary global note helps to ensure compliance with the restrictions.

18.2.2   Permanent global and definitive forms

Once any lock-up period expires, the temporary global note must be exchanged for either a permanent global note (as the name suggests, this is a permanent version of the temporary global note), or bonds in definitive form (in other words, separate certificates representing each bond).

18.2.2.1   Permanent global note

As with the temporary global note, this is a wordprocessed document (as opposed to being security printed) prepared by the lead manager's solicitor, and which represents all the bonds in issue. The permanent global note is issued on the closing date of the issue (see **21.10**), and is usually held by a bank known as the 'common depository' for safe-keeping on behalf of the clearing systems (but see 'New Global Notes' at **19.2.7**).

The main advantage of using a permanent global note rather than definitive bonds is cost, since the permanent global is not security printed. However, in circumstances where it is important to the investor that it has legal ownership of the debt obligation represented by the bond in which it has invested, an issuer cannot avoid providing the investor with definitive bonds. These circumstances are stated on the face of the permanent global notes. The most common are:

(a)   if any bondholder requires a definitive bond, in order to prove his legal entitlement to the bond in which he has invested, in connection with legal proceedings;

(b)   if the bondholder requires definitive forms in order to trade the bonds (ie, physically to deliver the bond certificates) because the clearing systems have for some reason ceased to operate, preventing trading through the clearing systems with reference to the global note; and

(c)   on or following a default.

When a bond is issued in permanent global form and held by the common depositary, the bondholders might potentially have problems in enforcing the debt against the issuer. This is because the legal owner of a bearer document is the person who physically holds the document. Even if the global note states that it is exchangeable for definitive bonds (providing the investor with legal ownership), the issuer may refuse to comply with that condition. There are various methods which practitioners use to avoid this problem. The first solution is to provide investors with direct rights of enforcement in the text of the global note itself, which is executed by the issuer. The second is for the issuer to execute a unilateral deed of covenant (a 'deed poll') in favour of the bondholders from time to time. This contains a declaration by the issuer to pay those persons shown as investors on the relevant accounts at the clearing systems, and provides a contractual link between the issuer and the investors on which an investor can sue the issuer for breach of the terms of the bonds. A third solution is to appoint a trustee to the issue which holds the issuer covenant to pay on trust for the bondholders: the trustee can then enforce on the bondholders' behalf.

18.2.2.2   Definitive form

A bond issued in 'definitive form' can be either a 'bearer' or 'registered' instrument.

Bearer bonds

The most familiar bearer instrument to most people is currency (eg, a £5 note), and bearer bonds share similar characteristics. They are security printed documents in order to make forgery very difficult, and the issuer's debt obligation is printed on the bond itself. Ownership of a bearer bond is transferred by physical delivery: the legal owner of a bearer bond, at least as far as the issuer and his agents are concerned, is the holder of the bond document. A bearer bond has the following basic features:

(a) *A promise to pay.* The face of the bond will include a simple statement to pay principal (and, if relevant, interest). For example:

I promise to pay the bearer $US10,000 on the 12th November 2012, in accordance with the terms and conditions contained herein.

The bearer bond will be signed by at least one officer of the issuer, although the signature is part of the security printing rather than being an original on each definitive bond instrument. However, each instrument is individually 'authenticated' (ie, signed) by the fiscal agent (or paying agent), and will not be valid until this is done.

(b) *Terms and conditions.* The terms and conditions of the bearer bond will be printed on the reverse of the bond itself, together with the addresses of the relevant paying agents. The main terms and conditions are reviewed in **Chapter 19**.

(c) *Coupons.* If the bond bears interest, coupons will be printed on the right-hand side of a bearer bond which must be torn off and surrendered to the paying agents in order to claim each interest payment as it falls due (the coupon is probably a bearer document itself). The name and address of the paying agents will be printed on the reverse side of each coupon.

(e) *Talons.* The maximum number of coupons which can be attached to a eurobond is 27 (under ICMA rules). If a bond carries more than 27 interest payment dates (eg, a bond paying semi-annual interest with a maturity of 14 years), it must attach a tear-off strip known as a 'talon' with the coupons. The talon will give the holder the right to claim a further sheet of coupons in relation to the remaining interest payments once all the coupons on the first sheet have been claimed.

Registered bonds

Registered bonds create a promise to pay the person whose name appears on a register of bondholders held by the issuer (or its agent for this purpose) rather than the holder of the actual bond certificate. Registered bonds can be transferred only by an entry on the register; title will not pass by physical delivery of the bond instrument. The terms and conditions of the bond will be printed on the reverse of the instrument.

Most eurobonds are issued in bearer form and registered eurobonds are rare. However, eurobond issues which are intended to be placed in the US but not registered with the Securities Exchange Commission are usually in registered form to take advantage of registration exemptions.

18.3   Legal nature of a eurobond

18.3.1   Transferability

In order to attract investors, the debt obligation of a bond must be easily transferable. Eurobonds will achieve transferability in one of two ways:

(a) creating the bond as a bearer instrument, allowing transfer by simple physical delivery. This is the most straightforward way to achieve transfer, although the vulnerability this creates means that bearer bonds will usually be traded through a clearing system; and

(b) making the bond a registrable instrument so that transfer is effected by a document of transfer and an entry on the register confirming that transfer has taken place (in a similar way to registered shares).

There is, however, an important legal difference between bearer bonds and registered bonds. Only bearer bonds are 'negotiable'.

18.3.2 Negotiability

Negotiability of a eurobond is of paramount importance in order to ensure that it is freely marketable (and should be distinguished from transferability or assignability (see **10.4.3**)).

18.3.2.1 Achieving negotiability

Eurobonds are, by their very nature, international instruments. In deciding on negotiability it will therefore first be necessary to decide which jurisdiction is applicable. Usually, the jurisdiction in which the 'negotiation' takes place is relevant: in the case of a eurobond this will be the place where the bond is delivered. In a conflict of laws situation, negotiable instruments are usually treated as chattels because the debt claim is represented by a tangible document rather than a simple 'book entry'.

Under English law, there are two ways in which negotiability can be achieved.

By statute

The Bills of Exchange Act 1882 confers negotiability on bills of exchange, promissory notes and cheques. However, the Act requires conditions as to amount and unconditionality of an instrument before they can be negotiable, and eurobonds invariably fall foul of those conditions (eg, a floating rate of interest or grossing-up provisions will make eurobonds 'uncertain' and therefore outside the provisions of the Act).

By mercantile custom

It is an established principle of English common law that an instrument can achieve negotiability simply because it is customarily treated as negotiable in the 'markets' in which it is usually traded. The financial community treats definitive bearer bonds (but not registered bonds) as negotiable, and therefore definitive bearer bonds have achieved negotiability by mercantile custom.

18.3.2.2 Consequences of negotiability

The consequences of negotiability work in favour of a transferee who purchases the bond bona fide, for value and without any actual notice of a defect in title (known as a 'holder in due course'). A negotiable bond purchased by a 'holder in due course' will have the following benefits:

(a)   the purchaser can obtain better title than the seller (eg, if the seller obtained the bond dishonestly);

(b)   the purchaser will take a clean legal title to the bond and is entitled to payment in full, notwithstanding any claims of set-off or other defence which the issuer may have had against any previous holder;

(c)   the purchaser can sue the issuer directly in the case of a dispute over the bond, and does not need to join the transferor in a claim (although a bond issued under a trust deed will usually give the trustee the power to act on behalf of the bondholders);

(d)   if a 'holder in due course' presents a stolen bond, the issuer must pay out on that bond as well as on any replacement bond it has issued to the original bondholder. Because of this risk, an issuer will not usually provide a replacement bond without first obtaining an indemnity from the original bondholder to the effect that he will recompense the issuer if it has to pay out on the original bond.

18.4 Comparing registered and bearer bonds

Having examined the legal consequences of negotiability, the differences between registered and bearer bonds can be examined.

18.4.1 Title

A bona fide purchaser for value without notice of a bearer bond can obtain better title than the seller; but the purchaser of a registered bond, which is not a negotiable instrument, will not obtain good title if the seller stole the bond certificate and was able to obtain a transfer in the register.

18.4.2 Claims and defences of an issuer

Negotiable bearer bonds will always be sold free from any claim the issuer might have against a previous holder. The purchaser of a registered bond is, in principle at least (although this may be varied under contract), subject to the rights the issuer might have against the transferor, such as set-off.

18.4.3 Priorities

A purchaser of a bearer bond will usually take the bond free of any equities (ie, third party claims), for example a person for whom the bond was held on trust. A purchaser of a registered bond will only take the bond free of competing interests of which he had no actual or constructive notice.

18.4.4 Anonymity

Bearer bonds can be held anonymously since the issuer will not know at any time who owns the bond. An issuer will know the identity of the registered holder of a registered bond, although the true beneficial ownership may lie behind a nominee holder.

18.4.5 Transfer

Bearer bonds are transferred by delivery. The similarity to cash of bearer bonds makes them vulnerable to theft if they are transferred by physical delivery, and most bearer bonds are therefore traded through clearing systems (see **17.8**). The transfer of a registered bond requires the execution of an instrument of transfer, and the filing of the instrument and the original bond certificate with the issuer or his agent for that purpose (whoever maintains the register of bondholders), and finally an amendment to the register. This whole process can take some time and is obviously a lengthier process than the physical delivery of a bearer bond, or its transfer within a clearing system which is effected by book entries.

Russia pays big premium on DM bond

By Edward Luce

The Russian government bowed to scepticism in the markets yesterday by agreeing to pay a higher than expected interest rate premium to buyers of its debut D-Mark bond issue.

The seven-year eurobond, only the second international bond to be issued by Russia since the Bolshevik revolution in 1917, was priced more generously than the markets had anticipated.

At an annual coupon of 9 per cent – considerably above the 8.75 per cent rumoured in the markets – the bond was priced to yield 200 basis points more than an equivalent seven-year issue by the Venezuelan government last month. This reflects the deterioration in bond market sentiment over the last two weeks.

"We needed to hit the psychological number of 9 per cent to attract investors," said an official from Credit Suisse First Boston, which jointly managed yesterday's deal with Deutsche Morgan Grenfell. "We decided it would be better to offer a more generous spread [risk premium] after talking extensively with investors in Germany and Switzerland."

The offering, which is the largest emerging market bond issued in D-Marks, was priced 3.7 percentage points higher than equivalent German government bonds. But in contrast to Russia's debut US$1bn eurobond last year, syndicate officials were unable to sell the entire offering on the day of the launch.

Market traders said worries over the possibility of a rise in US interest rates at the next meeting of the Federal Reserve on March 25 had damped investor demand for emerging market debt issues in the last fortnight. J.P Morgan's emerging market bond index, which measures the average spread of emerging market debt on the secondary markets, has fallen from 390 basis points to 450 points in the last two weeks.

"Considering how unlucky the timing was for Russia, the issue actually went quite well," one syndicate manager in London said yesterday. "It takes a while to sell bonds to Swiss and German retail investors, so the issue will probably take a few days to distribute."

Traders said they expected the debt, which is floating-rate as opposed to fixed-rate, to tighten over German government bonds if general market sentiment improved. Russia's $1bn offering last year was priced to yield 345 basis points more than US Treasury bonds but is now trading at a spread of 325 basis points over Treasuries. This reflects strong underlying appetite for Russian debt, say traders.

The Russian government plans to issue another US$2bn in eurobonds later this year. Officials say yesterday's issue is expected to be followed by Moscow's debut eurobond in the next two months. Other Russian cities plan to follow suit.

"Russian debt is very much in vogue," one trader in London said yesterday. "But the issue could have been timed much better."

Source: Financial Times.

Tunisia to tap Yankee bond sector

By Roula Khalaf

Tunisia is planning to tap the US bond markets in a Yankee bond issue of over $250m, marking its first foray into capital markets outside Japan.

According to bankers, the Yankee bonds – dollar-denominated bonds issued in the US by foreign banks or corporations – are expected to be sold by Merrill Lynch and should be marketed before the end of this year.

The issue is aimed at diversifying Tunisia's sources of financing and extending maturities of its debt to as much as 30 years.

The Yankee bonds will follow this week's Y12.5bn 20-year issue of Samurai bonds – the Japanese equivalent of Yankees – which was priced at 135 basis points above Japanese government bonds.

Middle East and North African countries are emerging as new issuers of debt on international markets. Eurobonds have been recently issued by governments or companies in Lebanon, Jordan and Oman. Egypt and Morocco are also planning to tap the market.

Tunisia, North Africa's smallest country, has been a regular bond issuer on the Japanese capital markets, raising a total of Y112.5bn since 1994. The funds are used to finance the budget deficit, which is expected to stand at about 3 per cent of gross domestic product this year. External financing on capital markets has largely replaced bilateral and multilateral credit.

According to a May report by Merrill Lynch, total external debt stands at $11.3bn, accounting for 57 per cent of GDP. The debt service ratio is estimated at 18.7 per cent.

The Tunisian government has annual borrowing needs of about $500m but it hopes to reduce the level of borrowing as foreign direct investment picks up.

Tunisia has been assigned a low investment grade rating. In a recent assessment of Tunisia, Standard & Poor's said its BBB– rating reflected the country's solid public finances, conservative monetary policy and moderate external debt and debt service. Tunisia's annual GDP growth has averaged about 4 per cent between 1990 and 1995 and inflation is in single digits.

The government is projecting a 5.7 per cent growth rate this year, but analysts say growth will depend on the level of rainfall, which affects cereal harvests.

But S&P also noted that Tunisia's credit standing is constrained by a high public debt burden – at about 74 per cent of GDP this year – and the fact that the public sector continues to weigh heavily on the economy, accounting for 40 per cent of GDP value added and 25 per cent of employment.

In spite of the government's stated commitment to privatisation, the programme has moved slowly.

Merrill Lynch says total privatisation receipts reached only $300m at the end of 1996 because the government had sold mainly small to medium-sized enterprises, with little progress made on the transfer of larger state companies to the private sector.

Source: Financial Times.

18.5   The legal effect on bearer bonds held in clearing systems

Since the majority of bearer bonds will be held in a clearing system, it is important to understand the legal rights of the various parties with respect to such instruments. Some investors may not actually be 'participants' in a clearing system (ie, they will not have their own accounts in a system), but will rely on a financial institution which is a participant to act as their nominee. The majority of bearer bond transactions will therefore involve a chain of parties:

Investor ⟶ Participant ⟶ Clearing System ⟶ Depository

In basic terms the investors (ie, bondholders) must give the bond to a participant (ie, an entity holding accounts with the clearing system – assuming the investor is not a participant itself), which must give the bond to the clearing system (eg, Euroclear or Clearstream), which in turn gives the instrument to a depositary bank for safekeeping. The danger for an investor is that if any of these parties goes into liquidation in possession of his bearer securities, the investor will be left to claim as an unsecured creditor. The way to avoid this risk is to ensure that the proprietary rights over the securities remain with the investor and are not vested in any of the other parties in the chain. In the event of another party's liquidation, the investor can therefore simply reclaim the bonds. The following sections examine each relationship in turn.

18.5.1   Investor – Participant

The law governing the relationship between the investor and the participant will usually be the governing law they have chosen in the documentation acknowledging their transaction (see also **9.8**). Under English law, the deposit of bearer securities with a participant will result in the investor passing legal title to the participant, but the investor retaining beneficial ownership. The participant therefore takes all the rights against the issuer such as payment of coupon and principal, and any conversion rights. However, the participant must account for any payments it receives, must comply with the investor's instructions as to any rights under the security, and must transfer the securities back to the investor at his request. The investor can also demand the return of the bonds in the event of the participant's liquidation and they will not become part of the participant's general pool of assets.

18.5.2   Participant – Clearing system

The two main clearing systems for bonds, Euroclear and Clearstream (see **17.8.1**), are (respectively) Belgian and Luxembourg entities, and the terms and conditions of the clearing systems will be construed in accordance with the local law. For the sake of simplicity, we will assume that the clearing system being used is Euroclear in Belgium.

Under general Belgian law, participants depositing bearer securities in Euroclear would have contractual rights against Euroclear for the return of their securities. However, general Belgian law is modified under a specific decree, so that the participants retain a proprietary right of ownership in the securities credited to their securities clearance account. Therefore, if Euroclear should become insolvent, the participants will not be unsecured creditors but will have the right to the return of the securities which are credited to their securities account.

18.5.3 Clearing systems – Depository

The final link in the chain is that between the clearing system and the depositary bank where the bearer instruments are held for safekeeping. This relationship is subject not only to the local law of the relevant clearing system, but also to the law of the jurisdiction in which the depository is situated. It is therefore important for the participant to ensure that the proprietory rights in the bearer securities are not in any way transferred to the depositary bank. The clearing systems will usually ensure that this is the case before using a depository; however, some participants may want a legal opinion from local lawyers to confirm that this is the case.

With careful planning and legal advice, therefore, an investor with bearer securities can avoid taking a credit risk on any of the other parties involved in the clearing system process.

18.6 Further reading

This chapter has provided a brief overview of the legal 'chain' of rights over a bond: for a more thorough examination, see the excellent *Interests in Securities* (Oxford University Press, 2000) by Dr Joanna Benjamin.

Russian contagion spreads to investment banks' core activities

Bond issues, syndicated loans and IPOs have been hit, say **William Lewis** and **Edward Luce**

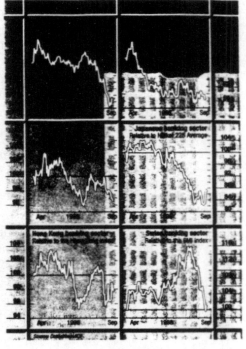

International banks and other financial groups have reported losses suffered in Russia of almost $9bn (£5.4bn) in recent days. But much worse could be in store as the knock-on effect of Russia's devaluation and other emerging market turmoil looks likely to dent investment bank revenues severely until the end of the year.

Even the most developed western markets have already seen sharply reduced activity in the most profitable areas for banks. "We're going to see many fewer bond issues, fewer syndicated loans and fewer IPOs between now and the end of the year," said John Leonard, an analyst at Salomon Smith Barney. "This will really have an impact on margins."

Already margins have been dented by trading losses in Russia. Among the worst hit are Salomon Smith Barney, which reported a net loss of $150m in July and August, and Chase Manhattan, which came close to making a loss from its trading activities in August.

Bankers Trust, the seventh largest bank holding company in the US, was one of the few to warn of the likely impact of the turbulence in global markets on other core investment banking areas.

While BT's investment banking operations appear to have been particularly badly hit because of its traditional focus on high yield bonds and leveraged lending, it appears to be far from alone in experiencing a slowdown.

Data provided by Securities Data Company show that US common stock trading volumes have plummeted in July and worsened in August. Total stock volumes, comprising initial public offerings and secondary offerings, were $9.8bn in July and $2.5bn in August. This compares with $17.6bn in June. In the last week of August volumes reached just $26.6m.

Similarly high yield debt volumes have also suffered. August saw volume of $2.7bn, compared with $15bn in July and $21bn in April. Donaldson, Lufkin & Jenrette was Wall Street's leading manager in this product area last year, and earlier this week it warned that it had made just $40m of pre-tax income so far in the third quarter.

"The volatility is impacting the IPO market especially," says Charles Rauch, an analyst in Standard & Poor's financial institutions group.

Mergers and acquisitions, one of the highest margin businesses for investment banks, has also been hit, with $146bn worth of deals announced in August in the US, and $150bn in July. This compares with $252bn in June and $210bn in May.

Senior bond officials said that almost all deals by borrowers rated below AAA or AA+ by the rating agencies had been put on ice for at least a few weeks. "If this continues into October then it will start to hit our balance sheet quite hard," said the head of a bond desk at a US investment bank in London.

Few, if any, of the 10 or 12 European high-yield – or "junk" – bond issues that were planned before the end of the year are likely to go ahead, say bankers. "Investors are fleeing any type of credit whether we're talking about AA rated or sub-investment grade," said Avinash Persaud, head of currency research at J.P. Morgan. "Only bonds which resemble US Treasury bonds, such as strong collateralised deals, are likely to get away in this climate."

Bankers were not prepared to make predictions about overall investment bank losses in the third and fourth quarters but all agreed that a large proportion of first-half profits would be wiped out in the next three months. More than half of investment banking income is derived from fees generated by underwriting public issues in the equity and fixed income markets.

Source: *Financial Times*.

Chapter 19

Issuing a Eurobond – the Parties and Documentation

19.1 Introduction

The next three chapters concentrate on the parties, documents and process involved in the issue of a eurobond. The reason for examining a eurobond is that bonds are the most common form of debt security, and the euromarket is the largest capital market centred on London. Many of the matters which are dealt with will, however, also apply to issues of other types of bond and indeed other debt securities.

The characteristics of a bond were explained at **17.5**, and the concept of eurocurrencies was explained at **17.3.2**: a eurobond is a bond which is issued to attract eurocurrencies. In other words, it is a bond denominated in a globally recognised currency which is not the currency of the country in which the bond is issued. It is generally agreed that the very first eurobond was issued in 1963 by Autostrade (the Italian motorway authority) in London, arranged by SG Warburg (now SBC Warburg Dillon Read) for US$15,000,000. However, the real increase in eurobond issues came in the early 1980s, reflecting a reduction in the size of the syndicated loan market caused by the imposition of more severe regulatory capital requirements (see **9.3.3**). Banks facing restrictions on lending turned instead to the lucrative fees available from underwriting eurobond issues.

19.2 Parties to a eurobond issue

19.2.1 The issuer

The various entities which might issue debt securities on the capital markets were listed at **17.10**. By their very nature, eurobonds will raise a currency that is not 'indigenous' to the country in which they are issued. If the issuer does not have a specific requirement for that currency, it will enter into a derivative or foreign exchange transaction to exchange the money for a currency it can use.

19.2.2 Lead manager

The lead manager to an issue will be a financial institution such as an investment bank, and have a role similar to the arranger in a syndicated loan (see **3.3.2**). It will be responsible for arranging the bond issue and managing the entire issue process, from receiving its mandate through to the issuer receiving funds. The lead manager will advise the issuer on the structure and timing of the issue, and so takes the credit for success and responsibility for the failure of a bond issue. If the issue is to be listed, the lead manager will usually be the 'sponsor' required by the UKLA to provide confirmations (eg, of compliance with the Listing Rules) for listing. Eurobond issues of sovereign, supranationals or frequent issuers are often identified with reference to the lead manager (eg, the Nomura International plc World Bank Euroyen Global Note).

19.2.3   Syndicate

The syndicate is the group of investment banks or securities houses (known individually as 'co-managers') who attempt to sell a bond issue to investors. They are effectively a distribution network for the issue, using their contacts and knowledge of the market to find investors ('making a book'). In most eurobond issues on the London market, the syndicate agree with the issuer to take all the bonds, even if they cannot find investors. This gives the issuer the reassurance of knowing the exact amount of the funds it will receive. The syndicate (in return for a fee) take the risk that the issue is not fully subscribed by investors, in which case they will buy the unsold bonds (they may sell any such bonds in the secondary market at a lower price in order to clear their books, or they may retain the bonds in the hope that demand for them increases and they make a profit on a sale). The names of the syndicate will appear on the offering document or listing particulars in order of contribution to the amount of the issue that they have sold, and if equal in alphabetical order. In some US issues and some high-yield UK issues, the syndicate will only have to use 'reasonable endeavours' to sell the securities, and a separate group of banks will 'underwrite' (ie, purchase) any unsold bonds to give the issuer certainty of funds.

19.2.4   Fiscal agent and trustee

A eurobond issue will use either a fiscal agent (under a fiscal agency agreement), or a trustee (under a trust deed). The legal effect of each arrangement is quite different.

19.2.4.1   Fiscal agent

The fiscal agent is appointed by, and is the representative and agent of, the issuer and not the bondholders. He is primarily responsible for paying principal and interest to the bondholders. The fiscal agent will also have certain administrative functions, including the publication of notices to the bondholders and acting as a depository for the issuer's accounts and other financial information which is open to inspection by the bondholders (although he has no duty to review or investigate such information). The fiscal agency agreement will appoint the fiscal agent and explicitly state that he does not owe the bondholders any duty of care.

19.2.4.2   Trustee

A trustee is initially chosen and appointed by the issuer (through its advisers), but represents the interests of the bondholders. The property held on trust is the issuer's covenant to pay the bondholders. The trustee's powers and duties are recorded in a trust deed, but he will also owe the bondholders a duty of care under common law trust principles. Trust arrangements are a concept peculiar to common law jurisdictions and will not usually be recognised by civil law jurisdictions. In a eurobond transaction, the trustee is likely to be either a professional trust association (eg, The Law Debenture Trust Corporation), or a subsidiary of a bank or other financial institution, whose sole function is to act as a trust corporation.

19.2.4.3   Choosing between a trustee and a fiscal agency

The majority of eurobond issues will use a fiscal agency rather than a trustee, primarily because of cost considerations. However, there are specific circumstances in which a fiscal agent is insufficient and a trustee must be appointed. These include the following.

Secured issues

If the bonds are secured, a trustee is required to hold the security. This is primarily due to the impracticality of providing individual bondholders with a right to part of the security, which would have to be transferred every time the bond changed hands. Any such transfer may restart 'hardening periods' (see **14.9**). Therefore, the trustee holds the security on trust for all the bondholders from time to time. A fiscal agent cannot perform this function since he is the agent of the issuer and so acts in the issuer's interests.

Subordinated issues

If bonds are to be issued which are subordinated to (ie, ranking behind) the repayment of another bond issue, the same trustee may be appointed to both senior and junior issues to ensure effective subordination (although it is now quite common to achieve subordination contractually through the terms of the issue, creating 'contingent debt').

By law

Certain jurisdictions have a statutory requirement for a trustee arrangement in order to protect the bondholders. However, most such legislation is 'domestic' in application and will not apply to international transactions.

19.2.4.4 Advantages of using a trust arrangement

Under a trust arrangement, the trustee has legal ownership of any claims that the bondholders (ie, the beneficiaries) have against the issuer. There are advantages of using a trust arrangement for both the issuer and the bondholders.

Advantages for the issuer

The advantages of using a trust arrangement from the issuer's perspective are based on the possibility of dealing with one sophisticated party representing the bondholders, rather than dealing with a group of individuals. For example:

(a)   Only the trustee can act in the event of a default by the issuer (albeit that he can act only within the terms of the trust deed under which he is appointed, or on the direction of a specific majority of bondholders). This will usually lead to a more considered approach towards a default than might be the case if the bondholders could precipitate action individually. The issuer can deal with a professional trustee rather than a disparate group of potentially less sophisticated bondholders with varying views and requirements. Furthermore, many trust deeds will provide the trustee with authority to waive technical events of default where he sees fit. The trustee therefore protects the issuer from 'rogue' bondholders.

Interestingly, in *Concord Trust v The Law Debenture Trust Corporation plc* [2005] UKHL 27, the House of Lords held that if a trustee mistakenly called an event of default (ie when no event of default had actually occurred), this was not a breach of contract, but simply an 'ineffective action'. This is some comfort to trustees who had feared they might be sued for wrongfully calling a default; however, an action in tort (for negligence or interference by unlawful means) may lie in some circumstances (though not on the facts in *Concord*).

(b)   A trustee can be given power to agree certain amendments to the terms of a bond without calling a meeting of bondholders (eg, to approve a restructuring of the issuer's group), providing the issuer with greater flexibility.

Advantages for the bondholders

There are a number of important advantages for a bondholder in creating an issue with a trust arrangement:

(a)   If an event of default occurs, the bondholders can rely on a professional entity (the trustee) to pursue the situation on their behalf. Individual action by each bondholder, which can be expensive and difficult to pursue, is not necessary since the trustee will act on their behalf. Class actions are fraught with difficulties because of the variety and disparity of bondholders.

(b)   Most bond issues are unsecured, and so if an issuer is facing financial difficulties, the bondholders are very vulnerable. A trustee acting on behalf of all the bondholders is more likely to achieve a moratorium, or a negotiated resolution with other creditors, than bondholders would if they acted as individuals.

(c)   If the bondholders need to make a collective decision, the trustee can chair any meetings and make recommendations.

(d)   After a default, an issuer must make any payment through the trustee rather than to individual bondholders. This avoids a powerful bondholder negotiating himself a good deal at the expense of minority bondholders.

(e)   A trustee will have investigative and monitoring powers which a fiscal agent will not. It is not, however, usual practice in eurobond issues for the trust deed to create any specific duties of investigation for the trustee: he will usually act simply as a medium for receiving certain information, such as the issuer's annual accounts, notices and certificates of compliance which must be available for inspection by the bondholders. The common law duty to act with due diligence in the best interests of the beneficiaries (ie, the bondholders) is still applicable irrespective of the contractual requirements of the trust deed, for example, if the trustee is given the power in the trust deed to request financial information from the issuer then he has a positive duty to do so if it would be in the best interests of the bondholders.

19.2.4.5   Advantages of using a fiscal agent

The primary advantage to the issuer of appointing a fiscal agent rather than a trustee is cost. A trustee will require his own solicitor (whose fees must be met by the issuer) to advise on the trust documentation, and a trustee's fees during the life of the eurobond will reflect the substantial responsibilities he must undertake. By way of contrast, there is considerable competition to take the high profile and prestigious role of fiscal agent. This drives down the fiscal agent's fees, and it is not unknown for institutions to take on the fiscal agency role for no remuneration provided that they are also awarded another role in the issue (eg, as the common depositary bank).

19.2.5   Listing agent

When listing on certain exchanges a listing agent must be appointed by an issuer to communicate with the listing authority on its behalf, to lodge the necessary documents with the listing authority, and to advise the issuer on the listing rules and process (see also **21.8**). The concept of Listing Agent for the UKLA was removed with the introduction of the FSMA 2000 on 1 December 2001.

19.2.6 Principal paying agent and paying agents

A paying agent is an agent of the issuer responsible for co-ordinating payments of principal and interest under the bond. It will receive payment monies from the issuer and distribute them to the appropriate paying agents, who pay the bondholders resident in their jurisdictions. If an issuer uses a fiscal agent, it will usually take the role of principal paying agent. However, if the issuer uses a trustee structure (or if the fiscal agent does not have a 'presence' in a jurisdiction in which interest payments must be made) a principal paying agent (or further paying agents) will be appointed.

19.2.7 Depository and common depository

A depository is a bank appointed on behalf of a clearing system dealing with a particular issue to act as 'safe keeper' of the temporary global note, the permanent global note, and any definitive bearer bonds traded through a clearing system. If an issue uses more than one clearing system, each system must use the same depository and it will be known as the 'common depository'. There are only a limited number of international commercial banks which have been approved by the clearing systems to perform the role of depository. The common depository will hold part of an issue for Euroclear and part for Clearstream, and transfers can be made between the two systems (see **17.8**).

As well as providing a 'hole in the ground', using a depository also allows the bonds to be kept in jurisdictions other than those of the clearing systems, giving rise to tax and other advantages. The use of a depository to hold the bonds is sometimes known as 'immobilisation' (not to be confused with 'dematerialisation', whereby paper securities are dispensed with altogether, and the rights are recorded and traded electronically).

There is one circumstance in which a global note cannot be placed with a common depository. Some issuers will want their securities to be recognised by the European Central Bank as 'eligible collateral' for the euro central banking system (known as 'Eurosystem'). These securities can be used to support exposure in Eurosystem and so are popular with certain investors. From July 2006, securities are only eligible as Eurosystem collateral if their global form is held by the clearing system themselves and not at a common depository. This new system is usually known as a 'New Global Note' structure (or sometimes an 'NGN structure', 'ECB structure' or 'ECB3 structure'!).

19.2.8 Legal advisers

Separate legal advisers will be appointed by the issuer and the lead manager. If the issue involves a trust arrangement, the trustee will also instruct solicitors, although they will sometimes use the same firm as the lead manager with a Chinese wall between the two sets of solicitors. Most eurobond issues are governed by English law. However, if the issue involves an overseas jurisdiction, irrespective of whether the eurobonds themselves are governed by English law, lawyers from that jurisdiction must be instructed to ensure compliance with local laws and regulations.

The role of legal advisers in an issue primarily involves the preparation of documentation (the principal documents will be produced initially by the solicitors to the lead manager – see **Chapter 21**). The solicitors will also be involved in the due diligence process, and will have to produce a legal opinion for the transaction.

19.2.9 Auditors

Auditors will be involved in the issue process whenever the issuer is an entity which produces accounts (primarily companies and certain quasi-governmental entities). The lead manager and its legal advisers will want to review the issuer's accounts for at least the previous three years. If the issue is to be listed, the audited accounts may have to be published, or incorporated by reference, in the prospectus (or listing particulars). The issuer's auditors will be asked to provide a comfort letter addressed to the lead manager and the syndicate, confirming that there has been no material change in the issuer's financial condition since the last published accounts, and a 'consent letter' consenting to the publication of their report in the offering document (see **19.3**).

INTERNATIONAL BONDS By Samer Iskandar and Edward Luce

The rise and rise of the jumbo bond

10-year benchmark bond yields

INTEREST RATES AT A GLANCE						
	USA	Japan	Germany	France	Italy	UK
Discount	5.00	0.50	2.50	3.30¹	5.50	7.25²
Overnight	n/a	n/a	3.32	3.32	6.25	n/a
Three month	5.19	0.37	3.40	3.42	5.96	7.45
One year	5.29	0.57	3.68	3.58	5.02	7.06
Five year	5.47	1.21	4.50	4.55	4.92	6.21
Ten year	5.53	1.90	4.96	5.00	5.34	5.97

(1) France-intervention rate. (2) UK-Base rate. Source: Reuters.

The recent trend towards larger bond issues is likely to be confirmed this week, as several borrowers are expected to launch benchmark deals with amounts of $1bn or more.

Cades, the French state-backed entity set up to manage the accumulated debts of the social security system, is planning to issue a third tranche of its multi-currency euro-fungible issue, denominated in guilders. The amount will be determined by market conditions, but the previous tranches were FFr8bn and DM3bn.

Fannie Mae, the largest US mortgage lender, is also expected to tap the market with the third issue in its "benchmark note" programme. Previous five-year and 10-year issues were in amounts of $4bn each.

Linda Knight, treasurer of Fannie Mae, says there is a pricing advantage in issuing large amounts: "There is a clear and direct benefit to our yield curve by issuing jumbo bonds."

The World Bank is also understood to be considering a $5bn issue, which would be the largest ever fixed-coupon bond.

"In theory, there is an immediate benefit to borrowers as investors are believed to be ready to give up some yield in exchange for greater liquidity," said one analyst in London.

This is already apparent on some existing deals. A FFr10bn three-year bond by Cades, for example, is trading at a yield spread of 10 basis points over French Treasury debt. This compares with a 14 basis points spread on a similar, FFr1bn

issue by CEPME, the financing agency for small companies whose debt is guaranteed by the French state.

"The cost saving from a jumbo issue amounts to between three and five basis points, depending on the maturity," says Christophe Frankel, head of funding at Cades.

Bankers estimate that Fannie Mae has also derived savings of three to five points from the massive size of its recent benchmark deals. Each basis point in yield costs the borrower $1m over the life of a $1bn issue of 10-year bonds.

However, for many issuers in the jumbo market, the benefits have not materialised immediately. "When a borrower launches its first jumbo deal, it sometimes needs to offer a more generous spread to attract new investors," says John Butler, chief fixed-income strategist at WestLB in London.

This was the case for several issues of global Pfandbrief bonds, which failed to meet their cost saving objectives. "But over time, they [jumbo Pfandbriefe issuers] will be able to issue at tighter levels because they will have a larger investor base," Mr Butler says.

There are other cost advantages to larger issues. These include lead managers' willingness to accept proportionately lower fees, and fees linked to documentation and legal paperwork, are also reduced.

"Every bond issue requires a prospectus, and these are often identical, regardless of the issue size," says a syndicate manager at a large US bank in London. "So it is

cheaper to write one prospectus for a billion-dollar deal than two prospectuses for two smaller issues."

Jumbo issuers are also pinning high hopes on building a complete yield curve. They believe investors will also expect to receive lower yields in exchange for arbitrage opportunities along the yield curve.

"Providing a liquid yield curve also gives you some kind of premium," Ms Knight says.

However, Mooyaart, a company which analyses bond prices relative to the performance of the most liquid benchmark issues, dismisses many of the arguments in favour of jumbo bonds as "pure marketing".

One put forward by borrowers such as KfW, the German federal development agency, is that issuers could establish a "surrogate" yield curve to the government bond yield curve.

This argument is "largely baseless", according to Brian Mooyaart, director of Moo-

yaart. "To provide the sort of liquidity a government provides, a borrower would have to issue at least $5bn a month and no borrower – not even the World Bank – can do that."

He also says that maintaining a full and liquid yield curve could prove to be more of a headache than a benefit. For example, the borrower might need eight to 10-year funds but the market would demand a two-year bond to keep the yield-curve fully supplied. "Pledging to maintain a liquid yield curve is one way of tying your hands behind your back," he says.

Analysts also say jumbo issuers are taking advantage of cyclical factors in their favour, including the "flight to safety" prompted by the Asian crisis and the popularity of the dollar. Once these disappear, supranational borrowers could return to the "opportunistic" habit of issuing in high-yield currencies to exploit good arbitrage opportunities.

Source: *Financial Times*.

19.3 Documentation of a eurobond issue

19.3.1 List of required documents

A typical eurobond issue involves a substantial number of documents. The principal documents required are listed below in two sections:

(a) documents relating to the underwriting, subscription and distribution of the bonds; and

(b) documents which relate to and constitute the bonds themselves.

19.3.1.1 Underwriting, subscription and distribution

(a) mandate letter;

(b) invitation telex;

(c) allotment telex;

(d) prospectus or other offering document;

(e) subscription agreement (or underwriting agreement);

(f) agreement among managers;

(g) auditor's report and consent letter;

(h) auditor's comfort letters;

(i) legal opinions.

19.3.1.2 Bonds and related documents

(a) fiscal agency agreement (including paying agency agreement) (or trust deed);

(b) paying agency agreement (if no fiscal agent);

(c) temporary global note;

(d) permanent global note (or definitive form bond);

(e) deed of guarantee (if the issue is guaranteed and there is no trust deed);

(f) deed of covenant (if no trustee, and bonds are in permanent global form).

19.3.2 Mandate letter

Once the issuer has awarded an institution the mandate to act as lead manager for the proposed eurobond issue, there will be a series of meetings and/or an exchange of correspondence which results in a letter (or sometimes telex or fax) which confirms the fundamental terms of the issue. This is known as the 'mandate letter'. It will also authorise the lead manager to announce the issue and allow him to invite other institutions (co-managers) to form a syndicate which will distribute the issue. The mandate letter is usually prepared by the lead manager.

19.3.3 Invitation telex

The invitation telex is the document sent by the lead manager to prospective co-managers (lead managers and co-managers together form the 'syndicate') inviting them to participate in the issue by subscribing for the eurobonds on their issue. If the issue is being underwritten (see **19.3.6**) the invitation telex will also request the co-managers to give an underwriting commitment. The invitation telex is prepared and sent by the lead manager (having usually been checked by its solicitors) on the day the issue is launched (see **21.7**). Note that the invitation telex (and allotment telex) is usually a fax or an e-mail rather than a telex.

The requirement to send an invitation telex, and its minimum content, are governed by ICMA rules. The telex must provide summary information about the issue and its basic terms and conditions. It may also provide a brief description of the issuer and its business, as well as any guarantor. The invitation telex will also outline the timetable of the issue.

19.3.4   Allotment telex

The invitation telex will have asked the co-managers to notify the lead manager of the maximum value of bonds for which they are prepared to subscribe on issue. Once he has received a response from all the co-managers, the lead manager will decide exactly how to divide the issue between them and will notify the co-managers by sending an allotment telex. The allocation is at the sole discretion of the lead manager, and is subject to the issue actually completing. The allotment telex will also contain a request for each co-manager's payment and transfer instructions for the bonds to which they are subscribing, which the lead manager will give to the clearing system at closing (see **21.10**).

ICMA rules require that allotments are made within 24 hours after the launch of the issue.

19.3.5   Prospectus or listing particulars

The prospectus is the document which provides detailed information about an issue for potential investors. If the issue is to be listed on the London Stock Exchange Professional Securities Market ('PSM') then this document is known as the 'listing particulars'. Since these 'selling documents' are at the heart of any eurobond issue, they are examined separately in **Chapter 20**.

19.3.6   Subscription agreement/underwriting agreement

The subscription agreement is a contract between the issuer, the lead manager and the co-managers which records the basis on which the issuer will sell, and the managers will buy, the bonds on issue. The syndicate members will be subscribing for the bonds on the basis that they will keep very few, or none, of those bonds for themselves ('for their own book'). Before they agree to subscribe (ie, before they sign the subscription agreement) the syndicate members will have lined up investors who want to take the bonds.

As explained at **19.2.3**, most (UK) eurobonds work on the basis that the syndicate will subscribe for all of the bonds between them, even if they cannot place them with investors. Under the terms of the subscription agreement, the liability of the syndicate members to the issuer of an issue is joint and several (compare this with a syndicated loan in which each bank's liability is restricted to its commitment). Therefore, whilst the managers will agree between themselves how many bonds they will each subscribe for (in the 'agreement among managers'), the subscription agreement allows an issuer to require any one manager to subscribe for the entire bond issue if necessary. If the issue uses underwriting banks instead, the subscription agreement will contain the terms of the underwriting (and may be called an 'underwriting agreement').

The subscription agreement will also cover the following matters:

(a)   Conditions precedent to the issue. These might include legal opinions to the managers, auditors' consent and comfort letters, and a closing certificate confirming there has been no material adverse change to the issuer's representations and warranties.

(b)   The pricing of the issue (ie, the interest rate payable on the eurobonds and, if appropriate, the price at which convertible bonds can be converted into shares).

(c)   Fees and commissions payable to the managers. These will usually include a 'selling commission' (also known as a 'selling concession') and a 'management/underwriting commission', both calculated as a percentage of the principal amount of the bonds.

(d)   Costs and expenses to be paid by the issuer. These are likely to include costs in connection with preparing and printing the bonds and documentation of the issue, any costs of listing, advertising costs, and the fees and expenses of the trustee (if one is used). There is also likely to be a provision under which the issuer pays for all or part of the syndicate's legal costs.

(e)   Representations and warranties given by the issuer to each of the managers. These will include representations of fact, for example that any (material) information supplied by the issuer in connection with the issue (particularly with respect to the offering circular) is true and accurate in all material respects, as well as representations of law, for example that the issuer is validly existing and incorporated (the subscription agreement will also contain indemnities given by the issuer to the managers in respect of any misrepresentation).

(f)   A representation from the managers that they will comply with all applicable selling restrictions (see **18.2.1**).

(g)   A force majeure clause (see **9.7**). There is a standard IPMA force majeure clause which is usually used.

19.3.7   Agreement among managers

The agreement among managers is a contract between the lead manager and the co-managers. Its main purpose is to record the number of bonds which each member of the syndicate has agreed to take. However, the agreement also covers payment and allocation of the managers' commission (these are governed by IPMA rules). The agreement among managers also delegates power to the lead manager to act on behalf of the syndicate in certain circumstances. IPMA has produced a standard form of agreement among managers which is adopted in most eurobond issues.

19.3.8   Auditor's report, consent letter and comfort letters

The prospectus or other offering document may include extracts from the latest set of accounts for the issuer, but not necessarily the entire set of statutory accounts filed at Companies House. The issuer's auditors will therefore be required to 'sign off' on the extract to confirm it is consistent with the annual accounts. This is sometimes contained in an 'auditor's report', which may be in the prospectus, and a typical format is given below.

The Directors
Issuer plc,
(address)

15 August 2009

Dear Sirs

Issuer plc (the 'Company')

We have examined the financial information set out on pages 15 to 19 of the Prospectus dated 15 August 2009 issued by the Company in respect of US$50,000,000 eurobonds due 2015.

In our opinion the financial information is consistent with the annual accounts of the Company for the three years ended 31 December 2008, which we audited in accordance with Auditing Standards and on which we reported without qualification.

Yours faithfully

Auditors

The auditors will be asked to provide a consent letter, consenting to the printing of their report in the prospectus (or listing particulars), and comfort letters, addressed to the managers, which essentially confirm:

(a)   that there has been no material adverse change in the issuer's financial position since the latest audited accounts; and

(b)   that any unaudited financial information contained in the offering document is correct.

There will usually be two comfort letters, the first given at the execution of the subscription agreement (the 'signing'), and the second, updating the first, at the time of the closing. The comfort letters are as important to the managers as the legal opinions, and will be legally binding on the auditors (although auditors will often attempt to limit their liability).

19.3.9   Legal opinions

Legal opinions are required by the lead manager and (usually) the co-managers and the trustee. One legal opinion will be required from the lead manager's solicitors with respect to the binding nature of the documentation, and a second will be required from the issuer's solicitors confirming the due incorporation of the issuer, that all necessary consents have been obtained, the position regarding taxation, and enforceability of the contractual documents against the issuer. Opinions from local lawyers will be required if the issue involves other jurisdictions.

19.3.10   Fiscal agency agreement

The fiscal agency agreement is a contract between the issuer, the fiscal agent (as fiscal agent and principal paying agent), and any other paying agents which have been appointed. The fiscal agency agreement records the structure through which the bondholders will receive payment of coupon and principal. Payments to bondholders are made through paying agents, because the issuer will not have the administrative capability to make the payments itself. If the issue uses a trust arrangement then it will require a 'principal paying agent' (usually a bank); if a fiscal agent is used, he will perform the function of a principal paying agent. Further paying agents will need to be appointed if an issue requires payments to be made in jurisdictions outside that of the principal paying agent (although they will often be branch offices of the principal paying agent).

Eurobonds will usually be held in a clearing system, and so payment will involve funds flowing through that system.

Example: A typical eurobond interest/principal funds flow

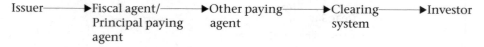

The fiscal agency agreement will also document the following matters:

(a)   the procedure for authentication of the temporary global note and definitive bonds;

(b)   the process necessary to exchange the temporary global note for definitive bonds;

(c)   the issue of replacement bonds (eg, on loss or theft of the original);

(d)   the procedures for convening the bondholders' meetings;

(e)   fees and expenses of the paying agents.

The fiscal agency agreement will also contain the full terms and conditions of the bonds, as well as the forms (if any) of temporary global notes, permanent global notes and definitive bonds, which will appear in a schedule to the agreement.

19.3.11   Paying agency agreement

If a bond issue uses a trust arrangement, the trustee is not responsible for making any payments of coupon or principal. A 'principal paying agent' (together with any other paying agents if necessary) must be appointed under a separate agreement with the issuer. This is known as the 'paying agency agreement', and it will cover similar payment matters to the fiscal agency agreement (see **19.3.10**).

19.3.12   Trust deed

If a trustee is employed as opposed to a fiscal agent (see **19.2.4**), a trust deed will be required to cover the following matters:

(a)   creation of the trust relationship;

(b)   the trust property (the issuer's covenant to pay);

(c)   the trustee's powers and duties;

(d)   appointment and removal of the trustee;

(e)   the requirements for, and organisation of, bondholders' meetings;

(f)   some monitoring of the issuer's financial position.

19.3.13   Deed of guarantee

Some corporate issuers (usually for tax reasons) may use a subsidiary company to issue securities and thereby raise finance for the parent or group. These subsidiaries may be formed solely for the purpose of the issue (often known as 'special purpose vehicles' or 'SPVs'), or they may be general finance vehicles through which the group does most, or all, of its financing. In either case they are often little more than shell companies with few assets. Such a company is unlikely to attain 'investment grade' status (see **17.11**), and therefore the parent company will need to guarantee the SPV's (or the finance vehicle's) obligations under the eurobond in order to lift the credit rating of the issue. The guarantee may be endorsed on the bond itself, or it may be made as a unilateral declaration of guarantee, by the parent company, in a deed of guarantee.

19.3.14   Deed of covenant

If a note is in permanent global form (ie, there are no definitive bonds) then the legal owner of the note is the common depositary bank since it is the bearer (holding the note on behalf of the clearing system). However, in the event of non-payment, the common depositary will not bring a claim against the issuer on the bondholders' behalf. Furthermore, whilst the global note is exchangeable for definitives, the issuer may be unwilling to comply with this condition if it is in a non-payment situation. The bondholders are left unable to enforce their claim.

One solution to this problem is to use a trust structure (see **19.2.4**), whereby the trustee holds the issuer's covenant to pay on trust for the bondholders. However, for those bond issues which do not use a trust structure, it is necessary to create a document which gives the bondholders a right to sue the issuer in accordance with their bond allocations shown in the clearing systems. That document is known as a deed of covenant: a promise to pay executed by the issuer in a deed poll (ie, a unilateral document), and which gives bondholders the right to claim against the issuer in accordance with their bond allocation shown on clearing system accounts.

19.4   Terms and conditions of a eurobond

19.4.1   Comparison with a facility agreement

The terms in a bond are generally both fewer and shorter than the terms in most commercial facility agreements. There are also standard terms for eurobonds which are used in international capital markets, and substantial variation from, or heavy negotiation of, the standard terms is unusual. The reason for this standardisation is to provide instruments which are familiar to investors, without complex terms, making them easily tradeable.

A bondholder will usually have five main concerns:

(a)   the issuer's and the issue's credit rating;

(b)   the amount of its investment;

(c)   the return it will receive on its investment;

(d)   when it is able to redeem its investment;

(e)   its rights on the issuer's default ranking pari passu with any other holders of the same or similar debt instruments of the issuer.

A bondholder will not be concerned with the detailed business of the issuer, or with intricate financial covenants unless it is a 'high yield' bond. Unlike the borrower in a loan transaction, the issuer of a eurobond will not make detailed representations and warranties to the investor. The issuer will provide information about itself and its finances in the prospectus (or listing particulars), and investors will normally rely on this in making their decision to invest. Liability for the content of these documents is discussed in **Chapter 20**.

19.4.2   Where are the terms and conditions found?

The terms and conditions of a bond govern how the instrument operates once it has been issued. Unlike most commercial loan transactions, a bond issue involves numerous documents relating to the funding. Several of those documents will contain a complete set of terms and conditions of the bond, for example:

(a)   in the temporary global note;

(b)   on the back of the definitive bearer (or registered) eurobond, or in the permanent global note;

(c)   as a schedule to the fiscal agency agreement (or trust deed);

(d)   sometimes in the paying agency agreement (if there is a trustee);

(e)   in the prospectus (or listing particulars).

The debt obligation is evident in the bond itself (whether in temporary global, definitive, or permanent global form) and is the property held on trust if a trustee is appointed (see the covenant to pay in the trust deed).

19.4.3   Specific terms and conditions of a eurobond

19.4.3.1   Preamble

The preamble is a short initial paragraph which may confirm the authorisation of the issue by the board (or other authorising body) of the issuer, and which lists the parties to, and dates of, all relevant contractual documents entered into in respect of the issue. This list will include the trust deed, fiscal agency agreement and paying agency agreement.

19.4.3.2   Form, denomination and title

This short clause will state the form (eg, bearer, registered or global) the bonds will take, the amounts in which they are issued (eg, US$10,000 and US$100,000 and also known as 'par value' or 'denomination'), and a statement as to how title to the bonds will pass (eg, for bearer bonds, title will pass by delivery).

19.4.3.3   Status

The status clause will specify the characteristic of the debt obligation and its ranking amongst other debt obligations of the issuer, indicating to the bondholder how it stands vis-à-vis other creditors of the issuer. Eurobonds are usually unsecured and rank pari passu with all other unsecured creditors. However, bonds may be secured or subordinated. (Banks may issue subordinated bonds so that the proceeds of the issue will supplement their 'Tier 2 Capital' for regulatory capital purposes: see **9.3.3**.)

19.4.3.4   Negative pledge

The negative pledge in a standard eurobond transaction will almost always be less onerous than the negative pledge required by the lenders in a commercial banking transaction (see **7.5.2.1**).

> #### Example
> So long as any of the Bonds or Coupons remains outstanding, the issuer will not create or permit to subsist any mortgage, charge, lien or other form of security interest or encumbrance upon the whole or any part of its undertaking, assets or revenues present or future to secure any present or future indebtedness in the form of bonds, notes, debentures, loan stock or other securities, or any guarantee of or indemnity in respect of such indebtedness, unless the Issuer's obligations under the Bonds and the Coupons are secured equally and rateably therewith or have the benefit of such other security, guarantee, indemnity or other arrangement as shall be approved by an Extraordinary Resolution of the Bondholders.

This form of negative pledge simply ensures that the issuer will not issue debt securities ranking higher than the current issue, unless the bondholders of this current issue receive identical rights. Any stronger form of negative pledge would be unworkable, since (unlike restrictive terms in a facility agreement) it would require a bondholders' meeting to obtain a waiver of this term.

19.4.3.5   Coupon

If a bond carries a fixed coupon, the rate will be determined on or before the launch date, and the coupon will be payable annually in arrear. If the coupon is at a floating rate, the method of calculation is explained in the interest clause, and the coupon payment dates are specified. The coupon payment dates will usually be the same dates in the appropriate months depending on the commencement date of the issue itself (eg, if quarterly – 15 August, 15 November, 15 February and

15 May). Since those days may not be days on which banks are open, a 'business day' definition must be introduced into this condition (see **11.7**).

The 365/365 basis for calculating domestic loan interest was explained at **4.9**. For fixed rate eurobonds issued *before* 1 January 1999, the convention was to use the '360/360' basis in which each calendar month is treated as having 30 days, so that one-twelfth of the annual interest rate will accrue for each month irrespective of the actual number of days in that month. However, fixed rate bonds issued *after* 1 January 1999 usually use the 'Actual/Actual' convention. Unfortunately, there are at least three different interpretations of this convention, but the most commonly adopted will probably be the ICMA method (r 251), ie actual days elapsed over the product of the number of days in a coupon period and the number of coupon periods. For floating rate notes (and syndicated loans, for most currencies other than sterling), the 'Actual/360' or '365/360' basis is usually used. This applies the 'annual' rate (x%) to the principal sum as if it were x% per 360 days. Over a calendar year, therefore, the interest charged is actually slightly more than the 'annual' rate and is different for months of different lengths.

Example

If the annual coupon is 6%, and the principal sum is £200, then the '365/360' basis requires interest of £12 to be paid every 360 days: ie 3.33p per day or approximately £12.17 per calendar year.

19.4.3.6   Payments

The mechanics for payment under a definitive bearer bond are relatively simple, requiring surrender of the bond for payment of principal, and surrender of the relevant coupon for interest. Surrender and payment are effected through the paying agents, who are agents of the issuer (in contrast with facility agreements where payments are made through the agent which is an agent of the lenders). Most eurobonds, however, will be held in clearing systems, and so payments will be made from the paying agents directly to the clearing systems which credit the money to the relevant cash account of each bondholder.

19.4.3.7   Redemption and purchase

The eurobond will usually specify three occasions on which it may be redeemed:

(a)   On maturity (usually 'at par', ie at face value).

(b)   For tax reasons. As with a facility agreement, an issuer will not want to maintain a bond issue if a change in tax law or practice renders its borrowing more expensive. A eurobond will therefore include a 'tax redemption clause' permitting redemption of the entire issue if, as a result of a change in tax laws, the issuer is required to gross up payments of interest or principal. The issuer must redeem the whole issue, and not just part.

(c)   Re-purchase. There is no legal reason why an issuer should not purchase its own bonds in the secondary market, and the terms will specifically permit this. However, if the bonds are listed on the London Stock Exchange, the Listing Rules generally require the issuer to notify all the bondholders of its intentions, through a Regulatory Information Service (RIS) – see Rule 12.5). Any purchases which are made by tender offer to the bondholders generally must be made to all the bondholders.

19.4.3.8   Taxation

An issuer will be required to gross up payments to investors in very limited circumstances, since the issuer has little control over the bondholder's identity and tax domicile. Any grossing-up obligation is usually restricted to taxes imposed by the issuer's own jurisdiction and would benefit only 'non-domestic' investors (see also **9.3.4**).

19.4.3.9 Events of default

The events of default in a bond issue are almost invariably less onerous and less detailed than in a facility agreement. Any default for non-payment of interest will have a grace period (often as much as 14 days) as a matter of course. Cross-default clauses are often subject to a high minimum threshold (ie, de minimis).

19.4.3.10 Prescription

The prescription period is the time in which a bondholder must claim principal and coupon, usually 10 years and five years respectively, from the due date for payment. The prescription periods avoid the issuer looking to statutes of limitation to limit its liability. At the end of the prescription period, the debt is actually extinguished not just action barred. (This is important to avoid the situation where an investor may search for an applicable jurisdiction with a limitation period which only views action barring as procedural, and with a longer limitation period than the prescription period.)

19.4.3.11 Replacement of bonds and coupons

This provision deals with lost, stolen, defaced or destroyed bonds. The risk to an issuer of simply replacing a 'lost' bearer instrument has already been mentioned: if the original bond is presented for payment, the issuer will have to honour the payment obligations on both original and replacement (this also applies to replacement coupons). The condition for replacement of bonds and coupons therefore provides that the bondholder claiming a replacement must indemnify the issuer in respect of any payments the issuer has to make on the original bond or coupon and pay all expenses of the issuer in making such a replacement (including any tax). Any mutilated or defaced bonds will have to be surrendered before a replacement is issued.

19.4.3.12 Meetings of bondholders and modification

The procedure for convening bondholders' meetings and the conducting of business thereat is provided for in the fiscal agency agreement (or trust deed). The trustee (or, if no trustee, the issuer) convenes meetings, either on its own initiative or at the request of bondholders holding at least 10% in aggregate of the principal amount of the bonds. Bondholder meetings are usually convened only when there is a problem with the issue or the issuer, or if any modifications of the terms and conditions are required. The conditions governing meetings are usually in standard form. Notice must generally be given to all bondholders through publication in an appropriate newspaper (eg, the *Financial Times*), and strict quorum requirements must be met for meetings to modify the terms and conditions. Matters on which bondholders might be asked to vote include the following:

(a) a postponement, reduction or cancellation of principal or interest;

(b) the release of any security or guarantee;

(c) a change in the currency of the bonds;

(d) waiver of any event of default;

(e) appointment of a new trustee;

(f) reorganisation of the issuer (eg, on a merger);

(g)   if there is no trustee, the appointment of a bondholders' committee to represent bondholders in a liquidation or reorganisation.

Under English law, there are no specific statutory requirements as to when a majority can bind a minority of bondholders. However, in order to protect the minority, English euromarket practice dictates that the majority of bondholders required to pass an extraordinary resolution is 75% (the matters listed above will usually require an extraordinary resolution). Certain civil law jurisdictions have precise statutory requirements as to which matters require a majority vote. A trustee is usually given power to approve minor modifications, or waive a minor breach of the terms and conditions, provided that such action is not materially prejudicial to the bondholders.

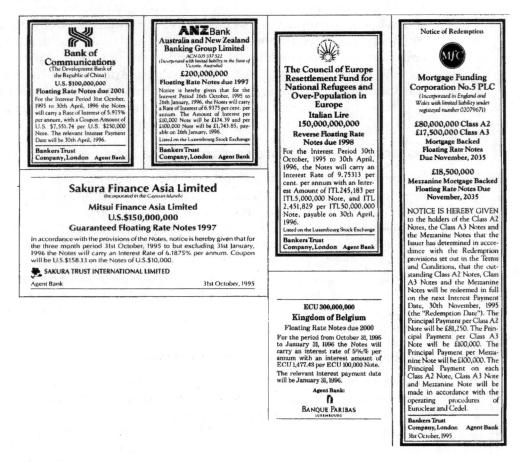

19.4.3.13   Notices

In a commercial loan transaction, the lenders' names and addresses appear in the parties clause, a schedule and on the signing pages of the loan document. However, the identity of bond investors will not be known, and therefore notice can be given only by one or more of an RIS, the FSA or a national newspaper (usually the *Financial Times* and, for issues listed on the Luxembourg Stock Exchange, the *Luxemburger Wort*) (see Rule 9.6). If bonds are listed on the London Stock Exchange, copies of any notices to bondholders must also be given to the Exchange. Notices of meetings for holders of London listed debt securities in bearer form must usually be placed in a leading national newspaper circulating in the UK, and a copy of the notice must be sent to the Company Announcements Office of the London Stock Exchange. When bonds are held in clearing systems, notices must also be sent to the systems, which have a duty to notify the relevant securities account holders.

50-year Swiss bond unlikely to set pulses racing

Lack of liquidity may restrict appeal of new sovereign issue, writes **William Hall**

The Swiss government's decision to issue a 50-year government bond breaks new ground in the maturity of debt issued by sovereign borrowers. But its initial reception suggests that Switzerland's "half-century" bond is unlikely to capture the imagination of the investment community.

Most governments in industrialised countries issue bonds of up to 30 years maturity. But Switzerland is the first country in recent memory to issue a 50-year bond. It carries a 4 per cent coupon and was priced to yield 4.095 per cent.

It is not Switzerland's first attempt to tap this segment of the market. In 1909 it issued a 50-year bond with a 3.5 per cent coupon. However, the gap between Switzerland's last 50-year bond and its latest issue suggests that demand for this maturity is limited, despite the country's triple-A credit rating. It is understood that the Swiss government took SFr200m of the new bond and total bids of SFr265m at the auction resulted in just SFr189m being sold.

The Swiss government has issued around SFr40bn of bond issues, so the SFr189m raised this week will not make much of a dent in its appetite for funds to finance a government debt which now tops SFr100bn.

The new bond is targeted at those Swiss investors which are required by law to earn a minimum 4 per cent on their funds under management. However, analysts questioned whether there would be much demand for the paper given its limited liquidity. Normally, investors prefer issues of between SFr2bn to SFr4bn.

Peter Thomann, who heads the Swiss government's treasury operations, admits that this week's issue is an experiment. Until recently Swiss government issues ranged between eight and 15 years. However, it now has issues ranging from two years to 30 years in its fund-raising armoury, and the latest bond fixes a new point on the yield curve.

Beat Schwab, of Credit Suisse First Boston, said the issue highlighted the steepness of the yield curve at the short end. The average yield on Swiss government bonds is 2.42 per cent and the gap between 10-year and 30-year

The new bond is targeted at those Swiss investors that are required by law to earn a minimum 4 per cent on their funds under management

government paper is around 120 basis points. By contrast, the 50-year bond is only yielding 35 basis points more than the 30-year bond.

Mr Schwab said the new bond might appeal to eurosceptic foreign investors bearish about the prospects for the single currency. The Swiss franc is a traditional safe haven, and short-term Swiss interest rates are 200 basis points below comparable German rates. But lack of liquidity will severely restrict its appeal.

Analysts are split on whether the Swiss franc will assume greater importance as investors seek to diversify their portfolios or will be marginalised by the Euro. But clearly the Swiss government at least believes its currency will still be circulating in 50 years' time.

Source: *Financial Times*.

19.4.3.14 Further issues

An issuer is usually permitted to issue further bonds with the same terms and conditions as the bonds in the issue: in other words, it may increase the size of the issue. Any such further issue will be allowed without the consent of the bondholders (which would be a time-consuming and difficult process). Any further issue will have the same ISIN number in the clearing systems and will be treated as part of the original issue once it has gone through the same 'lock up' provisions. In order for a further issue to be treated by the clearing systems as 'fully fungible' (ie, the new instruments are indistinct from those of the original issue), it must have exactly the same terms and conditions in all respects as the original issue.

19.4.3.15 Governing law and jurisdiction

These are standard boiler plate clauses (see **9.8**). The governing law will usually be English, with a submission to the non-exclusive jurisdiction of the English courts. For certainty and ease of enforcement, all documents in the issue process should have the same governing law.

Bond defaults lowest in years

By Edward Luce

The rate of defaults on worldwide corporate bond issues has fallen to its lowest level for 15 years, according to Moody's Investors Service, the New York-based credit rating agency.

The rare combination of strong profits growth and low global interest rates kept the default rate to 1.49 per cent of all issues in the first half of 1997, against 2.89 per cent in 1996. This was the lowest rate since 1982, Moody's said.

"What we are witnessing is ideal borrowing conditions, coupled with ideal business conditions," said Mr Sean Keenan, a Moody's economist.

Among other factors, low interest rates in Europe, Japan and the US have contributed to the buoyant debt market. Lower interest rates are usu-

ally associated with higher bond prices, which reduces the cost of funding for borrowers.

At the same time, strong economic growth in most parts of the world has contributed to low rates of insolvency among borrowers and strong liquidity for investors.

In the first six months of this year there were just 16 bond defaults on some $3.2bn (£1.91bn) of publicly held bonds. However, borrowers from emerging market countries, including Thailand, South Korea and Mexico, made up 31 per cent of defaults, a high in the 1990s for emerging market borrowers.

Among these, Thai property companies Sahaviriya City and Somprasong Land both defaulted on bonds of over $100m and South Korea's Hanbo Steel, now the focus of an investigation, defaulted

on $45m of debt in January.

Economists say the higher proportion of emerging market defaults reflects the increase in the number of issuers rather than any general problem with profitability.

"These figures are no reflection on the overall health of emerging markets," said one economist. "The proportion of emerging market defaults is bound to rise as emerging market borrowers make up an increasingly large proportion of the market."

Moody's says the rate of default among all corporate borrowers is almost certain to rise from the current low.

"All the risks are now on the upside," said Mr Keenan. "Economic conditions have little room to improve from here, and even marginally worse conditions could increase defaults in the second half."

Source: *Financial Times*.

Chapter 20

Eurobond Prospectus and Listing Particulars

20.1 Introduction

A eurobond issue may or may not be listed or admitted to trading on an exchange (the reasons for listing an issue are examined at **21.8.1**). If the issue is to be listed in the UK, it will be necessary to prepare a document which provides information about the issue for potential investors, and which satisfies the requirements of the FSA acting through the UK Listing Authority (UKLA). This 'disclosure document' is known either as a 'prospectus' (where the issue will be admitted to trading on the LSE's regulated market), or 'listing particulars' (where the issue will be admitted to trading on the LSE's non-regulated market, the Professional Securities Market ('PSM') – see **20.8**).

Thanks to the relentless EU crusade for market harmonisation (see **20.9**), the format and content of disclosure documents for most European bourses have recently been subject to considerable change. The key aim of these changes is to allow issuers to offer securities, or seek admission to trading, on any regulated market in the EU using a single disclosure document ('prospectus') approved by the issuer's home Member State. This is known as the 'passport' concept. This chapter gives an overview of the requirements for a prospectus in the London market, since that is the document most relevant to a stand-alone eurobond issue.

20.2 The new rulebooks

From 1 July 2005, issuers admitted to trading in the UK or making offers in the UK are governed by a new set of three sourcebooks within the FSA Handbook of rules and guidance:

(a) *The Listing Rules*. These apply to issuers listed (or applying for listing) on the UKLA's Official List. They stipulate the requirements for application and membership for both debt and equity securities, and also dictate the contents of listing particulars (for when a prospectus is not required – see **20.9**).

(b) *The Prospectus Rules*. These apply whenever a company is either:

    (i) making an offer of transferable securities to the public in the UK; or

    (ii) applying for admission to trading on a UK regulated market (eg the regulated market of the LSE, but not the PSM).

They implement the Prospectus Directive and apply provisions of the Prospectus Regulation with the aim of standardising prospectuses for most offers of transferable securities to the public. They deal primarily with when a prospectus is required, its content and format, and advertisement of the securities.

(c) *The Disclosure and Transparency Rules*. These rules apply to 'an issuer whose financial instruments are admitted to trading on a regulated market in the UK' (or for which a request to admission for trading has been made) – see DTR 1.1.1. The rules implement key aspects of the Market Abuse Directive and, since January 2007, the Transparency Directive in requiring ongoing disclosure and control of inside information by issuers.

Together, these sourcebooks replace the old Listing Rules (sometimes known as 'the Purple Book') and the Public Offers of Securities Regulations 1995 (the 'POS Regulations 1995'). Issuers of stand-alone eurobonds listed in London will usually need to look to parts of all three rulebooks to ascertain requirements for listing and disclosure.

20.3 Contents of a prospectus

20.3.1 Authority, format and general content

20.3.1.1 Authority

The UKLA derives its authority to insist upon the issue and publication of a prospectus or listing particulars from s 79 of the FSMA 2000, which provides that the Listing Rules can require that securities may not be admitted to the official list unless:

(a) listing particulars have been submitted to, and approved by, the competent authority and published, or

(b) in such cases as may be specified by listing rules, such document ... as may be so specified has been published.

20.3.1.2 General content

Assuming the eurobond issue requires a prospectus (see **20.9** for exceptions), Prospectus Rule 2.1 dictates the general content requirement by quoting three subsections of s 87A of the FSMA 2000 on the 'necessary information' to be contained in the prospectus:

(2) The necessary information is the information necessary to enable investors to make an informed assessment of —

(a) the assets and liabilities, financial position, profits and losses, and prospects of the issuer of the transferable securities and of any guarantor; and

(b) the rights attaching to the transferable securities.

(3) The necessary information must be presented in a form which is comprehensible and easy to analyse.

(4) The necessary information must be prepared having regard to the particular nature of the transferable securities and their issuer.

The level of detail required in a prospectus will depend on whether it is a 'retail' or 'wholesale' offer. The 'wholesale' regime requires less detailed disclosure, but only applies if the securities are denominated at or above €50,000 (or equivalent).

20.3.1.3 Prospectus format

The format of a prospectus is outlined at Prospectus Rule 2.2. There are two options for stand-alone eurobond issues: either a single document or as three separate documents. The three separate documents are:

(a) a 'registration document', which contains information relating to the issuer;

(b) a 'securities note', which contains the information relating to the bonds; and

(c) a 'summary', which 'must, briefly and in non-technical language, convey the essential characteristics of, and risks associated with, the issuer, any guarantor and the transferable securities to which the prospectus relates' (FSMA 2000, s 87A(5)). The summary should not generally exceed 2,500 words.

The advantage in using the three documents is that the registration document is valid for 12 months and so can be re-used for any number of issues during that period. However, most stand-alone issues since July 2005 have used a single document format.

Finally, Prospectus Rule 2.2.7 allows the issuer of a debt programme (eg an MTN programme) to use a 'base prospectus' (containing the main information on issuer and programme) and a 'final terms' document (which contains information on each particular securities issue under the programme). These are equivalent to the previous format of an offering circular supplemented by a pricing supplement.

20.3.1.4 Listing particulars

If a eurobond issue is to be admitted to trading on the PSM (this tends to be a minority), or is being admitted to trading on the LSE but does not require a prospectus under the Prospectus Directive, then listing particulars must be prepared. Listing Rule 4 details the content and format of listing particulars, and does so largely by incorporating selected parts of the Prospectus Rules. Listing particulars will therefore usually look like a 'low fat' version of a prospectus.

20.3.2 Responsibility for information

Section 84(1)(d) of the FSMA 2000 allows the Prospectus Rules to specify who is responsible for a prospectus, and this is covered by Prospectus Rule 5.5. For a eurobond (see Prospectus Rule 5.5.4) this includes:

(a) the issuer;

(b) anyone who accepts (and the prospectus states as accepting) responsibility;

(c) the offeror (if this is not the issuer);

(d) the person requesting admission to trading (if this is not the issuer);

(e) any guarantor (in relation to information on them or the guarantee); and

(f) anyone else who has authorised the contents of the prospectus.

In the case of a eurobond (and most other non-equity related securities) the issuer's directors are *not* required to take responsibility for the prospectus. The UK used its Member State discretion to derogate from the Prospectus Directive to ensure this was the case, thereby maintaining the status quo with the previous regime.

The Prospectus Rules require each of those responsible to make a declaration in the prospectus in the following form (see Prospectus Rules, Annex V, Appendix 3):

> [ ] accepts responsibility for the information contained in this document. To the best of their knowledge and belief (having taken all reasonable care to ensure that such is the case) the information contained in this document is in accordance with the facts and does not omit anything likely to affect the import of such information.

Liability for errors and omissions is considered in more detail at **20.6**.

20.3.3   Key information relating to the issuer

The minimum disclosure requirements for information relating to the issuer under the more onerous 'retail' regime (ie, where securities are denominated less than €50,000) are outlined in Annex IV, Appendix 3 of the Prospectus Rules. They include the following:

20.3.3.1   Persons responsible

The responsibility statement mentioned at **20.3** above.

20.3.3.2   Financial information

Audited accounts covering the last two financial years (unless the issuer is under two years old) to include a balance sheet, income statement (ie profit and loss account), cash flow statement and accounting policies. If the issuer prepares consolidated accounts it must use those in the registration document.

In a major change from the previous regime, all financial information must now be prepared in accordance with International Financial Reporting Standards ('IFRS' – see **6.9.5**) or an equivalent (US, Canadian or Japanese GAAPs are under consideration, but no ruling has yet been made as to equivalence due, in part, to the political nature of the process). To make this less burdensome for issuers there are transitional provisions, although these are proving complex to interpret. Moreover, the transitional provisions have now been extended to 1 January 2009 for some third country issuers (though not all) in view of the delays in determining equivalence.

20.3.3.3   Risk factors

Another new requirement is the 'prominent disclosure of risk factors that may affect the issuer's liability to fulfil its obligations under the securities to investors'. These will be factors specific to the issuer or maybe to its industry, for example risks relating to business cycles, competition, reliance on raw materials or product liability.

20.3.3.4   Information about the issuer

Unsurprisingly, and in accordance with the previous rules, information about the issuer itself is considered vital. So the name, registration number, place and date of registration, registered office address and any 'recent events particular to the issuer which are to a material extent relevant to the evaluation of the issuer's solvency' must all be included.

20.3.3.5   Business overview

The prospectus must describe the issuer's activities, new products and markets. It must also include a statement that there has been no material adverse change in the prospects of the issuer since its last published audited accounts (or explanation why this statement cannot be made). Any profits forecasts or estimates are strictly regulated.

20.3.3.6   Administrative, management, supervisory bodies and shareholders

Names, business addresses and functions of directors (or equivalent) must be disclosed and, to the extent known to the issuer, the identity of any 'controlling' shareholders.

20.3.3.7   Material contracts and displaying documents

The prospectus must summarise any material contracts 'not entered into in the ordinary course of the issuer's business' which could result in any member of the group being under an obligation or entitlement that is material to the issuer's obligations under the securities. Finally, the prospectus must indicate where certain 'display documents' (eg the memorandum and articles, reports, valuations, historical accounts etc) may be inspected.

This 'issuer information' appears in the registration document if a three-part prospectus is used.

20.3.4   Key information relating to the bonds

The minimum disclosure requirements for information relating to the bonds (where securities are denominated less than €50,000) are outlined in Annex V, Appendix 3 of the Prospectus Rules. They include the following:

20.3.4.1   Use of proceeds

The document must disclose why the money is being raised, the estimated total cost of the issue and some detail as to each principal intended use of the proceeds.

20.3.4.2   Information about the securities

Details as to the type (eg registered or bearer), currency, ranking, coupon, maturity and governing law of the securities must be included. The securities document must also give details of the terms and conditions of the offer, for example, the total amount, methods for paying up the securities and delivery back, pricing details, and the name and address of any paying agents.

20.3.4.3   Repeated information

Remember that the securities and registration documents may be issued as stand-alone documents, and so some of the information is common to both, for example the responsibility statement and risk factors.

Finally, Prospectus Rule 2.4 brings another departure from the previous rules in allowing an issuer to incorporate information by reference into the prospectus. However, incorporated information must first have been approved by the competent authority of the Home Member State, or filed with or notified to the FSA in accordance with the Prospectus Directive. The summary document must not incorporate information by reference (Prospectus Rule 2.4.4).

This 'bond information' appears in the securities document if a three-part prospectus is used.

20.4   General duty of disclosure

In drafting the prospectus it is important to remember the general disclosure obligation contained in s 87A of the FSMA 2000. This provides that the prospectus must contain all information which is 'necessary to enable investors to make an informed assessment of:

(a)   the assets and liabilities, financial position, profits and losses, and prospects of the issuer of the transferable securities and of any guarantor; and

(b)   the rights attaching to the transferable securities.

The prospectus must therefore contain information which the market reasonably needs and expects to receive so as to make an 'informed assessment' of the issuer's general position and the rights attached to the securities.

Section 87A also states that in determining what information is required to comply with this obligation, account must be taken of 'the nature of the transferable securities and their issuer.'

There is a similar general disclosure obligation for listing particulars in s 80 of the FSMA 2000, which also requires consideration of:

(a)   the nature of the persons who are likely to consider acquiring the securities;

(b)   the fact that certain matters may reasonably be expected to be within the knowledge of professional advisers of any kind which those persons may reasonably be expected to consult; and

(c)   any information available to investors or their professional advisers by virtue of requirements imposed by listing rules, by any other legislation or by a recognised investment exchange.

20.5   Omission of information

In most cases, if the Listing or Prospectus Rules require disclosure of information, the issuer's directors have little choice but to comply, however difficult or unpalatable that may be. The requirements for eurobonds are, however, generally less wide-ranging than for equity issues, reflecting the more sophisticated investor base of the former. The Rules list limited circumstances in which the UKLA can authorise the omission of information. Under Prospectus Rules 2.5 exemption from the duty to disclose (whether that duty arises under the Rules, s 87A or s 80) may be granted if:

(a)   disclosure would be contrary to the public interest, for example, information relating to important defence contracts;

(b)   disclosure would be seriously detrimental to the issuer of the securities (provided that omitting the information would not be likely to mislead a potential investor as to any facts the knowledge of which is essential in order to make an informed assessment); or

(c)   the information is of minor importance only and not such as to influence the assessment of the assets and liabilities, financial position, profits and losses and prospects of the issuer.

Since one of the issuer's responsibilities is to ensure compliance with the Listing and Prospectus Rules requirements, and to submit the listing particulars to the UKLA, both he and his solicitors will prepare the annotated copy of the listing particulars and the 'non-applicable' letter (see **21.8.3**). If it is within the specific requirements of the Listing or Prospectus Rules, or within the general duty under the FSMA 2000, the information must be included unless the UKLA allows omission. The consequences of failing to include the required information are examined at **20.6**.

20.6   Liability for prospectus and listing particulars

Misstatements in, and omissions from, the prospectus or listing particulars can give rise to both civil and criminal liability on the part of those responsible. All of the procedures outlined below apply to both a prospectus and listing particulars, but for simplicity this section refers only to 'prospectus'.

20.6.1   Civil liability

20.6.1.1   The Financial Services and Markets Act 2000

Compensation under s 90

Section 90 of the FSMA 2000 applies to both a prospectus and any supplementary prospectus (or listing particulars and supplementary listing particulars). It provides that anyone responsible for those documents is liable to compensate any person who acquires any of the securities and suffers loss in respect of them 'as a result of any untrue or misleading statement in the [prospectus] or any omission from them of any matter required to be included' under the general disclosure obligation. Certain defences are available, however.

Liability under the section is far-reaching. In this context, two points are particularly worthy of note. First, the section is concerned with a loss suffered by a person who has 'acquired' any of the securities. This may include not only the original investors on the marketing of the securities, but also subsequent purchasers on the secondary market. Secondly, the person concerned must establish that he suffered loss in respect of the securities 'as a result of' the offending statement or omission. Most commentators consider that this condition is satisfied if, for example, the price paid for the securities is higher than it would be but for the error or omission. It is not necessary for the investor to have relied on the prospectus in deciding to invest, or, indeed, even to have read them. That said, if the investor knows of the error or omission at the time of investing, his loss cannot be said to arise as a result of it.

Defences

A number of defences are available to a person facing a claim for compensation (see Sch 10 to the FSMA 2000):

(a)   That at the time the prospectus was submitted to the UKLA he reasonably believed, having made such enquiries (if any) as were reasonable, that the statement was true and not misleading, or that the matter the omission of which caused the loss was properly omitted. This is not sufficient on its own, however. The person must also establish one of four other facts, namely that:

    (i)   he continued in that belief until the time when the securities were acquired; or

    (ii)   they were acquired before it was reasonably practical to bring a correction to the attention of persons likely to acquire the securities in question; or

    (iii) before the securities were acquired he had taken all such steps as were reasonable for him to have taken to ensure that a correction was brought to the attention of those persons; or

    (iv)   he continued in that belief until after the commencement of dealings in the securities following listing, and the securities were acquired after such a lapse of time that he ought in the circumstances to be excused.

(b)   Where the alleged loss arises as a result of an expert's statement, and that the person defending the claim reasonably believed that the expert was competent to make or authorise the statement in the prospectus and had consented to its inclusion in the form and context in which it was included. Again, this defence is available only if one of four facts, broadly similar to those referred to in paras (i)–(iv) above, is also established. This is not a defence for the expert in question. It is a defence for the issuer if confronted with a claim arising out of some error contained in an expert's report which forms part of the prospectus (eg, the accountants' report).

(c)   That before the securities were acquired he had published a correction 'in a manner calculated to bring it to the attention of persons likely to acquire the securities' (or, as the case may be, a statement that the expert was not competent or had not consented); or, at the very least, that he had taken all such steps as were reasonable for him to secure such publication, which he reasonably believed had taken place before the acquisition.

(d)   That the loss arose from an official statement or one contained in a public official document, which had been accurately and fairly reproduced in the prospectus.

(e)   That the investor knew that the statement was false or misleading, or knew the matter which had been omitted.

(f)   Where the potential liability arose from a failure to provide a supplementary prospectus, and that he reasonably believed that the change or new matter did not warrant them.

20.6.1.2   *Hedley Byrne v Heller*: negligent misstatement

Misstatements in a prospectus may give rise to liability in tort under the rule in *Hedley Byrne & Co Ltd v Heller & Partners Ltd* [1964] AC 465. Liability arises if a person suffers loss having relied upon a misstatement and the person who made the misstatement owed a duty of care to the one suffering loss on the faith of it. For a duty of care to arise in these circumstances, a special relationship must exist between the person giving the information and the person relying on its accuracy.

Applying the principle to misstatements in a prospectus, it is thought that those assuming responsibility for the prospectus owe a duty of care to those applying for securities in the company on the marketing of those securities, but not to subsequent trading on the secondary market (see *Caparo Industries v Dickman* [1990] 1 All ER 568 and *Al Nakib Investments (Jersey) v Longcroft* [1990] 3 All ER 321). The inability of a subsequent purchaser to bring a claim for negligent misstatement contrasts with the position in relation to liability under the FSMA 2000 (see **20.5.1.1**); so too does the requirement that the claimant must have relied on the misstatement to his detriment.

20.6.1.3   The Misrepresentation Act 1967

A person may be able to rescind the contract for the acquisition of the securities and/or claim damages under the Misrepresentation Act 1967 if he acted upon an incorrect or misleading statement contained in the prospectus, or an omission from them. Under the 1967 Act, a claim for damages may be made only against the other party to the contract. So, for example, a manager, but not a purchaser in the secondary market, would have a claim against the issuer under the Act (see also **5.5.1**).

20.6.1.4   Contract

If an investor subscribes for and receives securities at the time of their issue (ie, in the primary market), he will have entered into a contract and the prospectus will form part of that contract because of the representations and warranties in the subscription agreement. If the prospectus is wrong or misleading, the investor may be entitled, under normal contractual principles, to rescind the contract and/ or sue the other contracting party for damages.

As part of the subscription arrangements, the syndicate of managers generally obtain a number of warranties from the issuer (see **19.3.6**). These warranties are usually supported by appropriate indemnities. If an investor, who does not have the benefit of those warranties, brings a claim against a member of the syndicate, that syndicate member may seek recompense from the issuer under the terms of the warranties and indemnities.

20.6.2 Criminal liability

20.6.2.1 The Financial Services and Markets Act 2000, s 397

Section 397 of the FSMA 2000 makes it a criminal offence for any person knowingly or recklessly to make a misleading, false or deceptive statement, promise or forecast, or dishonestly to conceal any material facts, if he does so for the purpose of inducing another person to enter, or offer to enter into a 'relevant agreement' (or refrain from doing so), or to exercise or refrain from exercising rights conferred by a relevant investment. Liability also attaches if the person is reckless as to whether such actions will produce this effect.

Section 397(3) of the FSMA 2000 goes even further by providing that a person is guilty of an offence if he:

> does any act or engages in any course of conduct which creates a false or misleading impression as to the market in or the price or value of any relevant investment ... if he does so for the purpose of creating that impression and of thereby inducing another person to acquire, dispose of, subscribe for or underwrite those investments.

A person charged with an offence under s 397(3) has a defence if *inter alia* he can prove that he reasonably believed that his act or conduct would not create such an impression.

Depending on the circumstances, a misstatement in the prospectus might give rise to charges on both counts. Each offence is punishable by imprisonment and/or a fine.

20.6.2.2 Other provisions

Errors in, and omissions from, the prospectus may also give rise to criminal penalties under other provisions, for example, s 19 of the Theft Act 1968 (misleading statements by a company's officers with intent to deceive the members or creditors).

20.7 Other jurisdictions

This chapter discusses liability for the information contained in listing particulars under English law only. Other jurisdictions may impose different liabilities, either statutory or common law, which may also apply to an issue irrespective of what law the issue is governed by as a result of the nationality of the investor. Liabilities imposed by US law can be particularly onerous.

20.8 Exemptions from preparing a prospectus

There are exemptions from the requirement to produce a prospectus available to issuers or offerors, and they are set out in s 86 of the FSMA 2000 and in Prospectus Rule 1.2. Remember, however, that a prospectus is required if there is *either* an 'application for admission to trading' *or* an 'offer to the public'. To avoid the former, an issuer would have to use a private placement and not admit the securities to a regulated market (using the PSM, for example, which was created for this purpose). To avoid an 'offer to the public' a eurobond issuer would usually need to rely on one of the following (PR 1.2.1):

(a)   an offer which is made to or directed at 'qualified investors' (for example, governments, central banks and entities authorised or regulated to operate in financial markets);

(b)   an offer which is made to or directed at fewer than 100 persons (other than 'qualified investors') per EEA State;

(c)   the minimum considation which may be paid by any person pursuant to the securities offer is €50,000 (or equivalent);

(d)   where the securities have a minimum denomination of €50,000 (or equivalent);

(e)   where the total consideration for the securities is less than €100,000.

A further 'exemption' is where a prospectus has already been approved by the competent authority of another Member State and any relevant requirements have been satisfied (known as 'passporting').

20.9   European regulatory reform

It is instructive to step back from the detail of the FSA listing requirements to consider the genesis of the recent changes to listing and disclosure rules.

In 1999, the European Commission launched the 'Financial Services Action Plan' (FSAP) with the three objectives of creating a single wholesale market in financial services, developing open and secure retail markets, and improving market rules and supervision. The breadth of the plan meant that a new regime of rule-making was required – the existing European regime was too cumbersome. A 'Committee of Wise Men' was formed which devised a streamlined process (sometimes called the 'Lamfalussy Process' after the Committee's chairman), with directives more concerned with principles than details, and power to implement the principles given to a Committee of European Securities Regulators (CESR).

A key limb of the FSAP is the Prospectus Directive, implemented in the UK from 1 July 2005. The aim of the Directive is that just one prospectus (approved by an EU regulator) should be required to list and sell an issue of securities across Europe. This is a welcome simplification, but does cause some problems: for example, there are restrictions on which regulator an issuer can choose to approve its prospectus, and a requirement in many cases to publish accounts under International Financial Reporting Standards (IFRS – see also **6.9.4**) or 'equivalent' standards (see **20.3.3.2**).

Another limb of the plan is the Transparency Obligations Directive, implemented in the UK on 20 January 2007. The Directive deals with the continuing disclosure obligations of EU listed companies (see **21.8.4**) and also requires issuers to publish consolidated accounts in accordance with IFRS or 'equivalent'. Lastly, the Market Abuse Directive, implemented in full in the UK on 1 July 2005, redefines the offences of insider trading and market manipulation, and attempts to bolster Member States' powers to investigate and prosecute offenders.

Chapter 21

Issuing a Eurobond – the Process

21.1 Introduction

Having briefly examined the parties and documents involved in a eurobond issue, this chapter concentrates on the actual process which an issuer must go through to issue the bonds.

One of the reasons why an issuer might choose to raise money on the euromarkets is the speed of the fund-raising process. The time between the issuer first instructing an investment bank to arrange the issue ('mandate') and when the issuer receives the money ('closing') may be as little as three weeks for a stand-alone bond (although five to six weeks is more usual). In order that an issue can be achieved this quickly, the eurobond market (through ICMA recommendations) has developed a guideline timetable for the issue process. Each party involved in the issue must be aware of the timetable, but it is usually the responsibility of the lead manager and its solicitors to monitor and 'police' the process.

21.2 The stages of a eurobond issue

The basic stages of a eurobond issue are as follows:

(a) Mandate.
(b) Due diligence.
(c) Documentation process begins.
(d) Marketing.
(e) Launch and syndication.
(f) Listing.
(g) Signing.
(h) Closing.

This is the usual order in which each stage of the issue process occurs, although not every stage will be completed before the next one begins. The substance of each stage is explained below.

21.3 Mandate

It should by now be clear that the question of the best way for a particular company to raise finance is a complex one. The company's directors will usually have lengthy meetings with investment banks and its own accountants before deciding whether an issue of debt securities is appropriate. Once the decision has been made, however, the first stage is for the company to instruct an investment bank to lead-manage the issue. This is known as the 'mandate'.

Once appointed, the lead manager will first advise as to the most appropriate structure for an issue (ie, which type of security) and the best market to target. For example, the lead manager may know that Japanese investors are particularly interested in the type of business the company runs, and suggest that the issue is targeted towards them. The lead manager will therefore approach its Japanese clients within its investor base, and will choose syndicate members which can 'bring in' Japanese investors.

The issuer and lead manager must first agree a number of important matters. These will include the marketing strategy, the decision whether to list, the identity of the fiscal agent (or trustee) and paying agents, and the fee structure. Once agreed, they will be recorded in the 'mandate letter' or 'term sheet', which is drafted by the lead manager. The basic terms and conditions of the bonds (such as price and status) will also be included in the mandate letter. The legal advisers will often have had little or no involvement up until the end of this mandate process.

21.4 Due diligence

The due diligence process for a loan facility was explained in **Chapter 2**. Bond issues will also require a due diligence process in which the lead manager ascertains and verifies the information it needs for the issue (which is driven primarily by the information required to be included in the information memorandum or listing particulars). The extent of the due diligence process will depend on a number of factors, including:

(a)   whether the lead manager already has a working relationship with the issuer;

(b)   the date of the issuer's latest audited accounts;

(c)   whether the issuer has previously issued euromarket securities and, if so, how recently;

(d)   the intended market for the issue (eg, an issue involving US investors will tend to require a more detailed due diligence process, since US investors are more litigious than most!);

(e)   the term of the bond (ie, the length of time until maturity);

(f)   whether the issue is rated: an unrated issue may require more due diligence than one which is fully rated; and

(g)   whether the issue is equity linked (eg, the debt is convertible into shares).

As a general rule, the due diligence process for an issue of equity linked securities will be more 'in depth' than for a straight debt issue, since investors in the former may become shareholders in the issuer (which represents a completely different risk to a straightforward debt investment).

Pre-Christmas rush to issue bonds after US Fed's glad tidings

The markets are open again but borrowers face higher costs, says **Edward Luce**

A wide range of borrowers – including the Polish city of Krakow and the French railway authority – took advantage yesterday of the improvement in market conditions to issue bonds.

The quarter-point reduction in US interest rates on Tuesday afternoon buoyed market sentiment and helped further reduce fears about a continued liquidity contraction in the bond markets.

However, the spreads on corporate bonds – the premium at which a bond trades above US Treasury or other government bonds – narrowed only marginally yesterday. Spreads, including those on emerging market bonds, have tightened by about 25 per cent since the last US rate cut in October.

This still leaves corporate bond spreads about 50 per cent wider than prior to the Russian domestic debt default in August, which led in effect to the closure of the corporate bond markets.

So the markets are open again, but at a cost. Companies still face substantially higher borrowing costs than they did a few months ago.

"The markets had already discounted this week's US interest rate cut in advance," said Xavier Werner, head of the European bond syndicate at ABN Amro. "If the US Federal Reserve had left rates untouched it could have had a very negative effect on sentiment."

Most bankers expect the market to continue to stabilise and liquidity to become gradually available for the less creditworthy borrowers, possibly including those rated below the investment grade threshold of BBB- for Standard & Poor's and Baa3 for Moody's Investors Service.

Yesterday Argentina, which has a rating of BB/Ba3, issued a $1bn bond, the largest emerging market offering since August. However, there are only two or three weeks left this year for borrowers to take advantage of the renewed confidence in the bond markets and tap fresh debt. The bond market traditionally grinds to a halt by mid-December as banks and investors tidy up their books for the end of the calendar year.

Economists also warned that the outlook for the credit markets remained mixed in spite of the surge of liquidity in US and Europe. A widely forecast slowdown in economic growth rates in 1999 is expected to restrain any exuberance.

In addition, corporate earnings growth is expected to slow in the US and this could hit share prices. Credit spreads, especially in the high-yield bond markets, closely track equity prices. "Spreads in the bond markets are linked to the economic cycle," said Ifty Islam, a senior economist at Deutsche Bank. "When growth rates fall, credit spreads normally widen."

But in the short-term, there is a large queue of borrowers hoping to issue bonds before Christmas. It includes Rolls-Royce and Continental AG, and several emerging market governments. Demand for new debt is expected to be underpinned by the growing mountain of cash available to investors, thanks to the large amount of redemptions of existing bonds since August and the absence of new issues to take their place.

In addition, the approach of European economic and monetary union is encouraging Asian and other central banks to redenominate a portion of their foreign exchange reserves into the euro or into leading pre-euro currencies, notably the D-Mark. As a result Asian and, in particular,

Japanese investors have provided an unusually high level of demand for recent bond issues, including more than 50 per cent of a DM500m bond offering by Finland this week.

The Bank of China is thought to be planning to denominate 15 to 25 per cent of its reserves in euros. This will provide a strong counter-cyclical demand base for bonds issued in euros. "The approach of Emu will keep the eurobond markets active unless there is another financial meltdown like Russia," said one bond syndicate official in Frankfurt. Bankers also said there was a strong chance in the near future of the first high-yield bond in a European currency since August.

Source: *Financial Times*.

The due diligence process will usually involve meetings between the lead manager and its solicitors, the relevant officers of the issuer (eg, the finance director, managing director, and other officers with particular knowledge of the business), and the issuer's auditors (both internal and external). The lead manager will usually conduct the meeting by asking detailed questions of the other parties in order to obtain sufficient information to be able to proceed with the issue and to prepare the prospectus (or listing particulars). An alternative approach to due diligence is for the lead manager to draft a list of detailed questions which is sent to the issuer. However, whilst this method is less time-consuming, it is also less flexible, and is more suited to frequent issuers, with high credit ratings, where there are likely to be few or no problems with the issuer and the information memorandum (or listing particulars) will be relatively straightforward.

The due diligence process provides the material for the prospectus (or listing particulars). The lead manager may be liable for any negligent misstatement or omission in these documents, and so he has a particular interest in checking that their contents are accurate and not misleading (see **20.5**). Obtaining the comfort letters in agreed form from the issuer's auditors (see **19.3.8**) is also part of the due diligence process following analysis of the issuer's accounts.

21.5 Documentation

The principal documentation involved in a eurobond issue was discussed at **19.3.1**. The preparation and negotiation of these documents is the responsibility of the lead manager's solicitors. Preparation of the contractual documentation is expedited by the fact that most of the documents required for a eurobond issue comply with market accepted standards (eg, the agreement among managers will almost invariably use the ICMA standard form, and will not require any input by the solicitors). If the eurobond issue is to be listed, a draft of the prospectus or listing particulars must be sent to the appropriate listing authority. The UKLA usually requires a period of at least 10 clear business days in which to review a prospectus prior to its intended publication (Prospectus Rule 3.1.3). However, early application is encouraged, and most solicitors would want the draft particulars to reach the Authority at least three weeks before publication.

Preparation of some of the documents will continue through signing, and the process is only really complete on closing when the last documents of the issue are executed. The solicitors will prepare agendas for both signing and closing, which act as checklists for the process at each stage.

21.6 Marketing

An important role of the lead manager is to help the issuer's directors in making presentations to potential investors (these are sometimes known as 'roadshows'). The roadshows are intended to familiarise potential investors with the issuer's business and portray the issue as a good investment. The roadshow may be held in a number of different countries in order to widen the audience of potential investors, although they are less necessary for well-known issuers for whose securities there is usually a regular demand. Solicitors are not usually involved in the roadshow process; however, the roadshow material should be scrutinised by the solicitors and the lead manager's compliance department to ensure it complies with ss 21, 25 and 98 of the FSMA 2000 (which put restrictions on advertising).

BANKS MOVE EXPECTED TO ADD MOMENTUM TO CHANGING STRUCTURE OF HOME LOANS MARKET

Abbey to securitise 10% of mortgage book

By Arkady Ostrovsky

Abbey National is planning to securitise 10 per cent of its £60bn mortgage book in an attempt to free up its balance sheet and increase its market share.

The bank will this week launch a £1bn mortgage-backed bond issue, adding momentum to the changing structure of the UK home loans market.

The bond is part of a programme that could allow Abbey National to take £6bn of debt from its balance sheet and repackage it as bonds, which would be sold to institutional investors.

The £1bn bond issue follows a successful £1bn mortgage-backed offering from the bank earlier this year and a £250m mortgage-backed bond issued last year.

The bank said the securitisation programme would allow it to manage its balance sheet more efficiently while providing an alternative source of funding.

UK banks traditionally kept high-yielding mortgages on their balance sheet. But increasing pressure from shareholders looking for better returns on capital means they have to free up their balance sheets. Cut-throat competition in the home loans market also means the margins of mortgage banks are being squeezed.

Last month Northern Rock, the former building society, launched £600m worth of mortgage-backed bonds, as part of its own programme to securitise its mortgage book.

Woolwich has meanwhile linked with Country-wide Credit, the US mortgage lender, to securitise its mortgages.

Fast-growing ex-mutuals, which need to raise lending volumes, are particularly keen to use bond markets as a new source of funding.

Abbey National said by using the bond market as a way to finance mortgages it could offer homeowners 30-year fixed rate mortgages, which are widely used in the US market.

An average maturity of a fixed-rated mortgage in the UK is 3-5 years.

Securitisation of mortgages also allows banks to reduce the amount of capital that regulators require them to set aside in case of default.

Abbey's £1bn bond, launched in February, released £45m of capital that Abbey used to hold as a cushion.

Bonds are usually launched through a special purpose vehicle, which is legally separate from the originator.

The proceeds from the sale of the bonds go to the the originator, while mortgage payments go to bond holders.

In the US, up to 40 per cent of mortgages are securitised, compared with about 3 per cent in the UK.

Source: *Financial Times*.

Sections 21–25 of the FSMA 2000 make it an offence for any person other than an 'authorised person' (ie, authorised to carry on regulated activity under the FSMA 2000) to 'in the course of business, communicate an invitation or inducement to engage in investment activity' (or to cause the same) in the UK, unless its contents have been approved by an authorised person (or an exemption applies). The prohibition is widely drafted, albeit with various exemptions.

21.7   Launch and syndication

The launch date is when the bond issue is confirmed by formal public announcement. The date will be agreed between the issuer and the lead manager. Launch must await the completion of any due diligence and marketing processes and will, so far as possible, be effected when market conditions are most favourable (eg, avoiding launches of other competing issues).

On the launch date, the issue will be announced to the market (usually through online trading screens) and the lead manager will send the invitation telex to the financial institutions he has chosen to invite into the syndicate (the lead manager will already have spoken to the syndicate to gauge their interest, and so the invitation telex is merely a formal communication). The invitation telex shows the 'price' of the bonds (unless it is an equity linked deal, when pricing will not be made until the date of signing of the subscription agreement) as well as the fees and commissions the syndicate banks will receive. These are sometimes referred to as the issuer's 'all in cost' of funds, although it does not include legal fees, printing costs and agency fees.

The co-managers are usually required to respond to the invitation telex within 24 hours of receipt. Acceptance (which is usually by telex) does not constitute a binding contract to subscribe: that is the purpose of the subscription agreement. It does, however, constitute a significant 'moral' obligation on the co-managers. Once all the co-managers have responded, the lead manager will know the level of interest in the issue, and can notify each co-manager of the number of bonds it is expected to take at issue by way of an 'allotment telex'.

Once the allotment telex has been sent, the draft subscription agreement is sent to each co-manager. ICMA recommendations allow the co-managers at least two working days in which to review the agreement before it is to be signed.

21.8   Listing

A listed bond is one which is formally quoted, listed or capable of being traded on a recognised stock exchange. Eurobond issues are not always listed, either through choice or an inability to comply with the stock exchange requirements. Most listed eurobonds will be listed on the stock exchanges in London or in Luxembourg.

21.8.1   Reasons for listing

Unlike most share issues, eurobond issues are not generally listed in order to use the exchange as a marketplace. Most trading (even of listed eurobonds) will take place away from the exchange (known as 'over-the-counter' trading) between banks and other financial institutions by telephone or online. The primary reason for listing a eurobond issue is to demonstrate that it has satisfied the requirements of the exchange. Since those requirements are generally intended to protect investors, attaining listed status makes securities more marketable. Some entities, such as pension funds and unit trust funds, are precluded (by legislation, regulation or their constitution) from investing in securities which are not listed. An issue must therefore be listed to attract their funds.

One specific advantage of obtaining a London listing of eurobonds is the 'quoted eurobond exemption' from UK withholding tax. This exemption allows a UK issuer to pay interest on the eurobonds gross (note that before 1 April 2001 this exemption applied only to bearer securities; it now applies to registered securities as well). A listing on a number of other stock exchanges, including Luxembourg, will also enable the securities to qualify for the same exemption.

There are two main disadvantages associated with listing an issue: cost and timing. Listing authorities will charge a fee, whilst legal fees and lead managers' fees will be considerably higher for a listed issue because of the additional time involved in a listing application (particularly for a first-time issuer).

The timetable for issuing a listed bond will usually be longer than an unlisted one (particularly with respect to new issuers), because the UKLA will require time to review the documentation of an issue and the due diligence process will often be more in-depth.

21.8.2 Listing requirements

The requirements of the UKLA for admission to listing with respect to a bond issue are found in Listing Rule 2. The Stock Exchange reserves the right to impose any special condition it considers appropriate in the interests of protecting investors. Specific requirements of most types of bond issuer include the following:

21.8.2.1 Status

The issuer is duly incorporated (or validly established) and is operating in conformity with its constitution. If the issuer is a UK incorporated company, it must not be a private company.

21.8.2.2 Securities

The main conditions relating to the securities are:

(a) the securities must conform with the law of the issuer's place of incorporation, be authorised under the issuer's constitution, and have any necessary statutory or other consents;

(b) the securities must be freely transferable;

(c) the securities must have an expected aggregate market value of at least £200,000 (unless securities of the same class are already listed). The Stock Exchange will allow a lower value if it is satisfied there will be an adequate market for the securities;

(d) the entire class of a security must be listed;

(e) convertible securities must convert into securities which are themselves listed on the London Stock Exchange or another 'regulated, regularly operating, recognised open market'.

The London Stock Exchange also has criteria for determining whether an applicant is suitable for membership.

21.8.3 Application procedure

The application procedure for listing eurobond securities on the London Stock Exchange is found in Listing Rule 3, supplemented by Listing Rule 17. The main requirements of the procedure include the following:

21.8.3.1   '10 clear business day documents'

In general, issuers (through their sponsor) must submit three copies of specified documents to the UKLA at least 10 clear business days prior to their intended publication (see Prospectus Rule 3.1.3). For a eurobond issue, these documents comprise the requisite application form, the prospectus (which must usually be annotated to indicate compliance with the relevant paragraphs of the Prospectus Rules), issuer board resolutions and two letters (the 'non-applicable' letter and the 'omission of information' letter) explaining why certain information does not appear in the prospectus and requesting the omission of information respectively. The 10-day time limit will not strictly apply to a eurobond issue, although a later submission might risk a delay to the listing. The UKLA will return copies of the documents with any comments it has.

21.8.3.2   Marked-up documents

Any 10-day documents which the UKLA amends (or which are altered after submission to the UKLA) must be re-submitted with the changes marked up.

21.8.3.3   '48-hour documents'

Listing Rule 3.4.4 requires the following documents, in final form, to be submitted at least two business days prior to the consideration of the listing application:

(a)   a complete application for admission of the securities; and either:

    (i)   the approved prospectus or listing particulars; or

    (ii)   a copy of a prospectus approved by another Member State (under the 'passporting' regime).

21.8.3.4   Listing charge

On the day of consideration of the listing application, the issuer must pay the appropriate listing fee (Listing Rule 3.2.2).

21.8.4   Continuing obligations

The responsibilities imposed on an issuer do not end once its securities are listed. There is a variety of 'continuing obligations' which the Listing Rules require an issuer to fulfil. For a eurobond issue, the main obligations are set out below.

21.8.4.1   Disclosures

Under Listing Rule 17.4, the issuer is required to notify a Regulatory Information Service ('RIS' – a service approved by the FSA for making market announcements, eg, Business Wire Regulatory Disclosure, First Sight and Announce) of:

(a)   any new issues (and related guarantee or security);

(b)   any change of guarantor or security of its listed securities (where the information is important for assessing the securities);

(c)   any change in the rights of listed securities;

(d)   any change in the paying agent; and

(e)   the publication of its annual accounts.

The issuer must immediately notify the CAO of any decision not to pay interest on the listed securities, as well as any change in the rights attached to the securities.

21.8.4.2 Equality of treatment

The issuer must ensure equal treatment of all the holders of the same class of listed debt securities.

21.8.4.3 Communications with bondholders

The issuer must notify an RIS of any notices to bondholders, no later than the date they are sent to the bondholders. The issuer is also under an obligation to publish notices informing the bondholders of significant events such as meetings, payment of interest, and exercise of conversion rights.

21.8.4.4 Paying agent

The issuer must maintain a paying agent in the UK until the date on which the securities are finally redeemed unless the issuer is a financial service provider and performs the paying agency role itself.

21.8.4.5 Bearer securities

If the debt securities are in bearer form, the issuer must advertise bondholder meetings in a national UK newspaper, and copies of the advertisements must be sent to an RIS at the same time. The requirement for a newspaper advertisement is waived if the securities are in global form and the issuer can confirm that it is able to notify all bondholders (although a copy of the notice must still be sent to an RIS).

21.8.4.6 Failure to meet continuing obligations

Failure to comply with any of the continuing obligations may lead to private or public censure, suspension or cancellation of the securities' listing.

21.9 Signing

A signing meeting is usually held within two weeks of the issue being launched, although it may be longer if the UKLA is slow to approve the prospectus. The signing is usually a simple meeting of the parties and their advisers, although it will occasionally be held as a more formal ceremony.

The lead manager and its solicitors must be sure that certain aspects of the issue process have been completed before the signing. Fundamentally, they must ensure that:

(a) the prospectus (or listing particulars) is in an agreed form (and agreed by the relevant listing authority);

(b) the other contractual documents (ie, paying agency agreement, trust deed (or fiscal agency agreement), legal opinions and auditors' comfort and consent letters) are in final form;

(c) the issuer (and any guarantor) has executed any resolutions necessary to authorise the issue, and has appointed an authorised signatory of the global note;

(d) the common depository has been appointed.

At the signing meeting, the subscription (or underwriting) agreement is executed by the issuer and the syndicate members, and takes contractual effect. If the issue is to be listed, final copies of the prospectus will be signed by the issuer to be sent to the UKLA. There is also a substantial number of peripheral documents to be produced and/or executed at the signing meeting, and the lead manager's solicitors will produce a signing agenda, which is distributed before the meeting, to ensure that nothing is overlooked.

21.10 Closing

The closing is the final stage of the issue process, and usually takes place approximately one week after signing. It is the time when the issuer receives its funds and the eurobonds come into being, creating the issuer's debt obligation.

The lead manager's solicitors will produce an agenda to ensure that all the necessary matters are completed. Essentially, there are two sets of procedures which must take place at closing: documentary procedures and payment procedures.

21.10.1 Documentary procedures

The following matters are the responsibility of the lead manager and its solicitors, and must be completed before the closing meeting:

(a) Admission to listing, if relevant, must be confirmed (subject to closing) by the relevant authorities.

(b) The conditions precedent to the subscription agreement must be satisfied.

(c) The auditors' closing comfort letter and the issuer's closing certificate must be in agreed form.

(d) The legal opinions must be in agreed form.

(e) All other documents associated with the issue must be executed or in an agreed form (those that have been executed in advance will be held 'in escrow').

It is vitally important that as many of these matters as possible are dealt with before the closing date to minimise the risk of any problems. This is primarily because the lead manager and 'would be' bondholders will have ensured that funds are already in place, awaiting instructions for transfer to the issuer on a successful completion. Any delay or, worse still, cancellation of the completion will be very expensive. The closing meeting is attended by the issuer (or its solicitor if it has already executed the necessary documents), the lead manager and its solicitors, the depository, and the fiscal agent (or trustee).

By the end of the completion meeting, the following documents should be executed (some may have been executed beforehand):

(a) Trust deed (if appropriate).

(b) Fiscal agency agreement or paying agency agreement.

(c) Auditors' closing comfort letter.

(d) Legal opinions.

(e) Issuer's closing certificate.

(f) Payment instructions from lead manager to the depository.

(g) The temporary global note.

(h) The permanent global note (if any).

(i) Receipts between issuer and lead manager acknowledging payment and delivery.

The temporary global note is authenticated (ie, signed) by the fiscal agent (or paying agent) in order to give it legal effect, and is delivered to the depository for safe-keeping.

After closing, any documents still to be lodged with the UKLA (or relevant exchange) must be sent by the listing agent; the definitive bearer bonds (if relevant) must be security printed (this may take several weeks) and authenticated before the temporary global note is exchanged for the definitive bonds (alternatively, the temporary global note is exchanged for the permanent global note), in either case only after the relevant lock-up period.

21.10.2 Payment procedures

The payment procedures, also known as the 'closing mechanics', or 'payment against delivery procedures', involve the depositary and are adopted in most eurobond transactions. Co-ordination of the payment procedures is the responsibility of the lead manager.

21.10.2.1 Prior to closing

The lead manager will have notified the clearing system of the names and amounts of bonds to be allotted to the account of each syndicate member. Each syndicate member will also give payment instructions to the clearing system to the effect that its cash account is to be debited with the amount of money it must pay for the bonds, and the money credited to the lead manager's new issues account. The instructions are phrased so that the debit will be made only if the syndicate member is credited with the requisite number of bonds in its securities account (payment against delivery). The lead manager will also instruct the clearing system to debit its new issues account with the total amount of the issue to be paid to the account of the common depositary, who will hold it until the temporary global note has been issued and delivered (ie, payment against delivery: see **21.10.3**).

21.10.2.2 At closing

The following matters occur 'simultaneously' at closing. The lead manager will authorise release of its payment instruction to the depository to transfer the money (already placed with the depository) representing the issue amount to the issuer. The depository will then transfer that money to the issuer's bank account once it receives the temporary global note.

The closing is now complete: the issuer has its funds and the depository holds the temporary global note on behalf of the clearing system. The clearing system will have credited the securities accounts of each syndicate member with an interest in the number of bonds for which they have subscribed, and each of their respective cash accounts will have been debited with the appropriate amounts.

21.10.3 Payment against delivery

The figure below shows the flow of payments and bonds at closing for both Euroclear and Clearstream participants.

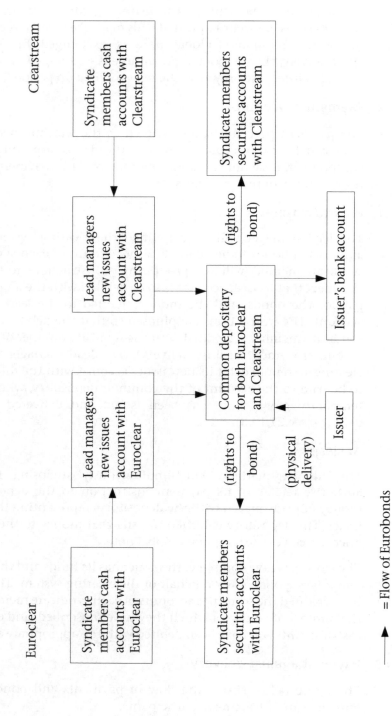

CLOSING PROCEDURES PAYMENT AGAINST DELIVERY

Euroclear

Clearstream

Syndicate members cash accounts with Euroclear

Lead managers new issues account with Euroclear

Syndicate members cash accounts with Clearstream

Lead managers new issues account with Clearstream

Common depositary for both Euroclear and Clearstream

Syndicate members securities accounts with Clearstream

Issuer's bank account

Syndicate members securities accounts with Euroclear

Issuer

(rights to bond)

(rights to bond)

(physical delivery)

= Flow of Eurobonds

= Flow of Cash

Stagecoach funds acquisition with asset-back bond

By Conner Middelmann and Motoko Rich

Stagecoach, the rapidly expanding bus and rail group, yesterday became the first publicly quoted company in the UK to fund a large acquisition by transforming corporate debt into bonds for sale to international investors.

The £545m bond transaction – known as a securitisation – provides a further boost to the fast-growing market for UK asset-backed securities. It will finance Stagecoach's recent purchase of Porterbrook Leasing, the rolling-stock company.

The bonds will be secured on lease payments due to Porterbrook from UK train operating companies (TOCs). About 80 per cent of these payments are backed by the UK government, to cover the possibility that the TOCs default on their payments. This makes the bonds low risk to investors.

Securitisation is a way for financial institutions or companies to remove assets from their balance sheets, freeing up capital and diversifying funding sources. Principal and interest payments on the securities are funded by the cash flows generated by the assets.

The Stagecoach offering follows Tuesday's £904m securitisation by financial institutions of rental income from former UK Ministry of Defence properties, which also has government backing.

"The asset base for securitisation has widened significantly from traditional assets like residential mortgage loans, and this trend is set to continue," said Ms Caroline Philips, associate director of asset securitisation at NatWest Markets, which is about to securitise $5bn of National Westminster Bank corporate loans.

Securitisation is being put to a widening array of uses. "The transaction illustrates how effectively securitisation can be used within acquisition financing," said Mr Keith Ballantine, of the Union Bank of Switzerland's securitisation team.

The Stagecoach securitisation, arranged in seven tranches by UBS, will refinance an acquisition facility the group set up in August to buy Porterbrook, and provide an additional £25m in funding. Stagecoach will pay an average interest rate of 7.4 per cent on the bonds.

Stagecoach is awaiting a decision from the Office of Fair Trading on whether the acquisition should be referred to the Monopolies and Mergers Commission. But Mr Keith Cochrane, finance director, said the funding package would not be affected by a referral.

"The transaction is entirely insular," said Mr Cochrane. "We have a stream of income based on the leases that we have with 16 TOCs, and we know what our fixed interest rate is, so we have raised the funding based on those figures."

Investors will have no recourse to Stagecoach if the projected leasing income does not materialise. For accounting purposes, the debt will still appear on Stagecoach's balance sheet, even though it is risk-free for the company.

Analysts welcomed the funding package, describing it as "innovative" and "cheap financing". But Stagecoach shares eased 4½p to 573p.

Source: *Financial Times*.

Glossary

Acceleration	Declaring a loan due and payable before the scheduled repayment date, usually as a result of an event of default
Accordion facility	Also known as a 'trombone facility', it allows the borrower to approach some or all syndicate members after signing and request an extension of available commitment. It is uncommitted, but if the borrower persuades some banks to lend more, the other syndicate members cannot object to the increased commitment being added to the loan
Accrued interest	The interest which is being earned on a loan, bond or other security on a daily basis between two interest payment dates. Secondary dealings in securities such as bonds or notes will usually take place on an accrued interest basis so that they will be bought and sold at a price which includes the accrued interest, ie market price plus interest which has been earned on that loan, bond or note but not yet paid (sometimes known as the 'dirty price')
Advance	A utilisation of money under a loan facility (now more commonly known as a 'loan')
All in cost	The entire cost of the transaction quoted to the borrower or issuer by the lenders or lead manager, which includes fees payable to the lenders or managers. All in cost will not usually include legal costs
Alphabet facilities	A facility with different tranches of debt repayable at different times, and usually labelled 'A', 'B' and 'C' facilities
Amortisation	The repayment of a debt in stages
Ancillary facility	A bilateral facility, for example an overdraft or derivatives facility, between a borrower and one of its syndicate banks which is drawn as part of a syndicated revolving credit facility
Arbitrage	Making a profit through the small differences in price between markets, for example buying shares on the Tokyo exchange and selling them in Singapore. Usually low risk, but requires high volume to make money
Arranger	Usually, the bank or financial institution responsible for arranging a loan transaction (including the syndication)
Asset backed security	A security which has its interest and capital repayments provided by a generic group of assets (eg, mortgages) which produce income (aka securitisation)
Asset stripping	Acquiring a business with a view to breaking it up and selling the most lucrative parts rather than developing it (euphemistically: 'rationalisation')

Authentication	In securities issues, the physical signing by the fiscal agent or principal paying agent of a security (eg, bond or note) in order to give it legal effect
Authorised institution	Under the provisions of the Financial Services and Markets Act 2000, in the UK only 'authorised institutions', as defined in the Act, may accept deposits in the course of a deposit-taking business
Availability period	The time during which a borrower may draw down (or 'utilise') advances under a loan (also known as 'commitment period')
Back office	The various 'non-profit centre' operational departments of a bank or financial institution which deal with the 'behind the scenes' activities of the organisation (eg, the settlement and accounts departments). 'Front office' activities include trading and lending
Balloon repayment	A final repayment of principal on a loan transaction which is substantially larger than earlier repayment instalments
Bankers' acceptance	A bill of exchange, drawn on and accepted by a bank. By accepting the bill of exchange the bank is accepting full liability to pay the bill on maturity as the primary obligor
Base rate	A fluctuating interest rate, peculiar to individual banks and used by them as a reference point for lending rates to individuals
Basel Convergence Agreement	Agreement on capital adequacy reached in July 1988 by the Committee on Banking Regulations and Supervisory Practices (which comprises representatives of the central banks from the G-10 countries). The agreement (also known as the 'Cooke report') contained proposals for the international convergence of capital measurement and capital standards and is implemented by way of Notices issued under the Banking Act 1987
Basis point	One hundredth of one percentage point (eg, 45 basis points is 0.45%)
Basis rate	The rate used as a basis for calculation of interest under a commercial loan transaction (eg, LIBOR)
Bells and whistles	Additional features of a debt transaction which are designed to attract investors
Bible	Complete set of conformed copy documents relating to a particular transaction
Bilateral facility	A loan facility between one bank and one borrower
Bill of exchange	A form of short-term IOU widely used to finance trade and provide credit
Bona fide	In good faith. A bona fide purchaser is one who believes he is entitled to buy, and the seller is entitled to sell
Bond or note	A debt instrument having a maturity of generally more than three years

Book loss or gain	The difference between the original cost or book value of a security and its current market value (excluding accrued interest), ie an unrealised loss or gain
Book runner	The institution responsible for the syndication, documentation, distribution, payment and delivery of a new market issue of securities (or loan facility)
Brady bond	Paper issued in exchange for distressed commercial bank debt (particularly emerging market countries)
Bridge financing	Interim financing used before the intended long-term financing is put in place
Broker	A person or institution acting as an agent for buyers and/or sellers and charging a commission for his services, but who does not buy for his own account
Bullet repayment	Repayment of a debt obligation in a single instalment at the maturity date of the debt (ie, no amortisation)
Business day	A day on which banks are open for business in the relevant financial centre
Call option	In relation to a bond or note issue, a term which gives the issuer the right, but not the obligation, to redeem its securities before their specified maturity, normally at a specified price on a specified or determinable date. A premium may be payable on the exercise of the call option (cf 'put option')
Carve out	An exception to a tight representation or undertaking
Certificate of deposit	A negotiable bearer instrument evidencing a time deposit with a commercial bank, either interest-bearing or issued at a discount
Chinese wall	An artificial barrier restricting communication between different areas within an organisation, allowing them to act for parties who may have conflicting interests. The concept originated in securities houses, but is commonly used within large firms of solicitors (aka an 'ethical wall' or 'information barrier' – particularly in institutions with Chinese clients)
Clawback clause	A clause enabling one party to retrieve money already paid out. Often found in the agency provisions of syndicated facility agreements enabling an agent to recover money already paid out by it to a party, wrongly believing that the agent had received the corresponding payment from another party. This allows an agent to distribute money (eg, repayment instalments) to the bank syndicate without confirming receipt of the payment from the borrower, knowing that if he does not receive the monies from the borrower he may 'clawback' the monies paid out to the syndicate
Clean down	A requirement for the borrower to reduce its drawing under a revolving credit facility to zero (or a specified reduced amount) for a given period (eg, five days in every year) to demonstrate it is not being used for capital expenditure

Clean-up period	The period (commonly 90 days) after an acquisition during which the new owners are allowed to remedy any events of default without the banks taking action
Clearing system	An organisation through which purchase and sale transactions of securities are handled and cleared. The main systems in the euromarkets for bonds and notes are Euroclear and Clearstream
Club loan	A facility provided by a small number of banks taking a similar level of commitment
Collateral	The assets over which security is granted
Commercial paper	Very short-term debt securities (eg, between a week and a few months' maturity) issued under a programme typically by borrowers requiring working capital funding
Commitment	The specified amount of money agreed to be lent by a bank in a 'committed facility', or agreed to be invested by a manager in a bond or note issue
Commitment fee	An annual percentage fee payable to a bank on the undrawn portion of its 'commitment' under a 'committed facility'. The commitment fee is usually paid quarterly in arrear
Commitment period	See 'Availability period'
Committed facility	A financing or credit arrangement in which a bank is obliged to lend up to a certain agreed limit of money for a defined period of time, usually subject to a predetermined set of conditions
Conformed copy	A record copy of a final executed document in which all signatures and any other handwritten words (eg, dates or alterations) are printed in typed form. Conformed copies are used to make up the transaction 'bible'
Coupon	Refers to both the stated rate of interest on a bond or note, and also to one of a series of actual coupon certificates attached to a bond or note, evidencing interest payable at a specified date
Credit default swap ('CDS')	A derivative used to hedge risk against default of an entity ('reference entity') or specific lending obligation (the 'reference obligation'). Essentially, the buyer pays a premium to the seller of the CDS to buy protection against loss on default. If the entity or obligation defaults, the seller will pay the buyer the par value of the defaulted obligation (usually a loan or bond): in return the buyer usually has to transfer the obligation in question to the CDS seller to recover what it can
Cross default	An event of default triggered by a default in the payment, or the potential acceleration of repayment, of other indebtedness of the same borrower or issuer
Data room	A place in which information about a target company up for sale can be viewed by potential purchasers. It may be a room at the vendor's solicitor, or may be a 'virtual' room online

Debt push down	Usually refers to moving debt around a group of companies (typically from parent companies down to operating companies) to maximise tax advantages. For example, an operating company making profits can use interest payments to reduce its corporation tax, whereas a holding company earning only dividends cannot
Deep discount securities	Non-interest bearing securities issued at a large discount to their face value
Dematerialised	Usually referring to securities which are not represented by physical certificates but are traded through an electronic exchange
Derivatives	Financial instruments that are a 'spin-off' from *(derived from)* more basic financial products and markets (examples include options, futures, swaps)
Discount	The difference between the price of a security and its face value
Distressed debt	Debt which is, or which the lender believes will be, non-performing (ie, repaid late, partially, or not at all) and which is usually sold for substantially less than the value of principal outstanding ('below par')
Double dipping	A means of structuring finance leases to utilise the tax benefits on capital investments in more than one jurisdiction
Double taxation treaty	An agreement between two countries intended to limit the double taxation of income and gains, under the terms of which an investor in one country may be able to apply for an exemption or reduction in the taxes imposed on his income or gains by another country, or from his own country on the basis that such income or gains have already had tax levied on them. This type of treaty encourages trade and financial transactions between countries
Drag along	Usually refers to certain investors being forced to accept something if a percentage of other (usually higher ranking) investors voted in favour
Drawdown	See 'Utilisation'
Drawstop	An event under a loan facility which prevents a borrower from utilising the loan
Earn out	In an acquisition finance, where the purchase price for the acquisition varies in accordance with the performance of the business post acquisition
Eligible bill	A banker's acceptance which can be re-discounted at (ie, sold to) the Bank of England
Emerging market	A jurisdiction in which the debt and capital markets are new or developing areas (often 'developing' countries) (see also 'LDC')

Equity cure	In an acquisition financing, the ability of the private equity 'owners' to put cash into the borrower which is treated as reducing debt or increasing profit (or cashflow) to 'cure' what would otherwise be a breach of financial covenants
Equity kicker	A warrant or option to buy, or exchange, debt for equity and which is attached to certain debt instruments (generally found in leveraged management buy-outs)
Equity of redemption	A mortgagor's right to reclaim mortgaged assets on repayment of the secured debt with interest and costs
Escrow arrangement	Documents held 'in escrow' are executed documents given by one executing party to a third party (usually a solicitor) to hold to its order until a certain condition is satisfied, or event occurs. On the satisfaction of such condition or occurrence of event, the third party will usually be instructed to release the documents out of escrow to the other executing party or as otherwise instructed
Exploding bridge	A facility in which the interest rate increases dramatically after a given period to act as an incentive to the borrower to refinance the facility
Face value	The nominal or par value of a security, rather than its market value at any particular time. It will be the amount due to the holder of the security on its maturity but exclusive of any interest or premium
Facility office	The branch or office of a bank through which the funds for a facility are provided. Also known as the 'lending office'
Finance lease	A means of financing whereby one lessee acquires the use of an asset for most of its useful life (eg, aircraft). Lease payments during the life of the lease are sufficient to enable the lessor to recover the cost of the asset, plus a return on its investment. The lessee must not be given an option to purchase the asset since this would be a hire-purchase agreement; however, if the lessor sells the asset at the end of the lease, any amount it receives is usually paid to the lessee
Finance vehicle	A subsidiary company, usually incorporated 'offshore', for use by its parent company for issuing debt securities and then 'on lending' the proceeds to the parent or other companies in the group. The finance vehicle (aka 'special purpose vehicle') will be used only for these purposes and is unlikely to have any assets of its own. The issue of securities by a finance vehicle will therefore have to be guaranteed (usually by the parent company)
Foreclosure	Forfeiture of a mortgagor's equity of redemption due to default in payment (of principal or interest)

Front end fee	A fee calculated as a percentage of the principal value of a loan or issue of securities, which is payable once at commencement of the loan or at issue of the securities, as opposed to an annual percentage fee payable each year (also known as 'arrangement fee')
Front running	A practice, usually prohibited in the commitment letter, in which an arranger sells part of its commitment outside of the normal process during primary syndication, thereby achieving an advantage over other arrangers in the syndicate
FSA	Financial Services Authority
FSA 1986	The Financial Services Act 1986, now superseded by FSMA 2000
FSMA 2000	The Financial Services and Markets Act 2000, which came into force from the end of November 2001 (a date known as 'N2')
Fungibility	An object is said to be 'fungible' if it can be replaced by another object and still fulfil any obligation to which it is subject. Fungible objects are therefore described by weight, quantity or value, rather than specific description (the most common example is cash)
Fungible securities	Securities of the same issue, which are kept in the clearing system where the book-keeping is such that no specific securities are assigned to customer accounts by their serial numbers
Gilts	Securities issued by the British Government
Governing law	The jurisdiction to which the terms and conditions of transaction are subject
Grace period	The period of time given to a borrower or issuer in which it is allowed to remedy an event of default
Grey market	The 'market' in a new security issue, among financial institutions, which commences on the launch of a new issue (ie, before it is available to trade to the 'public') and ends when the securities are formally available at closing of the issue
Gross-up	A borrower/issuer may be required to gross-up payments it has to make to the lenders/investors, meaning it must make additional payments to compensate for withholding taxes, or similar deductions, which would otherwise reduce the amounts actually received by the lenders/ investors
Headroom	Refers to the difference between a borrower's projected performance (eg, in its business plan) and the lower targets set for it to attain under its financial covenants
Hedge fund	A fund which is allowed to take relatively high-risk and 'innovative' positions with investors' money, agreeing to sell shares they do not yet own ('shorting' shares). The ethos behind hedge funds is to 'make good money in good markets but not lose money in down-turns'

Hedging	An activity employed by financial institutions or corporate treasurers to protect against loss due to market fluctuation in certain investments held by that organisation. Hedging is usually performed by counterbalancing a current sale or purchase of an investment by another future sale or purchase. The aim is to ensure that any loss on the current sale is offset by the profit on the future sale
High yield bonds	See 'Junk bonds'
Hive down	Refers to the transfer of assets from a parent down to one or more of its subsidiaries ('hive up' is the opposite)
ICMA	International Capital Markets Association, the regulatory body in the eurobond market, formed in July 2005 by the merger of the International Primary Markets Association (IPMA) and the International Securities Markets Association (ISMA)
Information memorandum	A document produced by the borrower and arranger of a syndicated facility to inform potential participants about the deal
Infrastructure finance	Providing finance for the acquisition of 'infrastructure' assets or businesses such as water, gas or electricity suppliers, ports, airports, telecommunications, windfarms, and transport franchises.
Interim facility	A short-form loan agreement, usually lasting only 30 days, which allows the bidder in an acquisition finance to demonstrate that it has immediate funds with which to purchase the target. The short-form facility is really just a negotiating tool to show serious intention to bid and to move quickly, and is often not utilised; the intention is to negotiate the usual 'long-form' loan documents to replace the short-form facility before it expires
IPO	'Initial Public Offering', ie the first ever issue of (usually equity) securities by a particular entity
Issuing house	The financial institution which organises and arranges the issue of new securities, also known as the 'lead manager'
Judgment currency indemnity	An indemnity sometimes included in credit facilities to protect the lenders against losses they may suffer if judgment is obtained against the borrower in a currency different to that in which the facility is denominated
Junk bonds	A bond (or note) with a low grade credit rating (ie, below investment grade), and which must therefore yield a higher rate of interest (or substantial discount) to attract investors (also known as 'high yield bonds')
Law Debenture Trust Corporation plc	A company often used by overseas borrowers and issuers as an agent for the service of process in England. Also used by issuers of securities as trustee for the bondholders or noteholders

LDC (Less Developed Country)	A common term for third world countries, primarily used to describe the debt of those countries, ie 'LDC debt' (see also 'Emerging market')
Lending office	See 'facility office'
Letter of credit	A written undertaking by a bank (the issuing bank) given at the request of, and in accordance with, the instructions of the applicant (the buyer) to the beneficiary (the seller), to effect a payment up to a stated amount of money, within a prescribed time-limit, and usually against the production of stipulated documents
LIBID (London Interbank Bid Rate)	The rate of interest quoted by banks operating in the London Interbank Market at which they are willing to borrow money (ie, bid for deposits in a particular currency)
LIBOR (London Interbank Offered Rate)	The rate of interest quoted by banks in the London Interbank Market at which they are willing to lend money, ie offer deposits in a particular currency
London Approach	Guidelines issued by the Bank of England encouraging support for troubled debtors rather than sale of distressed debt
London Code of Conduct	Published by the Bank of England: a guide to best practice in the wholesale money markets in London
London Stock Exchange	The London Stock Exchange plc (which trades as 'the London Stock Exchange') is the international stock exchange for the UK, but not the Republic of Ireland
Management buy-in (MBI)	The purchase of a business by 'external' managers. As with MBOs, most of the funding is from outside investors
Management buy-out (MBO)	The purchase of a business by its management (and sometimes employees). The managers invest a small amount of money, but most of the finance is provided by outside investors such as venture capitalists
Mandate	The authorisation from a borrower or issuer to his chosen arranger or lead manager to conduct the relevant transaction on the agreed terms. Usually given in the form of a letter signed by both parties
Margin	(a) in relation to floating interest rates, the rate of interest charged by the bank over and above the relevant cost of funding, such as LIBOR;
	(b) in relation to some financial markets (eg, the futures market), a deposit required to be paid by members of the relevant exchange for each transaction they carry out;
	(c) 'margin lending' is where the loan amount is of a lesser value than the amount of collateral given for the loan
Market flex	A term written into a commitment letter allowing the arranger unilaterally to change the terms of a facility if it cannot successfully syndicate

Matched funding	The process of matching a loan (asset) with a deposit (liability) of the same maturity
Maturity	The date upon which a debt is finally repayable
Mezzanine finance or debt	Usually high interest-bearing debt, where the lender receives little, if any, form of security for its loan and which ranks behind the 'senior debtors' so far as repayment is concerned. It is sometimes seen as halfway between debt and equity in terms of risk and reward
Monolines	Companies which provide a guarantee of debt securities issued by lower-rated issuers in return for an insurance premium. This 'monoline insurance' or 'wrap' can raise an issue rating from 'A' to 'AAA', so attracting more investors and reducing coupon for the issuer
New Global Note structure	A structure which requires global notes to be held by clearing systems (and not a common depository) to ensure they are eligible as collateral in the euro central banking system ('Eurosystem')
Non-recourse	A non-recourse loan is one with no comeback (or recourse) to a guarantor or parent company of the borrower. Non-recourse loans are usually used to finance a special project or purpose over which they are secured
Note	A widely used alternative label for 'bond' – see **17.5**
Off balance sheet liabilities	Obligations of a company which do not appear on its balance sheet. These can be of concern for lenders since they disguise the extent of the commitments entered into by a company
Opco/Propco finance	A finance technique in which an existing business puts ownership of its real property (ie, land and buildings) into one SPV (the 'Propco') and its operating assets into another (the 'Opco'). The Propco can raise finance for the business on very favourable terms because it only owns land, whilst the Opco leases the real property back from the Propco so that the business keeps trading
Option	The right, but not the obligation, to buy or sell an instrument at a specified price and up to a specified time in the future
Over-the-counter (OTC)	The purchase and sale of securities and other financial instruments which take place away from any stock exchange or other official financial exchange (eg, futures exchange). The eurobond secondary market is predominantly an over-the-counter market, irrespective of the fact that some of the securities traded will actually be listed on a stock exchange
Paper	Colloquially, securities such as bonds, notes, certificates of deposits and commercial paper
Par	The principal amount (the initial issue price) at which an issuer agrees to redeem its securities on their maturity (see also 'face value')

Parallel debt	A structure used in jurisdictions that do not recognise a security trustee. A parallel debt provision provides for a security agent to be owed an equivalent sum to that due under a loan facility (ie, two 'parallel' debts). This allows the security agent to hold security for the full amount of the loan. As the facility debt is repaid, the security agent debt is reduced 'in parallel' (and vice versa), so that the borrower only repays one debt.
Pari passu	Equally and without preference
Perpetual bonds or notes	Bonds or notes which have no scheduled maturity date and therefore are redeemable only under any call option that the issuer may have under their terms and conditions. Events of default in such issues will be very basic and will give rise to a winding-up procedure and not to redemption
PIK	Payment in kind, usually referring to a facility in which the borrower can roll-up interest and add it to principal to be paid when the loan matures (cf 'cash pay' where interest is paid as it falls due). Commonly found in mezzanine facilities for acquisition finance
Plain vanilla	A colloquial term used to describe securities or loan facilities with no additional features such as warrants, call options, multi-options, etc
Private equity	A private equity house (also referred to as the 'sponsors', 'venture capital', 'equity' or the 'investors') is an organisation that creates funds by raising money from institutions, banks and high net worth individuals to invest in the acquisition of other companies or groups.
Private placement	An offer of securities made to a limited and prearranged number of investors
Professional Securities Market ('PSM')	The PSM is a market created by the London Stock Exchange in July 2005 to enable companies to raise capital by issuing securities to professional or institutional investors. The key feature of the PSM is that it is 'unregulated' or, more precisely, 'exchange regulated' and so has a very flexible regulatory regime (eg, no requirement to report under IFRS, no restrictions on type or value of securities, etc).
Project finance	The financing of a specific project (eg, building a power station or toll road), the revenue from which will provide the lenders with repayment of their investment. The project also provides security for the lenders
Promissory note	An unconditional promise in writing, signed by the debtor, undertaking to pay a specific sum on demand, or at a fixed or determinable date in the future
Purple Book	Colloquial name for the old rules of the Financial Services Authority relating to listing on the London Stock Exchange. Now replaced by the Prospectus Rules, Listing Rules and Disclosure Rules

Put option	If contained within a bond or note issue, it will give the holder of the securities the right to call for an early redemption of the securities prior to their scheduled maturity (cf 'call option')
Redemption	The repurchase or repayment by an issuer (or borrower) of outstanding securities (or loans), in accordance with their terms, with the effect of extinguishing the outstanding debt
Repurchase agreements ('repos')	In capital markets, repos entail two simultaneous transactions: the purchase of securities (the 'collateral') by an investor from a bank or dealer; and the commitment by that bank or dealer to repurchase the securities at a specified higher price (or the same price with charges) on a specified future date (or on call). Repos are primarily used as a means of short-term funding and are governed by market standard terms and conditions
Rescheduling	In relation to debt obligations, the renegotiation and agreement of revised terms of a loan facility (usually involving the spreading of interest and capital repayments over a longer period) as a result of the borrower being unable to comply with the original terms
Reuters screen	A telecommunications system, subscribed to by banks and financial institutions, which provides regularly updated financial information relevant to banking and securities trading
Reverse flex	A clause in commitment documents for a loan that requires the arranger to push for lower pricing if the loan appears oversubscribed during syndication. The arranger is usually incentivised by taking a share of any cost saving
RIS	Regulatory Information Services: companies which provide information services to the capital markets and have been approved by the FSA Listing Rules as a vehicle for members to make announcements (see Listing Rules, Appendix 3 for a list of RISs)
Rollover	The renewal of a loan which has become repayable under a revolving credit loan facility
SEC (the Securities and Exchange Commission)	The US Federal Government agency charged with overseeing the US domestic securities market
Secondary market	The trading of securities which are already issued
Settlement	The process of clearing the paperwork involved in trading securities: ensuring the purchaser receives its securities and the seller its money. Purchases and sales must be reconciled between the different financial institutions involved in the trades. Settlement is dealt with by an institution's 'back office'
SPA	'Sale and purchase agreement' or 'share purchase agreement': the contract governing the acquisition of the target in an acquisition finance

Spread	Generally, the difference between two prices, but the term has other meanings in specific contexts
Standby letter of credit	A letter of credit issued by a bank as a form of guarantee. A beneficiary of arrangement will be able to make a drawing on the letter of credit merely by providing a certificate of non-payment of the underlying debt
Stapled financing	In an acquisition finance, where the bank advisers to the vendor offer a loan package to potential bidders for acquiring the target (the loan terms are 'stapled' to the back of the information memorandum relating to the target)
Stock lending	A transfer of securities from 'lender' to 'borrower' to meet a pre-existing contract of the borrower to sell securities. The 'loan' requires the borrower to replace the securities in due course, and cash collateral of 102–105% of the securities' value is usually taken
Structured finance	A financial structure specifically designed for a particular borrower
Subordination	A creditor is subordinated if its claim against the borrower ranks behind one or more other creditrs on insolvency. Subordination can be achieved by way of taking security, by contractual arrangements or by debt structuring (ie, lending at different levels of company within a group of companies) or a combination of all three
Swap	The exchange of one product for another, usually currencies, interest streams, or securities
T bill (Treasury bill)	A security issued by the US Government
Ticking fee	A fee to cover an arranger's commitment costs, and payable from when the arrangers underwrite a loan to when the loan documentation is signed
Toggle facility	Allows a borrower to chose whether to pay interest as it falls due, or roll it up and add it to the capital repayment ('payment in kind')
Tombstone	An announcement, usually placed in the financial press such as the *Financial Times*, made by either the borrower/issuer or the banks/lead manager, and announcing an issue of securities or provision of a loan facility. Tombstones are not intended as an advertisement to entice prospective purchasers, they simply contain a brief description of the issue or facility and a list of the participating banks or managers. The names of these banks or managers appear as a vertically presented list, hence the name 'tombstone'
UK Listing Authority ('UKLA')	The colloquial name for the division of the Financial Services Authority responsible for admission of securities to listing
Undertaking (of a company)	All of a company's present and future assets
Utilisation	The borrowing of money under a loan facility (sometimes known as 'drawdown')

Withholding tax	A tax deducted at source on certain payments (usually interest or dividend payments)
Workout	Common term for the long-term rescue of a defaulting borrower by its bank(s) (and other creditors)
Zero coupon bond/note	A non-interest bearing bond or note issued at a discount to its face value

Bibliography

Commercial lending

There are few, if any, books dedicated to the documentation of facility agreements; however, the following books address many of the legal issues that loan documentation raises:

Penn, Shea and Arora, *The Law and Practice of International Banking* (Banking Law vol 2) (2nd end, Sweet & Maxwell, 2000)

Philip Wood, *Law and Practice of International Finance* (Sweet & Maxwell, 1995)

This is a series of 6 volumes, of which the most relevant are *Comparative Law of Securities and Guarantees, Comparative Financial Law and International Loan, Bonds and Securities Regulations.*

Security

Ellinger and Lomnicka, *Modern Banking Law* (3rd edn, Clarendon Press, 2002)
Particularly useful review of secured lending.

Geoffrey Fuller, *Corporate Borrowing: Law and Practice* (4th edn, Jordans, 2009)
A good technical review of certain aspects of corporate borrowing.

Goode, *Commercial Law* (3rd edn, Penguin, 2004)
Professor Goode's well-known book covers a number of aspects of taking security, as well as being an invaluable reference work for general commercial practice.

Goode, *Legal Problems of Credit and Security* (3rd edn, Sweet & Maxwell, 2003)
A surprisingly readable collection of Professor Goode's lectures which covers a number of basic security issues in some depth.

Penn, Shea and Arora, *The Law Relating to Domestic Banking* (Banking Law vol 1) (2nd edn, Sweet & Maxwell, 2000)

Capital markets

Geoffrey Fuller, *The Law and Practice of International Capital Markets* (Butterworths, 2007)

A very useful guide.

Ravi Tennekoon, *The Law and Regulation of International Finance* (Butterworths, 2000)

Dr Joanna Benjamin, *Interests in Securities A Proprietary Law Analysis of the International Securities Markets* (Oxford University Press, 2001)

Stephen Valdez, *An Introduction to Global Financial Markets* (5th edn, Macmillan, 2006)

This is an excellent introduction to many different areas of banking and capital markets. Readable and informative.

General

Christopher Stoakes, *All you need to know about the City* (2005/2006 edn, Four by Four Publishing Limited)

A witty and readable demystification of the markets, players and products in the City of London. A very useful jargon-buster.

Michael Brett, *How to Read the Financial Papers* (5th edn, Century Business, 2003)

An unbeatable guide to jargon and concepts of the City in general and the financial world in particular. Aimed at laymen not lawyers, but contains very clear explanations and examples.

Michael Lewis, *Liar's Poker* (Coronet, 1999)

This is the story of the author's training and trading at the investment bank Salamon Brothers. The first half of this book is an hilarious account of investment banking; the second half is drier and more informative, but by this time you will be hooked. (Worth reading just to find out how to play 'liar's poker'.)

Index